LEARNING
OBJECT-ORIENTED
PROGRAMMING
IN C# 5.0

B. M. HARWANI

Cengage Learning PTR

CENGAGE
Learning·

Professional • Technical • Reference

Australia • Brazil • Japan • Korea • Mexico • Singapore • Spain • United Kingdom • United States

CENGAGE Learning

Professional • Technical • Reference

Learning Object-Oriented Programming in C# 5.0
B. M. Harwani

Publisher and General Manager, Cengage Learning PTR: Stacy L. Hiquet

Associate Director of Marketing: Sarah Panella

Manager of Editorial Services: Heather Talbot

Senior Marketing Manager: Mark Hughes

Product Manager: Heather Hurley

Project/Copy Editor: Karen A. Gill

Technical Reviewer: Joshua Smith

Interior Layout Tech: MPS Limited

Cover Designer: Mike Tanamachi

Indexer: Valerie Haynes Perry

Proofreader: Megan Belanger

For product information and technology assistance, contact us at **Cengage Learning Customer & Sales Support, 1-800-354-9706.**

For permission to use material from this text or product, submit all requests online at **cengage.com/permissions**.

Further permissions questions can be emailed to **permissionrequest@cengage.com**.

Microsoft, Windows, and Internet Explorer are either registered trademarks or trademarks of Microsoft Corporation in the United States and/or other countries.

All other trademarks are the property of their respective owners.

All images © Cengage Learning unless otherwise noted.

Cover background art: © Eugene Sergeev/Shutterstock.com.

Library of Congress Control Number: 2014933750

ISBN-13: 978-1-285-85456-4

ISBN-10: 1-285-85456-X

Cengage Learning PTR

20 Channel Center Street

Boston, MA 02210

USA

Cengage Learning is a leading provider of customized learning solutions with office locations around the globe, including Singapore, the United Kingdom, Australia, Mexico, Brazil, and Japan. Locate your local office at: **international.cengage.com/region**.

Cengage Learning products are represented in Canada by Nelson Education, Ltd.

For your lifelong learning solutions, visit **cengageptr.com**.

Visit our corporate website at **cengage.com**.

Printed in the United States of America
1 2 3 4 5 6 7 16 15 14

Today, the Internet is the most powerful source of information thanks to the amazing efforts of many, including the following:

- *Vinton Cerf, American Internet pioneer, who is recognized as the father of the Internet*

- *Robert Kahn, American engineer who, along with Vinton Cerf, invented the Transmission Control Protocol (TCP) and the Internet Protocol (IP), the communication protocols used on the Internet*

- *Tim Berners-Lee, British computer scientist also known as the inventor of the World Wide Web (WWW)*

I dedicate this book to them and to my mother, Nita Harwani. The person I am today is a product of the moral values she taught me.

ACKNOWLEDGMENTS

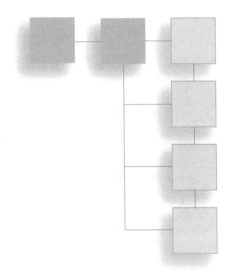

I am grateful to Heather Hurley, product manager at Cengage Learning, for believing in me and giving me an opportunity to create this work.

Thank you to Karen Gill who, as my project editor and copy editor, offered a significant amount of feedback that improved the chapters. She did first-class structural and language editing and played a vital role in improving the quality of information. I appreciate her efforts in enhancing the contents of this book and giving it a polished look.

I must thank Joshua Smith, the technical editor, for his excellent, detailed reviewing of the work and the many helpful comments and suggestions he made.

A great big thank-you to the editorial and production staff and the entire team at Cengage Learning who worked tirelessly to produce this book. I enjoyed working with each of you. Thanks, too, to MPS Limited for making the book look good on pages.

I also want to mention my family, my small world. To my wife, Anushka, and my wonderful children, Chirag and Naman, thank you for inspiring and motivating me and above all for forgiving me for spending so much time on my computer.

Speaking of encouragement, I must mention my dear students, who have been a good teacher for me. Their interesting problems and queries help me write books with a practical approach.

ABOUT THE AUTHOR

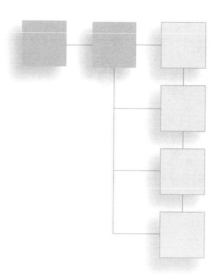

B. M. Harwani is the founder and owner of Microchip Computer Education (MCE), based in Ajmer, India, which provides computer education in all programming and web developing platforms. He graduated with a BE in computer engineering from the University of Pune, and he has a C Level diploma (Master's diploma in computer technology) from DOEACC, Government of India. As a teacher for more than 20 years, he has developed the art of explaining even the most complicated topics in a straightforward and easily understandable fashion. His published books include *Foundation Joomla* published by FriendsOfED, *jQuery Recipes* published by Apress, *Core Data iOS Essentials* published by Packt, *Introduction to Python Programming* and *Developing GUI Applications with PyQT* published by Cengage Learning, *Android Programming Unleashed* published by Sams Publishing, *The Android Tablet Developer's Cookbook (Developer's Library)* published by Addison-Wesley Professional, and *UNIX & Shell Programming* published by Oxford University Press, USA. To learn more, visit his blog at http://bmharwani.com/blog.

Contents

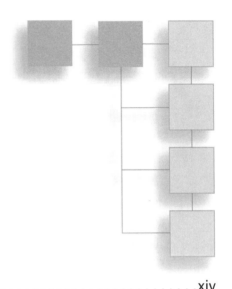

Introduction

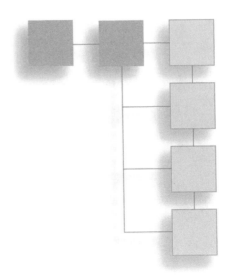

This book provides a thorough guide to the most valuable features of C# 5.0. It explains object-oriented programming (OOP) principles and their benefit in developing real-world applications, and it integrates in-depth OOP fundamentals when developing code in C#. It provides essential, straightforward information to help readers master the core capabilities of Visual C# 2013 and explores creating and using advanced class features such as generics, collections, and operator overloading. Readers will dig deep into web services, LINQ, multiple threading, and security features. This book also offers complete coverage of .NET features, including assemblies, interfaces, delegates, events, web application development, and ADO.NET.

What You'll Find in This Book

This book focuses on hands-on projects. It successfully presents readers with a comprehensive guide covering each major skill required for developing apps using C# 5.0. Here's what you'll find in this solid, comprehensive reference:

- Plenty of running examples

- A progression from easy examples to deeper, complex topics

- An explanation of object-oriented programming principles and their benefit in developing real-world applications

- Coverage of inheritance, polymorphism, interfaces, operator overloading, delegates, and events

- Application of generics and collections, managing errors and exceptions, implementing multiple threads, using ADO.NET, accessing information using LINQ queries, and developing web-based application development in .NET

- All topics that are required for developing apps in C# 5.0

WHO THIS BOOK IS FOR

The book addresses intermediate to advanced users, teaching different aspects of object-oriented programming in detail. The book explores valuable features of C# 5.0 with running examples. It begins with fundamental topics like data types, operators, expressions, branching and looping statements, arrays, and strings. After these fundamental topics, it gradually digs into the complex topics of reusability of code through classes, objects, inheritance, and polymorphism. The book covers interfaces, operator overloading, delegates, and events. Finally, it applies generics and collections, manages errors and exceptions, implements multiple threads, uses ADO.NET, and accesses information using LINQ queries.

The book is beneficial for developers and instructors who want to learn or teach C# 5.0 programming. For practical implementation, the book also explains web-based application development in .NET.

HOW THIS BOOK IS ORGANIZED

The book teaches different aspects of object-oriented programming. Here's a breakdown of topics covered by chapter.

Chapter 1, "The .NET Framework"—Covers introduction to C#, .NET Framework, CLR, CTS, CLS, and Assembly. It also introduces Visual Studio IDE, the requirements to install Visual Studio, and steps to run a C# program. The chapter concludes by using the Visual Studio IDE to develop C# programs.

Chapter 2, "Data Types"—Covers programming fundamental structs like identifiers, keywords, variables, and constants. You learn about predefined data types, including integer, floating-point, decimal, character, bool, nullable, and string types. In addition, the chapter explains implicitly typed variables, implicit type conversion, explicit type conversion, and streams. You perform console I/O, read input from the console, write comments, and create a Windows Form application.

Chapter 3, "Operators and Expressions"—Covers operators, precedence and associativity, and the `typeof`, `sizeof`, `checked`, and `unchecked` operators. You learn to use arithmetic, increment, and decrement operators along with sign, relational equality, logical Boolean, logical bitwise, shift, assignment, and ternary operators. Finally, you learn about the `Math` class.

Chapter 4, "Decision-Making and Looping"—Covers conditional statements that include `if-else-if` and `switch`. You learn to use the conditional operator and various loops. The chapter explains the `while` loop, `do-while` loop, `for` loop, `goto` statement, nested loops, and enumeration.

Chapter 5, "Arrays and Strings"—Covers both one-dimensional and multidimensional arrays. Also, you learn to initialize an array and use the `foreach` loop. In addition, this chapter explains using strings, passing command-line arguments to the main method, using `StringBuilder`, and using `ArrayList`.

Chapter 6, "Methods and Structures"—Covers methods, method parameters, method invoking, and method overloading. You learn about using optional and named parameters, C# parameter modifiers, passing by value, passing by reference, output parameters, and variable length parameters. The chapter also explains defining your own type (structures), using properties with struct, defining arrays in structures, and using array of structures and nested structs. Finally, the chapter covers the date and time structure, `DateTime` properties and methods, `TimeSpan`, date and time formatting, and application of custom and standard date and time formatting.

Chapter 7, "Classes and Objects"—Covers `class`, application of the `new` operator, accessing of public members, the difference between a struct and a class, methods in a class, and the `return` statement. The chapter also explains using method parameters, using private members, passing parameters by value and by reference, using output parameters, using method overloading, implementing encapsulation, using properties, and implementing the `this` keyword. Also covered are default constructors, parameterized constructors, copy constructors, constructor overloading, and constructor chaining. Finally, the chapter explains garbage collection, destructors/finalizers, static classes and members, static classes and constructors, namespace importing, namespace nesting, creation of a namespace alias, and the internal modifier.

Chapter 8, "Inheritance and Polymorphism"—Covers single inheritance, use of protected members, and base class constructor calling. The chapter also explains multilevel inheritance, hierarchical inheritance, hybrid inheritance, method overriding, virtual methods, sealed class and methods, method hiding, abstract classes, abstract properties, and polymorphism.

Chapter 9, "Interfaces"—Covers invoking interface members at the object level, implementing multiple interfaces, implementing interfaces explicitly, and verifying interface implementation. The chapter also explains implementing multilevel interfaces, implementing interface properties, understanding how a structure implements an interface, passing an interface as a parameter, and returning an interface.

Chapter 10, "Operator Overloading"—Introduces binary operator overloading, unary operator overloading, addition of a constant to an object, addition of two complex numbers, `true` and `false` operator overloading, comparison operators overloading, comparison of objects for equality, conversion operators overloading, creation of an implicit conversion operator, and creation of an explicit conversion operator.

Chapter 11, "Delegates and Events"—Covers declaring and instantiating delegates, invoking the referenced method, understanding instance versus static method targets, using multicast delegates, implementing covariance and contravariance, defining generic delegate types, using the anonymous method, distinguishing between delegates and interfaces, handling events, declaring an event, and declaring event accessors.

Chapter 12, "Generics and Collections"—Covers standard interfaces, `IEnumerators`, the generic collection classes, the hashtable, `SortedList`, `BitArray`, the stack and queue, generic types, generic collections, the `Generic List<T>` collection, `Queue<T>`, `Stack<T>`, `SortedSet`, `Dictionary`, and `LinkedList<T>`.

Chapter 13, "Managing Errors and Exceptions"—Covers errors, exceptions, the exception hierarchy, and keywords used in exception handling. The chapter also explains using multiple `try` and `catch` blocks, catching all types of exceptions, throwing an exception, rethrowing an exception, nesting `try` blocks, creating your own exception, and using the `checked/unchecked` operator.

Chapter 14, "Threads"—Introduces the main thread, child threads, use of the `Thread` class, and the life cycle of a thread. The chapter also explains thread properties and methods, multithreading, exclusive operations using `Monitor`, the `Lock` statement, and thread interruptions.

Chapter 15, "Streams"—Introduces streams, C# I/O classes, file handling, opening and closing of a file, random reading of a file, positioning of the file pointer using the `Seek` method, reading and writing of primitive types in binary format, and use of `BinaryWriter` and `BinaryReader`. You create character-based file I/O, use `StreamWriter`, utilize the `using` statement, implement `TextWriter` and `TextReader`, and use `StreamReader` and `StringWriter`. Also, you learn to read an entire file, hold data temporarily using `MemoryStream`, and manage a directory using `DirectoryInfo`.

Chapter 16, "ADO.NET"—Introduces major components of ADO.NET, data providers, creation and connection to a database, creation of a database table, data access from a database, connection to the server, and opening of the connection. The chapter also explains creating a `Command` object, executing commands, closing the connection, and releasing the resources. Finally, you learn to use `try ... catch ... finally`, administer the `using` keyword, display the table data through `GridView`, insert rows into a table, use parameters with the `Command` object, call stored procedures, and update the database table.

Chapter 17, "LINQ Queries"—Covers LINQ, implicitly typed local variables, and object and collection initializers. You learn to use lambda expressions, anonymous methods, extension methods, anonymous types, and LINQ categories.

Chapter 18, "Web-Based Application Development in .NET"—Explains Visual Studio toolbox, construction of your first web application, and use of the `CheckBox`, `RadioButton`, `ListBox`, `LinkButton`, and `HyperLink` controls. The chapter also explains using the `ImageButton` control, working with WCF, and creating a client application for web services.

Chapter 19, ".NET Assemblies"—Explains creation and use of a shared assembly.

COMPANION WEBSITE DOWNLOADS

You may download the companion website files from www.cengageptr.com/downloads.

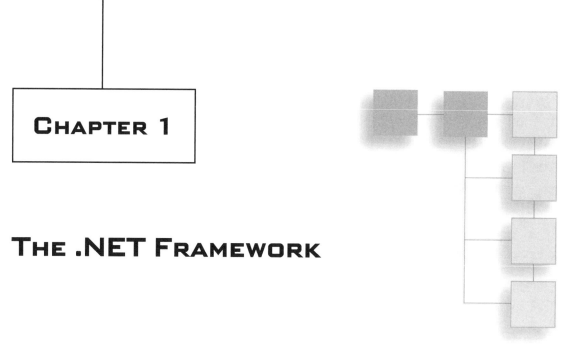

CHAPTER 1

THE .NET FRAMEWORK

This chapter's topics include the following:

- C# introduction
- .NET Framework structure
- Assembly use
- Visual Studio IDE overview
- Visual Studio installation
- Running a C# program
- Line-by-line explanation of code
- Modification of the Main() method

You'll begin your journey with an introduction to C#.

C# INTRODUCTION

C# was created at Microsoft in the late 1990s, and its chief architect was Anders Hejlsberg. As an object-oriented language, C# supports data encapsulation, inheritance, polymorphism, and method overriding. It is a powerful and simple language for building interoperable, scalable, and robust applications. Several of C#'s features are mentioned next:

- With C#, you can develop console windows as well as web applications.
- C# supports garbage collection and automatic memory management.

- C# includes native support for the Component Object Model (COM) and Windows-based applications.

- To avoid redundancy, the values of the primitive data types are automatically initialized to zeros, and reference types like objects and classes are initialized to null.

- C# produces portable code.

- Its programs execute in a secure, controlled, runtime environment.

- C# supports generics, partial types, and anonymous methods that expand the scope, power, and range of the language.

- It also supports language-integrated query (LINQ) and lambda expressions. LINQ enables you to write database queries in C# programming. Lambda expressions are used in LINQ expressions for efficient coding.

C# doesn't support unsafe type casts or pointers, and it doesn't accept 0 or 1 for Boolean values false and true, respectively.

Because C# automatically uses the .NET class library and it is automatically portable to all .NET environments, the next section covers the .NET framework and its relationship with C#.

.NET FRAMEWORK STRUCTURE

The .NET framework is a software development framework from Microsoft. It is a collection of tools, technologies, and languages that provides an environment to build and deploy robust enterprise applications easily. It also supports the development and execution of highly distributed, component-based applications. The .NET Framework sits on top of an operating system that includes Windows Vista, Windows 7, Windows 8, and Windows Server 2008. At the base of the .NET Framework is the Common Language Runtime (CLR) that manages the execution of the code (see Figure 1.1). Applications compiled for the .NET Framework are not compiled directly to native code but into an intermediate language called Microsoft Intermediate Language (MSIL). The CLR Just-In-Time (JIT) compiler compiles the MSIL code into native code before it is executed. The next layer up is the .NET Base Class Library, which contains classes and interfaces used for building applications. Above this layer is the ADO.NET and XML layer that supports the tasks related to data access, manipulating, parsing, and generating XML. The next layer is ASP.NET and Windows Forms, which build robust web applications and the standard Windows applications. The layer also develops and consumes web services. .NET supports cross-language integration. In other words, the code can be written in different programming languages that .NET supports. But different programming languages have different constructs. For making the languages compatible, Common Language Specification (CLS) is used. The CLS defines the reasonable subset of the CTS: the shared data type that helps in cross-language integration.

Because CTS is quite flexible, many languages adapt to the .NET platform. This means that you can develop web applications in several programming languages, including Visual Basic, C++, C#, JScript, and J#.

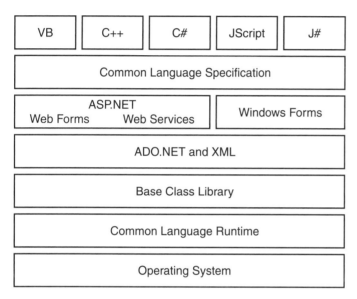

Figure 1.1
Structure of .NET Framework.
© 2015 Cengage Learning®.

.NET supports the following features:

- **Interoperability**—.NET includes a large library and supports several programming languages, allowing you to write code in different languages.

- **Common Language Runtime**—This is part of the .NET Framework that provides a runtime environment for the execution of code written in .NET languages. It manages the execution of .NET code, enables debugging and exception handling, and makes programs portable.

- **Language independence**—.NET supports several programming languages, including VB.NET, C#, J#, and C++, and the code in all the supported languages is compiled into Common Language Infrastructure (CLI) specifications, enabling you to exchange data types between programs developed in different languages.

- **Development for dynamic web pages**—.NET offers an integrated support for developing dynamic web pages, using a new technology.

- **Base Class Library**—This library contains classes, value types, and interfaces that are often used in application development. The classes are organized as namespaces, and the developers can easily use them just by including these namespaces in their programs.

- **ADO.NET**—ADO.NET provides access to relational databases and several data sources, such as Microsoft SQL Server and XML. You can use ADO.NET to connect to these data sources and retrieve, manipulate, and update data.

- **AJAX**—.NET supports AJAX, which developers can use to create highly responsive web applications with minimal effort.

- **Web services**—.NET has fully integrated support for developing web services.

- **Security**—.NET uses the assembly for code sharing instead of traditional DLL, which not only supports versioning but also implements security and allows only authorized categories of users or processes to call designated methods of specific classes.

Following are some important terms related to .NET that you need to understand before you move ahead.

Common Language Runtime (CLR)

The CLR is a runtime environment of the .NET Framework that manages the execution of .NET code and converts the source code into the MSIL. The MSIL is not an executable code but a portable assembly code; it is not dependent on a specific CPU. When the program is run, only the MSIL code is converted into executable code. The CLR activates the JIT compiler to convert MSIL into executable code. In other words, the MSIL can run in any environment for which the CLR is implemented, thereby implementing portability.

The CLR manages the code while executing. It also provides various services required in execution of an application, such as memory management, garbage collection, thread management, exception handling, and security checks. Furthermore, it manages versioning, deployment support, and debugging. Finally, it locates, loads, and manages different .NET types.

Note

> The code that is executed under the control of the CLR is known as *managed code.* The managed code is supposed to produce an MSIL file targeted for the CLR and use the .NET Framework library so that it can benefit from memory management, mixing languages, better security, and versioning control.

Common Type System

Common Type System (CTS) is a formal specification that documents how types are declared, used, and managed so the CLR can use them. Every language that is running on the .NET platform has a base set of data types that CTS provides. CTS ensures that the data types of objects written in various languages can interact with each other.

CTS supports both value types and reference types.

Value types represent built-in types like `int`, `float`, and `char`, user-defined types, and enumerations. Value types directly contain the data of the respective type and no reference. Instances of value types are allocated on the stack.

Reference types store a reference to the value's memory address and are allocated on the heap. Reference types can be arrays, pointer types, interface types, class types, or delegates.

Note

> C# has 15 predefined types, 13 value types, and 2 reference types.

Common Language Specification

The Common Language Specification (CLS) is a subset of CTS that ensures interoperability between the languages in the .NET environment. It defines the rules to support language integration so that the programs written in any .NET-compliant language can interoperate.

ASSEMBLY USE

Assemblies are basically the compiled code in .NET that contains the code in MSIL and a lot of other information that allows you to perform several tasks, including deployment, version control, reuse, activation scoping, and security permissions. In fact, every application in .NET is deployed as an assembly; in other words, the entire .NET code on compilation is converted into an intermediate language code and is stored as an assembly. There are two kinds of assemblies: executables that have the .exe file extension, and library assemblies that have the .dll file extension. These are also known as *class libraries* because they contain classes that you can directly use in your programs.

An *assembly* is a collection of class modules presented as a single .dll or .exe file. The assembly contains metadata that provides version information along with a complete description of methods, types, and other resources.

The metadata includes Manifest, which stores identification information, public types, and a list of other assemblies that are used in current assembly.

Each assembly has a 128-bit version number that is presented as a set of four decimal pieces: Major.Minor.Build.Revision. For example, an assembly might have the version number 8.0.1.7. The concept of versioning enables the developers to install new versions of the components that are not backward compatible. An assembly only uses types from the same assembly that it was built and tested with. If an assembly uses a type from version 8.0.1.7, for example, it does not use the same type from any other version. This helps developers in a couple of ways. First, the developers can define the same type in two assemblies without fear of collisions. Second, the developers can install a new version of the component(s) that is not backward compatible without fear of earlier applications that stop working.

There are two types of assemblies: private and shared. A private assembly is used by only one application, whereas a shared assembly is shared among several applications. By default, when a C# program is compiled, it produces a private assembly. The private assembly is placed in the same folder as the calling application. Because each application has its own copy of the assembly, there is no versioning problem in case of private assembly. In a shared assembly, to avoid a collision, you assign a unique name to it by using a strong name. A *strong name* is a combination of a filename, a public key, a version number, and a culture (locale information).

Private assemblies and shared assemblies are structurally identical. The real difference between private and shared assemblies depends on the way they are named and versioned and where they are deployed. Here are several distinctions between the two:

- Multiple applications can use a shared assembly. Only one application can use a private assembly.

- A shared assembly has to be registered in Global Assembly Cache (GAC). There's no need to register a private assembly; it is stored in the respective application's directory.

- A strong name has to be created for a shared assembly. A strong name is not required for a private assembly.

- A shared assembly can have multiple versions that are not backward compatible. If a private assembly has multiple versions that are not backward compatible, the application stops working.

- By default, all assemblies that you create are considered private assemblies. When you register a private assembly in GAC with a strong name, it becomes a shared assembly. The common utility that registers the assembly with a strong name in GAC is `gacutil.exe`, which is shipped with the .NET Framework.

After being introduced to C#, .NET, and its different terms, it's time to take a quick look at the steps required for running a C# program.

VISUAL STUDIO IDE OVERVIEW

To get started programming in C#, you need a compiler and an editor. Many editors and IDEs are available for this purpose. One of them that is popularly used is called Visual Studio. Visual Studio is Microsoft's integrated programming environment that enables you to edit, compile, run, and debug a C# program, all in one place. Visual Studio is basically a collection of software tools that is available in multiple editions: Professional, Premium, and Ultimate.

The Professional edition includes the basic features of the IDE to build applications on all .NET languages, including Visual Basic, C#, F#, and C++. It supports the writing, debugging, and testing of code. It enables development of all types of applications, including console, Windows, web, Windows Services, Cloud, WPF, Silverlight, Database, Office, and much more. In addition, it supports features that include unit testing, multicore development, office development, refactoring, access to Team Foundation Server (TFS), and Class Designer.

The Premium edition is an enhanced form of Professional edition that targets commercial enterprise application development. It supports database development tools and provides additional tools to verify, test, and check code. It also supports features that include profiling, code metrics, and user interface tests.

The Ultimate edition is an enhanced form of Premium edition that includes almost all tools required to develop different types of applications.

Visual Studio is also available in Express editions for developing applications for the web, Windows 8, and Windows Phone. The Express editions are free. Although they're not bundled with powerful tools, the Express editions are sufficient for developing small applications. They also have full language support and access to the .NET Framework libraries.

VISUAL STUDIO INSTALLATION

Visual Studio is compatible to 32-bit (x86) as well as 64-bit (x64) architectures. It supports operating systems that include Windows 7 (x86 and x64), Windows 8 (x86 and x64), Windows Server 2008 R2 (x64), and Windows Server 2013 (x64). It requires a 1.6GHz or faster processor, 1GB RAM, 10GB available hard disk space, 5400 RPM hard drive, and DirectX 9-capable video card running at 1024 × 768 or higher display resolution.

Visit http://www.visualstudio.com/en-us/downloads/download-visual-studio-vs.aspx to download the desired Visual Studio edition. An executable setup file is then downloaded to your computer. This book is being written while using Microsoft Visual Studio Express 2013 for Web.

1. Double-click the downloaded executable file to initiate the install of Visual Studio 2013.

2. Navigate to the location you'd like to install Visual Studio. The screen displays the hard disk space that the setup requires.

3. Agree to the license terms and conditions that are required before proceeding with the installation.

4. Click Next to move further. The next screen displays the list of optional features that you can install.

5. Select the check boxes of the desired features or choose Select All to select all the features.

6. Click the Install button. The next screen shows the progress of acquiring and applying the installation files.

7. Click the button to launch Visual Studio when the application process is completed.

When launched for the first time, Visual Studio displays a dialog box that prompts you to choose the default environment settings. Choose the General Development Settings option from the list of available environment settings and click on the Start Visual Studio button. The general development setting is applied, and your Visual Studio is ready for the application development. The first page that is displayed is known as the Start Page, and it is shown in Figure 1.2. As you can see in the figure, the Start Page contains a list of links to Visual Studio resources and web-based resources. You can return to the Start Page by selecting View, Start Page.

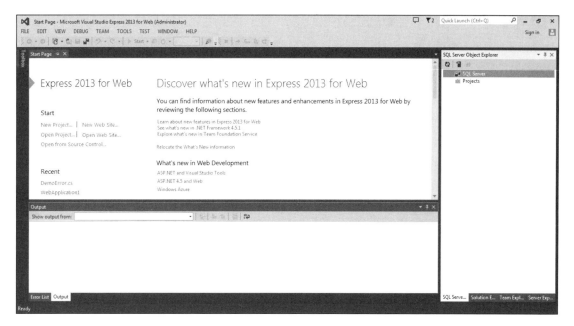

Figure 1.2
The Start Page after launching Visual Studio.
Used with permission from Microsoft.

The left column in the Start Page contains a Start section that displays links for building new applications. Below the Start section is the Recent section, which displays the links to projects that were recently created or modified. The right column contains the links to information about new features and improvements implemented in Visual Studio Express 2013 for Web. The column also contains the links to the new information in Web Development and various learning resources.

Now that you've learned how to install Visual Studio IDE, the next section explores the steps required for running a C# program.

RUNNING A C# PROGRAM

There are two ways to create, compile, and run a C# program. The first method is to use the Visual Studio IDE, and the second method is to use the command-line compiler csc.exe. First you'll look at using the Visual Studio IDE.

Using the Visual Studio IDE

To write a C# program in the Visual Studio 2013 IDE, launch it and select File, New Project or press Ctrl+Shift+N. A list of .NET-supported languages is displayed:

- **Visual Basic**—Developers who are familiar with Visual Basic or a similar language use this language to build type-safe, object-oriented applications.

- **Visual C#**—This option is designed for developers who are familiar with C-style languages, such as C, C++, and Java. Developers can use this language to rapidly develop type-safe, object-oriented applications.

- **Visual C++**—Specifically designed for C++ developers, this language can be used to build .NET managed applications as well as independent Windows-based applications that do not require .NET support.

- **Visual F#**—This language makes the task of developing applications related to science, engineering, and mathematical computations much easier.

Because you are interested in developing C# applications, select the Visual C# language from the left pane. After selecting a language, a list of project types that are supported by that language is displayed on the right. Here's a brief description of commonly used project types:

- **Windows Forms Application**—Creates a standalone Windows application–GUI-based application based on Windows Forms technology.

- **WPF Application**—Creates a project that uses a powerful Windows Presentation Foundation framework.

- **Console Application**—Creates command-line application executables. These applications don't support a graphical user interface and are executed at the command prompt.

- **ASP.NET Web Forms Application**—Creates web applications that can be deployed to a web server.

- **Class Library**—Creates reusable classes and components that can be shared with other projects. Specifically, this template enables you to build assemblies that can be shared with other applications.

- **Portable Class Library**—Creates and manages assemblies that work on more than one .NET Framework platform. That is, the assemblies can work on .NET 4, .NET 4.5, Silverlight 5, Windows Phone 8, and other platforms without modifications.

- **ASP.NET MVC 3/4 Web Application**—Creates a web application based on a web application development framework that splits applications into three layers: the model, the view, and the controller.

- **Silverlight Application**—Creates applications based on the application framework Microsoft Silverlight for developing rich Internet applications. These applications support multimedia, graphics, animation, languages, and development tools.

- **Silverlight Class Library**—Creates a Silverlight class library project that can be used by Silverlight applications.

- **Windows Forms Control Library**—Creates custom controls to use on Windows Forms.

From the list of project types displayed, select the Console Application type. Specify the name of the application as ConsoleApp, and then select the OK button (shown in Figure 1.3).

Note

If you don't find the Console Application type in your Visual Studio IDE, select the Class Library option.

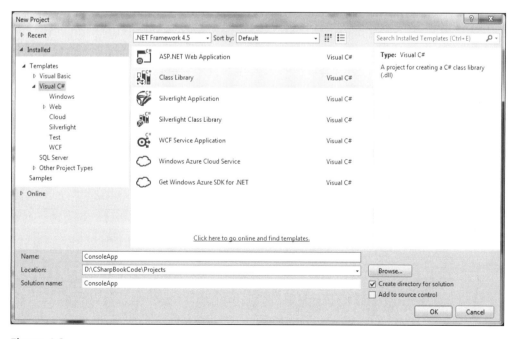

Figure 1.3
Selecting the Console Application template for creating a new application.
Used with permission from Microsoft.

The new console application appears, as shown in Figure 1.4. In the figure, notice certain windows and toolbars. Here's a description of them:

- **Solution Explorer**—In the Solution Explorer window (docked on the right side), you can see the default files that are created by the IDE. Only the editable files are displayed; other IDE-generated files are hidden by default. To display all the files, including the hidden ones, click the Show All Files icon located at the top of the Solution Explorer window. If it's hidden, select View, Solution Explorer to make the Solution Explorer window visible. Each project type that is selected while creating a new project provides a specific default code. The main file of the console application is Class1.cs, and it automatically shows up in the Editor window when the application is loaded. The Properties folder provides access to the project-level settings. References are a collection of assemblies that the application depends on. The project template automatically adds to the project references to commonly used class libraries (see Solution Explorer in Figure 1.4).

Note

Visual C# files use the .cs filename extension, which is short for "C#."

- **Properties Window**—Located below the Solution Explorer, this window displays the properties for the currently selected form, control, or object in the IDE. Properties display information about the selected item, such as its ID, text, size, and color. The left column lists the properties, and the right column displays the value of each property. You can modify the properties of the selected item as per your requirements, and the IDE automatically generates the related code. You can sort the properties either alphabetically by clicking the Alphabetical icon or category wise by clicking the Categorized icon. If the Properties window is hidden, select View, Properties Window to display it.

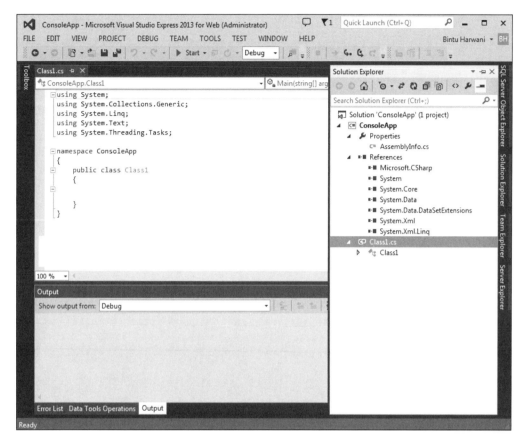

Figure 1.4
Visual Studio IDE showing default code for console application.
Used with permission from Microsoft.

- **Error List Window**—This window displays errors in the code if any exist and helps in pointing out and removing them. After you double-click the error that is shown in this window, the cursor jumps to the location of the error in the source code so you can correct it. The code that is causing the error is specifically marked with red wavy lines. The location of the error is specified as a line number. By default, line numbers aren't displayed in the VS text editor. To display the line numbers, select Tool, Options. From the Options dialog box, expand the Text Editor Node and select C# node and check the Line Numbers check box, as shown in Figure 1.5.

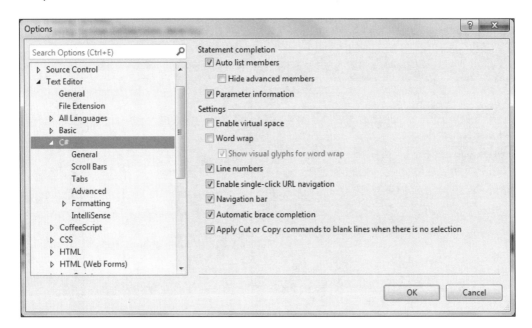

Figure 1.5
Options dialog box.
Used with permission from Microsoft.

- **ToolBox**—This shows the tools, also called *controls*, divided into related categories. If it's invisible, ToolBox can be displayed by selecting View, Toolbox. To use a control in GUI applications, just drag it from the desired category and drop it on the form, and the IDE automatically generates code for that tool. By default, the AutoHide feature is enabled for the ToolBox; consequently, the ToolBox appears when you click its title. The ToolBox appears over the Design window (in case of Forms) or the Editor window, thereby hiding the controls behind the ToolBox. Also, it makes it difficult to add controls to the form. To switch off the AutoHide feature—in other words, to keep the ToolBox visible on the left of the Design or Editor window—click the pushpin button in the upper-right corner of the ToolBox.

- **Menu Bar and Toolbar**—Menu Bar contains the groups of related commands used for managing and manipulating the IDE and the applications. When you choose a menu item from a menu, the designated task for that menu item is performed. The commonly used menu items are provided in the form of tools in the toolbar. The tools in the toolbar appear as icons. When you hover the mouse, a ToolTip appears indicating the task that the tool can perform.

The default code provided in the file Class1.cs is shown in Listing 1.1.

Listing 1.1 Default Code in Class1.cs File

```
using System;
using System.Collections.Generic;
using System.Linq;
using System.Text;
using System.Threading.Tasks;

namespace ConsoleApp
{
    public class Class1
    {
    }
}
```

You want to display the message Hello World! through this application. For this, add two statements, Console.WriteLine and Console.ReadLine with the Main method, to the preceding code. The Main method is an entry point of a C# console or Windows application. The file after adding the two statements appears as shown in Listing 1.2. Only the code in bold is newly added; the rest of the code is default.

Listing 1.2 Code Written in Class1.cs File

```
using System;
using System.Collections.Generic;
using System.Linq;
using System.Text;
using System.Threading.Tasks;

namespace ConsoleApp
{
    public class Class1
    {
        static void Main(string[] args)
        {
            Console.WriteLine("Hello World!");
            Console.ReadKey();
        }
    }
}
```

The `Console.WriteLine()` method is meant for displaying a message or a result of processing on the screen. In contrast, the `Console.ReadKey()` method is used for getting a key from the user through the keyboard.

Basically, when you run a console-based application in the Visual Studio IDE, the output appears in a console window, and control immediately comes back to Visual Studio IDE. (That is, the console window does not wait for sufficient time for the user to see the program output and goes back to the IDE immediately; consequently, you will not be able to view the output of the program.) To make the console window wait for enough time, enabling the user to view the output of the program, you need to add the `Console.ReadKey()` method to the program. The `Console.ReadKey()` method waits for the user to press any key on the keyboard, thereby displaying the output of the program. Only when the user presses a key does the console window disappear. To compile and run the program, select Debug, Start Debugging or press the F5 key. You get the output shown in Figure 1.6.

Note

If the application type chosen is `Class Library`, then we need to set its output type to Console Application. For doing so, right-click the project in Solution Explorer and select the Properties option. From the Properties dialog, click the Application tab, and in the Output Type drop-down, select the Console Application option.

Figure 1.6
Output of the console application.
Used with permission from Microsoft.

You can see that the text message `Hello World!` is displayed on the screen.

Now that you understand the way C# runs in the Visual Studio IDE, the next section covers how to run C# through the command-line compiler.

Using the Command-Line Compiler

The C# command-line compiler is convenient for compiling and running C# programs because you don't have to create a project for the program. So it is a bit faster and easier than using the IDE. Simply type the program in an editor, say Notepad.exe, and save the file with the extension .cs in any of the folders on your disk drive. For example, type the code as shown in Listing 1.3 in Notepad and save it with the name HelloWorld.cs.

Listing 1.3 Code Written in HelloWorld.cs File

```csharp
using System;
class HelloWorldClass
{
    static void Main(string[] args)
    {
        Console.WriteLine("Hello World!");
    }
}
```

To compile the program through the C# command-line compiler csc.exe, you need to open a command prompt window that is configured for Visual Studio. Select the Developer Command Prompt for VS2013 option from the Start menu. Thereafter, using the CD command, go to the folder where you have saved the HelloWorld.cs file. At the command prompt, execute the C# compiler csc.exe, specifying the name of the source file, as shown here:

```
D:\CSharpBookCode>csc HelloWorld.cs
```

The csc compiler shows errors in your program if any exist. If there are no errors, the csc compiler successfully compiles the program and creates a file called HelloWorld.exe that contains the MSIL version of the program (see Figure 1.7). Although MSIL is not executable code, it is still contained in an .exe file.

Figure 1.7
Compiling and running the C# program HelloWorld.
Used with permission from Microsoft.

The Common Language Runtime automatically invokes the JIT compiler after executing the file HelloWorld.exe. To run the program, just type its name at the command prompt, as shown here:

D:\CSharpBookCode>HelloWorld

When the program runs, the following output is displayed:

Hello World!

Note

If the csc command does not work, the path is not set. Set the following path for csc.exe: C:\Windows\Microsoft.NET\Framework\vX.X.XXX.

LINE-BY-LINE EXPLANATION OF CODE

```
1 using System;
2 class HelloWorldClass
3 {
4      static void Main(string[] args)
5      {
6          Console.WriteLine("Hello World!");
7      }
8 }
```

Line 1 indicates that the program is using the System namespace. A namespace defines a logical grouping that organizes related classes, structures, delegates, enumerations, interfaces, and other types. The idea of enclosing these members in namespaces is to avoid name conflicts. A class named A defined in namespace1 does not conflict with the class named A defined in namespace2. By using or importing a namespace in a program, you enable the importing program to access the members organized in the namespace. Because you are using the library class System.Console in your program, the using System; statement allows you to refer to this class simply as Console (without qualifying it by namespace as System). That is, you can access any of the members defined in the System namespace directly without qualifying it with the System namespace if you import it at the top of the program with the using statement. Most of the .NET types are defined in the standard System namespace. In this program, the goal is to access the WriteLine() method of the Console class defined in the System namespace for displaying a text message on the screen. The Console is the .NET base classes. Besides the Console class, there are many other classes defined in the System namespace that are used in almost every C# program. Therefore, you will be importing the System namespace with the `using` statement in almost all C# programs. You will learn about namespaces in detail in Chapter 5, "Arrays and Strings."

Note

The most fundamental namespace used in C# applications is `System`. It is not possible to build a functional C# application without using the `System` namespace.

Line 2 uses the keyword `class` to declare that a new class is being defined. The class is used for encapsulation. The name of the class is `HelloWorldClass`. The class definition begins with the opening curly brace (`{`) and ends with the closing curly brace (`}`). The elements between the two braces are members of the class.

Line 4 defines the `Main()` method and is the entry point of a C# program. (That is, it begins its execution from the `Main()` method.) The method has the static modifier, which means it can be called before an object of this class is created. This is because `Main()` is called at program startup. The keyword `void` indicates that the `Main()` method does not return a value. The `Main()` method has a single parameter: an array of strings (`string[] args`). You can use this parameter for passing command-line arguments. You will be learning about command line arguments in detail in Chapter 4, "Decision-Making and Looping." The empty parentheses that follow `Main` indicate that no information is passed to `Main()`. The opening curly braces (`{`) signal the start of `Main( )`'s body. All the code that comprises a method occurs between the method's opening and its closing curly brace.

For displaying output on the screen, you use the method `WriteLine()` of the `Console` class, as shown in line 6. The string passed to the `WriteLine()` method is displayed on the screen. Information that is passed to a method is called an *argument*. The line begins with `Console`, which is the name of a predefined class that supports console input/output (I/O). By calling the `WriteLine( )` method of the `Console` class, you display the desired output on the screen. You will learn about console I/O in detail in Chapter 2, "Data Types."

Note

C# is a case-sensitive language, and all its statements are terminated with a semicolon. You don't need to terminate the blocks with a semicolon; the blocks are used for grouping statements and begin and end with two curly braces, { and }, respectively.

MODIFICATION OF THE MAIN() METHOD

By default, Visual Studio generates a Main() method that has a void return value and a parameter: an array of string to be used for command-line arguments, as shown here:

```
static void Main(string[] args)
{
}
```

You can always modify the Main() method as per your requirement. You can remove the parameter and change the return type to int, and so on. The following Main() method has no return type and no parameter:

```
static void Main()
{
}
```

Similarly, the following Main() method returns a value of the int data type:

```
static int Main()
{
    ......
    return 0;
}
```

Likewise, the Main() method has a parameter and returns a value of the int data type:

```
static int Main(string[] args)
{
    ......
    return 0;
}
```

In short, you can use any type of Main() method depending on the program's requirement.

Next, you'll quickly write another program. The program shown in Listing 1.4 computes the area of a rectangle. The formula is length × breadth, and the values of length and breadth are given as 50 and 8, respectively.

Listing 1.4 Code Written in RectArea.cs File

```
using System;
class RectAreaClass
{
    static void Main()
```

```
    {
        int l,b,a;
        l=50;
        b=8;
        a=l*b;
        Console.WriteLine ( "The area of the rectangle is {0} ", a ) ;
    }
}
```

You can see that three variables, l, b, and a, are defined of int type (integer type). The variables l, b, and a are meant for storing the values of the length, breadth, and area of the rectangle, respectively. The variables l and b are assigned the given values 50 and 8, respectively. The computed area of the rectangle is assigned to the variable a and is thereafter displayed on the screen using the WriteLine() method of the Console class, as shown in Figure 1.8.

Note

The term int used in the previous example is a data type, and l, b, and a are variables. You will be learning about different data types and variables in the next chapter.

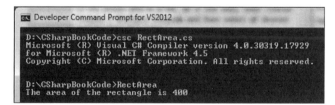

Figure 1.8
Compiling and running the C# program RectArea.
Used with permission from Microsoft.

The {0} used in the WriteLine() method is a format specifier that is replaced by the value of the argument or variable that is located after the double quotes. Therefore, the value of the variable a that is located after the double quotes replaces the {0}. Remember, the value 0 in curly braces { } represents the first variable, 1 represents the second variable, and so on. The following statement makes it clearer:

```
Console.WriteLine ( "Length is {0}, breadth is {1} and the area of the rectangle is {2}",
l,b,a ) ;
```

In the preceding statement, there are three variables, l, b, and a, after the double quotes. The value of variable l replaces the format specifier, {0}, the value of b replaces {1}, and the value of variable a replaces {2}, displaying the following output:

```
Length is 50, breadth is 8 and the area of the rectangle is 400
```

WriteLine() method supports concatenation, or the addition of expressions by using the + symbol. For example, if you don't like format specifiers, you substitute the above WriteLine() statement by the following:

```
Console.WriteLine ( "Length is " + l +", breadth is "+ b +" and the area of the rectangle is "+a ) ;
```

You can see that the variables l, b, and a in the preceding statement are used without quotes to display their value.

SUMMARY

This chapter introduced C# and the .NET Framework. You learned about different features and components of the .NET Framework, including the CLR, CTS, and CLS. You also came to understand the concept of assembly. You learned about the role of Visual Studio IDE in developing C# applications and how to download and install Visual Studio IDE. You also witnessed creating and running the C# programs through the Visual Studio IDE as well as through the command-line compiler. Finally, you saw how to modify the Main() method as per your requirement.

The next chapter covers identifiers, keywords, variables, and constants. You will learn about the two C# predefined data types: predefined value types and predefined reference types. You will also learn about integer, floating-point, decimal, character types, and Boolean types. In addition, you will read about string types. You will come to understand implicitly typed variables, implicit conversion, and explicit type conversion. You will learn about the predefined streams, console I/O, and reading input from the console. Finally, you will create a Windows Form application step by step.

CHAPTER 2

DATA TYPES

This chapter's topics include the following:

- Identifiers and keywords
- Variables
- Constants
- Predefined data types
- Predefined value types
- Nullable types
- Predefined reference types
- Implicitly typed variables
- Reference types
- Boxing
- Unboxing
- Streams
- Console I/O
- Comment Use
- Windows form application

Identifiers, keywords, variables, and data types play a major role in programming. You learn about them in detail next.

IDENTIFIERS AND KEYWORDS

Identifiers are the names programmers use to represent classes, methods, variables, and so on. For example, in the program shown in Listing 2.1, the identifiers are System, RectAreaClass, Main, l, b, a, Console, and WriteLine.

Listing 2.1 Code Written in RectArea.cs File

```
using System;
class RectAreaClass
{
    static void Main()
    {
        int l,b,a;
        l=50;
        b=8;
        a=l*b;
        Console.WriteLine ( "The area of the rectangle is {0} ", a ) ;
    }
}
```

An identifier must be a whole word and should be made up of Unicode characters. *Unicode* is a character-encoding standard that is widely accepted for handling and representing text. The identifiers start with a letter or an underscore and are case sensitive.

Keywords are names reserved by the compiler that cannot be used as identifiers. The keywords in the program shown in Listing 1.4 are using, class, static, void, and int.

The full list of C# keywords is shown in Table 2.1.

Table 2.1   C# Keywords

abstract	as	base	bool	break	byte	case
catch	char	checked	class	const	continue	decimal
default	delegate	do	double	else	enum	event
explicit	extern	false	finally	fixed	float	for
foreach	goto	if	implicit	in	int	interface
internal	is	lock	long	namespace	new	null
object	operator	out	override	params	private	protected
public	readonly	ref	return	sbyte	sealed	short
sizeof	stackalloc	static	string	struct	switch	this
throw	true	try	typeof	uint	ulong	unchecked
unsafe	ushort	using	virtual	void	while	

© 2015 Cengage Learning®.

You should avoid using an identifier that matches a keyword. But if it is necessary to use an identifier that matches a keyword, use it with the @ prefix to avoid a collision. For example, the following statement creates a problem because extern is a keyword:

```
int extern
```

But the next statement is correct:

```
int @extern
```

The preceding statements declare extern as an int variable.

VARIABLES

Variables, as the name suggests, refer to terms whose values vary. In other words, they keep a value that might change or are modified during processing. Following is the syntax for declaring variables in C#:

```
datatype identifier;
```

where datatype can be int, char, and so on.

For example:

```
int l;
```

The preceding statement declares an `int` variable named `l`. For safety reasons, you cannot use this variable in a program until you initialize it. After you declare it, you can assign a value to the variable using the assignment operator = as shown in the next statement:

```
l = 50;
```

You can declare a variable and initialize it simultaneously:

```
int l = 50;
```

You can declare and initialize more than one variable of the same data type using a single statement:

```
int l = 50, b =8;
```

You can modify the values in the variables `l` and `b` while processing.

CONSTANTS

As the name suggests, a *constant* is a variable whose value is fixed and cannot be changed. Constants are prefixed with the `const` keyword and are initialized at the time of declaration.

For example:

```
const float pi=3.1414F;
```

Because you cannot change the value of a constant, you cannot change `pi` throughout the program.

Constants make your programs easier to read and modify. They also help you prevent mistakes because the compiler displays an error if you make an attempt to change the value of a constant. Remember, you cannot initialize a constant through a variable. If you just change the value of the constant, the changes are automatically applied everywhere the constant is used.

PREDEFINED DATA TYPES

In C#, there are two types of predefined data types:

- **Value types**—These store the value directly. Data types such as `int`, `float`, `double`, `bool`, and `char` are value types that are stored on the stack.

- **Reference types**—These data types don't store the value; instead, they store a reference to the value. The class objects, strings, and dynamically created variables are known as *reference types* because they hold references to blocks of memory and are managed on the heap. The *heap* is basically all unallocated memory in an operating system. When you declare a variable, the compiler allocates a block of memory to store a corresponding value.

The following example makes it clearer:

```
int l=50;
int b=l;
```

Because the variable l is an `int` data type, 4 bytes of memory will be allocated for it. The value 50 that is assigned to the variable l is stored in the allocated block of memory. For the variable b, a separate block of 4 bytes of memory is allocated, and its value of 50 is stored in another memory block. The value of 50 is stored in two locations in memory; consequently, the changes made in either variable do not affect the other.

For example, if the value of variable l is incremented by 5:

```
l+=5
```

then only the memory block of variable l is updated to show the new value of 55. There is no change in the block of memory assigned to variable b.

Now consider the following example of a reference type. Assume that `Rect` is a class with two member variables: `length` and `breadth`. You will learn about classes and objects in detail in Chapter 7, "Classes and Objects."

```
Rect r=new Rect(50,8);
Rect s=r;
```

The values 50 and 8 are assigned to the member variables `length` and `breadth` of the object r. Remember: only one `Rect` object, r, is created. r and s point to the same memory location that contains the object. As reference types, the variables r and s just contain a reference; that is, they refer to the same object. The value of one object displays in another, and the changes made in either object affect the other. Because values 50 and 8 were assigned to the member variables `length` and `breadth`, the following example displays the value of member variable `length` (50):

```
Console.WriteLine(s.length);
```

Similarly, after you change the value of the member variable, the length of object s also makes the changes in the member variable of object r:

```
s.length=70;
Console.WriteLine(r.length);
```

The garbage collector claims the memory allocated to the reference types when there are no references left for them. Similarly, when the value types go out of scope, the memory allocated to them is released. Using `value` types increases performance because fewer objects on the managed heap reduce overloading of the garbage collector.

PREDEFINED VALUE TYPES

All the data types in C# are part of the .NET Framework. So whenever any variable of predefined value types—such as `int`, `float`, `double`, or `char`—is declared, internally an instance of a respective struct in the .NET Framework is also declared. For example, an `int` type in C# represents an instance of a .NET struct, `System.Int32`. In other words, all the predefined data types in C# are represented by a respective .NET type or struct known as Common Type System (CTS). The benefit of this concept is that all data types are treated as classes; therefore, they can invoke the respective methods. For example, to convert an `int` 1 to a string, you can call the method shown here:

```
string s = 1.ToString();
```

Note

CTS plays a major role to ensure cross-language interoperability.

Integer Types

C# supports the following eight predefined integer types, as shown in Table 2.2.

Table 2.2 Predefined Integer Types in C#

Name	CTS Type	Description	Range
sbyte	System.SByte	8-bit signed integer	–128 to 127 (-2^7 to $2^7 - 1$)
short	System.Int16	16-bit signed integer	–32,768 to 32,767 (-2^{15} to $2^{15} - 1$)
int	System.Int32	32-bit signed integer	–2,147,483,648 to 2,147,483,647 (-2^{31} to $2^{31} - 1$)
long	System.Int64	64-bit signed integer	–9,223,372,036,854,775,808 to 9,223,372,036,854,775,807 (-2^{63} to $2^{63} - 1$)
byte	System.Byte	8-bit unsigned integer	0 to 255 (0 to $2^8 - 1$)
ushort	System.UInt16	16-bit unsigned integer	0 to 65,535 (0 to $2^{16} - 1$)
uint	System.UInt32	32-bit unsigned integer	0 to 4,294,967,295 (0 to $2^{32} - 1$)
ulong	System.UInt64	64-bit unsigned integer	0 to 18,446,744,073,709,551,615 (0 to $2^{64} - 1$)

© 2015 Cengage Learning®.

You can see in Table 2.2 that in C#, an `int` is a 32-bit signed integer, a `byte` is an 8-bit unsigned type, an `sbyte` is a signed 8-bit type, a `short` is a 16-bit type, and a `long` is a 64-bit type. You need to append an integer with the characters `U`, `L`, `UL` to declare whether it is an unsigned, long or an unsigned long integer, as shown in the next statements:

```
uint a=10U;
long b=10L;
ulong c=10UL;
```

Floating-Point Types

The floating-point types represent the numbers that have fractional values. There are two kinds of floating-point types—`float` and `double`—which represent single- and double-precision numbers, respectively. The `float` type is 32 bits and has a range of `1.5E-45` to `3.4E+38`. The `double` type is 64 bits and has a range of `5E-324` to `1.7E+308`. So the `float` data type is used for smaller floating-point values, where less precision is required. Whenever a noninteger value is specified, the compiler interprets it as a `double` by default. To ensure the value will be treated as a floating-point value, append character `F` or `f` to the value.

Listing 2.2 evaluates the expression `3.0/7.0` and displays the result in `float` as well as in `double` format.

Listing 2.2 Code in FloatDouble.cs File

```
using System;
class FloatDouble
{
    static void Main()
    {
        float a;
        double b;
        a= 3.0F/7.0F;
        b= 3.0/7.0;
        Console.WriteLine ( "Float value of 3.0/7.0 expression is {0} and double value is
{1}", a,b ) ;
    }
}
```

Output:

```
Float value of 3.0/7.0 expression is 0.4285714 and double value is 0.428571428571429
```

The character F is appended to the expression 3.0/7.0 while assigned to variable a; otherwise, the compiler treats it as a double value. The expression 3.0/7.0 assigned to variable b is considered a double value. You can see the difference between the precision of the two fractional values in the output.

Next, you will read about another predefined value type supported by C#: the decimal type.

Decimal Types

The decimal type uses 128 bits to represent values within the range 1E-28 to 7.9E+28. The decimal type represents a value up to 28 decimal places, so it eliminates the rounding errors. The decimal type is preferred in monetary computations.

Note

The decimal constants are followed by the m or M suffix. Without the suffix, the values are interpreted as standard floating-point constants.

Listing 2.3 uses a decimal type for computing interest on some amount. Precisely, the program computes and displays 12.24% interest on the 100.50 amount using decimal type variables.

Listing 2.3 Code in DecimalType.cs File

```
using System;
class DecimalType {
    static void Main() {
        decimal amount, interest_rate, interest_amount, total_amount;
        amount = 100.50m;
        interest_rate = 12.24m;
        interest_amount = amount * interest_rate/100;
        totamount = amount+ interest_amount;
        Console.WriteLine("Original amount is {0}, interest is {1} and amount with
interest added is {2}", amount, interest_amount, total_amount);
    }
}
```

Output:

```
Original amount is 100.50, interest is 12.3012 and amount with interest added is
112.8012
```

Character Types

The C# `char` type is used to store a single character. It represents a single 16-bit (Unicode) character. In C#, the `byte` type and the `char` type are different bit sizes (`byte` is 8 bits, whereas `char` is 16 bits), so they cannot be implicitly converted. You need to explicitly convert the `byte` type to a `char` type and vice versa if you use it in an expression.

Literals of type `char` are enclosed in single quotation marks, as shown in this example:

```
char k= 'A';
```

The double quotation marks are used for the `strings` type. If a single character is enclosed in double quotations, you get a compilation error.

Next you'll look at different methods provided by the `char` class.

Character Methods

The `char` class includes several methods that you can use to check the content of individual characters. Following is the list of methods:

- **char.IsDigit(character)**—Returns `true` if the character is a digit 0 to 9.
- **char.IsLetter(character)**—Returns `true` if the character is a letter a to z or A to Z.
- **char.IsLetterOrDigit(character)**—Returns `true` if the character is a letter or a digit.
- **char.IsLower(character)**—Returns `true` if the character is a lowercase letter.
- **char.IsUpper(character)**—Returns `true` if the character is an uppercase letter.
- **char.IsPunctuation(character)**—Returns `true` if the character is a punctuation character.
- **char.IsWhiteSpace(character)**—Returns `true` if the character is a space, tab, or newline character.

The program shown in Listing 2.4 demonstrates using the `char` type and invoking different `char` class methods.

Listing 2.4 Code in CharType.cs File

```
using System;
class CharType {
    static void Main() {
        char a='A';
        char b='1';
```

```
        char c='a';
        char d='?';
        char e=' ';
        Console.WriteLine("The character in variable a is {0}", a);
        Console.WriteLine("The variable b contains {0} and it is a digit value: {1}", b,
char.IsDigit(b));
        Console.WriteLine("The variable c contains {0} and it is in lower case: {1}", c,
char.IsLower(c));
        Console.WriteLine("The variable d contains {0} and it is a punctuation: {1}", d,
char.IsPunctuation(d));
        Console.WriteLine("The variable e contains {0} and it is a white space: {1}", e,
char.IsWhiteSpace(e));
    }
}
```

Output:

```
The character in variable a is A
The variable b contains 1 and it is a digit value: True
The variable c contains a and it is in lower case: True
The variable d contains ? and it is a punctuation: True
The variable e contains     and it is a white space: True
```

You can see that the char class methods IsDigit(), IsLower(), IsPunctuation(), and IsWhiteSpace() methods return the Boolean value true. Basically, these methods help in decision-making when you use them in conditional statements, which you will be learning in the next chapter.

Bool Types

The C# bool type can store either of the Boolean values: true or false. The CTS type of bool data type is System.Boolean. The bool type is usually used in the logical expressions, such as in loops and conditional branching.

Example:

```
bool k=true;
```

NULLABLE TYPES

Recall that all the predefined value types in C#, such as int, float, double, and char, are represented by a respective .NET type or struct known as CTS (Common Type System). All these data types have a fixed range. For example, you can assign the int type in the range –2,147,483,648 to 2,147,483,647. Similarly, a bool type can be assigned either `true` or `false`. One thing to remember is that you can never assign `value` types `null`. For example, the next code snippet generates a compiler error:

```
using System;
class NullableType {
  static void Main() {
    int length=null;       //compiler error
    bool k=null;   //compiler error;
    Console.WriteLine("Length is {0}", length);
  }
}
```

Because `null` values are assigned to the `value` types `int` and `bool`, the preceding code generates a compiler error, as shown in Figure 2.1.

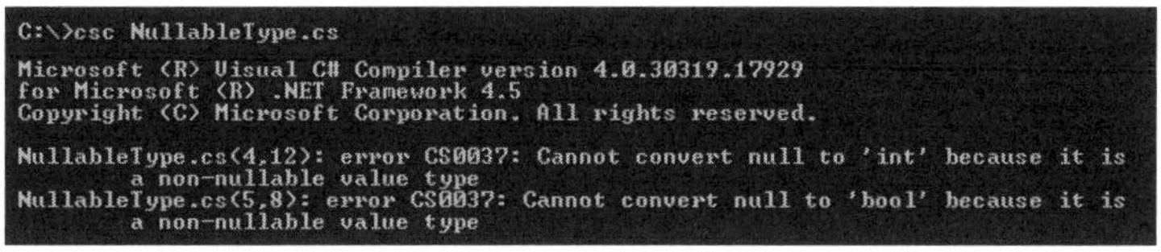

Figure 2.1
Compilation errors generated when you assign null values to value types.
Source: Visual Studio.

To enable a data type to accept a `null` value, C# supports the concept of `nullable` data types. A `nullable` type can represent all the values of its underlying type along with the `null` value. For example, you can assign a `nullable int` any value within its permissible range or `null`. Similarly, you can assign a `nullable bool` the three values `true`, `false`, or `null`. The `nullable` types help in initializing the variables that have no initial values. To define a `nullable` variable type, add a question mark symbol (?) to the underlying data type, as shown in the following syntax:

```
< data_type> ? <variable_name> = null;
```

Example:

```
int? length=null;
bool? k=new bool?();
```

The first example defines a `nullable int` variable `length`. The second example defines a `nullable boolean` variable `k`.

The program `NullableType.cs` shown in Listing 2.5 is a corrected format of the preceding code snippet.

Listing 2.5 Code in NullableType.cs File

```
using System;
class NullableType {
static void Main() {
int? length=null;
bool? k=null;
Console.WriteLine("Length is {0} and boolean variable k is {1}", length, k);
length=10;
k=true;
if(k !=null)
Console.WriteLine("Length is {0} and boolean variable k is {1}", length, k);
}
}
```

The output is shown in Figure 2.2.

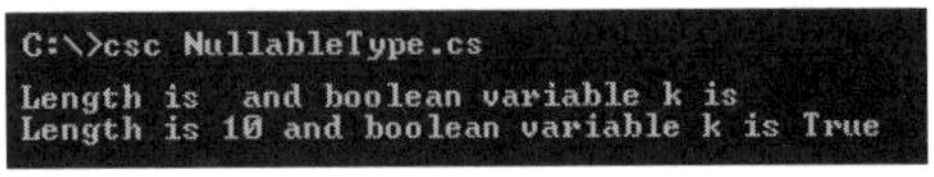

Figure 2.2
Output of the NullableType program.
Source: Visual Studio.

Note that `null` values are not displayed on the screen. They appear as white spaces.

As mentioned at the beginning of this chapter, C# reference types include objects, strings, and dynamically created variables.

PREDEFINED REFERENCE TYPES

Predefined reference types don't store the value but a reference to the value. The class objects, strings, and dynamically created variables are known as reference types because they hold references to blocks of memory. This book discusses objects and dynamically created variables in Chapter 6, "Methods and Structures." The `string` types are discussed next.

The `string` type represents a sequence of characters, as shown in the following example:

```
string a = "Hello ";
```

The `string` type is internally translated to the .NET class `System.String`, which in turn provides different methods to perform various operations on strings. For example, the following statements concatenate the two strings:

```
string a = "Hello";
string b = "World";
string c = a + b; // strings will be concatenated; i.e., c will have HelloWorld
```

There are two types of string literals in C#. The first are the regular string literals, as shown in the preceding examples, and the other are verbatim string literals. Regular string literals start and end with " (double quotes). The verbatim string literals are prefixed by @ and can span multiple lines. To store special symbols, the regular string literal has to be "escaped." (In other words, the special symbols must be represented by escape sequence characters.) The following examples will make it clear:

Statement	Output
`string a="Hello";`	`// Hello`
`string b=@"Hello";`	`// Hello`
`string c="\\Hello\\";`	`// \Hello\`
`string d=@"\Hello\";`	`// \Hello\`
`string e = "Hello \t World";`	`// Hello   World`
`string f = @"Hello \t World";`	`// Hello \t World`
`string g = "\"Hello\"";`	`// "Hello"`
`string h = @"""Hello""";`	`// "Hello"`
`string i="Hello\nWorld\nThanks";`	`// Displays Hello World and` `Thanks on separate lines`

`string j=@"Hello`
`World`
`Thanks";`
	`// Displays Hello World and`
	`Thanks on separate lines`

Note

Unlike C, C++, and Java, the strings in C# are not null terminated, and the text is stored as a collection of the `char` object. Consequently, the C# string can contain embedded `null` characters (`'\0'`).

The escape sequence was mentioned in the previous example. Now it will be discussed in detail. Table 2.3 displays a complete set of escape sequences.

Table 2.3 Set of Escape Sequence Characters

Escape Sequence	Purpose
\'	Single quotation mark
\"	Double quotation mark
\\	Backslash
\0	Null
\a	Alert
\b	Backspace
\f	Form feed
\n	Newline
\r	Carriage return
\t	Horizontal tab
\v	Vertical tab

© 2015 Cengage Learning®.

The program shown in Listing 2.6 demonstrates use of escape sequences and the job they perform.

Listing 2.6 Code in EscapeSequence.cs File

```
using System;
class EscapeSequence {
    static void Main() {
        Console.WriteLine("\'Hello\'");
        Console.WriteLine("\"Hello\"");
        Console.WriteLine("\\Hello\\");
        Console.WriteLine("There is a null value between Hello\0World");
        Console.WriteLine("Alert signal \a");
        Console.WriteLine("Yes\b\b\bNo");
        Console.WriteLine("Form feed: Hello\fWorld");
        Console.WriteLine("Hello\nWorld");
        Console.WriteLine("Carriage return without new line: Hello\rWorld");
        Console.WriteLine("Carriage return with new line: Hello\r\nWorld");
        Console.WriteLine("Hello\tWorld");
        Console.WriteLine("Vertical tab: Hello\vWorld");
    }
}
```

After running the program, you get the output shown in Figure 2.3.

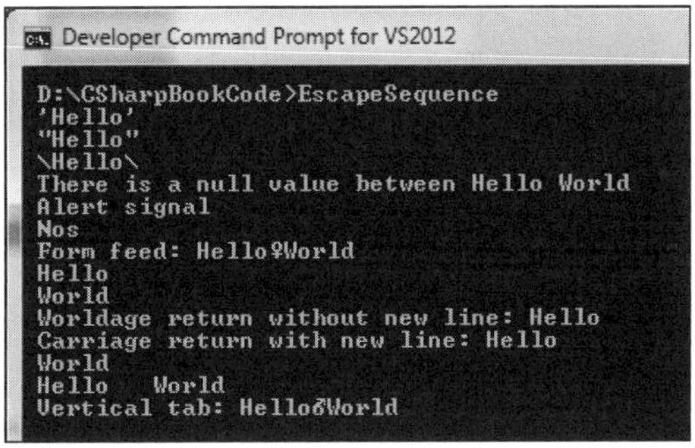

Figure 2.3
Output of the EscapeSequence program.
Source: Visual Studio.

You can see in the output shown in Figure 2.3 that displaying a single quote, a double quote, or a backslash requires an escape with a backslash (\). The null character \0 does not display on the screen and is represented by a whitespace. An alert signal \a results in a beep. The word Yes is displayed, and by using three times \b, the cursor is moved three characters back (on the character Y) and then is overwritten by the word No. In other words, the characters Ye of the word Yes are replaced by No, thereby displaying Nos on the screen. The newline character \n displays Hello and Word on two consecutive lines. The carriage return \r takes the cursor to the beginning of the same line (on the character C of the word Carriage). The word World overwrites the first five characters of the word Carriage, resulting in Worldage. The carriage return, along with newline character \r\n, takes the cursor to the beginning of the next line and the word World appears on the new line. The horizontal tab \t inserts spaces between the words Hello and World. The form feed and vertical tab perform on printers and not on the screen. The form feed takes you to the next page, and the vertical tab leaves vertical spacing while printing.

IMPLICITLY TYPED VARIABLES

Usually a data type of a variable is specified while declaring it. C# allows you to use implicitly typed variables, where the C# compiler itself determines the type of the variable based on the value that initializes it. An implicitly typed variable is declared by initializing it to some value and using the keyword var.

Example:

```
var pi = 3.1416;
```

Because pi is initialized with a floating-point literal of double type, pi is declared as a variable of the double data type. The following example declares the variable pi as a variable of the decimal type:

```
var pi = 3.1416M;
```

The suffix M represents decimal values and hence declares the variable pi of the decimal type.

You can declare only one implicitly typed variable at a time; in other words, declaring two implicitly typed variables together is not allowed. For example, the following statement generates an error:

```
var x = 10, y = 20;
```

While using implicitly typed variables, you must initialize the variable; otherwise, the compiler can't determine the type of the variable. The variable should not be initialized to null.

The program shown in Listing 2.7 uses implicitly typed variables for computing and displaying the area of a circle. The formula is pi*radius^2.

Listing 2.7 Code in ImplicitType.cs File

```
using System;
class ImplicitType {
   static void Main() {
      var pi = 3.1416;     // pi is implicitly defined of double type
      var radius = 5;      // radius is implicitly defined of int type
      var area=pi*radius*radius;
      Console.WriteLine("Area of circle is {0}", area);
   }
}
```

Output:

```
Area of circle is 78.54
```

You can see that the variables pi and radius are implicitly declared of double and int type based on the values used to initialize them. The area of a circle is computed using the given formula and displayed.

While writing expressions in a program, you come across variables of different types. You might need to convert variable(s) of one type to another. Next, you'll learn how these conversions take place.

Implicit Conversion

When you assign a value of one type to another, an implicit conversion takes place; that is, the value of the right side is automatically converted to the type on the left side. An implicit type conversion takes place automatically if the two types are compatible and if the destination type is larger than the source type.

Compatible types refer to similar types. For example, int, float, double, long, and byte are compatible types because they all belong to numerical types.

```
int a;
float b;
a=10;
b=a;
```

In the preceding example, the value in variable a is converted into float and assigned to variable b. Here's one more example:

```
long c;
double d;
c = 992200555L;
d = c;
```

This example implicitly converts the long value stored in variable c to a double data type. The reverse is not possible; a double cannot be implicitly converted to a long because the long data type is smaller in bit size than the double data type.

Explicit Type Conversion

You can explicitly convert data of one type to another. This conversion is also known as *casting*. Here's the syntax for performing explicit conversion:

```
(target_datatype) data_to_convert
```

where target_datatype refers to the data type in which you want to convert the data that is represented by data_to_convert:

Example:

```
double x;
int y;
y=(int) x;
```

In the preceding example, the data of the double data type in variable x is converted to the int data type. Remember: there is no implicit conversion from double to int type because int is of a smaller data type (in bit size) than double. Information may be lost while converting to the smaller data type. For example, while converting data of `float` type to `int`, the values after the decimal point are removed.

Now that you understand different predefined types supported by C# and how conversion takes place among them, you'll look at different operators supported by this programming language.

You have read about different value types. Now you'll learn about reference types in detail.

REFERENCE TYPES

By now, you know that reference types don't store the actual value; instead, they store a reference to the value. The reference types are categorized as built-in reference types and user-defined reference types:

- **Built-in reference types**—Built-in reference types include the following categories:
  - **Object**—The *object* data type is an alias for the `System.Object` class that is the base class of almost all C# data types. Values of any other data type (`numerical` types, `bool` types, `string` types, and so on) can be assigned to an object type after performing some type of conversion. The object type therefore acts as a general-purpose container that can be used to refer to any type. The process of converting a value type to an object type is known as *boxing*, and the reverse procedure of converting an object type to a value type is called *unboxing*.
  - **String**—A *string* is a built-in reference data type that represents a sequence of zero or more Unicode characters. You will learn about strings in Chapter 5, "Arrays and Strings."
- **User-defined reference types**—User-defined reference types include the following:
  - **Class**—A *class*, as mentioned earlier, is a user-defined structure that contains variables and methods.
  - **Delegate**—A *delegate* is a user-defined reference type that stores the reference of one or more methods. Chapter 11, "Delegates and Events," discusses delegates.
  - **Interface**—An *interface* is a type of user-defined class that is used for multiple inheritance. Chapter 9, "Interfaces," discusses interfaces in detail.

■ **Array**—An *array* is a user-defined data structure that contains values of the same data type. The values in an array are stored in consecutive memory locations. Chapter 5 discusses arrays.

Now you will learn how a `value` type is converted to an `object` type and vice versa.

Boxing

The variables of type `object` can refer to any object of any reference type. In addition, the variables of type `object` can refer to a `value` type, as shown in the next example:

```
int a = 10;
object b = a;
```

The variable `a`, which is a value type, is defined and initialized to value 10, and the variable `b`, an `object` type or reference type, is initialized to variable `a`. But there is a problem. The variable `a` is a `value` type, so it is managed on the stack. When the reference inside object `b` is set to refer to integer `a`, the reference needs to refer to the stack, which may deteriorate the runtime efficiency and is not allowed. All references must refer to objects on the heap and not to the items on the stack, so the runtime allocates a block of memory from the heap, copies the value of integer `a` to that memory block, and finally refers the object `b` to that memory block. This automatic copying of an item from the stack to the heap is known as boxing. If you modify the value of variable `a`, the value on the heap does not change, and vice versa. The preceding two statements show implicit boxing. You can rewrite the statements to perform explicit boxing:

```
int a = 10;
object b = (object) a;
```

Unboxing

In boxing, you saw how a variable of an `object` type can refer to a `value` type. Through unboxing, you can get back the boxed value from the object type variable. To access the boxed `int` value that the object `b` refers to, you can write the following assignment statement:

```
int a = b;
```

The preceding statements result in a compile-time error because a reference type cannot implicitly be converted to a `value` type:

```
int a = 10;
object b = a;  // Implicit Boxing
a = (int)b;    // Explicit Unboxing
```

The preceding code runs without error because here you explicitly convert the reference type to a value type. While performing explicit unboxing, you need make sure that the variable types match. In other words, if the value type boxed is of int type, you must unbox it to an int type variable. The following code generates a run-time error:

```
int a = 10;
int p;
float q;
object b = a;    // Implicit Boxing
p = (int)b;      // Explicit Unboxing
q = (float)b;    // Generates runtime error
```

You can see that unboxing to the variable p is okay because it matches the type (int) of the value type that is boxed, but unboxing to the variable q generates a runtime error because variable a is boxed as int type and therefore must be unboxed to int variable only.

It is recommended that you avoid boxing and unboxing. It severely reduces the performance of a program because of the overhead of checking on data types, allocation of heap memory, and so on.

In explicit boxing, you cast the object to a type assuming that the data referenced by the object has a specific type. If the type of object in memory does not match the cast, the InvalidCastException exception is thrown. C# provides two operators that confirm whether the data referenced by the object has a specific type that you can use before casting the object. Those two operators are is and as.

The is Operator

The is operator checks whether an object is compatible with a specific type. That is, it checks whether an object is of a specific type or is derived from a particular type. To check whether a variable is compatible with the object type, use the following code:

```
int a = 10;
object b=a;
if (b is a)
{
int c=(int) b;
}
```

You can see that the is operator takes two operands: one is an object type, and the other is a value type. If the type of the referenced object matches with the value type, it evaluates to true; otherwise, it evaluates to false. In the preceding code, explicit casting is performed only after you know that the object is compatible with a specific type.

The as Operator

The as operator performs explicit type conversions of reference types. It takes an object and a type as its operands. If the object (reference type) being converted is compatible with the specified type, conversion is performed successfully; otherwise, the operator returns the null value. The following code makes it clearer:

```
int a = 10;
object b=a;
int c= b as int;
string str = b as string;
```

You can see in the preceding example that the object b is set to refer to an int type. The first as operator, after finding that the object b is compatible with the int type, successfully converts it to the int type. The second as operator returns null because it finds that object doesn't refer to the string instance.

Whatever is displayed or produced as output by a program and whatever is entered in the program is referred to as a *stream*. You'll learn more about streams in the next section.

STREAMS

A *stream* is an object that transfers data in either direction (that is, reading data from the stream into the program or writing data from the program out to the stream). Stream in this case basically refers to the data in terms of bytes (byte stream); internally, all data is dealt with in terms of bytes only. Because bytes are harder for humans to understand, people often prefer to deal with character streams, which are in human-readable form. Because in C# char is a 16-bit type and byte is an 8-bit type, you need to convert character streams into byte streams and vice versa. The character stream classes are just wrappers that convert an underlying byte stream to a character stream. A stream class is an abstract class; therefore, it cannot be instantiated directly. All classes that represent streams inherit from the stream class.

At the top of the character stream hierarchy are the abstract classes TextReader and TextWriter. TextReader and TextWriter are base classes. The StreamReader and StringReader classes are derived from the abstract type TextReader class, whereas the

`StreamWriter` and `StringWriter` classes are derived from the abstract type `TextWriter` class. An outline of the mentioned classes is given here:

- **StreamReader**—Reads characters from a byte stream. This class wraps a byte input stream.

- **StreamWriter**—Writes characters to a byte stream. This class wraps a byte output stream.

- **StringReader**—Reads characters from a string.

- **StringWriter**—Writes characters to a string.

Methods Defined by stream Class

The methods defined by the `stream` class to read and write data are given next:

- **void Close( )**—Closes the stream.

- **void Flush( )**—Writes the contents of the stream to the physical device, preferably a file.

- **int ReadByte( )**—Reads a single byte from the input and returns it as an integer value. It returns –1 when the end of the stream is reached.

- **int Read( )**—Reads a specified number of bytes from the input into an array. Here's the syntax:

  ```
  int Read(byte[ ] buf, int offset, int num)
  ```

  Reads up to `num` number of bytes into the array `buf` starting at offset `buf [offset]`. The method returns the number of bytes that are successfully read from the input.

- **void WriteByte( )**—Writes the specified byte to an output stream. Here's the syntax:

  ```
  void WriteByte(byte b)
  ```

- **int Write( )**—Writes an array of bytes to an output stream. Here's the syntax:

  ```
  int Write(byte[ ] buf, int offset, int num)
  ```

  The `num` numbers of bytes from the byte array `buf` are written into the file beginning at `buf[offset]`. The number of bytes written is returned. If an error occurs during the writing process, an `IOException` is thrown. If the underlying stream is not opened for output, a `NotSupportedException` is thrown.

- **long Seek( )**—Sets the current position of the pointer in the stream to the specified offset from the specified origin. Here's the syntax:

  ```
  long Seek(long offset, SeekOrigin origin)
  ```

You will learn about the byte and character streams in detail in Chapter 15, "Streams." But for the time being, you need to understand the concept of predefined streams in C#.

The Predefined Streams

The three predefined streams that are provided in C# are `Console.Out`, `Console.In`, and `Console.Error`. Their outline is given here:

- **Console.Out**—Refers to the standard output stream. When you call `Console.WriteLine()`, it sends data to `Console.Out` (that is, monitor or screen) to display.
- **Console.In**—Refers to standard input, which is, by default, the keyboard. When you call `Console.ReadLine()`, it reads data from the keyboard.
- **Console.Error**—Refers to the standard error stream; displays errors on the console by default.

For using any of these three predefined streams, you have to import the `System` namespace in your program through the `using` statement.

Next, you'll see how the predefined streams are used in console I/O operations.

Console I/O

As the name suggests, console input and output are used for reading a line of text from the console window and for writing given data to the console window. First, you'll learn the methods used for sending output to the console window.

Sending Output to the Console

You use two methods for writing data to the console: `Console.Write()` and `Console.WriteLine()`:

The `Console.Write()` method writes the given data to the console window.

Like `Console.Write()`, the `Console.WriteLine()` method writes the given data to the console window, but `Console.WriteLine()` adds a newline character at the end of the data.

Here's the syntax:

```
Console.WriteLine("Data or text message to print and format specifiers ", arg0, arg1,
... , argN)
```

where `arg1, arg2....argN` are the comma-separated variables or argument list. The arguments are displayed inside the text message according to the format defined by the format specifiers. The format specifiers appear in the curly braces and determine the argument number to be displayed in the text message, its width, and its format, if any.

The format specifiers can have any of the following syntax:

- `{N}}`
- `{N, [+/-]width}`
- `{N, [+-]width: format[precision]]}`

where N refers to the argument numbers beginning with value 0 (that is, it represents the argument number to be inserted in the text message). For example, {0} refers to the argument arg0. Hence, {0} is replaced by the value in the argument arg0. Similarly, the format specifier {1} represents the location for substituting the value in argument arg1; the format specifier {2} represents the argument arg2; and so on.

Example:

```
int a=10, b=20;
Console.WriteLine("Value of a is {0} and value of b is {1}", a,b);
```

The output of the preceding statement will be as follows:

```
Value of a is 10 and value of b is 20
```

The output confirms that the format specifiers {0} and {1} are replaced by the values of the variables a and b, respectively.

The second syntax of the format specifier reports that you can also specify width for displaying the argument. In addition, you can justify the text within the width. If the width value is positive, the text has to be right justified within the given width. A negative value is used for left justifying the text in the given width.

Example:

```
int a=10, b=20;
Console.WriteLine("Value of a is {0,15} (right justified) and value of b is {1,-10}
(left justified)", a,b);
```

Here's the output of the preceding statement:

```
Value of a is              10 (right justified) and value of b is 20
(left justified)
```

You can see that the value of the variable a, 10, is assigned the width of 15 and is justified to the right within the given width. Similarly, the value of the variable b, 20, is assigned the width of 10 and is left justified within the given width.

The third syntax of the format specifier enables you to add a format string along with an optional precision value to format the argument while it's on display. A few of the format strings are shown in Table 2.4.

Table 2.4   List of Format Strings Used in Formatting Arguments

Format String	Description
C	Currency format.
D	Decimal format. Converts an integer to base 10. The precision specifier pads with leading zeros.
E	Scientific format. The precision sets the number of decimal places (6 by default). The case of the format string (e or E) determines the case of the exponential symbol.
F	Fixed-point format. The precision determines the number of decimal places.
G	General format. Uses E or F formatting, whichever is compact.
N	Number format. Uses commas as thousands separators.
P	Percent format.
X	Hexadecimal format. The precision specifier pads with leading zeros.

To understand the usage of the preceding format strings, look at the following example:

```
decimal a=1234.75M;
int b=1234;
Console.WriteLine("Currency format with precision, 2: {0,10:C2}", a);
Console.WriteLine("Decimal format with precision, 8: {0,10:D8}", b);
Console.WriteLine("Default scientific format {0,10:E}, and scientific format with 4
places of decimals : {1,10:e4}", a,a);
Console.WriteLine("Fixed point format with 3 number of decimal places: {0,10:F3}", a);
Console.WriteLine("General format: {0,10:G}", a);
Console.WriteLine("Number format: {0,10:N}", a);
Console.WriteLine("Percent format: {0,10:P}", a);
Console.WriteLine("Hexadecimal format with precision, 6: {0,10:X6}", b);
```

After applying the preceding format strings to the arguments in the `Console.WriteLine()` method, you get the output as shown here:

```
Currency format with precision, 2:   $1,234.75
Decimal format with precision, 8:    00001234
Default scientific format 1.234750E+003, and scientific format with 4 places of decimals : 1.2348e+003
Fixed point format with 3 number of decimal places:    1234.750
General format:     1234.75
Number format:    1,234.75
Percent format: 123,475.00 %
Hexadecimal format with precision, 6:      0004D2
```

You can see that `C2` format string displays numbers in two-decimal format. The format string `D8` displays the integer to base 10, and because the integer is four digits, it is padded with leading four 0s. The format string `E` displays the number to six places of decimals with an exponential symbol displayed in uppercase. The `e4` format string displays the number to four places of decimals and displays an exponential symbol in lowercase. The format string `F3` displays the number to three places of decimal. The format string `G` displays the number in exponential or fixed point format. In the preceding above, your number is displayed in fixed-point format. The format string `N` displays the number with thousand separators `(,)`. The format string `P` multiplies the number by 100 and displays it two places of decimals along with the percent symbol. The format string `X6` displays the number in hexadecimal format. Because the hexadecimal number is three digits, it is padded with three leading zeros.

Reading Input from the Console

To get data from the console (keyboard), you can use the following two methods:

- **Console.Read( )**—Reads a single character from the console (that is, the keyboard). The character read is returned as an `int`, so you must cast it to `char`. After entering a character, you need to press the Enter key so it's sent into the program for processing.
  Here's the syntax:
  ```
  Console.Read()
  ```

- **Console.ReadLine( )**—Reads characters from the keyboard until you press the Enter key and returns them in the form of a `string` object.
  Here's the syntax:
  ```
  Console.ReadLine()
  ```

To understand how you can get data from the user, you need to rewrite the program for computing the area of rectangle. But this time, instead of assuming some fixed values for length and breadth, you will ask the user to enter values for them. The program that computes the area of a rectangle by using the length and breadth values entered by the user is shown in Listing 2.8.

Listing 2.8 Code Written in RectAreaInput.cs File

```
using System;
class RectAreaInput
{
    static void Main()
    {
        int l,b,a;
        Console.Write("Enter Length: ");
        l = int.Parse(Console.ReadLine());
        Console.Write("Enter Breadth: ");
        b = int.Parse(Console.ReadLine());
        a=l*b;
        Console.WriteLine ( "The area of the rectangle is   {0} ",a ) ;
    }
}
```

Output:

```
Enter Length: 5
Enter Breadth: 10
The area of the rectangle is 50
```

In the preceding program, the user is asked to enter values for length and breadth through the Console.ReadLine() function. The values of length and breadth that the user enters are in string form, and you need to convert them to int type through the int.Parse() method. The values of length and breadth, when converted to int type, are multiplied to calculate the area of a rectangle. You can also convert the string type into the int type using the System.Convert.ToInt32() method. The System.Convert class contains various methods to perform different data type conversions.

As said earlier, Main() is an entry point for a program. You might wonder if there can be more than one entry point or Main() method in a program. The answer is yes!

Next, you'll combine the two classes RectAreaClass and RectAreaInput into one program. Create the program TwoRect.cs with the code shown in Listing 2.9.

Listing 2.9 Code Written in TwoRect.cs File

```
using System;
class RectAreaClass
{
    static void Main()
    {
        int l,b,a;
        l=50;
        b=8;
        a=l*b;
        Console.WriteLine ( "The area of the rectangle is " + a ) ;
    }
}
class RectAreaInput
{
    static void Main()
    {
        int l,b,a;
        Console.Write("Enter Length: ");
        l = int.Parse(Console.ReadLine());
        Console.Write("Enter Breadth: ");
        b = int.Parse(Console.ReadLine());
        a=l*b;
        Console.WriteLine ( "The area of the rectangle is   {0} ",a ) ;
    }
}
```

Compiling the TwoRect.cs program leads to an error, as shown in Figure 2.4. The error appears because, by default, the compiler looks for exactly one Main() method in any class to use as the entry point for the program.

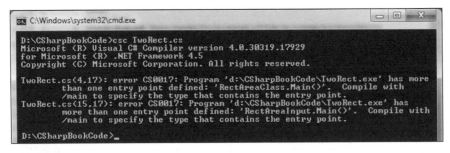

Figure 2.4
Errors displayed while compiling the C# application TwoRect.cs.
Source: Visual Studio.

When there is more than one `Main()` method, you need to inform the compiler which of these methods should be used as the entry point for the program. You do so by using the `/main` switch, with the full name of the class to which the `Main()` method belongs. For example, to use the `Main()` method of the `RectAreaInput` class, you need to compile the program as shown here:

```
csc TwoRect.cs /main:RectAreaInput
```

By the preceding statement, the compiler knows that the `Main()` method of the `RectAreaInput` class must be used as the entry point of the program. So, after running the program `TwoRect`, you get the output of the `RectAreaInput` class (see Figure 2.5). Similarly, to use the `Main()` method of the `RectAreaClass`, you can compile the program as shown here:

```
csc TwoRect.cs /main:RectAreaClass
```

The previous statement shows that the `Main()` method of the `RectAreaClass` will be used. So, after running the `TwoRect` program, the output of `RectAreaClass` will follow, as shown in Figure 2.5.

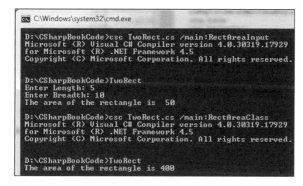

Figure 2.5
Compiling the C# application TwoRect.cs with desired Main() methods.
Source: Visual Studio.

Sometimes you want to write comments in a program to inform the reader why you're using certain code. The next section explains how to write comments in C#.

COMMENT USE

Comments represent the code that is not compiled. They increase the readability of the code and are used for documentation. Not only do comments remind the programmer why a certain formula or statement is used, but they inform what might be the result of using particular statements. Remember, the compiler ignores comments.

There are three types of comments:

- **Single-Line Comment**—This type of comment is one line long. It begins with a double slash (//) and concludes at the end of the line.
  Example:

  ```
  // This program calculates the area of a rectangle
  ```

- **Trailing Comment**—This type of comment appears at the end of a statement. The statement is followed by the comment symbol, a double slash (//). The statement before the comment symbol is executed and the text following the comment symbol are ignored.
  Example:

  ```
  a=l*b;    // This formula computes the area of a rectangle
  ```

- **Multiline Comment**—This type of comment is enclosed within /* and */. As the name suggests, a multiline comment can be several lines long, and the compiler ignores anything between the two comment symbols /* and */.
  Example:

  ```
  /*
  For calculating the area of a rectangle
  The user is asked to enter values of length and breadth
  The length and breadth values are multiplied to compute the area of a rectangle */
  ```

All the C# applications that you made up until now were console based. Now you'll create a GUI-based Windows application and see how you can write C# code in it.

WINDOWS FORM APPLICATION

You will create a Windows Form application that is an exact replica of the console-based application that you created earlier. In other words, you will create a Windows Form application that prompts the user to enter length and breadth values. The TextBox controls are displayed, where the user can enter length and breadth values. When the user clicks the Button control after entering the length and breadth values, the area of rectangle is displayed on the screen.

To create a simple Windows Form application, launch Visual Studio and select the File, New, Project option. Select the Windows Forms Application project type, assign the name WindowsFormsRectApp to the project, and click OK to create the project.

The rectangle in the Design area is titled Form1. (See Figure 2.6 in the main window of the Windows Forms application. It is on this window that you will be placing a control and creating a graphical user interface, or GUI.) The ToolBox on the left displays the list of controls divided into the related categories that you can drag and drop on Form1.

Note

You can have multiple forms or windows in an application.

Click the ToolBox and select the All Windows Forms tab to display the list of controls contained in it.

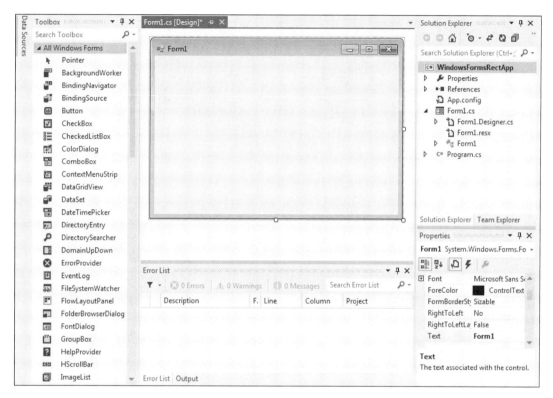

Figure 2.6
Screen after creating a Windows Form application.
Source: Visual Studio.

Drag and drop three Label, three TextBox, and a Button control on the form, as shown in Figure 2.7 (left). By default, the three Label controls have the names label1, label2, and label3, respectively. Similarly, the default names assigned to the three TextBox controls are textBox1, textBox2, and textBox3, respectively. The name of the Button control is button1 by default. Now perform the following steps on the seven controls:

1. Set the Text property of the label1 control to Enter Length:.

2. Set the Text property of the label2 control to Enter Breadth:.

3. Set the Text property of the label3 control to The area of rectangle is.

4. Set the Text property of the button1 control to Calculate.

5. Set the Name property of the textBox1 control to txtLength.

6. Set the Name property of the textBox2 control to txtBreadth.

7. Set the Name property of the textBox3 control to txtRectArea.

8. Set the Name property of the button1 control to btnCalculate.

9. Set the ReadOnly property of the txtRectArea control to True because you don't want the user to be able to edit the value displayed in this text box.

After you perform these tasks, the form appears, as shown in Figure 2.7 (right).

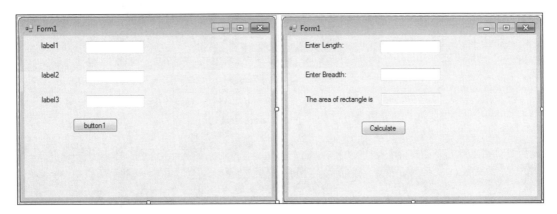

Figure 2.7
(left) Form after placing the Label, TextBox, and Button controls; (right) form after setting the Name and Text properties of the controls.
Source: Visual Studio.

Earlier you read about the process of dragging and dropping controls on the Form1.cs[Design] window. Because you want the area of the rectangle to be calculated and displayed when the user clicks the Button control, double-click the Calculate button on the form to open the Form1.cs window. Write the following code in the btnCalculate_Click method:

```
private void btnCalculate_Click(object sender, EventArgs e)
{
        int l = Convert.ToInt32(txtLength.Text);
        int b = Convert.ToInt32(txtBreadth.Text);
        int a = l * b;
        txtRectArea.Text = a.ToString();
}
```

The preceding code accesses the `length` and `breadth` values that the user enters in the `txtLength` and `txtBreadth` TextBox controls. The values accessed from the `TextBox` controls are converted to integer values, and the area of a rectangle is computed, which is then assigned to variable `a`. The area of the rectangle in variable `a` is converted to string format before it's assigned to the `txtRectArea` TextBox for display.

When you create a GUI in the `Form1.cs[Design]` window (that is, drag and drop controls on the form and set their `Name`, `Text`, and other properties), Visual Studio automatically generates the corresponding code in the `Form1Designer.cs` file. Listing 2.10 shows the code in the `Form1Designer.cs` file that is auto-generated for you and that represents the controls and their properties that you placed on the form.

Comments in C# are represented by different symbols. The single-line comments are specified using the symbol //. The multiline comments are specified using the symbol /* */. The XML tags, text strings, and API documentation are represented by the third type of comment symbol: ///.

Listing 2.10 Code Auto-Generated in Form1Designer.cs File

```
namespace WindowsFormsRectApp
{
    partial class Form1
    {
        /// <summary>
        /// Required designer variable
        /// </summary>
        private System.ComponentModel.IContainer components = null;

        /// <summary>
        /// Clean up any resources being used
        /// </summary>
        /// <param name="disposing">true if managed resources should be disposed;
otherwise, false</param>
        protected override void Dispose(bool disposing)
        {
            if (disposing && (components != null))
            {
                components.Dispose();
            }
            base.Dispose(disposing);
        }

        #region Windows Form Designer generated code

        /// <summary>
        /// Required method for Designer support - do not modify
```

```
/// the contents of this method with the code editor
/// </summary>
private void InitializeComponent()
{
    this.label1 = new System.Windows.Forms.Label();
    this.label2 = new System.Windows.Forms.Label();
    this.label3 = new System.Windows.Forms.Label();
    this.txtLength = new System.Windows.Forms.TextBox();
    this.txtBreadth = new System.Windows.Forms.TextBox();
    this.txtRectArea = new System.Windows.Forms.TextBox();
    this.btnCalculate = new System.Windows.Forms.Button();
    this.SuspendLayout();
    //
    // label1
    //
    this.label1.AutoSize = true;
    this.label1.Location = new System.Drawing.Point(27, 9);
    this.label1.Name = "label1";
    this.label1.Size = new System.Drawing.Size(71, 13);
    this.label1.TabIndex = 0;
    this.label1.Text = "Enter Length:";
    //
    // label2
     //
    this.label2.AutoSize = true;
    this.label2.Location = new System.Drawing.Point(27, 57);
    this.label2.Name = "label2";
    this.label2.Size = new System.Drawing.Size(75, 13);
    this.label2.TabIndex = 1;
    this.label2.Text = "Enter Breadth:";
    //
    // label3
    //
    this.label3.AutoSize = true;
    this.label3.Location = new System.Drawing.Point(27, 97);
    this.label3.Name = "label3";
    this.label3.Size = new System.Drawing.Size(122, 13);
    this.label3.TabIndex = 2;
    this.label3.Text = "The area of rectangle is ";
    //
    // txtLength
    //
    this.txtLength.Location = new System.Drawing.Point(155, 9);
    this.txtLength.Name = "txtLength";
```

```
            this.txtLength.Size = new System.Drawing.Size(100, 20);
            this.txtLength.TabIndex = 3;
            //
            // txtBreadth
            //
            this.txtBreadth.Location = new System.Drawing.Point(155, 54);
            this.txtBreadth.Name = "txtBreadth";
            this.txtBreadth.Size = new System.Drawing.Size(100, 20);
            this.txtBreadth.TabIndex = 4;
            //
            // txtRectArea
            //
            this.txtRectArea.Location = new System.Drawing.Point(155, 97);
            this.txtRectArea.Name = "txtRectArea";
            this.txtRectArea.ReadOnly = true;
            this.txtRectArea.Size = new System.Drawing.Size(100, 20);
            this.txtRectArea.TabIndex = 5;
            //
            // btnCalculate
            //
            this.btnCalculate.Location = new System.Drawing.Point(138, 155);
            this.btnCalculate.Name = "btnCalculate";
            this.btnCalculate.Size = new System.Drawing.Size(75, 23);
            this.btnCalculate.TabIndex = 6;
            this.btnCalculate.Text = "Calculate";
            this.btnCalculate.UseVisualStyleBackColor = true;
            this.btnCalculate.Click += new
System.EventHandler(this.btnCalculate_Click);
            //
            // Form1
            //
            this.AutoScaleDimensions = new System.Drawing.SizeF(6F, 13F);
            this.AutoScaleMode = System.Windows.Forms.AutoScaleMode.Font;
            this.ClientSize = new System.Drawing.Size(416, 262);
            this.Controls.Add(this.btnCalculate);
            this.Controls.Add(this.txtRectArea);
            this.Controls.Add(this.txtBreadth);
            this.Controls.Add(this.txtLength);
            this.Controls.Add(this.label3);
            this.Controls.Add(this.label2);
            this.Controls.Add(this.label1);
            this.Name = "Form1";
            this.Text = "Form1";
            this.ResumeLayout(false);
```

```
            this.PerformLayout();

        }
        #endregion
        private System.Windows.Forms.Label label1;
        private System.Windows.Forms.Label label2;
        private System.Windows.Forms.Label label3;
        private System.Windows.Forms.TextBox txtLength;
        private System.Windows.Forms.TextBox txtBreadth;
        private System.Windows.Forms.TextBox txtRectArea;
        private System.Windows.Forms.Button btnCalculate;

    }
}
```

The C# code was written to handle the click event of the btnCalculate button in the Form1.cs file. Listing 2.11 shows the complete code in the Form1.cs file.

Listing 2.11 Complete Code of Form1.cs File

```
using System;
using System.Collections.Generic;
using System.ComponentModel;
using System.Data;
using System.Drawing;
using System.Linq;
using System.Text;
using System.Threading.Tasks;
using System.Windows.Forms;

namespace WindowsFormsRectApp
{
    public partial class Form1 : Form
    {
        public Form1()
        {
            InitializeComponent();
        }

        private void btnCalculate_Click(object sender, EventArgs e)
        {
            int l = Convert.ToInt32(txtLength.Text);
            int b = Convert.ToInt32(txtBreadth.Text);
            int a = l * b;
            txtRectArea.Text = a.ToString();
        }
    }
}
```

Your application is now ready to run. Run the application by selecting the Debug, Start Debugging option or by pressing the F5 key. After entering the `length` and `breadth` values in the first two `TextBox` controls, when you click the Calculate button, the area of the rectangle is computed and displayed in the third `TextBox` control, as shown in Figure 2.8.

Note

You cannot edit the area displayed in the third `TextBox` control because it is set to Read-Only mode.

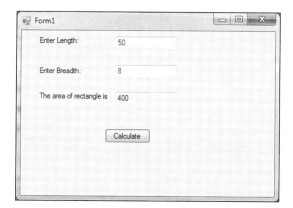

Figure 2.8
Area of rectangle displayed after clicking the Calculate button.
Source: Visual Studio.

This application confirms that the Visual Studio IDE performs most of the work when developing applications. All the files, folders, and code for developing Windows applications are auto-generated for you. You simply place the controls, set the properties, and handle the events. That's it.

SUMMARY

In this chapter you learned about identifiers, C# keywords, variables, and constants. You learned about different types of predefined value types and saw how to use `integer`, `float`, `decimal`, `character`, and `bool` types. You also saw different types of integers, their CTS types, and their range. You discovered how predefined reference types are different from predefined value types. You explored implicitly typed variables and implicit and explicit type conversion. In addition, you learned about streams, console I/O, and the methods of reading input from the console. You also saw how comments are added to a program. Finally, you discovered how to create a Windows Form Application step by step.

The next chapter is focused on understanding different operators, including their precedence and associativity. You will learn about the `typeof`, `sizeof`, `checked`, and `unchecked` operators. You will also read about arithmetic, increment and decrement, and sign operators. In addition, you will find out how relational, equality, logical Boolean, and logical bitwise operators are used in a C# program. Also, you will learn to use Shift, the assignment operators, and ternary operators in C# programs. Finally, you will learn about the math class and different methods provided by this class.

CHAPTER 3

OPERATORS AND EXPRESSIONS

This chapter's topics include the following:

- Operators
- Precedence and associativity
- Arithmetic operators
- Relational operators
- Equality operators
- Logical Boolean operators
- Logical bitwise operators
- Shift operators
- Assignment operators
- Ternary operator (conditional operator)
- The Math class

You'll start with learning the operators and their different types.

OPERATORS

Operators are the symbols that represent a specific mathematical or logical processing. Operators process the data, also known as *operands*. Depending on the number of operands that operators deal with, the operators are classified into the following three categories:

■ **Unary**—Operates on a single operand

■ **Binary**—Operates on two operands

■ **Ternary**—Operates on three operands

Mostly, the operators belong to the binary category. The ternary operator is also known as a *conditional* operator.

When more than one operator is used in an expression, the order of evaluation of operators in the expression is determined by the precedence and associativity of the operators. The *associativity* of an operator is a property that determines how operators of the same precedence are grouped in the absence of parentheses. C# has a rich set of operators. Table 3.1 displays common C# operators and their associativity. The operators in the table are arranged in order of precedence from highest to lowest.

Table 3.1   Common C# Operators and Their Associativity

Category	Operators	Associativity
Primary	`[]`, new, typeof, `sizeof`, `x++`, `x--`, checked, unchecked	Left to right
Unary	`!`, `~`, `+`, `-`, `++x`, `--x`, `()`	Left to right
Arithmetic	`*, /, %`	Left to right
Sign	`+, -`	Left to right
Shift	`<<, >>`	Left to right
Relational and type	`<, <=, >, >=`, is, as	Left to right
Equality	`==, !=`	Left to right
Logical bitwise	`&, ^, I`	Left to right
Logical Boolean	`&&, ||`	Left to right
Ternary	`?:`	Right to left
Assignment	`=, *=, /=, %=, +=, -=, &=, ^=, |=, <<=, >>=`	Right to left

PRECEDENCE AND ASSOCIATIVITY

Operator precedence and associativity define a set of rules that indicate the order in which the operator should be evaluated in an expression. When two or more operators are used in an expression, the operators with the higher precedence are executed first, followed by the operators of lower precedence. Consider the following expression:

```
a= 2 + 3 * 4
```

The precedence of the multiplication operator is higher than the plus operator, and the assignment operator has the lowest precedence. Therefore, 3 * 4 is evaluated first, and the result is added to 2. When operators of the same precedence are used in an expression, they are evaluated based on associativity. *Left-associative operators* are evaluated in order from left to right. *Right-associative operators* are evaluated in order from right to left. According to Table 3.1, the assignment operators and the ternary operator (?:) are right associative. All other binary operators are left associative.

So the following expression

```
a=2*3/4
```

would be evaluated as

```
a = (2 * 3) /4
```

Similarly, the following expression

```
a = b = c;
```

would be evaluated as

```
a = (b = c);
```

Adding Parentheses

You can control the operator precedence and associativity by using parentheses. The content of the parentheses is evaluated first. Consider the following expression:

```
a=2 * 3 / 4
```

Using the parentheses, you can make the expression evaluate as shown here:

```
a = 2 * ( 3 / 4 )
```

Go back to the operators listed in Table 3.1. The square brackets ([]) are used for arrays, indexers, and attributes. They are discussed in detail in Chapter 5, "Arrays and Strings." The new operator is related to classes and objects, so it is discussed in Chapter 7, "Classes and Objects." The is operator is used to check whether an object is compatible with a specific type. The as operator is used to perform explicit type conversions of reference types. Because these operators require knowledge of classes and objects, they are discussed in detail in Chapter 7. The increment and decrement operators, ++ and --, can be used as a suffix as well as a prefix. They behave differently in the two modes, as you will see later in this chapter.

The typeof Operator

The typeof operator is used to obtain the System.Type object for a type. Recall from the previous chapter that the int type is an alias for System.Int32. Similarly, the float type is an alias for the System.Single type, and so on. The typeof operator is used with the following syntax:

```
typeof(type)
```

where type represents the type for which the System.Type object is obtained.

The sizeof Operator

You use the sizeof operator to obtain the size of a value type in bytes. The format of using this operator is shown here:

```
sizeof(type)
```

For example, the size of the int type is 4 bytes, so the following statement returns the value 4:

```
sizeof(int);
```

The TypeInfo.cs program shown in Listing 3.1 displays the size and obtains the System.Type object of different value types.

Listing 3.1 Program Code in TypeInfo.cs File

```
using System;
public class TypeInfo
{
    static void Main()
    {
        Console.WriteLine("Size of int is {0}", sizeof(int));
        Console.WriteLine("Size of char is {0}",sizeof(char));
        Console.WriteLine("Size of float is {0}",sizeof(float));
        Console.WriteLine("Size of double is {0}",sizeof(double));
        Console.WriteLine("Size of int 64 is {0}",sizeof(Int64));
        Console.WriteLine("Type of int is {0}",typeof(int));
        Console.WriteLine("Type of char is {0}",typeof(char));
        Console.WriteLine("Type of float is {0}",typeof(float));
        Console.WriteLine("Type of double is {0}",typeof(double));
    }
}
```

When you run the program, you get the output shown in Figure 3.1.

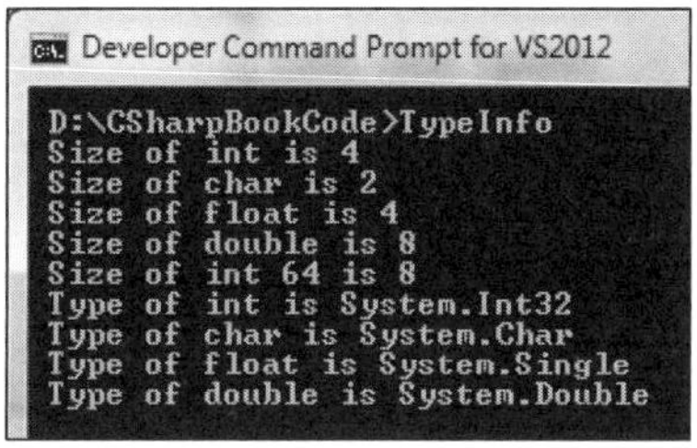

Figure 3.1
Size and System.Type objects of different value types.
Source: Visual Studio.

In the output, you can see that the size of int, char, float, double, and int 64 types are displayed as 4, 2, 4, 8, and 8 bytes, respectively. Also, the System.Type object of the int type is obtained as System.Int32, the char type as System.Char, the float type as System.Single, and double as System.Double, respectively.

Is there any way to detect overflow if it happens in an expression? Yes, read on.

Checked and Unchecked Operators

The checked operator is used to implement overflow checking for integral-type arithmetic operations and conversions. *Overflow* means assigning a value to a data type that is outside its range. By default, the expressions that contain only constant values cause a compiler error if the expression results in an overflow. For example, the upper range of short int is 32767. If you attempt to assign value 32768, it will be declared an overflow operation. If the expression contains one or more nonconstant values, the compiler does not detect the overflow and returns incorrect results. In other words, the expressions that include nonconstant values are not checked for overflow at runtime, and an overflow exception is not raised. In such expressions, you can use the checked operator.

The checked operator enables overflow checking. If case overflow is detected in any expression, the checked operator raises an OverflowException error. On the other hand, the unchecked operator is used to prevent overflow checking. In other words, no exception is raised even if overflow occurs in a calculation.

The CheckUncheck.cs program shown in Listing 3.2 explains the role of checked and unchecked operators in overflow detection.

Listing 3.2 Program Code in CheckUncheck.cs File

```
using System;

public class CheckUncheck
{
    static void Main()
    {
        int a=2000000000;
        int b=2000000000;
        // int c=2000000000 + 2000000000;  //Displays compiler error - "operation
overflows"
        int c= a+b;
        Console.WriteLine("Value of c= {0}",c);
        Console.WriteLine("Unchecked - preventing overflow checking. Value of c={0}",
unchecked(a+b));
        Console.WriteLine("Checked - checking overflow at run time. Value of c={0}",
checked(a+b));
    }
}
```

The program displays a compiler error if you remove the comment mark from the statement that adds two 2000000000 values because these are constants. The statement is currently commented out, so no compiler error is generated (see Figure 3.2). Overflow goes undetected when the values are added using the variables a and b, so a negative value, -294967296, is displayed on the screen. Similarly, the overflow is not detected while using the unchecked operator, thereby displaying the negative value again. The checked operator, as expected, checks for overflow and raises the overflow exception after detecting it, as shown in Figure 3.2.

Figure 3.2
Overflow exception displayed in checked expression.
Source: Visual Studio.

Next up is a quick look at arithmetic operators.

ARITHMETIC OPERATORS

Arithmetic operators are used to perform different math operations on numerical data. C# defines the arithmetic operators shown in Table 3.2.

Table 3.2 Arithmetic Operators Used in C#

Operator	Meaning
+	Addition
-	Subtraction/unary minus
*	Multiplication
/	Division
%	Modulus

© 2015 Cengage Learning®.

You can apply the arithmetic operators to any numeric data type. The +, -, *, and / operators are common and are used in addition, subtraction, multiplication, and division tasks. The modulus operator, %, computes the remainder of an integer division. You can apply it to both integer and floating-point types. The + and - operator in Table 3.2 can be a unary or a binary operator depending on the number of operands used with it. As unary operators, + and - are also known as sign operators, as you will soon see.

Note

In C/C++ languages, the modulus operations are allowed only on integer values.

Increment and Decrement Operators

C# includes the following unary operators for incrementing and decrementing counters:

- ++ **(increment operator)**—Increments the value of the variable by one each time it is used.

- −−**(decrement operator)**—Decrements the value of the variable by one each time it is used.

The increment and decrement operators behave differently depending on their location. If the operators are prefixed to a variable, they are termed *preincrement/predecrement operators*, and they first increase or decrease the value of the variable by one and thereafter use the resulting value in the expression. If these operators are suffixed to the variable, they are known as *post increment/decrement operators*, and they use the current value of the variable in the expression and then increase or decrease the value of the variable.

Examples:

```
int b=10;

a=++b;    //The value of variable b will be incremented by 1 and then assigned to variable
a. That is, the value of both variables a and b will become 11.

int b=10;

a=b++;    //The value of variable b will be assigned to variable a and then be incremented
by 1. That is, variable a will be 10 and variable b will become 11.
```

The decrement operator works similarly:

```
int b=10;

a=--b;    //The value of variable b will be decremented by 1 and then assigned to variable
a. That is, the value of both variables a and b will become 9.

int b=10;

a=b--;    //The value of variable b will be assigned to variable a and then be decremented
by 1. That is, variable a will be 10 and variable b will become 9.
```

Sign Operators

There are two sign operators, + and -, that indicate or change the sign of a value. The format for using them in unary form is given here:

```
var1 = +var2;
```

The preceding statement assigns the value of the variable var2 to the variable var1 without changing the sign of var2. The plus sign indicates that you have a positive number and is usually omitted in arithmetic expressions. The following example will make it clearer:

```
a=+b;
```

If the value of variable b is 10, it will be assigned as such to the variable a. If the value of variable b is -10, it will be assigned as -10 (without affecting the sign) to variable a.

Of course, the unary operator - (minus) affects the sign of the variable. (It reverses the sign of the source variable before assigning it to the target variable.) Precisely, the source variable is multiplied by -1 before it's assigned to the target variable, as explained in the following example:

```
a=-b;
```

If the value of variable b is 10, it will be assigned as -10 to the variable a. If the value of the variable b is -10, it will be assigned as +10 to the variable a.

The program shown in Listing 3.3 explains how you can use arithmetic, increment, decrement, and sign operators in arithmetic expressions.

Listing 3.3 Program Code in ArithmeticOp.cs File

```
using System;
public class ArithmeticOp
{
    static void Main()
    {
        int a = 5;
        int b = 3;
        int add = a + b ;
        int sub = a - b;
        int mult = a * b;
        int div = a/b;
        int rem = a% b;
        double remdr=5.123%3.123;
        int c= +a;      //value of variable a will be assigned to variable c
        int d= -a;      //value of variable a will be multiplied by -1 and then assigned to
variable c
        Console.WriteLine("Addition of {0} and {1} is {2}", a, b, add);
        Console.WriteLine("Subtracting {0} from {1} results into {2}", b, a, sub);
        Console.WriteLine("Multiplication of {0} and {1} is {2}", a, b, mult);
        Console.WriteLine("Dividing {0} by {1} results into {2}", a, b, div);
        Console.WriteLine("Remainder when integer {0} is divided by {1} is {2}",
a, b, rem);
        Console.WriteLine("Remainder when float 5.123 is divided by 3.123 is
{0}", remdr);
        Console.WriteLine("Sign Operators - Value in c variable is {0} and in d is {1}",
c, d);
        int e=a + ++b;
        Console.WriteLine("Pre-increment operation. Value in a is {0}, b is {1} and e is
{2}", a, b, e);
        b--;
        int f=a + b++;
        Console.WriteLine("Post increment operation. Value in a is {0}, b is {1} and f
is {2}", a, b, f);
        int g= --b;
        Console.WriteLine("Pre-decrement operation. Value in g is {0} and b is {1}",
g, b);
    }
}
```

Results of addition, subtraction, multiplication, and division operations on variables a and b are assigned to variables add, sub, mult, and div, respectively. Figure 3.3 shows the result of these operations. The result of modulus operation on integer and double values is assigned to rem and remdr variables, respectively. The plus and minus sign operators are applied to the variable a, and the results are stored in variables c and d, respectively. The value of variable b is preincremented and then added to the value of variable a before it is assigned to variable e. Similarly, the value of variable b is added to the value of variable a, and the result of the addition is assigned to variable f. After the addition operation, the value of variable b is incremented by 1. Again, the value of variable b is decremented by 1, and then the result is assigned to variable g (see Figure 3.3).

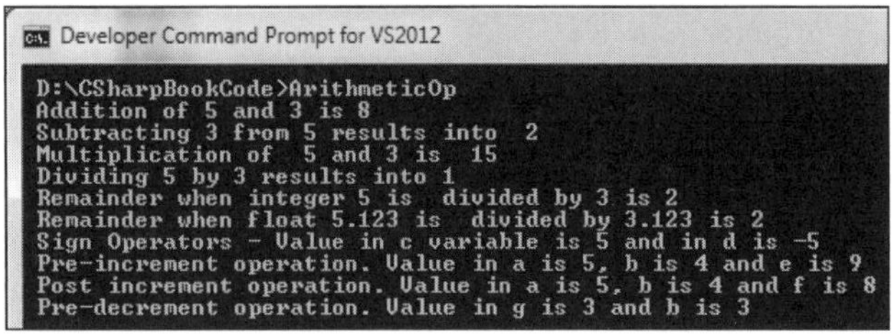

Figure 3.3
Output of ArithmeticOp.cs program.
Source: Visual Studio.

RELATIONAL OPERATORS

As the name suggests, the relational operators help in determining the relationship among different values. In other words, you can compare the values with these operators. The expressions created by using relational operators are known as *relational expressions*, and they result in Boolean values true and false. The relational operators in C# are given in Table 3.3.

Table 3.3 Relational Operators Used in C#

Operator	Meaning
>	Greater than
<	Less than
>=	Greater than or equal to
<=	Less than or equal to

© 2015 Cengage Learning®.

Examples:

The following expression returns true if the current value of variable a is greater than 5:

```
bool b= (a >5);
```

The returned Boolean value will be assigned to variable b. Actually, the relational operators are used in conditional branching and loops, as shown in the following example:

```
if (a > 5)
```

If the value of variable a is greater than 5, the preceding statement executes the block of statements associated with the if statement; otherwise, the block of statements associated with the else statement is executed.

Note

> The if statement used in the preceding example is called a *decision-making statement*. You will learn about it in detail in the next chapter.

Similarly, the following statement returns true if the value of the variable a is less than or equal to 5:

```
bool b=(a <= 5);
```

EQUALITY OPERATORS

Equality operators are used for checking whether the two operands are equal or not equal. Table 3.4 shows the two equality operators.

Table 3.4 Two Equality Operators in C#

Operator	Meaning
==	Equal to
!=	Not equal to

© 2015 Cengage Learning®.

The equal to operator (==) returns the Boolean value true if its two operands are equal; otherwise, it returns false.

```
int a=5;
int b=5;
bool c= a==b;
```

The preceding statement returns true because the values of variables a and b are equal.

Similarly, the inequality operator (!=) returns false if its two operands are equal; otherwise, the operator returns true. Example:

```
bool c= a!=b;
```

The preceding statement returns true if the values of variables a and b are unequal; otherwise, it returns false.

Like the relational operators, the equality operators are used in conditional statements and loops, as shown in the next example:

```
while (a !=5) { }
```

The preceding statement executes the while loop as long as the value of variable a is not equal to 5. You will be learning about loops in the next chapter.

LOGICAL BOOLEAN OPERATORS

Logical Boolean operators are used in creating logical expressions. The logical expressions return the Boolean value true or false, which in turn is used in conditional branching, loops, and other flow control statements. The logical Boolean operators in C# are listed in Table 3.5.

Table 3.5 Logical Boolean Operators Used in C#

Operator	Meaning
||	OR
&&	AND
!	NOT
^	XOR

© 2015 Cengage Learning®.

The OR (||) operator returns `true` if one of the two logical expressions evaluates to `true`; otherwise, it returns `false`. For example, the following example evaluates to `true` if either of the expressions is `true`:

```
if ((a < 5) || (b < 10))
```

The `if` statement used in the previous example is called a *conditional branching* statement. You will learn about it in detail in the next chapter.

The AND (&&) operator returns `true` only if both the logical expressions evaluate to `true`. The following example returns `true` if both the logical expressions evaluate to `true`:

```
if ((a < 5 ) && (b < 10))
```

The NOT (!) operator simply inverts the value of a Boolean variable or expression. For example, if the value of the Boolean variable or expression is `true`, the NOT operator inverts it to `false` and vice versa. Assuming the value of variable `a` is more than 5, the following logical expression evaluates to `true`:

```
if (a <5)
```

By application of the NOT (!) operator, the following logical expression evaluates to `false`:

```
if (!(a <5))
```

The XOR (^) operator returns `true` if one and only one of the two logical expressions evaluates to `true`. For example, the following example returns `true` only if either of the two logical expressions is `true` and not both:

```
if ((a < 5) ^ (b < 10))
```

LOGICAL BITWISE OPERATORS

Besides arithmetic, relational, and logical operators, C# provides bitwise operators. The bitwise operators are applicable only to integers and not on `bool`, `float`, `double`, or `class` types. Every number that is entered in a computer is internally represented in the form of binary digits. For example, the decimal value 25 is internally represented in the form of binary digits as 11001. The bitwise operators operate on these binary digits to give desired results. Table 3.6 shows the bitwise operators that are used in C#.

Table 3.6   Bitwise Operators Used in C#

Operator	Meaning
&	Bitwise AND
|	Bitwise OR
^	Bitwise exclusive OR (XOR)
~	One's complement (unary NOT)

© 2015 Cengage Learning®.

Considering x and y as two operands, following are the shifting and bitwise operators:

■ **x & y (bitwise AND)**—Corresponding bits of x and y are compared. It returns 1 if the corresponding bit of x and of y is 1; otherwise, 0 is returned.

■ **x | y (bitwise OR)**—Corresponding bits of x and y are compared. It returns 0 if the corresponding bit of x and of y is 0; otherwise, it returns 1. That is, if either of the bits of x or y is 1, the operator returns 1.

■ **x ^ y (bitwise exclusive OR - XOR)**—Corresponding bits of x and y are compared. It returns 1 if either of the bits of x or y is 1; otherwise, it returns 0. That is, the operator returns 0 if the corresponding bits of x and of y are the same.

■ **~ x (NOT)**—It returns the complement of x; that is, bit 1 is converted to 0, and 0 is converted to 1.

SHIFT OPERATORS

Like the bitwise operators, the shift operators are applicable only to integers and not to bool, float, double, or class types. These operators shift the bits of the operand's binary digits to the left or right as specified. Table 3.7 shows the two shift operators used in C#.

Table 3.7   Shift Operators Used in C#

Operator	Meaning
>>	Shift right
<<	Shift left

© 2015 Cengage Learning®.

Considering x and y as two operands, following are the shifting and bitwise operator:

- **x << y (binary shift left)**—It returns x with the bits shifted to the left by y places. The digit is padded with 0s on the right side. This operation is the same as multiplying x by 2**y.

- **x >> y (binary shift right)**—It returns x with the bits shifted to the right by y places. The digit is padded with 0s on the left side. This operation is the same as dividing x by 2**y.

Note

In the case of a right-shift on a signed value, the sign bit is preserved. The negative numbers are represented by setting the high-order bit of an integer to 1. Thus, if the value being shifted is negative, each right-shift adds a 1 bit on the left. If the value is positive, each right-shift adds a 0 bit on the left.

The program shown in Listing 3.4 explains how bitwise operators AND, OR, XOR, and NOT (&, |, ^, and ~) and shift operators (<< and >>) are applied on integers and their results.

Listing 3.4 Program Code in Bitwise.cs File

```
using System;
class Bitwise
{
    static void Main()
    {
        int a,b,c,d,e,g,h;
        a=10;
        b=7;
        c=a&b;
        d=a ^ b;
        e=a | b;
        Console.WriteLine ("The result of 10 and 7 operation is {0}", c);
        Console.WriteLine ("The result of 10 exclusive or 7 operation is {0}", d);
        Console.WriteLine ("The result of 10 or 7 operation is {0}", e);
g=a<<2;
        Console.WriteLine ("Left shifting - Multiplying 10 by 4 becomes: {0}", g);
        h=a>>1;
        Console.WriteLine ("Right shifting - Dividing 10 by 2 becomes: {0}",h);
        Console.WriteLine ("The bitwise negation of {0} is {1}", a, ~a);
    }
}
```

Output:

```
The result of 10 and 7 operation is 2
The result of 10 exclusive or 7 operation is 13
The result of 10 or 7 operation is 15
Left shifting - Multiplying 10 by 4 becomes: 40
Right shifting - Dividing 10 by 2 becomes: 5
The bitwise negation of 10 is -11.
```

The bits of the integers 10 and 7 and the result of applying the & (AND) operator on them is shown in Figure 3.4(a). The AND operator returns 1 if the respective bits of both the integers are 1; else, it returns 0. Figure 3.4(b) shows the result of applying the exclusive OR operator on the two integers 10 and 7. You can see that the exclusive OR operator returns 1 if either of the respective bits of the two integers is 1. Figure 3.4(c) shows the result of applying the OR operator on the two integers; it returns 1 if either or both of the respective bits of the integers are 1.

```
10  ▶ 0 0 0 0 1 0 1 0              10  ▶ 0 0 0 0 1 0 1 0              10  ▶ 0 0 0 0 1 0 1 0
 7  ▶ 0 0 0 0 0 1 1 1               7  ▶ 0 0 0 0 0 1 1 1               7  ▶ 0 0 0 0 0 1 1 1
10&7 ▶ 0 0 0 0 0 0 1 0  (2)      10^b ▶ 0 0 0 0 1 1 0 1  (13)      alb  ▶ 0 0 0 0 1 1 1 1  (15)

          (a)                             (b)                             (c)
```

Figure 3.4
(a) Bitwise AND (&) operator applied on values 10 and 7 (b) Bitwise XOR (^) operator applied on values 10 and 7 (c) Bitwise OR (!) operator applied on values 10 and 7.
Source: Visual Studio.

Figure 3.5(a) shows the result of left-shifting the value 10 by two bits. You can see that two 0 bits are added to the right in the number. On every left-shift, the value of the number is multiplied by 2. In other words, when you left-shift a number by two bits, the number is multiplied by 4, thereby giving the result of 40. Figure 3.5(b) shows the number 10 shifted one bit to the right. The rightmost bit of the number is dropped, and a 0 bit is added to its left, dividing the number by 2 and giving the result of 5.

```
  10  ▶ 0 0 0 0 1 0 1 0                10  ▶ 0 0 0 0 1 0 1 0
10<<2 ▶ 0 0 1 0 1 0 0 0  (40)       10>>1 ▶ 0 0 0 0 0 1 0 1  (5)

          (a)                               (b)
```

Figure 3.5
(a) Value 10 shifted two bits to the left (multiplied by 4) (b) Value 10 shifted one bit to the right (dividing by 2).
Source: Visual Studio.

Next, you'll see how assignment and compound assignment operators are used in different expressions.

ASSIGNMENT OPERATORS

As the name suggests, the assignment operator (=) assigns a value or the result of the expression to a variable. A *variable* is a placeholder where a value is kept. The format of assigning a value to a variable follows:

```
var1 = value/var2/expression;
```

Example:

```
a=10;     //Value 10 will be assigned to variable a
a=10 *2; //Assigns the result of expression; i.e., 20 to variable a
a=b;      //Value in variable b will be assigned to variable a.
a=b-c+d; //Result of the expression will be assigned to variable a.
```

You can chain assignment operators to assign the same value to multiple variables. For example, to assign value 10 to three variables, a, b, and c, you can use the following statement:

```
int a,b,c;
a = b = c = 10;
```

You cannot assign a value to a literal. The following statement results in a syntax error:

```
10 = x;
```

The assignment operator is right associative. Observe the following given code:

```
int a, b, c;
c = 5;
a=b=c+10;
```

The preceding statement will compute c+10 and assign the result to variable b. Finally, the result will be assigned to variable a, as shown here:

```
a=(b=c+10);
```

Compound Assignment Operators

You can combine assignment operators with an arithmetic or a logical operator. These compound assignment operators are usually used when an expression is evaluated, and the result is supposed to be assigned to one of the operands. For example, the following expression adds the values of the variables a and b and assigns the addition to variable a:

```
a = a+b;
```

You can combine the preceding assignment operator with the + operator to create a compound assignment operator:

```
a += b;
```

You can combine any arithmetic and logical operator with an assignment operator. Table 3.8 shows the list of assignment and compound assignment operators.

Table 3.8   Assignment and Compound Assignment Operators Used in C#

Operator	Syntax	Task Performed
=	var1 = var2;	Value of var2 variable is assigned to variable var1.
+=	var1 += var2;	Value of var1 and var2 is added, and sum is assigned to variable var1. It acts as the following statement: var1=var1+var2
-=	var1 -= var2;	Value of var2 variable is subtracted from value of variable var1.
*=	var1 *= var2;	Value of var2 variable is multiplied with value in variable var1, and result is assigned to variable var1.
/=	var1 /= var2;	Value of var1 variable is divided by value in variable var2, and result is assigned to variable var1.
%=	var1 %= var2;	Value of var1 variable is divided by value in variable var2, and remainder is assigned to variable var1.
&=	var1 &= var2;	Logical AND operation is applied to values in variables var1 and var2, and result is stored in variable var1.
|=	var1 |= var2;	Logical OR operation is applied to values in variables var1 and var2, and result is stored in variable var1.
^=	var1 ^= var2;	Logical exclusive OR operation is applied to values in variables var1 and var2, and result is stored in variable var1.
<<=	var1 <<= var2,	Variable var1 is left-shifted by var2 number of bits, and result is stored in variable var1.
>>=	var1 >>= var2;	Variable var1 is right-shifted by var2 number of bits, and result is stored in variable var1.

The program `AssignmentOp.cs` shown in Listing 3.5 demonstrates using assignment and compound assignment operators on different operands.

Listing 3.5 Program Code in AssignmentOp.cs File

```
using System;
public class AssignmentOp
```

```
{
    static void Main()
    {
        int a=10;
        int b=7;
        int c=a;
        int d=7;
        Console.WriteLine("Value of variable a assigned to variable c. a= {0} and c =
{1}", a,c);
        a+=b;
        Console.WriteLine("Value in variable, b is added in variable, a. Value in a =
{0} and b = {1}", a, b);
        a-=b;
        Console.WriteLine("Value in variable, b is subtracted from variable, a. Value
in a = {0} ", a);
        a*=3;
        Console.WriteLine("Value in variable, a after multiplying by 3 becomes {0} ", a);
        b/=2;
        Console.WriteLine("Value in variable, b after divided by 2 becomes {0} ", b);
        a%=2;
        Console.WriteLine("Value in variable, a is divided by 2. The remainder is {0} ", a);
        c&=d;
        Console.WriteLine("Bitwise AND operation applied between the values 10 and 7.
Result is {0} ", c);
        c=10;
        c|=d;
        Console.WriteLine("Bitwise OR operation applied between the values 10 and
7.Result is {0} ", c);
        c=10;
        c^=d;
        Console.WriteLine("Bitwise Exclusive OR operation applied between the values
10 and 7. Result is {0} ", c);
        c=10;
        c<<=2;
        Console.WriteLine("Left shifting value 10 by 2 bits i.e. multiplying 10 by 4.
Result is {0} ", c);
        c=10;
        c>>=1;
        Console.WriteLine("Right shifting value 10 by 1 bit i.e. dividing 10 by 2.
Result is {0} ", c);
    }
}
```

Figure 3.6 shows the output of the application of assignment operators and compound assignment operators on values 10 and 7.

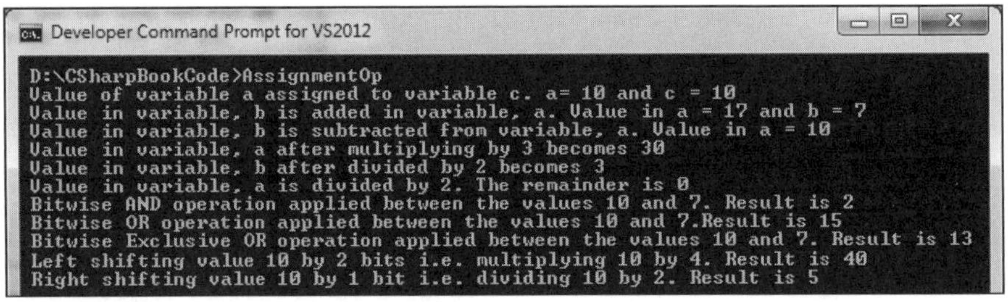

Figure 3.6
Output of AssignmentOp.cs program.
Source: Visual Studio.

Besides the assignment operator, another operator that is right associative is the ternary operator.

TERNARY OPERATOR (CONDITIONAL OPERATOR)

Also known as the conditional operator, the ternary operator acts as a shortcut of a decision-making statement. In other words, out of two statements, this operator chooses one statement to execute depending on the Boolean value returned by the included logical expression.

Here's the syntax:

```
[logical_expression] ? [statement_to_execute_if_true] :
[statement_to_execute_if_false]
```

If logical_expression evaluates to true, statement_execute_if_true is executed; otherwise, statement_to_execute_if_false is executed.

The following statement assigns the value 10 to variable a if the logical expression a>5 is true; otherwise, value 20 is assigned to variable b.

```
b=a>5?10:20;
```

The next chapter discusses the ternary operator in detail.

Before this chapter concludes, you'll learn about the Math class and its different methods that perform complex calculations with ease.

THE MATH CLASS

The System.Math class includes several methods that perform a variety of calculations for you. An outline of different methods it provides is given here:

- **Pow( )**—Raises a number to the given power.
- **Exp( )**—Raises the constant e to the given power.
- **Log( )** and **Log10**—Returns the natural and 10-based logarithm, respectively.
- **Sqrt( )**—Returns the square root of the given number.
- **Sign( )**—Returns the sign of the specified number. Returns -1 and 1 for negative and positive numbers, respectively.
- **Abs( )**—Returns the absolute value of a given number.
- **Ceiling( )**—Returns the smallest integral value larger than or equal to a fractional number.
- **Floor( )**—Returns the largest integral value smaller than or equal to the given fractional number.
- **Round( )**—Returns the number after rounding it to the nearest integral value.
- **Truncate( )**—Returns the number after removing its fractional part.
- **Sin( )**—Returns the sine of the specified angle.
- **Cos( )**—Returns the cosine of the specified angle.
- **Tan( )**—Returns the tangent of the specified angle.

The Math class also defines the following two properties:

- **Math.PI**—Represents the value of pi, 3.14269....
- **Math.e**—Represents the exponent constant, e, 2.71828....

The program MathMethods.cs, shown in Listing 3.6, demonstrates use of different methods of the Math class.

Listing 3.6 Different Methods of the Math Class in MathMethods.cs File

```
using System;
public class MathMethods
{
    public static void Main(string[] args)
    {
        double a = -10.15;
        double b=Math.Abs(a);
```

```
            double c=90;
            double d=Math.Cos(c);
            double e=Math.Pow(2,3);
            double f=1.2;
            double g=Math.Exp(f);
            double h=12.3456789;
            double i=Math.Floor(h);
            double j=-12.3456789;
            double k=Math.Floor(j);
            double l=Math.Ceiling(h);
            double m=Math.Ceiling(j);
            double n= Math.Truncate(h);
            double o= Math.Sqrt(2);
            Console.WriteLine("The absolute value of {0} is {1}.", a, b);
            Console.WriteLine("The cosine of an angle of {0} rad is {1}.", c, d);
            Console.WriteLine("2 to the power 3 is {0}", e);
            Console.WriteLine("e to the power {0} is {1}.", f, g);
            Console.WriteLine("The largest integer less than or equal to {0} is {1}.", h, i);
            Console.WriteLine("The largest integer less than or equal to {0} is {1}.", j, k);
            Console.WriteLine("The smallest integer greater than or equal to {0} is {1}.",
h, l);
            Console.WriteLine("The smallest integer greater than or equal to {0} is {1}.",
j, m);
            Console.WriteLine("Value of Pi is {0}", Math.PI);
            Console.WriteLine("The truncated value of {0} is {1}", h, n);
            Console.WriteLine("The square root of 2 is {0}",o);
            Console.WriteLine("Sign of h is {0} and of j is {1} ", Math.Sign(h),
Math.Sign(j));
            Console.WriteLine("The natural logarithm of 100 is {0}", Math.Log10(100));
        }
}
```

Figure 3.7 shows the output of the application of different methods of the Math class.

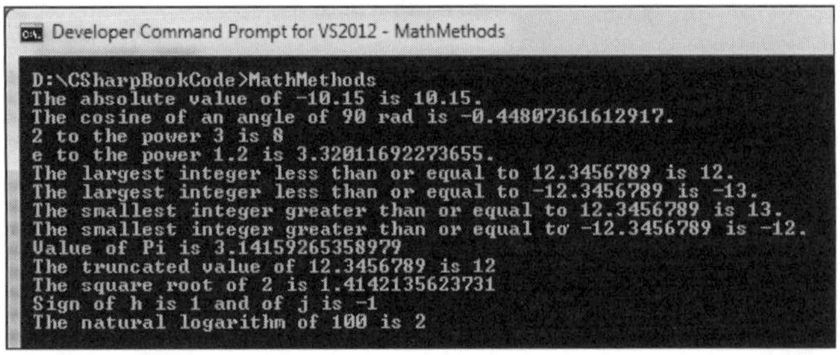

Figure 3.7
Output of MathMethods.cs program.
Source: Visual Studio.

SUMMARY

In this chapter, you learned about different operators, their precedence, and their associativity. You learned to use `typeof`, `sizeof`, `checked`, and `unchecked` operators in C# programs. You also learned about different arithmetic operators, their range, and increment, decrement, and sign operators. You learned how relational, equality, logical Boolean, and logical bitwise operators are used in creating logical expressions. You saw the usage of shift operators, assignment operators, and ternary operators in C# programs. Finally, you learned to use the `Math` class and its different methods.

In the next chapter, you will learn to use conditional statements and loops in C# programs. You will learn to use the `if-else-if` statement, `switch` statement, `break` command, and conditional operator. Also, you will learn to repeat a set of statements using the `while` loop, the `do-while` loop, and the `for` loop. You will learn to use `continue` and `goto` statements. Finally, you will learn to use nested loops and enumeration.

CHAPTER 4

DECISION-MAKING AND LOOPING

In this chapter, you learn about the statements that control the flow of your program. In other words, you learn to divert the normal sequential flow of execution of statements in a program to a block of desired statements as per your requirements. This chapter's topics include the following:

- Conditional statements
- The conditional operator
- Loops
- The continue statement
- The goto statement
- Enumeration

You'll begin this chapter by exploring conditional statements.

CONDITIONAL STATEMENTS

Conditional statements allow you to branch your code depending on the value of the logical expression or variable. The two statements that are popularly used for branching code in C# follow:

- **if-else-if statement**—Includes a logical expression and, depending on its value, provides two-way branching. If you have more than two blocks of statements to branch at, you can nest `if-else` statements.

- **switch statement**—Includes a logical expression and provides multiway branching, allowing you to execute a block of statements out of several blocks depending on the value of the logical expression.

First, you'll learn the concept of an `if-else-if` statement.

The if-else-if Statement

The `if-else-if` ladder or `if-else-if` statement helps in choosing a set of statements from two or more sets depending on the validity of the logical expression (condition) included.

Syntax:

```
if(condition)
    statement;
[else if(condition)
    statement;
else if(condition)
    statement;

    .
    .
    .

else
    statement;]
```

The conditions are evaluated, and the condition that evaluates to `true` results in execution of the associated statement. If none of the condition is found `true`, the final `else` clause is executed.

The program `IfElse1.cs`, shown in Listing 4.1, asks the user to enter marks (the number a student acquires in some tests). If the marks the user enters are greater than or equal to `60`, the message `First Division` is displayed on the screen. Otherwise, the message `Second Division` is displayed on the screen.

Listing 4.1 Program Code in IfElse1.cs File

```
using System;
class IfElse1 {
    static void Main() {
        int m;
        Console.Write("Enter marks: ");
        m = Convert.ToInt32(Console.ReadLine());
```

```
      if(m >=60)Console.WriteLine("First Division");
      else Console.WriteLine("Second Division");
   }
}
```

Output:

```
Enter marks: 80
First Division

Enter marks: 50
Second Division
```

The preceding program is an example of a simple if-else statement. Try using an if-else statement that is nested inside an else statement.

The program IfElse2.cs, shown in Listing 4.2, asks the user to enter marks. If the marks the user enters are greater than or equal to 60, the message First Division is displayed on the screen. If the marks entered are greater than or equal to 45 but less than 60, the message Second Division is displayed on the screen; otherwise, the message Third Division is displayed.

Listing 4.2 Program Code in IfElse2.cs File

```
using System;
class IfElse2 {
   static void Main() {
      int m;
      Console.Write("Enter marks: ");
      m = Convert.ToInt32(Console.ReadLine());
      if(m >=60)Console.WriteLine("First Division");
      else if (m>=45) Console.WriteLine("Second Division");
         else Console.WriteLine("Third Division");
   }
}
```

Output:

```
Enter marks: 80
First Division

Enter marks: 50
Second Division

Enter marks: 40
Third Division
```

The program CharacterFunc.cs shown in Listing 4.3 asks the user to enter a character and reports whether the entered character is a digit, a letter in lowercase, a letter in uppercase, a punctuation symbol, whitespace, or something else. This program uses the character methods discussed in Chapter 2, "Data Types." The focus of this program is to teach you how to use if-else-if ladder in decision-making.

Listing 4.3 Program Code in CharacterFunc.cs File

```
using System;
class CharacterFunc {
    static void Main() {
        char n;
        Console.Write("Enter a character: ");
        n = (char)Console.Read();
        if (char.IsDigit(n))Console.WriteLine("You have entered a digit");
        else
            if (char.IsLetter(n))
            {
                if (char.IsLower(n))
                    Console.WriteLine("You have entered a letter in lowercase ");
                else
                    Console.WriteLine("You have entered a letter in uppercase ");
            }
            else
                if   (char.IsPunctuation(n))Console.WriteLine("You     have     entered
punctuation");
                else
                    if  (char.IsWhiteSpace(n))Console.WriteLine("You    have    entered
whitespace");
                    else
                        Console.WriteLine("You have entered something else");
    }
}
```

Output:

```
Enter a character: 3
You have entered a digit

Enter a character: E
You have entered a letter in uppercase

Enter a character: r
You have entered a letter in lowercase

Enter a character:
You have entered whitespace
```

```
Enter a character: ?
You have entered punctuation

Enter a character: ~
You have entered something else
```

You can see that the IsDigit(), IsLetter(), IsLower(), IsPunctuation(), and IsWhiteSpace() methods are used to check whether the character entered is a digit, an uppercase letter, a lowercase letter, punctuation, or whitespace. Accordingly, the message is displayed on the screen.

What follows is one more program on if-else-if ladder. The program IfElse3.cs, shown in Listing 4.4, asks the user to enter a number between 1 and 4 and prints it in words.

Listing 4.4 Program Code in IfElse3.cs File

```
using System;
class IfElse3 {
    static void Main() {
        int n;
        Console.Write("Enter a number between 1 and 4: ");
        n = Convert.ToInt32(Console.ReadLine());
        if(n==1)Console.WriteLine("One");
        else if (n==2) Console.WriteLine("Two");
        else if (n==3) Console.WriteLine("Three");
        else if (n==4) Console.WriteLine("Four");
        else Console.WriteLine("The number is out of range");
    }
}
```

Output:

```
Enter a number between 1 and 4: 1
One

Enter a number between 1 and 4: 3
Three

Enter a number between 1 and 4: 5
The number is out of range
```

You might be thinking of the many if-else statements that have been used for testing numbers 1 to 4. What if you have to test numbers from 1 to 10? The shortcut is to use the switch statement.

The switch Statement

You use the `switch...case` statement to select a block of statement from several blocks based on the value of the given variable or expression. The variable or expression is written within the `switch` statement, and its expected values are written with different `case` statements. The block of statements associated with the `case` statement whose value matches the value or expression specified in the `switch` statement is executed. The block of statements continues to execute until a `break` statement appears in the block of the statement being executed. A `default` keyword is used to represent the block of statements that you want to execute if no case match occurs. The syntax for using the `switch` statement follows:

```
switch (variable_name)
{
    case value_1:
        statement;
        . . . . . . . . . . . . .
        break;
    case value_2:
        statement;
        . . . . . . . . . . . . .
        break;
        . . . . . . . . . . .
        . . . . . . . . . . .
    default:
        statement;
        . . . . . . . . . . . . .
        break;
}
```

Because the `break` statement is used in a `switch` statement, here's a quick introduction to the `break` statement before getting into the `switch` statement.

Breaking Out

You can terminate and exit from a loop using a `break` statement. After you encounter the `break` statement, the remaining code in the loop is bypassed and the program continues its execution from the statement following the loop. You can use any number of `break` statements in a program. When used inside a set of nested loops, the `break` statement breaks out of only the innermost loop.

Syntax:

```
break
```

The program Switch1.cs, shown in Listing 4.5, asks the user to enter a number between 1 and 4 and prints it in words. The program uses a switch statement instead of the if-else statement that you used in Listing 4.4.

Listing 4.5 Program Code in Switch1.cs File

```
using System;
class Switch1 {
    static void Main() {
        int n;
        Console.Write("Enter a number between 1 and 4: ");
        n = Convert.ToInt32(Console.ReadLine());
        switch (n) {
            case 1: Console.WriteLine("One");
                    break;
            case 2: Console.WriteLine("Two");
                    break;
            case 3:
                    Console.WriteLine("Three");
                    break;
            case 4:
                    Console.WriteLine("Four");
                    break;
            default:
                    Console.WriteLine("The number is out of range");
                    break;
        }
    }
}
```

Output:

```
Enter a number between 1 and 4: 1
One

Enter a number between 1 and 4: 3
Three

Enter a number between 1 and 4: 5
The number is out of range
```

You can see that when many decisions have to be made, the switch statement is much easier than the if-else-if ladder. The value the user enters is converted into the int type and assigned to variable n. Using the switch statement, the value in variable n is tested. The message one is displayed if the value in variable n is 1, two is displayed if the value in variable n is 2, and so on. If the value in variable n is not between 1 and 4, the default block is executed, displaying a message The number is out of range. The break statement in the preceding program is used to exit from the switch block.

Now you'll see how characters are compared in a switch statement.

The focus of the program Switch2.cs, shown in Listing 4.6, is to demonstrate how to use a character in a switch statement. The program asks the user to enter a character between a and d and prints the word Apple if the user enters the character a, Bat if the user enters the character b, Cat if the user enters the character c, and Dog if the user enters the character d.

Listing 4.6 Program Code in Switch2.cs File

```
using System;
class Switch2 {
    static void Main() {
        char n;
        Console.Write("Enter a character between a and d: ");
        n = (char)Console.Read();
        switch (n) {
            case 'a': Console.WriteLine("Apple");
                    break;
            case 'b': Console.WriteLine("Bat");
                    break;
            case 'c': Console.WriteLine("Cat");
                    break;
            case 'd': Console.WriteLine("Dog");
                    break;
            default: Console.WriteLine("The character entered is out of range");
                    break;
        }
    }
}
```

Output:

```
Enter a character between a and d: a
Apple

Enter a character between a and d: c
Cat

Enter a character between a and d: e
The character entered is out of range
```

The character entered in variable n is tested to see if it is a, b, c, or d and, accordingly, the message is displayed on the screen. If the character in variable n does not match the specified conditions, the message The character entered is out of range is displayed.

The preceding program always displays the message The character entered is out of range when letters are entered in uppercase. The reason is quite simple: the switch statement compares only lowercase characters. To avoid this error, you can add the following statement before the switch statement:

```
n=char.ToLower(n);
```

The preceding statement uses the char.ToLower method, which converts uppercase letters to lowercase letters. In other words, the character the user enters will be converted to lowercase before being compared in a switch statement. The char.ToLower method changes only the uppercase letters, not the lowercase ones. Except for uppercase letters, the char.ToLower method leaves everything unchanged.

Note

Similar to the char.ToLower method, C# provides a method called char.ToUpper that converts lowercase letters to uppercase.

Recall that if the value mentioned in the case statement matches the expression specified in the switch statement, the block of statements associated with the case statement is executed. The statements continue to execute until a break statement is encountered. The following program uses this strategy.

Switch3.cs, shown in Listing 4.7, asks the user to enter a character and reports whether the entered character is a vowel or a consonant.

Listing 4.7 Program Code in Switch3.cs File

```
using System;
class Switch3 {
    static void Main() {
        char n;
        Console.Write("Enter a character : ");
        n = (char)Console.Read();
        n=char.ToLower(n);
        switch (n) {
            case 'a':
            case 'e':
            case 'i':
            case 'o':
            case 'u':
```

```
                    Console.WriteLine("The character entered is a vowel");
                    break;
            default: Console.WriteLine("The character entered is a consonant");
                    break;
        }
    }
}
```

Output:

```
Enter a character : e
The character entered is a vowel

Enter a character : m
The character entered is a consonant
```

You can see that if the character in variable n is a, e, i, o, or u, the statement associated with the case statement is executed. Because no break statement is used except the last case statement (u), whenever any of the vowel character appears in variable n, the statement associated with the case statement (u) is executed, therefore displaying the message The character entered is a vowel. When no match occurs, the message The character entered is a consonant is displayed.

If the user enters any character in uppercase, it is converted to lowercase by application of the char.ToLower method before it is compared in a switch statement.

THE CONDITIONAL OPERATOR

The *conditional operator*, also known as the *ternary operator*, is often used to replace if-else statements that contain a single statement body. For example, the if-else statement with a single statement body is shown here:

```
if (logical expression)
    statement1;
else
    statement2;
```

You can see that the if-else statement has a single statement to execute depending on the outcome of the logical expression. You can replace the preceding if-else statement with the conditional operator, as shown here:

```
logical expression? statement1 : statement2;
```

where statement1 is executed if the logical expression is true; otherwise, statement2 is executed.

The focus of the program `CondOperator1.cs` shown in Listing 4.8 is to explain how the conditional operator is used. The program asks the user to enter the available quantity of a product. If the available quantity is less than 100, the quantity to be ordered for the product is 500; otherwise, it's 250.

Listing 4.8 Program Code in CondOperator1.cs File

```
using System;
class CondOperator1 {
    static void Main() {
        int avqty, ordqty;
        Console.Write("Enter available quantity: ");
        avqty = Convert.ToInt32(Console.ReadLine());
        if(avqty <100) ordqty=500;
        else ordqty=250;
        Console.WriteLine("Available Quantity: {0} and Ordered Quantity: {1}", avqty,
ordqty);
        ordqty=avqty<100?500:250;
        Console.WriteLine("Available Quantity: {0} and Ordered Quantity: {1}", avqty,
ordqty);
    }
}
```

Output:

```
Enter available quantity: 200
Available Quantity: 200 and Ordered Quantity: 250
Available Quantity: 200 and Ordered Quantity: 250
```

Here is one more example demonstrating use of the conditional operator. The program `CondOperator2.cs`, shown in Listing 4.9, asks the user to enter a number and determines whether the entered number is even or odd.

Listing 4.9 Program Code in CondOperator2.cs File

```
using System;
class CondOperator2 {
    static void Main() {
        int n;
        Console.Write("Enter a number: ");
        n = Convert.ToInt32(Console.ReadLine());
        Console.WriteLine(n%2==0?"Number is an even number":"Number is an odd number");
    }
}
```

Output:

```
Enter a number: 20
Number is an even number

Enter a number: 7
Number is an odd number
```

If the condition mentioned in the ternary operator is true (that is, if the modulus operator applied to the variable n evaluates to 0), the message Number is an even number is displayed on the screen. Otherwise, the message Number is an odd number is displayed.

Loops

A *loop* refers to the construct that enables you to execute a set of statement(s) repetitively as long as the given logical expression evaluates to true. This section discusses the following three loops:

- The while loop
- The do-while loop
- The for loop

The while Loop

The while loop executes a set of statements as long as the logical expression evaluates to true. The Boolean expression is included at the beginning of the loop. Until it evaluates to true, the body of the loop is not executed.

Syntax:

```
while(logical expression)
{
    .........................
    ........................
    // body of the loop
}
```

When the logical expression evaluates to false, the program control passes to the statement immediately following the loop.

Note

The curly braces are optional if the body of the loop consists of a single statement.

The program while1.cs, shown in Listing 4.10, prints the sequence numbers from 1 to 10.

Listing 4.10 Program Code in while1.cs File

```
using System;
class while1 {
    static void Main() {
        int k;
        k = 1;
        Console.WriteLine("The sequence numbers from 1 to 10 are:");
        while(k <=10) {
            Console.WriteLine(k);
            k++;
        }
    }
}
```

Output:

```
The sequence numbers from 1 to 10 are:
1
2
3
4
5
6
7
8
9
10
```

You can see that the variable k is initialized to 1. The while loop is set to execute as long as the value in variable k is less than or equal to 10. In the body of the while loop, the value in variable k is displayed on the screen, and then its value is incremented by 1. Therefore, the loop displays the sequence numbers from 1 to 10.

The program while2.cs, shown in Listing 4.11, prints the characters from a to z.

Listing 4.11 Program Code in while2.cs File

```
using System;
class while2 {
    static void Main() {
        char k;
        k = 'a';
        while(k <= 'z') {
```

```
            Console.Write("{0} ",k);
            k++;
        }
    }
}
```

Output:

a b c d e f g h i j k l m n o p q r s t u v w x y z

The variable k is initialized to the character a. A while loop is set to execute until the value in variable k becomes greater than z. In the while loop, the character assigned to variable k is displayed and is incremented by 1. After incrementing the variable, the next character in sequence is assigned to variable k.

The program while3.cs, shown in Listing 4.12, prints the sequence numbers between the two limits the user enters.

Listing 4.12 Program Code in while3.cs File

```
using System;

class while3 {
    static void Main() {
        int k,m,n;
        Console.WriteLine("Enter the beginning and ending limits of the sequence number
you wish to print");
        m = Convert.ToInt32(Console.ReadLine());
        n = Convert.ToInt32(Console.ReadLine());
        k = m;
        Console.WriteLine("The sequence numbers from {0} to {1} are:", m,n);
        while(k <=n) {
            Console.WriteLine(k);
            k++;
        }
    }
}
```

Output:

```
Enter the beginning and ending limits of the sequence number you wish to print
5
9
The sequence numbers from 5 to 9 are:
5
6
7
8
9
```

The variable k is initialized to the upper limit the user enters in variable m. The while loop is set to execute as long as the value in variable k is less than or equal to the lower limit entered in variable n. Therefore, the sequence numbers between the entered range m and n are displayed on the screen.

The do-while Loop

Like the while loop, the do-while loop is used to execute a set of statements as long as the included logical expression evaluates to true. The only difference between the while and do-while loop is that the logical expression is evaluated at the bottom of the loop instead of at the beginning. Also, the do-while loop executes at least once even if the logical expression evaluates to false. The syntax of the do-while loop is given here:

```
do {
    . . . . . . . . . . . . . .
    . . . . . . . . . . . . . .
    //body of the loop
} while(logical expression);
```

Because the logical expression is evaluated after the loop has executed, the loop runs at least once whether the logical expression evaluates to true or false.

The program dowhile1.cs, shown in Listing 4.13, prints the sequence numbers from 1 to 10.

Listing 4.13 Program Code in dowhile1.cs File

```
using System;
class dowhile1 {
    static void Main() {
        int k;
        Console.WriteLine("The sequence numbers from 1 to 10 are:");
        k = 1;
        do {
            Console.WriteLine(k);
            k++;
        }while(k <=10);
    }
}
```

Output:

```
The sequence numbers from 1 to 10 are:
1
2
```

```
3
4
5
6
7
8
9
10
```

If, in the preceding program, you set the initial value of variable k to 15, the loop still executes once, displaying the value 15 on the screen. This occurs because the logical expression in the do-while loop is evaluated at the end.

The benefit of using the do-while loop is that it executes at least once. Therefore, you can use it to obtain data from the user and make a decision based on the data received. The program dowhile2.cs, shown in Listing 4.14, adds the numerical values the user entered. The program continues to add numerical values the user entered until 0 is entered.

Listing 4.14 Program Code in dowhile2.cs File

```csharp
using System;
class dowhile2 {
    static void Main() {
        int k,s;
        s=0;
        Console.WriteLine("Enter the number you wish to add, enter 0 to quit:");
        do {
            k = Convert.ToInt32(Console.ReadLine());
            s+=k;
        }while(k !=0);
        Console.WriteLine("The sum of the numbers entered is {0}", s);
    }
}
```

Output:

```
Enter the number you wish to add, enter 0 to quit:
9
1
5
0
The sum of the numbers entered is 15.
```

Next, you'll look at another loop: the for loop.

The for Loop

The for loop is used to repeat a set of statement(s) a specified number of times.

Syntax:

```
for(initializing variables(s); condition; increment/decrement)
{
   statement1;
   statement2;
   ............
   ............
}
```

where initializing variables means assigning an initial value to the variable that plays a major role in executing the loop. The condition is a Boolean expression. The for loop continues to execute as long as the Boolean expression (condition) evaluates to true. When condition becomes false, the program control exits from the for loop and resumes program execution from the statement that follows the for loop. The increment/decrement determines the value to be added or subtracted from the variable on each iteration of the loop.

Note

The curly braces are optional if the number of statements used in the body of the for loop comprises only one statement.

The program ForLoop1.cs, shown in Listing 4.15, displays sequence numbers from 1 to 10 using the for loop.

Listing 4.15 Program Code in ForLoop1.cs File

```
using System;
class ForLoop1 {
   static void Main() {
      int i;
      Console.WriteLine("Sequence numbers from 1 to 10:");
      for(i = 1; i <=10; i++)
         Console.WriteLine(i);
   }
}
```

Output:

```
Sequence numbers from 1 to 10:
1
2
```

3
4
5
6
7
8
9
10

The program ForLoop2.cs, shown in Listing 4.16, demonstrates how the break state-ment terminates and exits from a loop. The program displays the sequence numbers from 1 to 10.

Listing 4.16 Program Code in ForLoop2.cs File

```
using System;
class ForLoop2 {
    static void Main() {
        int i;
        Console.WriteLine("Sequence numbers from 1 to 10:");
        for(i = 1; i <=15; i++)
        {
            if(i>10)break;
            Console.WriteLine(i);
        }
    }
}
```

Output:

```
Sequence numbers from 1 to 10:
1
2
3
4
5
6
7
8
9
10
```

The for loop is set to execute as long as the value of the variable i is less than or equal to 15. In the body of the loop, the if statement is used to break out of the loop if the value of the variable i is more than 10. Therefore, the loop terminates after displaying 10.

The program `BreakExample.cs`, shown in Listing 4.17, is another example of a `break` statement. The program displays the sequence numbers from 1 to 10. The program also demonstrates how to run a `for` loop without its three statements: `initializing variable(s)`, `condition`, and `increment/decrement`.

Listing 4.17 Program Code in BreakExample.cs File

```
using System;
class BreakExample {
    static void Main() {
        Console.WriteLine("Sequence numbers from 1 to 10:");
        int k=1;
        for( ; ; ) {
            if(k>10)break;
            Console.WriteLine(k);
            k++;
        }
    }
}
```

You can see in the program that the variable `k` is initialized to value 1 before the `for` loop. In the `for` loop, an `if` statement is used to specify the `exit` condition from the loop, and the variable `k` is incremented within the body of the `for` loop. After running the program, you get the sequence numbers from 1 to 10.

The program `SumSeq.cs`, shown in Listing 4.18, prints the sum of sequence numbers from 1 to 10.

Listing 4.18 Program Code in SumSeq.cs File

```
using System;
class SumSeq {
    static void Main() {
        int i, sum;
        sum = 0;
        for(i=1;i<=10;i++)
            sum += i;
        Console.WriteLine("Sum of first 10 sequence numbers is " + sum);
    }
}
```

Output:

```
Sum of first 10 sequence numbers is 55
```

You can see that the variable sum, where the addition of sequence numbers will take place, is initialized to value 0. A counter i is set to have the values from 1 to 10 through a for loop. Each value of the counter i is added to the sum variable. When the for loop completes, the variable sum adds all the values represented by the counter i.

THE CONTINUE STATEMENT

The continue statement skips the body of the loop and resumes with the next iteration of the loop. Unlike the break statement, the continue statement doesn't terminate and exit from the loop; instead, it just skips the rest of the statement of the loop and executes the loop with the next iterative value.

The program ContinueExample.cs, shown in Listing 4.19, displays the sequence numbers from 1 to 10 except value 7.

Listing 4.19 Program Code in ContinueExample.cs File

```
using System;
class ContinueExample {
    static void Main() {
        int i;
        Console.WriteLine("Sequence numbers from 1 to 10 except 7:");
        for(i = 1; i <=10; i++)
        {
            if(i==7)continue;
            Console.WriteLine(i);
        }
    }
}
```

Output:

```
Sequence numbers from 1 to 10 except 7:
1
2
3
4
5
6
8
9
10
```

The for loop is set to execute ten times by initializing variable i to 1 and setting the for loop to execute as long as the value of variable i is less than or equal to 10. On each

iteration of the loop, the variable i is incremented by 1. In the loop, the value of variable i is displayed to print the sequence numbers on the screen. An if statement is
used in the loop to check whether the value of variable i is equal to 7. If the value of
the variable i is equal to 7, the body of the for loop is bypassed through the continue
statement, so it does not display the value 7 on the screen. Also, the value of variable i
is incremented by 1 for the next iteration. So the program displays all the values of the
variable i from 1 to 10 except the value 7.

The program AddEven.cs, shown in Listing 4.20, asks the user to enter a few numbers
and prints the sum of only even numbers entered.

Listing 4.20 Program Code in AddEven.cs File

```
using System;
class AddEven {
    static void Main() {
        int n,i,k,sum;
        sum=0;
        Console.WriteLine("How many numbers are there? ");
        k = Convert.ToInt32(Console.ReadLine());
        Console.WriteLine("Enter {0} numbers", k);
        for(i = 1; i <=k; i++)
        {
            n = Convert.ToInt32(Console.ReadLine());
            if(n%2!=0)continue;
            sum+=n;
        }
        Console.WriteLine("The sum of even numbers entered is {0}",sum);
    }
}
```

Output:

```
How many numbers are there? 5
Enter 5 numbers
8
1
20
6
9
The sum of even numbers entered is 34
```

The user is prompted to specify the count of the numbers to be entered. A for loop is
set to execute for the specified count. Within the for loop, the user is asked to enter a
value. The modulus operator is applied on the entered value to determine if it is an even

or odd number. The even numbers are added to the variable sum. After the for loop terminates, the addition of entered even numbers in variable sum is displayed on the screen.

THE GOTO STATEMENT

goto is an unconditional jump statement that makes the program control jump to the specified statement and continue its normal execution from there. The use of the goto statement is not recommended because it makes the program highly unstructured.

Syntax:

```
goto label;
```

The preceding statement makes the program control jump to the statement that is prefixed with label:.

Note

You can also use goto to jump to any case or default label within a switch. However, you cannot jump into the switch from the code outside the switch.

The program GotoExample.cs, shown in Listing 4.21, demonstrates how the goto statement is used to jump to any statement in the program. The program prints the sequence numbers from 1 to 10.

Listing 4.21 Program Code in GotoExample.cs File

```
using System;
class GotoExample {
    static void Main() {
        int n=1;
        Console.WriteLine("The sequence numbers from 1 to 10 are: ");
printval:Console.WriteLine(n);
        n++;
        if(n<=10) goto printval;
    }
}
```

Output:

```
The sequence numbers from 1 to 10 are:
1
2
3
4
5
```

6
7
8
9
10

The variable n is initialized to the value 1. The label printval is prefixed to the statement Console.WriteLine() in the program. The value in variable n is displayed on the screen. After printing the value in variable n, it is incremented by 1. An if statement checks whether the value in variable n is less than or equal to 10. The if statement makes the program control jump to the statement that is prefixed with label printval if the value of the variable n is less than or equal to 10. When the program control jumps to the said label, the value of the variable n is displayed, its value is incremented by 1, and again, the statement checks whether the value of the variable n is less than or equal to 10. In other words, the program is set to print the value in variable n and increment its value by 1 until its value becomes greater than 10.

A *nested loop* means one loop inside the other. The main thing to remember in a nested loop is that the outer loop begins its next iteration only after the inner loop completes its iteration and exits. Also, the inner loop executes (completely) for the number of times the outer loop executes. In other words, with every iteration of the outer loop, the inner loop is reinitialized and is set to execute until its condition becomes false.

If you use a break statement in a for loop (whether inner or outer), it exits from the current level of loop. That is, if the break statement is used in the inner loop, it exits from the inner loop and continues to execute the outer loop. The outer loop continues to execute with its next iterative value, resulting in execution of the inner loop again.

The program NestedLoop1.cs, shown in Listing 4.22, prints the sequence numbers from 1 to 5 three different times.

Listing 4.22 Program Code in NestedLoop1.cs File

```
using System;
class NestedLoop1 {
    static void Main() {
        int i,j;
        Console.WriteLine("The sequence numbers from 1 to 5 three times:");
        for(i = 1; i <=3; i++)
        {
            for(j = 1; j <=5; j++)
```

```
            {
                Console.Write("{0}\t",j);
            }
            Console.WriteLine();
        }
    }
}
```

Output:

```
The sequence numbers from 1 to 5 three times:
1     2     3     4     5
1     2     3     4     5
1     2     3     4     5
```

You can see that the outer and inner for loops are set to execute for three and five times, respectively. The inner loop prints the sequence numbers from 1 to 5 by initial-izing variable j to 1 and incrementing its value by 1 on every iteration. The inner loop terminates and exits when the value of the variable j becomes greater than 5. When the inner loop terminates, the outer loop increments its variable i by 1 and begins the next iteration. Therefore, it re-executes the inner loop, reinitializing its variable j to 1.

The program NestedLoop2.cs, shown in Listing 4.23, prints the sequence numbers in the pattern shown here:

```
1
1     2
1     2     3
1     2     3     4
1     2     3     4     5
```

Listing 4.23 Program Code in NestedLoop2.cs File

```
using System;
class NestedLoop2 {
    static void Main() {
        int i,j;
        for(i = 1; i <=5; i++)
        {
            for(j = 1; j <=i; j++)
            {
                Console.Write("{0}\t",j);
            }
            Console.WriteLine();
        }
    }
}
```

Output:

```
1
1    2
1    2    3
1    2    3    4
1    2    3    4    5
```

You can see that the outer loop is set to execute five times. It initializes the variable i to 1 and sets it to execute until the value of variable i becomes greater than 5. The execution of the inner loop depends on the value of the variable of the outer loop, which is i. As expected, the value of the variable i of the outer loop increments by 1 whenever the inner loop completes its execution and terminates. With every iteration of the outer loop, the value of the variable i increments by 1. When the value of variable i is 1, the inner loop executes once, thereby printing the value 1 on the screen. When the value of variable i becomes 2, the inner loop executes twice, printing the sequence numbers 1 and 2.

ENUMERATION

An *enumeration* is a user-defined integer type to which you can assign a set of values. The instance of enumeration can contain only the value from the specified set, or a compilation error is generated. The set can define strings as well as integers. Enumeration represents each value or datum defined in the set, whether it is a string or a numerical value, as an integer. You use enumeration when you want to apply constraint on the range of values that can be assigned to an object, ensuring that the variable(s) in your program are assigned only valid values.

The program Enum1.cs, shown in Listing 4.24, demonstrates how you can use enumeration to apply a constraint on the value that can be assigned to a variable. The program also shows that every value defined in the enumeration represents an integer value. It defines an enumeration named weekdays and defines an instance w of type enumeration.

Listing 4.24 Program Code in Enum1.cs File

```
using System;
enum weekdays{Sunday, Monday, Tuesday, Wednesday, Thursday, Friday, Saturday}
class Enum1
{
    public static void dispday(weekdays d)
    {
```

```
       switch(d)
       {
          case weekdays.Sunday: Console.WriteLine("Sunday");
                                break;
          case weekdays.Monday: Console.WriteLine("Monday");
                                break;
          case weekdays.Tuesday: Console.WriteLine("Tuesday");
                                break;
          case weekdays.Wednesday: Console.WriteLine("Wednesday");
                                break;
          case weekdays.Thursday: Console.WriteLine("Thursday");
                                break;
          case weekdays.Friday: Console.WriteLine("Friday");
                                break;
          case weekdays.Saturday: Console.WriteLine("Saturday");
                                break;
       }
    }
    public static void Main(String[] args)
    {
       weekdays w;
       w = weekdays.Tuesday;
       Console.WriteLine("Weekday is {0}", w);
       Console.WriteLine("Position of Tuesday in Enumerations is {0}", (int)w);
       dispday(w);
    }
}
```

Output:

```
Weekday is Tuesday
Position of Tuesday in Enumerations is 2
Tuesday
```

The enumeration weekdays is defined and contains the days of the week, such as Sunday, Monday, and Tuesday. An instance w of the enumeration weekdays type is defined. The instance w is assigned the element Tuesday, which is subsequently defined in the weekdays enumeration. Because every element in the enumeration represents an integer beginning with value 0, the Tuesday element, as the third element in the set, represents an integer value 2. The integer value of the element Tuesday that is assigned to instance w is displayed on the screen and is passed to the switch statement to display the text Tuesday.

SUMMARY

In this chapter, you learned to use conditional statements and loops in C# programs. You read about how decision-making is accomplished using the `if-else-if` and `switch` statements and about how to exit from the loop using the `break` command. Also, you saw how a ternary or conditional operator behaves as a shortcut to an `if-else` statement. You learned to use different loops, including `while`, `do-while`, and `for`. You explored the role of the `continue` statement within the loop and how branching is done using the `goto` statement. Finally, you learned to use nested loops and enumeration in C#.

The next chapter covers strings and arrays. You will learn to use one-dimensional arrays and discover how they are initialized. You will also come to know how a `foreach` loop is used in accessing elements in an array and learn the usage of `StringBuilder` and `ArrayList`. Finally, you will learn to use multidimensional arrays and generics in C#.

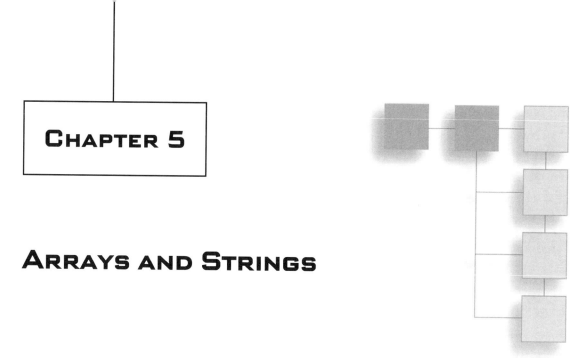

CHAPTER 5

ARRAYS AND STRINGS

This chapter's topics include the following:

- Using arrays
- Using strings
- Passing command-line arguments to Main()
- Using StringBuilder
- Using ArrayList

Arrays are one of the collections that C# provides. But prior to reading a discussion of arrays, you need a quick overview of collections. Collections are a standard set of classes used to store and manage a group of objects. These classes are shown here:

- `Array`—A fixed size allocation of memory where data can be accessed randomly using the integer `subscript` or `index`.
- `ArrayList`—A collection that behaves as a dynamic array. In other words, the size can be dynamically increased as required. It can store objects of any derived type.
- `List`—Stores a strongly typed list of objects that `index` can access.
- `Hashtable`—A lookup data structure that uses a hash code to find elements quickly. Therefore, a hashtable is considered an extremely efficient way to store keys for lookup.
- `Dictionary`—A collection of keys and values that is an implementation of a hashtable.

- **Stack**—Represents a LIFO (last in, first out) collection of objects. The procedure for adding an item to the stack is called *pushing*, and that of removing an item is called *popping*.

- **Queue**—Supports a FIFO (first in, first out) structure. The procedure for adding an item in the queue is called *enqueue*, and removing an item in the queue is called *deque*.

This chapter focuses on arrays and ArrayLists. It also looks at strings, which are another form of array. The remaining collections are discussed in Chapter 9, "Interfaces." It's important for you to have a solid understanding of classes and objects first.

USING ARRAYS

An *array* refers to a collection of values, usually of the same type, that is stored in consecutive memory locations. The advantage of storing values in an array is that you can access them randomly by specifying the index or subscript. An array can store data of any type, including integer, float, and strings.

Arrays are of two types:

- One-dimensional

- Multidimensional

One-Dimensional Arrays

As the name suggests, one-dimensional arrays have either rows or columns to store their values linearly. In C#, arrays are implemented as objects. To define an array, you first declare a variable that refers to an array followed by creating an instance of the array through the new operator. The syntax for defining a one-dimensional array is given here:

```
data_type[] array_name = new data_type[size];
```

where data_type refers to the type of data that will be stored in the array and size in square brackets refers to the allowable number of values that can be stored in the array.

Following are the two ways to define an integer array p of size 10 elements:

```
int[] p = new int[10];
```

```
int[] p;
p = new int[10];
```

The memory that is required to accommodate 10 integers will be allocated to the array p, as shown in Figure 5.1.

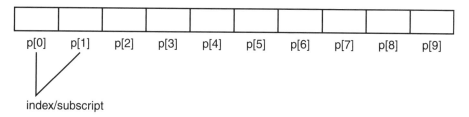

Figure 5.1
Memory allocations in the array p.
© 2015 Cengage Learning®.

You can see that the first element has a zero index. You can reference any element in the array by specifying its index or subscript in square brackets. For example, the following statement accesses the array element at index location 3 and assigns it to the integer k:

```
k=p[3];
```

Now you'll write a program that stores a few integers. The OneDimArray.cs program shown in Listing 5.1 prompts the user to enter 10 numerical values that are accommodated into an integer array. The entered values are then displayed on the screen.

Listing 5.1 Program Code in OneDimArray.cs File

```
using System;
class OneDimArray{
    static void Main() {
    int[] p = new int[10];
    int i;
    Console.WriteLine("Enter ten numbers");
    for(i = 0; i <=9; i++)
       p[i] =Convert.ToInt32(Console.ReadLine());
    Console.WriteLine("\nThe numbers entered in the array are");
    for(i = 0; i <=9; i++)
       Console.WriteLine(p[i]);
    }
}
```

Output:

```
Enter ten numbers
4
0
9
1
3
6
2
8
5
7
The numbers entered in the array are
4
0
9
1
3
6
2
8
5
7
```

The memory to store 10 integers is allocated to array p. The user is asked to enter 10 integer values which, using the for loop, are stored in the specific index or subscript location. For example, the first value the user enters is stored in index location p[0], the second value in p[1], and so on. After the entered values are assigned and stored in the respective memory allocated to the array p, each array element is accessed via its index and displayed on the screen.

Initializing an Array

If the values for the array elements are known, you can use them to initialize the array while creating it. The syntax for initializing a one-dimensional array is given here:

```
data_type[] array_name = { value1, value2, value3, ... , valueN };
```

The values value1, value2.... valueN are assigned to the array array_name to initialize it. The values are assigned sequentially beginning with index value 0.

Example:

The following statement initializes an array p to 10 integer values. The values are stored at index locations p[0], p[1]...... p[9].

```
int[] p = {4,0,2,8,1,7,3,9,5,6};
```

Because 10 blocks of memory are allocated to the array p, its Length property displays 10.

The ArrayInit.cs program shown in Listing 5.2 defines and initializes an array with the given 10 numerical values and then displays them on the screen.

Listing 5.2 Program Code in ArrayInit.cs File

```
using System;
class ArrayInit{
    static void Main() {
        int[] p = {4,0,2,8,1,7,3,9,5,6};
        int i;
        Console.WriteLine("The numerals entered in the array are");
        for(i = 0; i <p.Length; i++)
            Console.WriteLine(p[i]);
    }
}
```

Output:

```
The numerals entered in the array are
4
0
2
8
1
7
3
9
5
6
```

The values 4, 0, 2, 8, 1, 7, 3, 9, 5, and 6 are assigned to the array p for initializing it as shown in Figure 5.2. The first value is assigned to index location p[0], the second to p[1], and so on. The Length property of the array represents value 10, so a for loop is set to execute from 0 until one less than the Length property to access and display all array elements.

Figure 5.2
Integer values assigned and accommodated in the array p.
© 2015 Cengage Learning®.

Using the foreach Loop

The `foreach` loop cycles through the elements of a collection. Here's the syntax for using the `foreach` loop:

```
foreach(data_type variable in collection) statement;
```

where `data_type` variable specifies the data type of an iteration variable. The iteration variable accesses the value of the next element in the collection each time the `foreach` loop is executed. Because the element of the collection is assigned to the iteration variable, its data type must match the data type of the collection.

You'll use the `foreach` loop to access and display array elements. The `ArrayForEach.cs` program shown in Listing 5.3 initializes an array with 10 numerical values and displays its elements using the `foreach` loop. The program also sorts the array and redisplays the sorted values.

Listing 5.3 Program Code in ArrayForEach.cs File

```
using System;
class ArrayForEach{
    static void Main() {
        int[] p = {4,0,2,8,1,7,3,9,5,6};
        Console.WriteLine("The original order of numerals in the array is:");
        foreach(int x in p) {
            Console.WriteLine(x);
        }
        Array.Sort (p);
        Console.WriteLine("\nThe array in sorted order is: ");
        foreach(int x in p) {
            Console.WriteLine(x);
        }
    }
}
```

The first element in the array `p` is assigned to iteration variable `x`, which is then displayed. With each subsequent iteration of the `foreach` loop, the next element from the array `p` is accessed and assigned to the variable `x`. For example, in the first iteration, value 4 is assigned to variable `x`, which is subsequently displayed on the screen. In the next iteration, the second value 0 is assigned to the variable `x` and hence displayed on the screen. The iteration of the `foreach` loop terminates when all the elements of the array are accessed.

For sorting, the `Array` class has the built-in `Sort()` method that sorts an entire array. The `Sort()` method requires the array to contain built-in C# types like `int` and `string`.

In the preceding code, the array p is sorted by passing it to the Sort() method, and the sorted elements are then displayed on the screen.

Output:

```
The original order of numerals in the array is:
4
0
2
8
1
7
3
9
5
6
The array in sorted order is:
0
1
2
3
4
5
6
7
8
9
```

A one-dimensional array contains either rows or columns. Now you'll read about arrays that have both.

Multidimensional Arrays

A multidimensional array is an array that has two or more dimensions. In other words, its elements are stored and retrieved through a combination of two or more indices. The most popular multidimensional array is a two-dimensional array.

Two-Dimensional Arrays

In a two-dimensional array, the array elements are arranged in rows as well as in columns fashion. That is, the elements are arranged in tabular form and hence are stored and accessed by using two indices: one refers to the row and the other refers to the column location.

Here's the syntax for defining a two-dimensional array:

```
data_type[,] array_name = new data_type[size1, size2];
```

where [,] indicates that a two-dimensional array reference variable is being defined. The size1 and size2 refer to the number of rows and columns in the array, respectively.

Example:

```
int [,] p=new int[2][4];
```

The preceding command defines an array p consisting of two rows and four columns. The indices by which the array elements of this two-dimensional array are accessed are shown in Figure 5.3.

	0	1	2	3
0	p[0][0]	p[0][1]	p[0][2]	p[0][3]
1	p[1][0]	p[1][1]	p[1][2]	p[1][3]

Figure 5.3
Memory allocations in the two-dimensional array p[2][4].
© 2015 Cengage Learning®.

To access an array element, you need to specify both row and column indices, as shown here:

```
k=p[1][2];
```

By the preceding statement, the array element at row 1 and column 2 location will be accessed and assigned to variable k. Now you'll quickly write a program that defines a two-dimensional integer array. The program TwoDimArray.cs, shown in Listing 5.4, prompts the user to enter a few integers that will be stored in a two-dimensional array sized 2 by 4. The array elements are then displayed on the screen.

Listing 5.4 Program Code in TwoDimArray.cs File

```
using System;
class TwoDimArray {
    static void Main() {
        int[,] p = new int[2, 4];
        int i,j;
        Console.WriteLine("Enter elements for an array of order 2 x 4");
```

```
for(i = 0; i <=1; i++)
{
    for(j = 0; j <=3; j++)
    {
        p[i,j] =Convert.ToInt32(Console.ReadLine());
    }
}
Console.WriteLine("\nThe elements in the two-dimensional array are");
for(i = 0; i <=1; i++)
{
    for(j = 0; j <=3; j++)
    {
        Console.Write(p[i,j]+"\t");
    }
    Console.WriteLine();
}
    }
}
```

Output:

```
Enter elements for an array of order 2 x 4
4
3
9
1
2
6
8
5
The elements in the two-dimensional array are
4    3    9    1
2    6    8    5
```

The values are stored in the array in "row major" form by default. "Row major" form means that the first row is filled, followed by the second row, and so on. In other words, the values the user enters are sequentially stored in the first row of the two-dimensional array (in p[0][0], p[0][1], p[0][2], and p[0][3] locations). After you fill the first row, values are stored in the second row (in p[1][0], p[1][1], p[1][2], and p[1][3] locations).

The next section discusses strings, which are an array of characters.

USING STRINGS

A string represents a sequence of zero or more Unicode characters. The strings are immutable, meaning that you cannot change the contents of a string object after the object is created. Remember, in C#, the strings are objects.

Example:

```
string str="Hello";
```

You can also create a string from a char array, as shown in this example:

```
char[] k = {'H', 'e', 'l', 'l', 'o'};
string str = new string(k);
```

The preceding example defines a char array, k, consisting of five characters and a string object, str, which is created and initialized using the char array. That is, the string str is initialized to "Hello". You can access the elements of the string (the characters stored in it) via index/subscript. For example, the preceding string str has the characters stored in the format shown in Figure 5.4.

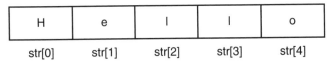

Figure 5.4
Characters stored in memory allocated to the string str.
© 2015 Cengage Learning®.

The first character in the string, str, is accessed via str[0]. Similarly, the second character in the string is accessed as str[1], and so on.

The [] operator provides read-only access to the individual characters. You cannot use it to modify the content of the string. Look at the following example:

```
string str="Hello";
char k=str[0];
```

The character k gets the first character of the string str (that is, H). Now, if you try to modify the content of the string through the [] operator, you get an error.

For example, the following statement:

```
str[0]='K';
```

displays the error Property or indexer 'string.this[int]' cannot be assigned - it is read only. You will use StringBuilder for mutable strings that you will learn about later in this chapter.

The String class provides several methods to perform different operations on strings. Here are a few of its methods:

- **static string Copy(string str)**—Returns a copy of the string str.

- **static bool IsNullOrEmpty(string str)**—Returns true if the specified string str is null or an empty string.

- **static string Substring(int index, int count)**—Returns a new string consisting of the specified portion of the invoking string. The method returns the count number of characters from the location index from the invoking string.

- **int CompareTo(string str)**—Compares the string str with the invoking string and returns value 0, <0, or >0. Value 0 is returned if both strings are equal. Value <0 is returned if the invoking string is less than str. Value >0 is returned if the invoking string is greater than str.

- **int IndexOf(string str)**—Searches the string str in the invoking string and returns the index of the first occurrence. The method returns -1 if str is not found in the invoking string.

- **int LastIndexOf(string str)**—Searches the string str in the invoking string and returns the index of the last occurrence. The method returns -1 if str is not found in the invoking string.

- **Length property**—Returns the length of the string.

Now you'll try a couple of the String class methods. The program String1.cs shown in Listing 5.5 extracts and displays the first three characters of an input string.

Listing 5.5 Program Code in String1.cs File

```
using System;
class String1 {
    static void Main()
    {
        string s;
        Console.Write("Enter a string ");
        s = Console.ReadLine();
        if (string.IsNullOrEmpty(s))
            Console.WriteLine("The string is empty");
        else
        {
            string substr = s.Substring(0,3);
```

```
        Console.WriteLine("Original string is {0}, its length is {1} and its first
three characters are {2}",s,s.Length, substr);
        }
    }
}
```

Output:

```
Enter a string
The string is empty

Enter a string manish
Original string is manish, its length is 6 and its first three characters are man
```

The string the user enters is assigned to string object s. Then the Substring() method is called on string object s to extract the first three characters from the string object s, assign them to another string object substr, and display them.

The program String2.cs shown in Listing 5.6 displays all the characters in an input string one below the other.

Listing 5.6 Program Code in String2.cs File

```
using System;
class String2 {
    static void Main()
    {
        string s;
        int i,n;
        Console.Write("Enter a string ");
        s = Console.ReadLine();
        Console.WriteLine("The character wise display of the string {0} is ", s);
        n=s.Length;
        for(i=0;i<=n-1;i++)
        {
            Console.WriteLine("{0}", s.Substring(i,1));
        }
    }
}
```

Output:

```
Enter a string Sanjay
The character wise display of the string Sanjay is
S
a
n
j
a
y
```

The string that the user enters is assigned to string object s. A for loop is executed from index 0 until one less than the length of the entered string. In the for loop, the Substring() method is called on string object s to extract each of its characters and display them.

The program StringConcat.cs shown in Listing 5.7 shows how two strings are concatenated.

Listing 5.7 Program Code in StringConcat.cs File

```
using System;
class StringConcat {
    static void Main()
    {
        string str1="Hello";
        string str2="World!";
        Console.WriteLine("The string two strings are {0} and {1}", str1, str2);
        str1+=" ";
        str1+=str2;
        Console.WriteLine("The string after concatenation is {0}", str1);
    }
}
```

Output:

```
The string two strings are Hello and World!
The string after concatenation is Hello World!
```

The strings Hello and World!, stored in objects str1 and str2, are concatenated with a space in between through the + (plus operator). The concatenation is applied to string object str1 and displayed.

The StringCompare.cs program shown in Listing 5.8 compares the two strings and indicates whether one is smaller, larger, or equal to another string.

Listing 5.8 Program Code in StringCompare.cs File

```
using System;
class StringCompare {
    static void Main()
    {
        string s1,s2;
        int n;
        Console.Write("Enter two strings ");
        s1 = Console.ReadLine();
        s2 = Console.ReadLine();
```

```
        n=s1.CompareTo(s2);
        if(n==0) Console.WriteLine("The two strings {0} and {1} are equal", s1,s2);
        if(n<0) Console.WriteLine("The string {0} is smaller than {1} ", s1,s2);
        if(n>0) Console.WriteLine("The string {0} is greater than {1} ", s1,s2);
    }
}
```

Output:

```
Enter two strings manish
manoj
The string manish is smaller than manoj

Enter two strings manish
manish
The two strings manish and manish are equal

Enter two strings manish
dharmendra
The string manish is greater than dharmendra
```

The strings that the user enters are stored in the two objects, s1 and s2. The CompareTo() method is called on object s1, and object s2 is passed to it as a parameter. The method returns values 0, <0, and >0 depending on whether object s1 is equal to, less than, or greater than the object s2.

Note that you can also compare string objects using the equality operators (== and !=). For example:

```
string str1="Hello";
string str2="Hello";
Console.WriteLine(a == b);
```

will display True, indicating that the two strings objects are equal.

The SearchPattern.cs program shown in Listing 5.9 checks whether a string pattern exists in another string.

Listing 5.9 Program Code in SearchPattern.cs File

```
using System;
class SearchPattern {
    static void Main()
    {
        string s1,s2;
        int n;
        Console.Write("Enter a string ");
        s1 = Console.ReadLine();
```

```
        Console.Write("Enter pattern to search ");
        s2 = Console.ReadLine();
        n=s1.IndexOf(s2);
        if(n!=-1)
           Console.WriteLine("The pattern {0} is found in {1} at location {2}", s2,s1,
n+1);
        else
           Console.WriteLine("The pattern {0} is not found in {1}", s2,s1);
     }
}
```

Output:

```
Enter a string sandeep
Enter pattern to search deep
The pattern deep is found in sandeep at location 4

Enter a string sandeep
Enter pattern to search dep
The pattern dep is not found in sandeep
```

The main string that the user enters is stored in the string object s1. The string pattern to search is entered and stored in string object s2. The method IndexOf() that is called on string s1 determines whether the string object s2 occurs in it. Recall that the IndexOf() method returns the location of the pattern if found; otherwise, it returns -1.

The CountVowels.cs program shown in Listing 5.10 demonstrates using the switch statement to count the number of vowels in an entered string.

Listing 5.10 Program Code in CountVowels.cs File

```
using System;
class CountVowels {
   static void Main()
   {
      string s;
      int i,n,c;
      Console.Write("Enter a string ");
      s = Console.ReadLine();
      n=s.Length;
      c=0;
      for(i=0;i<=n-1;i++)
      {
         switch(s[i]){
              case 'a':
              case 'A':
```

```
            case 'e':
            case 'E':
            case 'i':
            case 'I':
            case 'o':
            case 'O':
            case 'u':
            case 'U':
                        c++;
                        break;
        }
    }
    Console.WriteLine("The number of vowels in {0} is {1}", s, c);
  }
}
```

Output:

```
Enter a string Education
The number of vowels in Education is 5
```

```
Enter a string jklmn
The number of vowels in jklmn is 0
```

The string that the user enters is stored in string object s. The counter c is initialized to the value 0. A for loop is executed from value 0 until one less than the length of the entered string to access each character. Each character of the entered string is checked to see if it is a vowel. On occurrence of a vowel, the counter c is incremented by 1. Finally, the counter c is displayed.

The Palindrome.cs program shown in Listing 5.11 checks whether the entered string is a palindrome. Palindrome strings are those that are the same whether read forward or backward. Examples are radar and madam.

Listing 5.11 Program Code in Palindrome.cs file

```
using System;
class Palindrome {
    static void Main()
    {
        string s;
        int i,n,e;
        Boolean p=true;
        Console.Write("Enter a string ");
        s = Console.ReadLine();
        n=s.Length;
```

```
        e=n-1;
        for(i=0;i<n/2;i++)
        {
            if(s[i] !=s[e])
            {
                Console.WriteLine("The string {0} is not a palindrome", s);
                p=false;
                break;
            }
            e--;
        }
        if(p)Console.WriteLine("The string {0} is a palindrome", s);
    }
}
```

Output:

```
Enter a string pallap
The string pallap is a palindrome
```

```
Enter a string pallak
The string pallak is not a palindrome
```

To discover whether the string is a palindrome, you compare the first and last character of the string. If they are the same, you compare the second character with the second to the last character. Again, if they are the same, you compare the third character of the string with the third to the last character. The process continues until you reach the middle of the string. If any mismatch occurs during the comparison, the string is declared as not palindrome; otherwise, the string is declared palindrome.

Here are a few more string functions:

- **StartsWith(string str)**—Returns the Boolean value true if the invoking string begins with the specified pattern str.

- **EndsWith (string str)**—Returns the Boolean value true if the invoking string ends with the specified pattern str.

- **Contains(string str)**—Returns the Boolean value true if the invoking string contains the specified pattern str anywhere in it.

- **PadLeft(int n)**—Returns the invoking string padded with whitespaces on its left. The amount of padding is computed by subtracting the width of the invoking string from the specified total width, n.

- **PadRight(int n)**—Returns the invoking string padded with whitespaces on its right. The amount of padding is computed by subtracting the width of the invoking string from the specified total width, n.

- **`Replace(string str1, string str2)`**—Returns the string after replacing the pattern `str1` with pattern `str2` in the invoking string.

- **`Insert(int index, string str)`**—Returns the string after inserting the given string `str` at the specified `index` location in the invoking string.

- **`TrimStart()`**—Removes the leading trim characters from the invoking string.

- **`TrimEnd()`**—Removes the trailing trim characters from the invoking string.

- **`Trim()`**—Removes the leading and trailing trim characters from the invoking string. If no trim characters are specified in any of the three `trim()` methods, all whitespace characters including tabs are removed.

- **`Split(char c)`**—Returns a string array by splitting the invoking string into parts based on the specified character `c`.

- **`Join(string str, string[] strArray)`**—Returns the string after joining all the elements of the given string array `str`. The array is separated by the specified string pattern `str`.

- **`ToLower()`**—Converts a string to lowercase.

- **`ToUpper()`**—Converts a string to uppercase.

The `StringFunc1.cs` program shown in Listing 5.12 demonstrates the usage of the different `String` class methods that include `StartsWith()`, `EndsWith()`, `Contains()`, `ToLower()`, `ToUpper()`, `PadLeft()`, and `PadRight()`.

Listing 5.12 Program Code in StringFunc1.cs File

```
using System;
class StringFunc1 {
    static void Main()
    {
        string str1,str2;
        str1="Hello";
        if(str1.StartsWith("H"))
            Console.WriteLine("The string {0} starts with H", str1);
        if(str1.StartsWith("Hell"))
            Console.WriteLine("The string {0} starts with Hell", str1);
        if(str1.StartsWith("hell"))
            Console.WriteLine("The string {0} starts with hell", str1);
        else
            Console.WriteLine("The string {0} does not start with hell", str1);
        if(str1.EndsWith("o"))
            Console.WriteLine("The string {0} ends with o", str1);
```

```
        if(str1.Contains("Hell"))
            Console.WriteLine("The string {0} contains the word Hell", str1);
        if(str1.Contains("hell"))
            Console.WriteLine("The string {0} contains the word hell", str1);
        else
            Console.WriteLine("The string {0} does not contain the word hell", str1);
        str2=str1.ToLower();
        Console.WriteLine("The original string {0} appears as {1} in lower case", str1,
str2);
        str2=str1.ToUpper();
        Console.WriteLine("The original string {0} appears as {1} in upper case", str1,
str2);
        str2=str1.PadLeft(10);
        Console.WriteLine("Original string {0} appears as {1} after padding on its left",
str1,str2);
        str2=str1.PadRight(10);
        Console.WriteLine("Original  string  {0}  appears  as  {1}  after  padding  on  its
right", str1,str2);
    }
}
```

Output:

```
The string Hello starts with H
The string Hello starts with Hell
The string Hello does not start with hell
The string Hello ends with o
The string Hello contains the word Hell
The string Hello does not contain the word hell
The original string Hello appears as hello in lower case
The original string Hello appears as HELLO in upper case
Original string Hello appears as      Hello after padding on its left
Original string Hello appears as Hello      after padding on its right
```

The StringFunc2.cs program shown in Listing 5.13 demonstrates usage of the different String class methods that include Replace(), Insert(), TrimStart(), TrimEnd(), Trim(), Split(), and Join().

Listing 5.13 Program Code in StringFunc2.cs File

```
using System;
class StringFunc2 {
    static void Main()
    {
        string str1,str2, str3,str4;
        str1="Hello";
```

```
        str2=str1.Replace('l','w');
        Console.WriteLine("The string, {0} after replacing l by w appears as {1}", str1,
str2);
        str2=str1.Insert(5, " World!");
        Console.WriteLine("The string, {0} after inserting a word, World! appears as
{1}", str1,str2);
        str3=str2.Replace("World!", "John!");
        Console.WriteLine("The string, {0} after replacing World! by John! will appear as
{1}", str2,str3);
        str3=" Hello ";
        str4=str3.TrimStart();
        Console.WriteLine("The string {0} appears as {1} after removing leading space",
str3,str4);
        str4=str3.TrimEnd('\t');
        Console.WriteLine("The string {0} appears as {1} after removing trailing tabs",
str3,str4);
        str4=str3.Trim();
        Console.WriteLine("The string {0} appears as {1} after removing spaces and tabs
from either side", str3,str4);
        str3="You are Welcome";
        string[] stringArray=str3.Split(' ');
        Console.WriteLine("The string {0} is split into three parts: {1}, {2} and {3}",
str3,stringArray[0], stringArray[1], stringArray[2]);
        str3=string.Join(",",stringArray);
        Console.WriteLine("The three parts of the array, {0}, {1} and {2} after joined with,
(comma) separator appears as {3}", stringArray[0], stringArray[1], stringArray[2],
str3);
    }
}
```

Output:

```
The string, Hello after replacing l by w appears as Hewwo
The string, Hello after inserting a word, World! appears as Hello World!
The string, Hello World! after replacing World! by John! will appear as Hello John!
The string      Hello         appears as Hello            after removing leading space
The string      Hello         appears as       Hello after removing trailing tabs
The string      Hello         appears as Hello after removing spaces and tabs from
either side
The string You are Welcome is split into three parts: You, are and Welcome
The three parts of the array, You, are and Welcome after joined with , (comma) separator
appears as You,are,Welcome
```

You have an understanding now about the String class and its methods. Now you'll see how an array of strings is defined.

The StringArray.cs program shown in Listing 5.14 prompts the user to enter five fruit names and stores them in a string array. The entered fruit names are then displayed on the screen.

Listing 5.14 Program Code in StringArray.cs File

```
using System;
class StringArray{
    static void Main() {
        string[] fruits = new string[5];
        Console.WriteLine("Enter the name of five fruits");
        for(int i = 0; i <=4; i++)
            fruits[i] =Console.ReadLine();
        Console.WriteLine("The elements in the string array are:");
        foreach(string f in fruits) {
            Console.WriteLine(f);
        }
    }
}
```

Output:

```
Enter the name of five fruits
Orange
Banana
Apple
Mango
Grapes
```

```
The elements in the string array are:
Orange
Banana
Apple
Mango
Grapes
```

If you already have the fruit names, you can use them to define and initialize the string array simultaneously. You can modify the StringArray.cs program that you saw in Listing 5.14 to initialize a string array with five strings. The code in Listing 5.15 shows the modified StringArray.cs file.

Listing 5.15 Program Code in Modified StringArray.cs File

```
using System;
class StringArray{
    static void Main() {
```

```
        string[] fruits = {"Apple", "Mango", "Banana", "Grapes", "Orange"};
        Console.WriteLine("The elements in the string array are:");
        foreach(string f in fruits) {
            Console.WriteLine(f);
        }
    }
}
```

Output:

```
The elements in the string array are:
Apple
Mango
Banana
Grapes
Orange
```

The SplitSentence.cs program shown in Listing 5.16 prompts the user to enter a sentence that is then split to form a string array. The words in the sentence that are stored in the string array are then displayed on the screen, each word on a separate line.

Listing 5.16 Program Code in SplitSentence.cs File

```
using System;
class SplitSentence{
    static void Main() {
        string sentence;
        Console.Write("Enter a sentence: ");
        sentence = Console.ReadLine();
        string[] stringArray=sentence.Split(' ');
        Console.WriteLine("The words in the sentence are:");
        foreach(string s in stringArray) {
            Console.WriteLine(s);
        }
    }
}
```

Output:

```
Enter a sentence: Today is Monday
The words in the sentence are:
Today
is
Monday
```

PASSING COMMAND-LINE ARGUMENTS TO MAIN( )

You can pass command-line arguments to the program using the Main() method. A parameter that is in the form of a string array is passed to the Main() method. Using this array, you can access all the commands or options that are passed to the program while executing. The array is usually called args, but it can be called by any name. The command-line arguments are passed after the name of the program, as shown in the output of the program. The CommandArgs1.cs program shown in Listing 5.17 demonstrates how the command-line arguments are passed to a Main() method. The program also checks whether arguments are passed to it. All the passed arguments are displayed on the screen, one on each row.

Listing 5.17 Program Code in CommandArgs1.cs File

```
using System;
class CommandArgs1
{
    public static void Main(string[] args)
    {
        if(args.Length >0)
        {
            Console.WriteLine("The supplied command-line arguments are:");
            for (int i = 0; i < args.Length; i++)
                Console.WriteLine(args[i]);
        }
        else
            Console.WriteLine("No command-line arguments are supplied");
    }
}
```

Output:

```
C:\>CommandArgs1
No command-line arguments are supplied

C:\>CommandArgs1 a.bat 2 35 letter.txt
The supplied command-line arguments are:
a.bat
2
35
letter.txt
```

USING STRINGBUILDER

You have worked with strings and know that the String class provides several methods for dealing with strings. The only drawback with the String class is that it is an immutable data type; once the string object is initialized, you cannot change it. A new string is created whenever you try to modify the content of an existing string. That is, the original string remains unchanged, and a new string object with applied modifications is created, making it highly unsuitable for frequent modifications. To create mutable type strings (the modifiable strings), Microsoft provides the `System.Text.StringBuilder` class. The `StringBuilder` class enables you to perform several operations that include replacing, removing, inserting, and appending text without creating a new object.

While creating a `StringBuilder` object, you should allocate more memory to it to make room for the modifications that can be applied to it. If you don't specify the size of memory to be allocated to the `StringBuilder`, the memory equal to the size of the string that the `StringBuilder` instance is initialized with is allocated to it.

While creating a `StringBuilder` object, you can specify a capacity that represents the memory to be allocated to it for holding the string and to accommodate modifications that might be applied to it. It is better to assign too much capacity so that you avoid relocation if the size of the stored string increases.

Note

You have to include `System.Text` reference in your program to use the `StringBuilder` class.

You can build `StringBuilder` objects in several ways. Following are three ways for doing so.

The first way is to specify the initial string and the capacity as shown here:

```
StringBuilder sb =new StringBuilder("Hello", 50);
```

The preceding code creates a `StringBuilder` object named sb with the initial capacity of 50 memory locations, the first 5 of which are filled with the string Hello. The rest of the 45 memory locations are left uninitialized and are meant to accommodate any modifications that may be applied to the object.

The second way is to specify only the initial string:

```
StringBuilder sb = new StringBuilder("Hello");
```

The third way is to create an empty `StringBuilder` with a given capacity:

```
StringBuilder sb = new StringBuilder(50);
```

You can also specify the maximum capacity that the `StringBuilder` object can grow:

```
StringBuilder sb = new StringBuilder(50, 100);
```

The preceding example creates a `StringBuilder` object `sb` of initial capacity 50 memory locations, allowing it to grow to 100 memory locations. An exception is thrown if the size of the string stored in the `StringBuilder` object increases more than the given maximum capacity.

The `StringBuilder` class has the following two main properties:

- `Length`—Shows the length of the string that it actually contains.
- `Capacity`—Shows the maximum length of the string that can be stored in the `StringBuilder` object.

Using the `Capacity` property, you can set the capacity of the `StringBuilder` object at any time.

Example:

```
sb.Capacity=75;
```

If the value assigned is less than the length of the currently stored string in the `StringBuilder` object or is more than the maximum capacity assigned at the time of creating the object, an exception is thrown. Table 5.1 lists the main `StringBuilder` methods.

Table 5.1 Main StringBuilder Methods

Method	Purpose
Append()	Appends a string to the current string.
AppendLine()	Appends a string to the current string after a line break. That is, the appended string appears on the next line.
AppendFormat()	Appends a string as per the format specifiers applied.
Insert()	Inserts a substring into the current string at the given index location.
Remove()	Removes the desired number of characters from the current string beginning from the given index location.
Replace()	Replaces a given string or character with another character or string.
ToString()	Returns the string object.

© 2015 Cengage Learning®.

Note

To convert from `StringBuilder` to `string`, you have to do explicit casting using the `ToString()` method.

Now you'll write a program that demonstrates creating a modifiable string using the `StringBuilder` class. The `StringBuilder1.cs` program shown in Listing 5.18 creates a `StringBuilder` object and modifies it by adding a couple of strings to it. Precisely, the program prompts the user to enter a few fruit names that are then appended to the `StringBuilder` object. Finally, the fruit names are displayed when you show the `StringBuilder` object on the screen.

Listing 5.18 Program Code in StringBuilder1.cs File

```
using System;
using System.Text;
class StringBuilder1{
    static void Main() {
        StringBuilder sb = new StringBuilder();
        int i,n;
        Console.Write("How many fruits are there? ");
        n =Convert.ToInt32(Console.ReadLine());
        Console.WriteLine("Enter the names of {0} fruits", n);
        for(i = 0; i <=n-1; i++)
            sb.AppendLine(Console.ReadLine());
        Console.WriteLine("\nThe fruit names entered are");
        Console.WriteLine(sb);
    }
}
```

Output:

```
How many fruits are there? 3
Enter the names of 3 fruits
Mango
Apple
Banana

The fruit names entered are
Mango
Apple
Banana
```

We can see that a `StringBuilder` object, sb is created. User is asked for the count of the fruit names that will be entered. Using a `for` loop, a specified number of fruit names will be entered and appended to the StringBuilder object, sb. The fruit names are then displayed by displaying the StringBuilder object, sb.

The StringBuilder2.cs program shown in Listing 5.19 demonstrates application of Replace() and Remove() methods in modifying the StringBuilder object. The program demonstrates replacing of a word as well as a character from the StringBuilder object. Finally, the StringBuilder object is converted into a string object.

Listing 5.19 Program Code in StringBuilder2.cs File

```
using System;
using System.Text;
class StringBuilder2{
    static void Main() {
        string str;
        StringBuilder sb = new StringBuilder("It is hot today");
        Console.WriteLine("Original string builder is: {0} ", sb);
        sb.Replace("is", "was");
        Console.WriteLine("Modified string builder is: {0}", sb);
        sb[0]='A';
        Console.WriteLine("The string builder after replacing first character is: {0}",
sb);
        sb.Remove(7,3);
        Console.WriteLine("The string builder after removing a word is: {0}", sb);
        str=sb.ToString();
        Console.WriteLine("The string builder converted into string: {0}", str);
    }
}
```

Output:

```
Original string builder is: It is hot today
Modified string builder is: It was hot today
The string builder after replacing first character is: At was hot today
The string builder after removing a word is:  At was   today
The string builder converted into string: At was   today
```

You can see that the StringBuilder object sb is created and initialized to the string It is hot today. Using the Replace() method, the word is is replaced by was, converting the string to It was hot today. Thereafter, the first character of the string I is replaced by A, making the string At was hot today. Then three characters from the seventh index location (hot in the string) are deleted, making the string At was today. Finally, the StringBuilder object is converted into a string.

The StringBuilder3.cs program shown in Listing 5.20 demonstrates application of the AppendFormat(), Insert(), and Append() methods in modifying the StringBuilder object. The program creates an empty StringBuilder object, adds formatted content, inserts a word in the StringBuilder object at the specific location, and adds a word to the end of the object without a newline character.

Listing 5.20 Program Code in StringBuilder3.cs File

```
using System;
using System.Text;
class StringBuilder3{
    static void Main() {
        StringBuilder sb = new StringBuilder();
        sb.AppendFormat("Value1: {0}, Value2: {1}, Addition is {2}", 10,20,30);
        Console.WriteLine("Original string builder is: {0} ", sb);
        sb.Insert(24, "and ");
        Console.WriteLine("The string builder after inserting a word is: {0} ", sb);
        sb.Append(" units");
        Console.WriteLine("The string builder after appending a word is: {0} ", sb);
    }
}
```

Output:

```
Original string builder is: Value1: 10, Value2: 20, Addition is 30
The string builder after inserting a word is: Value1: 10, Value2: 20, and Addition is 30
The string builder after appending a word is: Value1: 10, Value2: 20, and Addition is 30
units
```

You can see that the empty StringBuilder object sb is created. Using the AppendFormat() method, three numerical values are added to the sb object in the specific format, making the object appear as Value1: 10, Value2: 20, Addition is 30. Then, using the Insert() method, the word and is added to the object at the twenty-fourth index location (before A of Addition, making the string appear as Value1: 10, Value2: 20, and Addition is 30. Finally, the word units is added to the string, making the sb object appear as Value1: 10, Value2: 20, and Addition is 30 units.

USING ARRAYLIST

The ArrayList is like a dynamic array. Traditional arrays have many limitations, like these:

■ You need to specify the size of array at the time of declaration.

■ You cannot add more elements than the specified size.

- The allocated size of the array goes to waste if the number of elements stored in the array is less than the number that is possible.

- Inserting and deleting an element in between the array requires a lot of shuffling.

- Arranging an element in an array requires some coding.

`ArrayList` overcomes all these limitations of arrays. It enables you to add new items with no bounds on size. Also, it enables you to insert an element in between other elements, remove an element from the list, search an element, arrange elements in the list, and destroy the list. The `ArrayList` class is defined in the `System.Collections` namespace.

The methods supported by `ArrayList` class are briefly described in Table 5.2.

Table 5.2   ArrayList Class Methods

Method	Description
`Add()`	Appends a new element object to the end of the `ArrayList`. The number of elements that can be added to the `ArrayList` is limited by your computer's memory.
	Syntax:
	`ArrayList.Add(object);`
	The specified object is added to the `ArrayList`. Because objects are appended, the value that is being appended is boxed (the value is converted to an object) before being appended to the `ArrayList`. When you're reading values from the `ArrayList`, the element is unboxed to the original data type (where it was converted to object).
`AddRange()`	Adds the elements of the supplied `ArrayList` to the invoking `ArrayList`, as shown in the following statement:
	`ArrayList.AddRange(ArrayList2);`
	where `ArrayList2` is the `ArrayList` whose elements must be added to the invoking `ArrayList`.
`Clear()`	Clears the invoking `ArrayList`. (All the elements of the invoking `ArrayList` will be deleted.)
`RemoveRange()`	Removes the given range of elements from the invoking `ArrayList`.
	Syntax:
	`ArrayList.RemoveRange(x,y);`

(Continued)

Table 5.2 ArrayList Class Methods (*Continued*)

Method	Description
	Removes y number of elements from the ArrayList beginning with the index location x.
	Example:
	`list.RemoveRange(0,2);`
	The preceding statement removes two elements beginning from 0th index location from the ArrayList list. (The 0th and 1st element from the ArrayList will be deleted.)
RemoveAt()	Removes the specified element from the ArrayList.
	Syntax:
	`ArrayList.RemoveAt(n);`
	The nth element from the ArrayList will be deleted.
Insert()	Inserts an element in the ArrayList at the specified index location. All the elements in the ArrayList are shifted to accommodate the newly inserted element.
	Syntax:
	`ArrayList.Insert(n,e);`
	The element e will be inserted at index location n in the invoking ArrayList.
GetRange()	Fetches the given number of elements from the specified index location from the invoking ArrayList.
	Syntax:
	`ArrayList.GetRange(x,y);`
	The y number of elements from index location x from the ArrayList are accessed.
IndexOf()	Searches for the specified object in the ArrayList and returns the index location if it is found. The method returns -1 if the value is not found in the ArrayList. If the object is found more than once in the ArrayList, the index location of its first occurrence is returned.
	Syntax:
	`ArrayList.IndexOf(o, [s],[e]);`
	where o is the object to search and s and e are the optional parameters that refer to the starting and ending index locations in the ArrayList to limit the search range for the given object.

LastIndexOf()	Searches for the specified object in the ArrayList and returns the index location of its last occurrence.
	Syntax:
	ArrayList.LastIndexOf(o,[s],[e]);
	where o refers to the object to search and s and e are the optional parameters that refer to the starting and ending index locations in the ArrayList to limit the search range for the object.
CopyTo()	Copies the contents of the ArrayList into an array.
	Syntax:
	ArrayList.CopyTo(array);
	All the elements of the invoking ArrayList are copied into the specified array.
Sort()	Sorts all the elements of the invoking ArrayList.
	Syntax:
	ArrayList.Sort([x],[y]);
	The parameters x and y are used for sorting a specific range of elements in the ArrayList (that is, y number of elements beginning from x index location will be sorted).
Reverse()	Reverses the order of all the elements in the invoking ArrayList.
	Syntax:
	ArrayList.Reverse([x],[y]);
	The parameters x and y are optional and are used to reverse a particular range of elements in the ArrayList. The parameters reverse y number of elements beginning from x index location in the ArrayList.
Count	A virtual property that returns the number of elements in the specified ArrayList.

© 2015 Cengage Learning®.

Now you'll write a program to understand the concept of the ArrayList collection and methods it provides. The ArrayList1.cs program shown in Listing 5.21 is a simple one that demonstrates use of the ArrayList object. The program prompts the user to enter a few fruit names, which are then added to the ArrayList object.

Listing 5.21 Program Code in ArrayList1.cs File

```
using System;
using System.Collections;
class ArrayList1{
    static void Main() {
        ArrayList al = new ArrayList();
        int i,n;
        Console.Write("How many fruits are there? ");
        n =Convert.ToInt32(Console.ReadLine());
        Console.WriteLine("Enter the names of {0} fruits", n);
        for(i = 0; i <=n-1; i++)
            al.Add(Console.ReadLine());
        Console.WriteLine("\nThe fruit names entered are");
        foreach (string f in al)
        {
            Console.WriteLine(f);
        }
        Console.WriteLine("\nThe fruit names entered are");
        for(i=0;i<al.Count;i++)
        {
            Console.WriteLine(al[i]);
        }
    }
}
```

Output:

```
How many fruits are there? 3
Enter the names of 3 fruits
Apple
Mango
Orange

The fruit names entered are
Apple
Mango
Orange

The fruit names entered are
Apple
Mango
Orange
```

In the preceding program, you see that an empty ArrayList object called al is created. The user is prompted to enter a few fruit names that are added to the al object using the Add() method. The content in the ArrayList object al is printed on the screen through the foreach loop as well as through the indices or subscripts.

Now you'll learn how elements in an ArrayList object are inserted, removed, and merged into another ArrayList object. The ArrayList2.cs program shown in Listing 5.22 creates two ArrayList objects, adds elements of one ArrayList object into the other, removes the specified range of elements from the ArrayList, and inserts elements at a specified location in the ArrayList.

Listing 5.22 Program Code in ArrayList2.cs File

```
using System;
using System.Collections;
class ArrayList2{
    static void Main() {
        ArrayList al1 = new ArrayList();
        ArrayList al2 = new ArrayList();
        al1.Add("Apple");
        al1.Add("Mango");
        al1.Add("Orange");
        al2.Add("IceCream");
        al2.Add("Sandwich");
        Console.WriteLine("The first ArrayList contains {0} elements", al1.Count);
        Console.WriteLine("\nThe second ArrayList contains {0} elements", al2.Count);
        al1.AddRange(al2);
        Console.WriteLine("\nThe first ArrayList now contains {0} elements as shown
below:", al1.Count);
        foreach (string f in al1)
        {
            Console.WriteLine(f);
        }
        al2.Clear();
        Console.WriteLine("\nThe  second  ArrayList  now  contains  {0}  elements",
al2.Count);
        al2.AddRange(al1.GetRange(3,2));
        Console.WriteLine("\nThe second ArrayList now contains {0} elements as shown
below:", al2.Count);
        foreach (string f in al2)
        {
            Console.WriteLine(f);
        }
        al1.RemoveAt(0);
        Console.WriteLine("\nThe first ArrayList after removing the first element has
the following elements left:");
```

```
        foreach (string f in al1)
        {
            Console.WriteLine(f);
        }
        al1.RemoveRange(2, 2);
        Console.WriteLine("\nThe first ArrayList after removing the last two elements
has the following elements left:");
        foreach (string f in al1)
        {
            Console.WriteLine(f);
        }
        al1.Insert(0, "Apple");
        Console.WriteLine("\nThe first ArrayList after inserting an element at the top
has the following elements:");
        foreach (string f in al1)
        {
            Console.WriteLine(f);
        }
        ArrayList al3 = al1.GetRange(0, al1.Count);
        Console.WriteLine("\nThe third ArrayList is a copy of the first ArrayList and it
has the following elements:");
        foreach (string f in al3)
        {
            Console.WriteLine(f);
        }
    }
}
```

Output:

The first ArrayList contains 3 elements

The second ArrayList contains 2 elements

The first ArrayList now contains 5 elements as shown below:
Apple
Mango
Orange
IceCream
Sandwich

The second ArrayList now contains 0 elements

The second ArrayList now contains 2 elements as shown below:
IceCream
Sandwich

```
The first ArrayList after removing the first element has the following elements left:
Mango
Orange
IceCream
Sandwich
```

```
The first ArrayList after removing the last two elements has the following elements
left:
Mango
Orange
```

```
The first ArrayList after inserting an element at the top has the following elements:
Apple
Mango
Orange
```

```
The third ArrayList is a copy of the first ArrayList and it has the following elements:
Apple
Mango
Orange
```

The following things are happening in the preceding program:

- Two ArrayList objects called a11 and a12 are created.

- Three strings, Apple, Mango, and Orange, are added to the object a11, and two strings, IceCream and Sandwich, are added to the object a12.

- The count of the two objects a11 and a12 is displayed on the screen.

- All the elements or strings in object a12 are appended to the object a11. That is, now the a11 objects have five strings: Apple, Mango, Orange, IceCream, and Sandwich.

- All the elements in the a12 object are deleted.

- Two elements from the a11 object are accessed starting from the third position (that is, from IceCream location) and added to the a12 object. That is, the a12 object now has two elements: IceCream and Sandwich.

- The count of elements and the name of the elements of the a12 object are displayed on the screen.

- Remove the first element from the object a11, leaving four elements: Mango, Orange, IceCream, and Sandwich.

- Four elements in the a11 object are displayed on the screen.

- Two elements from the a11 object are removed starting from the second location (IceCream and Sandwich will be deleted from a11), leaving only two elements: Mango and Orange.

- Insert a string, Apple, at location 0 (at the top in the all object). Now the all object will have three elements: Apple, Mango, and Orange.

- A new ArrayList object, al3, is created and initialized to all elements of the object all. That is, Apple, Mango, and Orange are added to the al3 object.

- The elements in the third object, al3, are displayed on the screen.

Summary

In this chapter, you learned about both types of arrays: one-dimensional and multidimensional. You read about the process of initializing arrays and printing those using indices and the foreach loop. You learned to use strings and manipulate them using different String class methods. You also passed command-line arguments to Main() and discovered how to use StringBuilder to call different methods to modify strings. Finally, you learned to use ArrayList and call its methods to insert, delete, merge, and replace elements.

In the next chapter, you will learn to write methods, pass parameters, and invoke them. You will discover how to nest methods inside each other. You'll unlock the difference between pass by value and pass by reference and read about the concept of method overloading. The next chapter also focuses on structures, structs with methods, and nested structs. Finally, you will explore the difference between classes and structs.

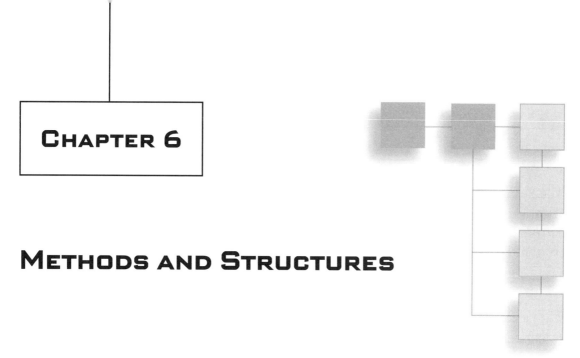

CHAPTER 6

METHODS AND STRUCTURES

This chapter's topics include the following:

- Methods
- Optional and named parameters
- C# parameter modifiers
- Your own type: structures
- Nested structs
- Date and time structure

METHODS

Methods are a group of statements meant to accomplish a specific task. A name is given to a method so that the caller can call it. The caller can also pass data in the form of parameters to the method for processing. A method can return the processed data to the caller. Dividing an application into small chunks of code (that is, in methods) provides the following benefits:

- Makes the application manageable
- Helps in quick debugging
- Supports scalability
- Enhances teamwork

A method is defined in this format:

```
accessibility returnType MethodName(parameter list) {
    . . . . . . . . . . . .
    . . . . . . . . . . . .
    . . . . . . . . . . . .
}
```

The MethodName is always followed by parentheses. Also, you need to define its return type. The return type of the method indicates the data type of the value returned by the method. For example, if the method returns a value of data type integer, the return type of the method is set to int. Similarly, if the method returns the value of data type float, the return type of the method is set to float, and so on. If the method does not return anything, the return type is set to void.

The accessibility of the method determines whether the method is private (can be called only in the class where it is declared) or can be publicly called by all the other classes in your application. If accessibility is not specified, the method is declared as private by default.

Note

A method can return, at most, a single datum. In other words, a method cannot return more than one value.

For example, the following statements define a private method called getrect that returns nothing:

```
private void getrect() {
    int l,b,a;
    l=50;
    b=8;
    a=l*b;
    Console.WriteLine("Area of rectangle is {0}", a);
}
```

The next statements define a public method called getrect that returns an integer value:

```
public int getrect() {
    int l,b,a;
    l=50;
    b=8;
    a=l*b;
    return a;
}
```

Return Statement

When a method is called, the program control jumps to the method to execute the code enclosed in its body. The control returns to the caller function either when the method completes (you encounter its closing curly braces) or when it returns something to the caller via the return method. The statement return in a method terminates the execution of a method, and the program control returns to the caller.

Here's the syntax of the return statement:

```
return [value];
```

where value is optional and represents the value that the method returns.

You can have any number of return statements in a method, though that is not recommended. The value that a method returns not only helps in knowing the type of computation performed by a method but helps in knowing the status of the method (whether the execution of the method was a success or a failure).

Method Parameters

Methods can also accept information through parameters. By convention, parameter names always begin with a lowercase letter. What follows is an example of a method that accepts two parameters, l and b, of int type. The method calculates the area of a rectangle using the parameters that are passed to it:

```
public int getrect(int l, int b) {
    int a;
    a=l*b;
    return a;
}
```

Method Invocation

Methods are invoked by typing the method name followed by parentheses. The values, if any, that you want to pass to the method are enclosed within the parentheses. The values that are passed to the method are also known as *arguments*. If the method does not return data, it can be called as shown in the next examples:

```
getrect(50, 8);
```

In the preceding statement, the getrect method is called and the values, 50 and 8, are the arguments that will be assigned to the method parameters for further actions. If no data is required to be sent to the method, you can call it without the arguments, as shown here:

```
getrect();
```

If the method returns some data, it can be displayed directly, as shown here:

```
Console.WriteLine("Area of rectangle is {0}", getrect());
```

Alternatively, you can assign the returned data to some variable. For example, the following statement assigns the value returned by the getrect method to the variable x:

```
int x=getrect();
```

The next example calls the getrect method with two arguments: 50 and 8. The value that the method returns is assigned to variable z :

```
int z=getrect(50, 8);
```

The DemoMethod.cs program shown in Listing 6.1 demonstrates calculating the area of a rectangle through a method. While you're calling the method, the length and breadth values are passed as arguments to the method, which in turn is assigned to its parameters. The method computes the area of a rectangle from the values received through parameters and returns the result to the caller.

Listing 6.1 Program Code in DemoMethod.cs File

```
using System;
class DemoMethod
{
    static int getrect(int l, int b)
    {
        int a=l*b;
        return a;
    }
    static void Main()
    {
        int u = 50, v = 8;
        int z=getrect(u,v);
        Console.WriteLine("Area of rectangle is {0}",z);
    }
}
```

Output:

```
Area of rectangle is 400
```

You can see that the method getrect is defined with two parameters: l and b. The method is set to return a value of int type. From the Main method, the getrect method is called passing the arguments, u and v, that are initialized to values 50 and 8, respectively. The area of the rectangle returned by the getrect method is assigned to variable z, which in turn displays the area of the rectangle on the screen.

Method Overloading

C# supports method overloading, which means you can create more than one method with the same name but with a different signature (with a different number of parameters and types). For example, the following statements define three overloaded versions of `getrect` methods, each with a different set of parameters:

```
public int getrect() {
    int l,b,a;
    l=50;
    b=8;
    a=l*b;
    return a;
}
public int getrect(int l) {
    int b,a;
    b=10;
    a=l*b;
    return a;
}
public int getrect(int l, int b) {
    int a=l*b;
    return a;
}
```

You can see that the first `getrect` method is without a parameter, the second one has a single parameter of `int` type, and the third `getrect` method contains two parameters of `int` type.

You might be thinking that the compiler will become confused while determining which method to choose when called. The Common Language Runtime (CLR) automatically chooses the correct version of the method by examining the supplied arguments. The benefit of method overloading is that it provides flexibility in supplying arguments. For example, it enables supplying a different number of arguments of different data types to the same common method name.

You can call the `getrect` method in three ways: with no arguments, by supplying only the value of the `length` argument, and by supplying both `length` and `breadth` arguments, as shown in the following statement:

```
int x,y,z;
x=getrect();
y=getrect(20);
z=getrect(30,5);
```

The CLR automatically determines which overloaded method to call depending on the number and the type of supplied arguments. For example, getrect(30,5) results in invoking the method that has two integer parameters. Remember, if no version matches, an error occurs. The next statement results in an error because no overloaded getrect method has float type parameters:

```
float z=getrect(30.10, 5.15);
```

Note

You cannot overload a method with versions that have the same signature (with the same number of parameters and parameter data types) because the CLR cannot distinguish them.

The MethodOverloading.cs program shown in Listing 6.2 demonstrates method overloading by defining the getrect method with each signature.

Listing 6.2 Program Code in MethodOverloading.cs File

```
using System;
class MethodOverloading
{
    static int getrect()
    {
        int l,b,a;
        l=50;
        b=8;
        a=l*b;
        return a;
    }
    static int getrect(int l)
    {
        int b,a;
        b=10;
        a=l*b;
        return a;
    }
    static int getrect(int l, int b)
    {
        int a=l*b;
        return a;
    }
    static void Main()
    {
        int x,y,z;
        x=getrect();
```

```
      y=getrect(20);
      z=getrect(30, 5);
      Console.WriteLine("Area of first rectangle is {0}",x);
      Console.WriteLine("Area of second rectangle is {0}",y);
      Console.WriteLine("Area of third rectangle is {0}",z);
   }
}
```

Output:

```
Area of first rectangle is 400
Area of second rectangle is 200
Area of third rectangle is 150
```

You can see that three getrect methods are defined. One has no parameter, the second has a single int type parameter, and the third has two int type parameters. All three methods are set to return data of the int type. In the Main method, the getrect method is invoked three times. The first method is called without arguments, so it invokes the getrect method, which has no parameter. In the second method call, the integer value 20 is passed. This method invokes the getrect method that has one parameter. Because the third method is called with two integer arguments, it invokes the getrect method that has two parameters. The values that the three methods return are assigned to three variables, x, y and z, which are then displayed on the screen.

As mentioned earlier, you can overload the methods by using parameters of different types. The example shown in Listing 6.2 overloads the getrect method while dealing with only int type parameters. Now you'll see how the getrect method can return an area of the rectangle of long and double types. You can modify the code in Listing 6.2 to appear as shown in Listing 6.3. Only the code in bold is modified; the rest is identical to Listing 6.2.

Listing 6.3 Program Code in MethodOverloadArea.cs File

```
using System;
class MethodOverloadArea
{
   static int getrect()
   {
      int l,b,a;
      l=50;
      b=8;
      a=l*b;
      return a;
   }
```

```
static int getrect(int l)
{
    int b,a;
    b=10;
    a=l*b;
    return a;
}
static int getrect(int l, int b)
{
    int a=l*b;
    return a;
}
static long getrect(long l, long b)
{
    long a=l*b;
    return a;
}
static double getrect(double l, double b)
{
    double a=l*b;
    return a;
}
static void Main()
{
    int x,y,z;
    x=getrect();
    y=getrect(20);
    z=getrect(30, 5);
    long larea=getrect(99999999999,888888 );
    double darea=getrect(99999999999.2222222222,88888888888.5555555555);
    Console.WriteLine("Area of first rectangle is {0}",x);
    Console.WriteLine("Area of second rectangle is {0}",y);
    Console.WriteLine("Area of third rectangle is {0}",z);
    Console.WriteLine("Area of fourth rectangle is {0}",larea);
    Console.WriteLine("Area of fifth rectangle is {0}",darea);
}
}
```

Output:

```
Area of first rectangle is 400
Area of second rectangle is 200
Area of third rectangle is 150
Area of fourth rectangle is 88888799999111112
Area of fifth rectangle is 8.88888888878642E+21
```

You can see that the getrect method is overloaded to contain parameters of long and double types. The arguments are sent while the method call determines which method needs to be invoked.

OPTIONAL AND NAMED PARAMETERS

You can define optional parameters in methods. *Optional parameters* are ones that have default values. The caller can supply values for the optional parameters and can even omit them if they're not necessary. When the caller omits the optional parameters, C# uses their default values for processing. If the method includes both normal parameters and optional parameters, the optional parameters must be placed at the end in the parameter list. The following code shows a getrect method that has an optional parameter, b:

```
public int getrect(int l, int b=10) {
    int a;
    a=l*b;
    return a;
}
```

In this method, the b parameter is optional and has a default value of 10. You can call the getrect method in the following two ways:

By passing the value for the b parameter explicitly as shown here:

```
x=getrect(50,8);
```

By not passing the value for the b parameter, thereby asking the method to use its default value:

```
x=getrect(50);
```

You can also define multiple optional parameters in a method as shown here:

```
public float getaverage(int p, int q=10, r=20) {
    float avg;
    avg=(float)(p+q+r)/3;
    return avg;
}
```

When you're calling methods, the argument values are assigned to the parameters by position. (The first value in the method call is assigned to the first parameter, the second value to the second parameter, and so on.) By using the named parameters, you can pass values for the parameters in any order you like. All you need to do is specify each parameter by its name using a colon operator.

When calling the getaverage method, you can specify the name of the parameters that you want to set in any order, as shown here:

```
float z=getaverage(50, r:80);
```

In this method call, you have supplied the value 50 for the parameter p. Also, you supplied the value for the parameter r as 80. The parameter q takes its default value. This feature of supplying values for the parameters by specifying their names is called *named parameters*.

Note

When using named parameters in a method, the positional parameters must be listed before any named parameters.

The OptionalParam.cs program shown in Listing 6.4 computes the area of a rectangle using optional and named parameters.

Listing 6.4 Program Code in OptionalParam.cs File

```
using System;
class OptionalParam
{
    static int getrect(int l=50, int b=8)
    {
        int a=l*b;
        return a;
    }
    static void Main()
    {
        int w, x,y,z;
        w=getrect();
        x=getrect(20);
        y=getrect(b:10);
        z=getrect(30,5);
        Console.WriteLine("Area of first rectangle is {0}",w);
        Console.WriteLine("Area of second rectangle is {0}",x);
        Console.WriteLine("Area of third rectangle is {0}",y);
        Console.WriteLine("Area of fourth rectangle is {0}",z);
    }
}
```

Output:

```
Area of first rectangle is 400
Area of second rectangle is 160
Area of third rectangle is 500
Area of fourth rectangle is 150
```

The first call to the `getrect` method is without arguments; therefore, the method executes taking the default values of the parameters `l` and `b`. The computed area of a rectangle is returned and assigned to variable `w`. The second `getrect` method is called with a single argument, `20`, which is assigned to parameter `l`. The parameter `b` then takes its default value. The third `getrect` method call uses the named parameter mechanism to pass the value `10` to parameter `b`. The parameter `l` in this case takes its default value. The final method call passes a value for both parameters `l` and `b`.

C# PARAMETER MODIFIERS

As discussed earlier, the methods take parameters. There are many ways to pass parameters to the methods. C# provides several parameter modifiers to control how parameters are passed to a method. These parameter modifiers are listed in Table 6.1.

Table 6.1   C# Parameter Modifiers

Parameter	Meaning
(None)	If no parameter modifier is specified, it is assumed to be passed by value. That is, the method receives a copy of the original parameter, and the caller cannot see the modifications that the method makes on the parameters.
out	Output parameters enable methods to return more than one value to the caller. The method assigns the value to the output parameter(s), which the caller can see and access. The compiler error is generated if the method does not assign a value to the output parameter.
ref	The reference of the parameters is passed to the method. The caller can see modifications that the method makes to the parameters.
params	Enable sending a variable number of arguments to the method as a single logical parameter. A method can have only a single params modifier, and it must be the final parameter of the method.

Now you'll learn the technique of passing parameters to a method beginning with the pass by value method.

Passing By Value

By default, the parameters are passed to a method by value. In this behavior, a copy of the data is passed to the method. Therefore, if the method modifies the value of the parameters, the caller never knows about the changes made. After invoking the method, when control reaches back to the caller, the caller picks up its original parameter values (the values while invoking the method). The PassByValue.cs program shown in Listing 6.5 demonstrates passing parameters to a method by value.

Listing 6.5 Program Code in PassByValue.cs File

```
using System;
class PassByValue
{
    static int getrect(int l, int b)
    {
        int a=l*b;
        l=10;
        b=20;
        return a;
    }
    static void Main()
    {
        int u = 50, v = 8;
        Console.WriteLine("Before calling method. Value of u={0} and v={1}",u,v);
        int z=getrect(u,v);
        Console.WriteLine("Area of rectangle is {0}",z);
        Console.WriteLine("After calling method. Value of u={0} and v={1}",u,v);
    }
}
```

Output:

```
Before calling method. Value of u=50 and v=8
Area of rectangle is 400
After calling method. Value of u=50 and v=8
```

From the output, you can see that the values in the arguments u and v are copied to the parameters l and b of the getrect method. Therefore, the modifications done in the values of the parameters l and b in the getrect method are visible only within the scope of the method. When they come back to the caller, the modifications made in the parameters are lost. The arguments u and v pick up their original values, 50 and 8.

Passing By Reference

The modifications that the called method performs on the supplied arguments are usually lost when they're returned to the caller. When using the pass by reference method, the changes that the called method makes on the supplied arguments persist in the caller, too. In other words, the caller method can see the modifications that the called method makes on the supplied arguments. Pass by reference is implemented using the ref modifier, which is applied to the variables whose reference you want to pass to the method. Remember: you must initialize the reference parameters before you pass them to the method.

The PassByReference.cs program shown in Listing 6.6 demonstrates passing parameters to a method by reference.

Listing 6.6 Program Code in PassByReference.cs File

```
using System;
class PassByReference
{
    static int getrect(ref int l, ref int b)
    {
        int a=l*b;
        l=10;
        b=20;
        return a;
    }
    static void Main()
    {
        int u = 50, v = 8;
        Console.WriteLine("Before calling method. Value of u={0} and v={1}",u,v);
        int z=getrect(ref u,ref v);
        Console.WriteLine("Area of rectangle is {0}",z);
        Console.WriteLine("After calling method. Value of u={0} and v={1}",u,v);
    }
}
```

Output:

```
Before calling method. Value of u=50 and v=8
Area of rectangle is 400
After calling method. Value of u=10 and v=20
```

In the preceding code, you can see that the arguments u and v are initialized to values 50 and 8. The references of both the arguments are sent while calling the getrect method. Because the arguments are passed by reference, the parameters l and b in the method refer to the same memory locations that are allocated to the arguments u and v. In the method getrect, the modifications made in the values of parameters l and b are actually applied to the arguments u and v. So, after the method call, the changes made in the parameters l and b are visible in the arguments u and v.

Using Output Parameters

Methods define the out modifier (output parameter[s]) for storing the result of processing. The values that a method assigns to the output parameters are automatically available to the caller. Consequently, such methods need not return a value, and their return type is set to void.

Note

If the method using the out modifier doesn't assign a value to the output parameter(s), compiler errors are generated.

Calling a method with output parameters also requires use of the out modifier. In other words, you must use the out modifier with arguments as well as with parameters. The variables that are passed as output arguments must not be initialized. If they are, their value is lost after the method call.

The OutParam.cs program shown in Listing 6.7 demonstrates using output parameters in a method. The method computes the area of a rectangle and assigns the result to the output parameter. The method does not return anything. The caller displays the area of the rectangle through the output parameter that was sent while invoking the method.

Listing 6.7 Program Code in OutParam.cs File

```
using System;
class OutParam
{
    static void getrect(int l, int b, out int a)
    {
        a=l*b;
    }
    static void Main()
    {
        int u = 50, v = 8;
        int z;
        getrect(u, v, out z);
```

```
        Console.WriteLine("Area of rectangle is {0}",z);
    }
}
```

Output:

```
Area of rectangle is 400
```

You can see that the variable z is used with the out modifier while calling the getrect method. The argument z is assigned to the parameter a in the getrect method. Note that the out modifier is used with the parameter a, too. The method assigns the result of computation to the parameter a. As expected, the value assigned to the parameter a in the method is visible in the caller through the argument z. Therefore, the computation that the method performs is displayed through the argument z.

You can use the out modifier to get multiple outputs from a method. In other words, using the output parameter, you can overcome the method's limitation of returning only a single value. The ReturnMultipleVal.cs program shown in Listing 6.8 returns more than one value through the output parameter. The method defines three parameters without a modifier. The addition, multiplication, and division of two normal parameters that are sent to the method are assigned to the parameters using the out modifier. In this way, all three operations—addition, multiplication, and division— are performed for the caller.

Listing 6.8 Program Code in ReturnMultipleVal.cs File

```
using System;
class ReturnMultipleVal
{
    static void mathop(int a, int b, out int c, out int d, out float e )
    {
        c=a+b;
        d=a*b;
        e=(float) a/b;
    }
    static void Main()
    {
        int u = 10, v = 20;
        int add, mult;
        float div;
        mathop(u, v, out add, out mult, out div);
        Console.WriteLine("Value of u={0} and v={1}. Their addition is {2},
multiplication is {3}, and division is {4}",u,v,add,mult, div);
    }
}
```

Output:

Value of u=10 and v=20. Their addition is 30, multiplication is 200, and division is 0.5

Note

You must use the `out` modifier in both places while implementing the method and while invoking the method.

Sending Variable Length Parameters

C# supports the `params` modifier that enables you to send arrays or comma-delimited lists as parameters to the method. In other words, you can pass a variable number of identically typed parameters to the method as a single logical parameter. The `VariableLengthParam.cs` program shown in Listing 6.9 demonstrates passing an array to a method. The method uses the `params` modifier with the string array that is supplied to it as a parameter. The string arrays of different lengths are supplied to the method to display their elements.

Listing 6.9 Program Code in VariableLengthParam.cs File

```
using System;
class VariableLengthParam
{
    static void DisplayNames(params string[] names)
    {
        if(names.Length ==0)
            Console.WriteLine("No names provided");
        else
        {
            for (int i = 0; i < names.Length; i++)
                Console.WriteLine(names[i]);
        }
    }
    static void Main()
    {
        string[] programmers = {"John", "Kelly", "Caroline", "Paula", "David" };
        string[] developers = {"Nancy", "Cynthia", "Mike"};
        Console.WriteLine("List of programmers is: ");
        DisplayNames(programmers);
        Console.WriteLine("\nList of developers is: ");
        DisplayNames(developers);
    }
}
```

Output:

```
List of programmers is:
John
Kelly
Caroline
Paula
David

List of developers is:
Nancy
Cynthia
Mike
```

YOUR OWN TYPE: STRUCTURES

C# provides a way to define your own data type, and that is through structures, or *structs*. The structs are similar to classes. In the next chapter, you will learn the difference between the two. For the time being, it is enough to know that structs are value types, whereas classes are reference types. Value types provide better performance because their instances are allocated in a stack and the memory allocated to them is automatically released when their scope ends. The structs derive from `System.ValueType`; they cannot derive from any other class or struct.

To declare your own structure, you use the `struct` keyword followed by the name of the type that you want to define, followed by the body of the struct between opening and closing braces.

```
struct type_name {
    field1….. // body of the structure
    field2
    …..
}
```

Example:

```
struct Product {
    public string code;
    public string product_name;
    public double price;
}
```

The preceding code defines a struct named `Product` that contains two public fields of string and double type.

Note

The fields, methods, and properties that you define within a struct are known as its *members*.

You cannot initialize the `struct` fields while defining a struct. For example, the following lines display errors:

```
struct Product {
    public string code="L102";              //error - cannot initialize fields
    public string product_name="Laptop";    //error - cannot initialize fields
    public double price;
}
```

You need to initialize the fields of a struct before you can use them. You can initialize the `struct` fields in any of the following ways:

Instantiating the `Product` struct using the default constructor as shown here:

```
Product p1 = new Product();
```

With the preceding command, the built-in default constructor is invoked, the struct variable p1 is allocated on the stack, and all its fields are initialized to `null` or 0.

Note

For the structs, C# implicitly defines the default constructor; you don't need to implement the default constructor yourself.

You can also initialize the `struct` fields explicitly by using the following commands:

```
Product p1;
p1.code="L102";
p1.product_name="Laptop";
p1.price=800;
```

One more way to initialize the `struct` fields is to use the parameterized constructors and methods. The following code defines a parameterized constructor that initializes the fields of the `Product` struct:

```
public Product(string c, string n, double p) {
    code=c;
    product_name = n;
    price= p;
}
```

Again, the structs cannot have a default parameterless constructor. Also, you cannot define destructors for structs.

The StructExample.cs program shown in Listing 6.10 demonstrates how a struct is defined to store product information. The program also explains how the struct fields are initialized explicitly and through a constructor. Finally, the program shows how the content in one struct is assigned to another.

Listing 6.10 Program Code in StructExample.cs File

```
using System;
struct Product {
    public string code;
    public string product_name;
    public double price;
    public Product(string c, string n, double p) {
        code=c;
        product_name = n;
        price= p;
    }
}
class StructExample {
    static void Main() {
    Product p1=new Product("C101", "Camera", 15.75);
    Product p2, p3;
    Console.WriteLine("Information of first product - Product Code: {0}, Product
Name: {1}, Product Price {2}", p1.code, p1.product_name, p1.price);
    p2=p1;
    Console.WriteLine("Information of second product - Product Code: {0}, Product
Name: {1}, Product Price {2}", p2.code, p2.product_name, p2.price);
    p3.code="L102";
    p3.product_name="Laptop";
    p3.price=800;
    Console.WriteLine("Information of third product - Product Code: {0}, Product
Name: {1}, Product Price {2}", p3.code, p3.product_name, p3.price);
    }
}
```

Output:

```
Information of first product - Product Code: C101, Product Name: Camera, Product Price
15.75
Information of second product - Product Code: C101, Product Name: Camera, Product Price
15.75
Information of third product - Product Code: L102, Product Name: Laptop, Product Price
800
```

You can see that variable p1 of the Product type is created and uses the constructor, and its three fields—code, product_name, and price—are initialized to C101, Camera, and 15.75, respectively. Then two more variables, p2 and p3, of the Product type are created. The content in variable p1 is assigned to variable p2. That is, the values in the three fields—code, product_name, and price—of the p2 variable are used to initialize the field values of variable p1. Finally, the code, product_name, and price fields of Product variable p3 are explicitly initialized to L102, Laptop, and 800, respectively.

Using Properties with Struct

Now you'll use properties with the struct type. Properties simplify the task of accessing members of the structure as well as the class. You will be reading more about properties in the next chapter. For the time being, it's important to know that a property behaves like a field, allowing you to get and set its value. At the same time, it acts like a method. It consists of a name along with get and set methods. The get and set methods are used to get and set the value of a member. The get methods are known as *accessors*, whereas the set methods are known as *mutators*. After using a property's name, the respective accessor and mutator are invoked automatically.

The StructExample2.cs program shown in Listing 6.11 demonstrates the use of properties with a struct. The program assigns and accesses the data in the struct fields through the respective accessors and mutators.

Listing 6.11 Program Code in StructExample2.cs File

```
using System;
struct Product
{
    private string code;
    private string product_name;
    private double price;
    public Product(string c, string n, double p) {
        this.code = c;                              // #1
        this.product_name = n;
        this.price = p;
    }
    public void Show()
    {
        Console.WriteLine("Information of product - Product Code: {0}, Product
Name: {1}, Product Price {2}", Code, Product_Name, Price);        //    #2
    }
    public string Code                              //    #3
    {
```

```
      get { return code; }                         //    #4
      set { code = value; }                        //    #5
   }
   public string Product_Name
   {
      get { return product_name; }
      set { product_name = value; }
   }
   public double Price
   {
      get { return price; }
      set { price = value; }
   }
}
class StructExample2
{
   static void Main(string[] args)
   {
      Product p1=new Product("C101", "Camera", 15.75);
      p1.Show();
   }
}
```

Output:

```
Information of product - Product Code: C101, Product Name: Camera, Product Price 15.75
```

Statement #3 defines a property named Code of the string type. The property has a get and a set (accessor and mutator) method. Whenever the code member is accessed in any statement, the respective method is called automatically. For example, statement #1 invokes the set method defined in statement #5. The value to be assigned to the code member is assigned to the parameter value, from which it is assigned to the member code.

Similarly, when the code member is accessed as shown in statement #2, the get accessor (in statement #4) is called, returning the value in the member code to be displayed on the screen.

Defining Arrays in Structures

You learned about arrays in the previous chapter. Now you'll discover how to use them as a structure member. The ArrayInStruct.cs file shown in Listing 6.12 stores information about a product in a struct called Product. The Product struct has two public members: code of string type, and a string array called product_info. The product_info array stores a product's name, its price, and its date of manufacturing.

Listing 6.12 Program Code in ArrayInStruct.cs File

```
using System;
struct Product {
    public string code;
    public string[] product_info;
}
class ArrayInStruct {
    static void Main() {
        Product p1=new Product();
        p1.product_info = new string[3];
        p1.code="C101";
        p1.product_info[0]="Cell Phone";
        p1.product_info[1]="12.99$";
        p1.product_info[2]="11/07/2013";
        Console.WriteLine("Information of the product is - Product Code: {0},
Product Name: {1}, Product Price: {2}, Date of Manufacturing: {3}", p1.code,p1.
product_info[0], p1.product_info[1],
        p1.product_info[2]);
    }
}
```

Output:

```
Information of the product is - Product Code: C101, Product Name: Cell Phone, Product
Price: 12.99$, Date of Manufacturing: 11/07/2013
```

You can see that a `Product` struct is defined with two fields: `code` and `product_info`. The `product_info` array is simply declared in the struct and not defined. The `Product` struct is instantiated, creating the variable `p1`. The `code` field is set to the value `C101`. Three memory blocks are allocated to the `product_info` array. In other words, the `product_info` array is defined, thereby allowing this array to store three strings. The product name, its price, and its date of manufacturing are stored as string elements in the array `product_info`. Finally, the information in the structs `members`, `code`, and `product_info` are accessed and displayed on the screen.

The program `ArrayInStructInit.cs` shown in Listing 6.13 uses an array in the `Product` struct to store product information. The program demonstrates how a struct containing an array member is initialized when it's instantiated.

Listing 6.13 Program Code in ArrayInStructInit.cs File

```
using System;
struct Product {
    public string code;
    public string[] product_info;
```

```
    public Product(string c, string[] pinfo) {
        code=c;
        product_info=new string[3];
        product_info[0]=pinfo[0];
        product_info[1]=pinfo[1];
        product_info[2]=pinfo[2];
    }
}
class ArrayInStructInit {
    static void Main() {
        string[] pfo=new string[3];
        pfo[0]="Cell Phone";
        pfo[1]="12.99$";
        pfo[2]="11/07/2013";
        Product p1=new Product("C101", pfo );
        Console.WriteLine("Information of the product is - Product Code: {0}, Product
Name: {1}, Product Price: {2}, Date of Manufacturing: {3}", p1.code,
p1.product_info[0], p1.product_info[1], p1.product_info[2]);
    }
}
```

Output:

```
Information of the product is - Product Code: C101, Product Name: Cell Phone, Product
Price: 12.99$, Date of Manufacturing: 11/07/2013
```

You can see that the Product struct is defined consisting of two fields. One is a string named code, and the other is a string array named product_info. The string array product_info is simply declared, not defined in the Product struct. A constructor is defined to initialize both the fields. In the constructor, the field product_info is defined as an array of three elements. The elements in the string array pinfo that is passed as a parameter are used to initialize the elements of the array field product_info. In the Main method, a string array named pfo, which is three elements, is defined. The three elements of the string array are initialized to represent the product code, its price, and its date of manufacturing. A struct variable, p1, is created by invoking the constructor. The product code C101 and the string array pfo are passed to the constructor. The constructor initializes the two fields: code and the string array named product_info. The information in the struct variable p1 is then displayed on the screen.

In the previous chapter, you learned to create an array of different types, such as int and string. You saw how an array of a type is used for storing several elements of the same type. The question is whether you can define an array of a struct type. Why not?

Using an Array of Structures

Up until now, you have been storing information for one product in the Product struct. What if you want to store information of more than one struct? The answer is simple: create an array of structs. Like other data types, C# enables you to create an array of struct types. Recall that structs are nothing but custom data types. The program ArrayOfStructs.cs shown in Listing 6.14 defines an array of the Product struct. In other words, each array element stores a Product struct. The size of the array is set to three elements, so information about three products can be stored in the array. The program asks information about the code, product_name, and price of three products. The entered information is stored sequentially in the Product structs that are defined in the array elements.

Listing 6.14 Program Code in ArrayOfStructs.cs File

```
using System;
struct Product {
    public string code;
    public string product_name;
    public double price;
}
class ArrayOfStructs {
    static void Main() {
        Product[] p=new Product[3];
        Console.WriteLine("Enter information for three products");
        for (int i = 0; i <=2; i++)
        {
            p[i] = new Product();
            Console.Write("Enter product code: ");
            p[i].code = Console.ReadLine();
            Console.Write("Enter product name: ");
            p[i].product_name = Console.ReadLine();
            Console.Write("Enter product price: ");
            p[i].price = Convert.ToDouble(Console.ReadLine());
        }
        Console.WriteLine("Information of products is:");
        for (int i = 0; i <=2; i++)
        {
            Console.WriteLine("Product Code: {0}, Product Name: {1}, Product Price {2}",
p[i].code, p[i].product_name, p[i].price);
        }
    }
}
```

```
Enter information for three products
Enter product code: C101
Enter product name: Camera
Enter product price: 9.99
Enter product code: L102
Enter product name: Laptop
Enter product price: 30.00
Enter product code: T103
Enter product name: Tablet
Enter product price: 15.99
Information of products is:
Product Code: C101, Product Name: Camera, Product Price 9.99
Product Code: L102, Product Name: Laptop, Product Price 30
Product Code: T103, Product Name: Tablet, Product Price 15.99
```

A `Product` struct is defined and consists of the fields `code`, `product_name`, and `price`. A struct array, p, is defined and consists of three `Product` structs. A `for` loop is set to execute three times to enter `code`, `name`, and `price` information for three products. The `Product` stuct is instantiated and assigned to each index location of the `struct` array so that each element of the `struct` array, p, is able to store information of one product. The `code`, `name`, and `price` the user enters are assigned to the `code`, `product_name`, and `price` fields of each `Product` struct. Finally, the information for the three products is displayed on the screen.

You know that you can initialize a struct when it's defined. An array of structs consists of more than one struct. The program `ArrayOfStructsInit.cs` shown in Listing 6.15 defines an array of the `Product` struct. The program demonstrates how an array of structs is initialized (that is, how the struct defined in each array element is initialized).

Listing 6.15 Program Code in ArrayOfStructsInit.cs File

```
using System;
struct Product {
    public string code;
    public string product_name;
    public double price;
    public Product(string c, string n, double p) {
        code=c;
        product_name = n;
        price= p;
    }
}
```

```
class ArrayOfStructsInit {
    static void Main() {
        Product[]  p=  {  new  Product("C101",  "Camera",  9.99),  new  Product("L102",
"Laptop",30), new Product("T103", "Tablet", 15.99) };
        Console.WriteLine("Information of products is:");
        for (int i = 0; i <=2; i++)
        {
            Console.WriteLine("Product Code: {0}, Product Name: {1}, Product Price {2}",
p[i].code, p[i].product_name, p[i].price);
        }
    }
}
```

Output:

```
Information of products is:
Product Code: C101, Product Name: Camera, Product Price 9.99
Product Code: L102, Product Name: Laptop, Product Price 30
Product Code: T103, Product Name: Tablet, Product Price 15.99
```

Here, a constructor is defined to initialize the three fields: code, product_name, and price. In the Main method, the struct array p is defined and initialized with three Product struct objects. After you define and initialize the struct array, the information about the three products stored in it is displayed on the screen.

NESTED STRUCTS

In C#, a struct can be nested inside another struct. The nested struct acts as a member of the parent struct. The access modifier used while declaring the nested struct defines its accessibility. There are two ways of nesting the C# structs inside each other. The first way is nesting the whole declaration of a struct inside the other struct, as shown here:

```
struct S1
{
    // public member variables of struct S1
    public struct S2
    {
        // public member variables struct S2
    }
}
```

In the preceding syntax, you see that the entire struct S2 is declared inside the struct S1 body. The second way of nesting a struct is to use the struct as a member variable of another struct, as shown here:

```
struct S1
{
    // public member variables
}
struct S2
{
    // public member variables
    public S1 s;   // struct S1 declared as member variable of struct S2
}
```

The NestedStruct.cs program shown in Listing 6.16 demonstrates nesting of structs. A Product stuct is defined and consists of three members: code of string type, product_name of string type, and price of double type. Nested inside the Product struct is another struct called Specifications. The struct Specifications consists of three members of the string type called color, weight, and size.

Listing 6.16 Program Code in NestedStruct.cs File

```
using System;
struct Product {
    public string code;
    public string product_name;
    public double price;
    public struct Specifications
    {
        public string color;
        public string weight;
        public string size;
    }
}
class NestedStruct {
    static void Main() {
        Product p1;
        p1.code="L102";
        p1.product_name="Laptop";
        p1.price=800;
        Product.Specifications spec;
        spec.color="silver";
        spec.weight=".25 pound";
        spec.size="8 inches";
```

```
        Console.WriteLine("Information of the product - Product Code: {0}, Product Name:
{1}, Product Price {2}", p1.code, p1.product_name, p1.price);
        Console.WriteLine("Product Color: {0}, Weight: {1}, Size: {2}", spec.color,
spec.weight, spec.size);
    }
}
```

Output:

```
Information of the product - Product Code: L102, Product Name: Laptop, Product Price 800
Product Color: silver, Weight: .25 pound, Size: 8 inches
```

You can see that the `Specifications` struct consisting of three members is declared inside the `Product` struct. The `Product` struct is the parent struct consisting of three members. In the `Main` method, a structure variable p1 of the `Product` type is created. The members `code`, `product_name`, and `price` of the `Product` struct are initialized to `L102`, `Laptop`, and `800`, respectively. Thereafter, the struct variable `spec` of `Product.Specifications` is created. The main thing to observe is that you access the nested struct by specifying the parent struct followed by a . (period) followed by the nested struct name. The member variables `color`, `weight`, and `size` of the `Specifications` struct are initialized to `silver`, `.25` pound, and `8 inches`, respectively. Finally, the values in the member variables of both `Product` and `Specifications` are displayed on the screen.

You might be wondering whether it is possible to initialize the nested struct's members while instantiating it. The answer is yes.

The `NestedStructInit.cs` program shown in Listing 6.17 demonstrates how the parent and the nested struct's members are initialized while instantiating them.

Listing 6.17 Program Code in NestedStructInit.cs File

```
using System;
struct Product {
    public string code;
    public string product_name;
    public double price;
    public struct Specifications
    {
        public string color;
        public string weight;
        public string size;
        public Specifications(string clr, string wgt, string siz) {
```

```
            color=clr;
            weight = wgt;
            size= siz;
    }
}
public Product(string cde, string nme, double prc) {
    code=cde;
    product_name = nme;
    price= prc;
    }
}
class NestedStructInit {
    static void Main() {
        Product p1 =new Product("L102", "Laptop", 800);
        Product.Specifications spec = new Product.Specifications("silver", ".25 pound",
"8 inches");
        Console.WriteLine("Information of the product - Product Code: {0}, Product Name:
{1}, Product Price {2}", p1.code, p1.product_name, p1.price);
        Console.WriteLine("Product Color: {0}, Weight: {1}, Size: {2}", spec.color,
spec.weight, spec.size);
    }
}
```

Output:

```
Information of the product - Product Code: L102, Product Name: Laptop, Product Price 800
Product Color: silver, Weight: .25 pound, Size: 8 inches
```

To initialize struct members, both the parent and the nested structs define their respective constructors. While instantiating the Product struct, the values for the three members are passed, which the parameterized constructor uses to initialize the code, product_name, and price members. Similarly, while instantiating the nested struct, Specifications values are passed, which invoke its constructor to initialize its color, weight, and size members. Finally, the values in the members of the parent and the nested struct are displayed on the screen.

The program StructAsMember.cs shown in Listing 6.18 demonstrates how you can treat a struct as a member of another struct. The Specifications struct is defined and consists of three members: color, weight, and size of string type. A constructor is also defined to initialize its members. After the Specifications definition, another struct called Product is defined consisting of four members: code and product_name of string type, price of double type, and spec of Specifications type. (Through the spec member, the Product struct can access members of Specifications.)

Listing 6.18 Program Code in StructAsMember.cs File

```
using System;
struct Specifications
{
    public string color;
    public string weight;
    public string size;
    public Specifications(string cl, string wt, string sz) {
        color=cl;
        weight = wt;
        size= sz;
    }
}
struct Product {
    public string code;
    public string product_name;
    public double price;
    public Specifications spec;
    public Product(string cde, string nme, double prc,string clr, string wgt,
string siz ) {
        code=cde;
        product_name = nme;
        price= prc;
        spec= new Specifications(clr, wgt, siz);
    }
}
class StructAsMember {
    static void Main() {
        Product p1 =new Product("L102", "Laptop", 800, "silver", ".25 pound",
"8 inches");
        Console.WriteLine("Information of the product - Product Code: {0}, Product
Name: {1}, Product Price {2}", p1.code, p1.product_name, p1.price);
        Console.WriteLine("Product Color: {0}, Weight: {1}, Size: {2}", p1.spec.color,
p1.spec.weight, p1.spec.size);
    }
}
```

Output:

```
Information of the product - Product Code: L102, Product Name: Laptop, Product Price 800
Product Color: silver, Weight: .25 pound, Size: 8 inches
```

You can see that the Product struct is instantiated by passing six values to it. The Product constructor is called to initialize its members. In other words, the first three values passed to the constructor initialize the `Product` struct's members, and the remaining three values are used to invoke the `Specifications` struct's constructor to initialize its `color`, `weight`, and `size` members. The values assigned to the members of the two structs are then displayed on the screen.

Now you know how to work and use structs in C# programs. The `DateTime` struct is a frequently used built-in struct that C# provides. By its name, it is clear that the `DateTime` struct stores the date and time. The next section explores it in more detail.

DATE AND TIME STRUCTURE

The `DateTime` structure represents the date and time. It is a value type structure, not a reference type. The value of `DateTime` is between 12:00:00 midnight, January 1, 0001 and 11:59:59 P.M., December 31, 9999 A.D. You can create the `DateTime` object using any of the following methods:

```
DateTime today_date = DateTime.Today; // Creates the DateTime instance from the current
date and time values
DateTime custom_date1 = new DateTime(2012, 11, 5); // Creates the DateTime instance
consisting of only date
DateTime custom_date2 = new DateTime(2012, 11, 5, 10, 30, 15); // Creates the DateTime
instance from the supplied date and time values
string dateStr = "11/5/2013 10:30:15 AM";
DateTime custom_date3 = DateTime.Parse(dateStr); // Creates the DateTime instance from
the date and time values supplied in the given string
DateTime custom_date4 = new DateTime(1000000); // Creates the DateTime instance from
the supplied number of Ticks
```

A *tick* represents one hundred nanoseconds, or one ten-millionth of a second.

Note

If time is not specified along with the date, the `DateTime` class constructor sets the time to 12:00 a.m.

The `DateTime` object stores day, month, year, hour, minute, second, and millisecond values as a separate property, allowing each to be accessed individually through `Properties`.

Using the DateTime Properties and Methods

The `DateTime` properties return the desired components from the date and time contained in the `DateTime` structure. Table 6.2 offers a brief description of `DateTime` properties.

Table 6.2 DateTime Properties

Property	Description
Hour, Minute, Second, Millisecond, Year, Month, and Day	The property name itself depicts the component it returns.
DayOfWeek	Displays the day of the week (Monday, Tuesday, Wednesday, Thursday, Friday, Saturday, or Sunday).
DayOfYear	Returns the day of the year.
TimeOfDay	Returns the time element in the DateTime structure.
Date	Returns the date component of the DateTime structure. The time value is set to 12 midnight (00:00:00).
Day, Month, Year	Returns the values of the day, month, and year from the supplied DateTime object.
Now	Returns the current date and time values. Example: 7/3/2013 9:43:16 AM
Today	Gets the current date in the form of a DateTime instance. Does not include time information. The time value is set to 12:00:00. Example: 7/3/2013 12:00:00 AM
Ticks	Returns the number of ticks in the DateTime structure.
UtcNow	Returns a DateTime in Coordinated Universal Time (UTC).
Kind	Indicates whether the time represented by the DateTime instance is based on local time, Coordinated Universal Time (UTC), or neither.

Now you'll take a quick look at the different methods that the DateTime struct provides. Table 6.3 shows a description of a few of the DateTime methods.

Table 6.3 DateTime Methods

Method	Description
Add	Adds/subtracts the value of the specified TimeSpan object to the DateTime object.
AddDays	Adds/subtracts the specified number of days to the DateTime object. Pass a positive value to this method to add and a negative value to subtract.
Subtract	Returns the difference between the two dates in terms of a TimeSpan structure.
AddHours	Adds/subtracts the specified number of hours to the DateTime object.
AddMilliseconds	Adds/subtracts the specified number of milliseconds to the DateTime object.
AddTicks	Adds/subtracts the specified number of ticks to the DateTime object. One tick is considered 100 nanoseconds.
AddMinutes	Adds/subtracts the specified number of minutes to the DateTime object.
AddMonths	Adds/subtracts the specified number of months to the DateTime object.
AddSeconds	Adds/subtracts the specified number of seconds to the DateTime object.
AddYears	Adds/subtracts the specified number of years to the DateTime object.
Parse	Converts the date and time that is in string form into the DateTime object.

When called through a DateTime object, the preceding methods do not change the object's value. Instead, they return a new DateTime object with the impact of the method applied (with modified date and time).

The DateTimeDemo1.cs program shown in Listing 6.19 demonstrates creating a DateTime object in the following four ways:

- From the system's current date and time
- From the supplied day, month, and year

- From the date and time values stored in string format
- By supplying ticks value

The program also demonstrates determining yesterday's and tomorrow's dates by adding and subtracting days from the current date using the `AddDays` method. It explains copying of the `DateTime` structure. It also extracts day, month, year, day of week, and day of year from the current date and displays it on the screen.

Listing 6.19 Program Code in DateTimeDemo1.cs File

```
using System;
class DateTimeDemo1
{
    static void Main()
    {
        DateTime today_date = DateTime.Today;
        DateTime custom_date1 = new DateTime(2012, 11, 5);
        DateTime date1 = custom_date1;
        string dateStr = "11/5/2013 10:30:15 AM";
        DateTime custom_date2 = DateTime.Parse(dateStr);
        DateTime custom_date3 = new DateTime(1000000);
        DateTime yest_date = DateTime.Today.AddDays(-1);
        DateTime tom_date = DateTime.Today.AddDays(+1);
        Console.WriteLine("Today's date is {0}", today_date);
        Console.WriteLine("Custom date is {0}", custom_date1);
        Console.WriteLine("Copy of custom date, {0} is {1}", custom_date1, date1);
        Console.WriteLine("Date created through string is {0}", custom_date2);
        Console.WriteLine("Date created through 1000000 ticks is {0}", custom_date3);
        Console.WriteLine("Yesterday's date was {0}", yest_date);
        Console.WriteLine("Tomorrow's date is {0}", tom_date);
        Console.WriteLine("Current day is {0}, month is {1}, and year is {2}",
today_date.Day, today_date.Month, today_date.Year);
        Console.WriteLine("Weekday is {0}, and the day of the year is {1}",
today_date.DayOfWeek, today_date.DayOfYear);
    }
}
```

Output:

```
Today's date is 7/3/2013 12:00:00 AM
Custom date is 11/5/2012 12:00:00 AM
Copy of custom date, 11/5/2012 12:00:00 AM is 11/5/2012 12:00:00 AM
Date created through string is 11/5/2013 10:30:15 AM
Date created through 1000000 ticks is 1/1/0001 12:00:00 AM
```

```
Yesterday's date was 7/2/2013 12:00:00 AM
Tomorrow's date is 7/4/2013 12:00:00 AM
Current day is 3, month is 7,and year is 2013
Weekday is Wednesday, and the day of the year is 184
```

You can see that several DateTime objects are created in the preceding code. For example, the today_date object is created using the current system's date, custom_date1 is created by supplying the year, month, and day values, custom_date2 is created from the supplied string, and custom_date3 is created by supplying the number of ticks. The custom date in the custom_date1 object is copied into another DateTime object, date1, so date1 will have the same date and time as custom_date1. By invoking the AddDays method on the today_date object, tomorrow's and yesterday's dates are computed and displayed on the screen. Using the Day, Month, Year, DayOfWeek, and DayOfYear properties of the DateTime object, today_date is accessed to display the current day, month, year, day of week, and day of year, respectively.

One structure that goes hand in hand with the DateTime struct is TimeSpan.

Using TimeSpan

TimeSpan is a structure that represents a time interval. You can instantiate TimeSpan by using one of its constructors. The following example initializes a TimeSpan structure to the specified number of hours, minutes, and seconds.

```
TimeSpan time_interval = new TimeSpan(10, 30, 15);
```

A few of the TimeSpan properties are as follows:

- **Days**—Returns the days component of the time interval represented in the TimeSpan structure.

- **Hours**—Returns the hours component of the time interval represented in the TimeSpan structure.

- **Minutes**—Returns the minutes component of the time interval represented in the TimeSpan structure.

- **Seconds**—Returns the seconds component of the time interval represented in the TimeSpan structure.

- **TotalDays**—Converts the entire value stored in the TimeSpan object into days and returns a double value.

The DateTime struct consists of several components, such as day, month, year, hour, and minute. While programming, sometimes you don't want all DateTime structs, but only a few. So, is there a way to display only the required DateTime components or to format the DateTime struct in a desired format? Of course! Read on.

Formatting Dates and Times

There are numerous techniques in C# for displaying dates and times in desired formats. There are predefined formatting methods along with the series of custom format specifiers that can be used with the `ToString` method. The basic formatting methods to format the date and time in long and short formats follow:

- `ToLongDateString`—Displays the date in long format. Example: Monday, July 01, 2013
- `ToLongTimeString`—Displays time in long format. Example: 10:47:38 AM
- `ToShortDateString`—Displays the date in short format. Example: 7/1/2013
- `ToShortTimeString`—Displays time in short format. Example: 10:47 AM

These built-in methods provide many formatting features. Therefore, C# supports customized date and time formatting.

Custom Date and Time Formatting

C# provides several custom format specifiers that you can use to format date and time as required. These format specifiers are used with the `ToString` method. The `ToString` method formats the `DateTime` struct according to the supplied format specifier and returns it in the form of a string. Table 6.4 shows the list of custom specifiers that the `ToString` method supports.

Table 6.4 Custom Specifiers Supported by the ToString Method of the DateTime Struct

Format Specifier	Description
h	Displays the hour in one digit. If the hour is greater than 9, the hour is displayed in two digits. Range: 1–12.
hh	Displays the hour in two-digit format. Adds a leading 0 if the hour is one digit. Range: 01–12.
H	Displays the hour in a single digit that is also military format. Range 0–23.
HH	Displays the hour in two digits in military format, in the range 00–23. Adds a leading 0 if the hour is one digit.
m	Displays minutes in one digit. Range: 0–59.
mm	Displays minutes in two digits. Displays a leading zero if the number is only one digit long. Range: 00–59.

s	Displays seconds in a single digit. Range: 0–59.
ss	Displays seconds in two digits. Shows leading zero if the seconds are one digit long. Range: 00–59.
d	Displays the numeric value for the day of the month. Will be one or two digits long.
dd	Displays the numerical value of the day in two digits, with a leading 0 if necessary.
ddd	Displays the current weekday in three-letter string. Example: Mon.
dddd	Displays the current weekday in full string. Example: Monday.
M	Displays the month in numeric form, in one digit preferably. Displays two digits if the month is greater than 9. Example: 1
MM	Displays the month in two digits. Displays leading zero if the month is in one digit. Example: 01.
MMM	Displays the first three letters of the month. Example: Jan.
MMMM	Displays the full month string. Example: January.
y, yy, yyy, yyyy	Displays the year in one digit, two digits, three digits, and four digits format, respectively.
t	Displays A when the time is in A.M. and P when the time is in P.M.
tt	Displays complete AM or PM depending on the time.
gg	Displays AD on the date.

The focus of the DateTimeExample.cs program shown in Listing 6.20 is on formatting the date and time. In all, it does the following tasks:

■ Displays the current date in long and short format.

■ Displays the current day, month, and year in the desired number of digits or characters.

■ Displays the current weekday in three-character format and in complete format.

■ Counts the number of days between the two dates.

■ Computes the TimeSpan between the two dates (that is, the difference of the number of days, months, years, hours, minutes, and seconds between the two dates).

- Determines the new date after adding a `TimeSpan` to a specific date.

- Determines whether the supplied year is a leap year.

Listing 6.20 Program Code in DateTimeExample.cs File

```
using System;
class DateTimeExample
{
    static void Main()
    {
        DateTime today_date = DateTime.Today;
        DateTime custom_date = new DateTime(2012, 11, 5);
        Console.WriteLine("Today's date in long format is {0} and in short format is {1}",
today_date.ToLongDateString(), today_date.ToShortDateString());
        Console.WriteLine("The current day in two-digit form is {0}, month in string form
is {1}, and year in two-digit form is {2}", today_date.ToString("dd"), today_date.
ToString("MMM"), today_date.ToString("yy"));
        Console.WriteLine("The weekday in three-character format is {0} and in complete
format is {1}", today_date.ToString("ddd"), today_date.ToString("dddd"));
        TimeSpan elapsed = today_date.Subtract(custom_date);
double daysdiff = elapsed.TotalDays;
        Console.WriteLine("The number  of  days  between  {0}  and  {1}  dates  is  {2}",
today_date.ToString("d"), custom_date.ToString("d"), daysdiff);
        DateTime work_started = new DateTime(2013, 11, 5, 9, 0, 0);
        DateTime work_finished = new DateTime(2013, 11, 6, 22, 30, 15);
        TimeSpan time_taken = work_finished - work_started;
        Console.WriteLine("The total time taken to finish this work is {0} i.e. {1} day,
{2} hours, {3} minutes, and {4} seconds", time_taken, time_taken.Days,
time_taken.Hours, time_taken.Minutes, time_taken.Seconds);
        DateTime date_timespan = DateTime.Today.Add(time_taken);
        Console.WriteLine("Today's date {0} after adding the time span {1} will become
{2}", today_date, time_taken, date_timespan);
        if (DateTime.IsLeapYear(today_date.Year))
            Console.WriteLine("The current year is {0}, and it is a leap year",
today_date.Year);
        else
            Console.WriteLine("The current year is {0}, and it is not a leap year",
today_date.Year);
    }
}
```

Output:

```
Today's date in long format is Wednesday, July 03, 2013 and in short format is 7/3/2013
The current day in two-digit form is 03, month in string form is Jul, and year in two-digit
form is 13
The weekday in three-character format is Wed and in complete format is Wednesday
The number of days between 7/3/2013 and 11/5/2012 dates is 240
The total time taken to finish this work is 1.13:30:15 i.e. 1 day, 13 hours, 30 minutes,
and 15 seconds
Today's date 7/3/2013 12:00:00 AM after adding the time span 1.13:30:15 will become
7/4/2013 1:30:15 PM
The current year is 2013, and it is not a leap year
```

You can see that the current date and time in today_date are displayed in long and short formats by calling the ToLongDateString and ToShortDateString methods. Using the format specifiers dd, MMM, and yy with the ToString method on the today_date object, the current day is displayed in two digits, the month in three characters, and the year in two digits. Again, using the ddd and dddd format specifiers with the ToString method on the today_date object, the current weekday is displayed in three characters as well as in complete format.

A TimeSpan object called elapsed is created by subtracting a custom date from the current date. Using the TotalDays property, the value stored in the TimeSpan object elapsed is converted into the number of days and returned. Two DateTime objects, work_started and work_finished, are created supplying the respective year, month, day, hour, minute, and second values. That is, the work_started and work_finished represent the date and time information of starting and finishing some work. A TimeSpan object called time_taken is created containing the difference of the date and the time in work_started and work_finished objects. The number of days, hours, minutes, and seconds that take place in finishing the work is displayed through the Days, Hours, Minutes, and Seconds properties of the TimeSpan object time_taken.

A DateTime object called date_timespan is created by adding a TimeSpan, time_taken to the current day. Finally, the IsLeapYear method is called on the today_date object to determine if the current year is a leap year.

Besides the previously mentioned custom format specifiers that help in precise date and time formatting, C# supports standard single-character format specifiers.

Standard Date and Time Formatting

C# provides certain preset standard date and time formats that can be used by supplying the standard format specifiers. Table 6.5 shows the single-character format specifiers that you can use with the ToString method to format the date and time.

Table 6.5 Preset Single-Character Format Specifiers Supported by ToString Method

Specifier	DateTimeFormat	Pattern
d	Short date pattern	M/d/yyyy
D	Long date pattern	dddd, MMMM dd, yyyy
t	Short time pattern	h:mm tt
T	Long time pattern	h:mm:ss tt
f	Full date/short time pattern	dddd, MMMM dd, yyyy h:mm tt
F	Full date/long time pattern	dddd, MMMM dd, yyyy h:mm:ss tt
g	General (short date/time pattern)	M/d/yyyy h:mm tt
G	General (short date and long time pattern)	M/d/yyyy h:mm:ss tt
m, M	Month/may pattern	MMMM dd
y, Y	Year/month pattern	MMMM, yyyy
r, R	RFC1123 pattern	ddd, dd MMM yyyy HH:mm:ss GMT
s	Sortable date/time pattern	yyyy-MM-ddTHH:mm:ss
u	UniversalSortable date/time pattern	yyyy-MM-dd HH:mm:ssZ

© 2015 Cengage Learning®.

The program DateTimePatterns.cs shown in Listing 6.21 demonstrates usage of single-character specifiers in formatting dates and times.

Listing 6.21 Program Code in DateTimePatterns.cs File

```
using System;
class DateTimePatterns
{
    static void Main()
    {
        DateTime datetime = DateTime.Now;
        Console.WriteLine("Date in M/d/yyyy pattern " +datetime.ToString("d"));
```

```
      Console.WriteLine("Date time in dddd, MMMM dd, yyyy pattern " + datetime.
ToString("D"));
      Console.WriteLine("Date time in dddd, MMMM dd, yyyy h:mm tt pattern " + datetime.
ToString("f"));
      Console.WriteLine("Date time in dddd, MMMM dd, yyyy h:mm:ss tt pattern " +
datetime.ToString("F"));
      Console.WriteLine("Date time in M/d/yyyy h:mm tt pattern " + datetime.
ToString("g"));
      Console.WriteLine("Date time in M/d/yyyy h:mm:ss tt pattern " + datetime.
ToString("G"));
      Console.WriteLine("Date time in MMMM dd pattern " + datetime.ToString("m"));
      Console.WriteLine("Date time in ddd, dd MMM yyyy HH:mm:ss GMT pattern " +
datetime.ToString("r"));
      Console.WriteLine("Date time in yyyy-MM-ddTHH:mm:ss pattern " + datetime.
ToString("s"));
      Console.WriteLine("Date time in h:mm tt pattern " + datetime.ToString("t"));
      Console.WriteLine("Date time in h:mm:ss tt pattern " + datetime.ToString("T"));
      Console.WriteLine("Date time in yyyy-MM-dd HH:mm:ssZ pattern " + datetime.
ToString("u"));
      Console.WriteLine("Date time in MMMM, yyyy pattern " + datetime.ToString("y"));
   }
}
```

Output:

```
Date in M/d/yyyy pattern 7/1/2013
Date time in dddd, MMMM dd, yyyy pattern Monday, July 01, 2013
Date time in dddd, MMMM dd, yyyy h:mm tt pattern Monday, July 01, 2013 6:34 PM
Date time in dddd, MMMM dd, yyyy h:mm:ss tt pattern Monday, July 01, 2013 6:34:23 PM
Date time in M/d/yyyy h:mm tt pattern 7/1/2013 6:34 PM
Date time in M/d/yyyy h:mm:ss tt pattern 7/1/2013 6:34:23 PM
Date time in MMMM dd pattern July 01
Date time in ddd, dd MMM yyyy HH:mm:ss GMT pattern Mon, 01 Jul 2013 18:34:23 GMT
Date time in yyyy-MM-ddTHH:mm:ss pattern 2013-07-01T18:34:23
Date time in h:mm tt pattern 6:34 PM
Date time in h:mm:ss tt pattern 6:34:23 PM
Date time in yyyy-MM-dd HH:mm:ssZ pattern 2013-07-01 18:34:23Z
Date time in MMMM, yyyy pattern July, 2013
```

You can see how the current dates and times are converted into different patterns on application of preset single character format specifiers using the ToString method.

Whereas the `DateTimeDemo1.cs` program shown in Listing 6.19 and the `DateTimeExample.cs` program shown in Listing 6.20 were focused on formatting dates, the `DateTimeDemo2.cs` program shown in Listing 6.22 focuses on displaying the time in different formats. The program demonstrates application of different `DateTime` methods and format specifiers to display the time in the required pattern. Specifically, the program performs the following tasks:

- Displays the current date and time. Also, it extracts only the time from the `DateTime` object and prints it.

- Formats the date and time in specific patterns.

- Prints the time in long and short formats.

- Adds the desired number of hours to the current time to obtain the new time.

- Displays hours and minutes in single- and two-digits forms. Also, it displays the hours in military format.

- Displays the minutes and seconds in two-digit form.

- Adds the specific number of ticks to the current time to obtain the new time.

Listing 6.22 Program Code in DateTimeDemo2.cs File

```
using System;
class DateTimeDemo2
{
    static void Main()
    {
        DateTime current_time = DateTime.Now;
        Console.WriteLine("Current date and time is {0}", current_time);
        Console.WriteLine("Current time is {0}", current_time.ToString("T"));
        Console.WriteLine("Current time is {0}", current_time.TimeOfDay);
        Console.WriteLine("Display only AM or PM: {0}", current_time.ToString("tt"));
        string format1 = "MMM ddd d HH:mm yyyy";
        Console.WriteLine("Current date and time in MMM ddd d HH:mm yyyy format is {0}",
current_time.ToString(format1));
        string format2 = "M d h:mm yy";
        Console.WriteLine("Current date and time in M d h:mm yy format is {0}",
current_time.ToString(format2));
        Console.WriteLine("Current time in long format is {0} and in short format is {1}",
current_time.ToLongTimeString(), current_time.ToShortTimeString());
        Console.WriteLine("Date and time after 5 hours will be {0}. Only time after 5
hours will be {1}", current_time.AddHours(5), current_time.AddHours(5).ToString
("T"));
```

```
        Console.WriteLine("Hour:Minutes in single-digit format is {0} and in two-digit
format is {1}", current_time.ToString("h:mm"), current_time.ToString("hh:mm"));
        Console.WriteLine("Hour:Minutes in military format. Single-digit format is {0}
and two-digit format is {1}", DateTime.Now.ToString("H:mm"),
current_time.ToString("HH:mm"));
        Console.WriteLine("Minutes in two-digit format are {0} and seconds in two-digit
format are {1}", current_time.ToString("mm"), current_time.ToString("ss"));
        DateTime current_time2 = current_time.AddTicks(5000000);
        Console.WriteLine("Current time after adding 5000000 ticks becomes {0}",
current_time2.TimeOfDay);
    }
}
```

Output:

```
Current date and time is 7/3/2013 9:43:16 AM
Current time is 9:43:16 AM
Current time is 09:43:16.4530698
Display only AM or PM: AM
Current date and time in MMM ddd d HH:mm yyyy format is Jul Wed 3 09:43 2013
Current date and time in M d h:mm yy format is 7 3 9:43 13
Current time in long format is 9:43:16 AM and in short format is 9:43 AM
Date and time after 5 hours will be 7/3/2013 2:43:16 PM. Only time after 5 hours will be
2:43:16 PM
Hour:Minutes in single-digit format is 9:43 and in two-digit format is 09:43
Hour:Minutes in military format. Single-digit format is 9:43 and two-digit format is
09:43
Minutes in two-digit format are 43 and seconds in two-digit format are 16
Current time after adding 5000000 ticks becomes 09:43:16.9530698
```

You can see that the system's current date and time are assigned to the DateTime object called current_time. From the current_time object, only the time is accessed and displayed by using the T format specifier and the TimeOfDay property. Then AM or PM is displayed, depending on the current time. The format specifiers are combined and used with the ToString method to display the time in different formats. Using built-in DateTime methods, the time is displayed in long as well as in short formats. The code also displays the resultant time when 5 hours and 5000000 ticks are added to the current time. The code displays hours and minutes in single digit, double digit, and military format.

SUMMARY

In this chapter, you learned how to define methods and their parameters and how to invoke methods. You also discovered how to implement method overloading. You read about how to use optional and named parameters and C# parameter modifiers and how to implement pass by value and pass by reference. You saw how to use output parameters and send variable length parameters to the methods. You learned to use structures, use properties with `struct`, define arrays in structures, and use an array of structures. You learned to nest structures within structures, use the date and time structure, use `DateTime` properties and methods, use `TimeSpan`, format dates and times, apply custom date and time formatting, and use standard date and time formatting.

The next chapter is focused on classes. You will learn to use the `new` operator and access public members. You will also learn the difference between a struct and a class, use methods in a class and method parameters, use the `return` statement, use private members, pass parameters by value and reference to the methods in a class, use output parameters, and apply method overloading to the class methods. You will discover how to implement encapsulation and how to use properties, the `this` keyword, constructors, default constructors, parameterized constructors, copy constructors, constructor overloading, and constructor chaining. You will use garbage collection, destructors/finalizers, and static classes and members. You will learn to use namespaces, import them, nest them, create a namespace alias, and use the internal modifier.

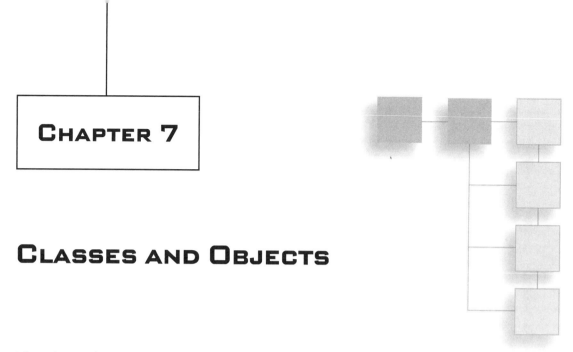

CHAPTER 7

CLASSES AND OBJECTS

This chapter's topics include the following:

- Class
- Encapsulation
- Use of properties
- The `this` keyword
- Constructors
- Garbage collection
- Static classes and members
- Namespaces
- Internal modifier

CLASS

The class is a structure or a template that defines data and methods. The methods and data defined in a class are called *members* of the class. The methods, as expected, are the small modules that contain the code to process the data members of the class. The data members of a class are also known as *instance variables*. A class is created by using the keyword `class`, as shown in the following syntax:

```
class classname {
    access type variable1;
    access type variable2;
```

```
. . . . . . . . . . . .
. . . . . . . . . . . .
access type variableN;
access return_type method1(parameters) {
    // body of method
}
access return_type method2(parameters) {
    // body of method
}
. . . . . . . . . . . . .
. . . . . . . . . . . . .
access return_type methodN(parameters) {
    // body of method
}
}
```

Each `instance` variable and method is preceded with an access type that refers to the access specifier that determines accessibility or visibility of the member. Using the access specifier is optional. There are five access specifiers: private, public, protected, internal, and protected internal. By default, the members are private to the class. The outline of the five access specifiers is given here:

- **Private**—Only other members of the same class can access private members.

- **Public**—Public members can be accessed by an object, from any derived class, and from other parts of the program using the `dot` (.) operator. Even the methods defined inside other classes can access them.

- **Protected**—Members of the same class and inheriting members of the same class can access protected members. Other parts of the program cannot access protected members using the `dot` (.) operator.

- **Internal**—Internal members are accessible only within a file of the same assembly. We cannot reference an internal member outside the assembly within which it is declared.

- **Protected internal**—The members defined in the containing assembly and the inheriting members of the class can access the protected internal member.

The objects or instances of the class get the structure of the class. (Each object gets an individual copy of the instance variables and methods.)

The new Operator

The new operator is meant for allocating memory for the object being created. The allocated memory is then filled with the data members, also known as *fields*, of the class.

Syntax:

```
class_name object_name=new class_name(arguments_list)
```

where arguments_list is used while defining the parameterized constructor in the class (explained later in this chapter). The arguments_list is also used to initialize the instance variables of the object.

Examples:

```
RectArea rect1 = new RectArea();
RectArea rect2 = new RectArea(5, 8);
```

The first example defines an object or instance, rect1, of the RectArea class. Memory that is sufficient to store the data members (if any) is allocated to the instance, rect1. Until the default constructor is used (explained later in this chapter), this example will not initialize the data members of the object. The second example defines another object, rect2, and uses the arguments 5 and 8 that are passed to it to invoke the parameterized constructor. The parameterized constructor uses the supplied values 5 and 8 to initialize the object's data members l and b.

As said earlier, an object can directly access the members of the class that are declared public, from any derived class and from other parts of the program using the dot (.) operator. The next section explains how.

Public Members

The public members of a class are declared by using the public specifier. As the name suggests, the public members are accessible from outside the class. The ClassDemo1.cs program shown in Listing 7.1 defines a class, RectArea, consisting of three public data members: l, b and a. The class computes and displays the area of the rectangle. The focus of this program is to explain how the public data members l, b, and a are accessed from outside the class and through the object directly.

Listing 7.1 Program Code in ClassDemo1.cs File

```
using System;
class RectArea {
    public int l,b,a;
}
```

```
class ClassDemo1 {
    static void Main() {
        RectArea rect = new RectArea();
        rect.l=5;
        rect.b=8;
        rect.a=rect.l*rect.b;
        Console.WriteLine("Area of rectangle is {0}", rect.a);
    }
}
```

Output:

```
Area of rectangle is 40
```

In this program, the variables l, b, and a are the data members or instance variables of the class. In the code, you see two classes: RectArea and ClassDemo1.

■ **RectArea class**—This is the class through which you will be computing the area of a rectangle. This class contains the data members required for finding the area of a rectangle.

■ **ClassDemo1 class**—This is the main class that instantiates and uses the RectArea class. This class defines the Main method, which is the entry point of a C# program. The program begins its execution from this method. The object(s) of the RectArea class is created in this main class. It is in this main class that the object(s) of the RectArea class accesses the members of the RectArea class.

In the program, you can see that the data members l, b, and a are accessible outside the body of the RectArea class because they are declared as public members. The program assigns values to the data members l and b, computes the area of a rectangle, and assigns the result to the data member a. The result in data member a is then displayed on the screen. If you declare the instance variables l, b, or a as private, you get errors as shown here:

```
Microsoft (R) Visual C# 2010 Compiler version 4.0.30319.1
Copyright (C) Microsoft Corporation. All rights reserved.
ClassDemo1.cs(13,6): error CS0122: 'RectArea.l' is inaccessible due to its protection
level
ClassDemo1.cs(4,13): (Location of symbol related to previous error)
ClassDemo1.cs(14,6): error CS0122: 'RectArea.b' is inaccessible due to its protection
level
```

You might be thinking that the classes are similar to the structures that you learned in the previous chapter. To understand the relationship between the two, you need to recall the difference between the `Value` and `Reference` types (from Chapter 2, "Data Types").

What do value and reference types have to do with struct and class? Read on.

Difference Between a Struct and a Class

The data types such as `int`, `float`, `double`, and `char` are called value types and are stored on the stack. In contrast, the class objects, strings, and dynamically created variables are known as reference types because they hold references to blocks of memory and are managed on the heap. For the class types, a block of memory is not allocated; instead, a small piece of memory is allocated to hold the address (that is, the reference of another block of memory where the class object is stored). The memory for the actual class object is allocated only when the `new` keyword is used to create the object.

Now that you've learned the difference between value and reference types, you can easily understand the difference between a struct and a class. Following are the points that clearly differentiate a struct from a class:

- The structs are value types. After instantiating a struct, it is created on the stack. On the other hand, classes are reference types. After instantiating a class, it is allocated on the heap.
- The structs derive from `System.ValueType`, whereas the classes derive from `System.Object` or one of its descendants.
- The structs cannot derive from any other class/struct, nor can they be derived.
- The structs cannot have a default parameterless constructor, but classes can.
- The structs can be assumed as a lightweight alternative to a class. But they cannot inherit like a class can.
- The structs store the values in each field together. They do not store referenced data.

In the previous chapter, you learned to use methods independently. Now you'll learn to use methods inside a class.

Methods Defined in a Class

Methods defined in a class are the subroutines that make the data of the class accessible to perform necessary processing on the class data. Each method has a name through which it is called. You cannot use `Main` or any C# keyword for the method name. Recall from the previous chapter that the method name is followed by parentheses that may or may not contain parameters. Syntax for defining methods in a class is given here:

```
access return_type name(parameter_list) {
    // body of method
}
```

where:

- access is an access modifier that determines the accessibility of the method. It is private by default.

- return_type specifies the data type of the value returned by the method. A method may or may not return a value. If the method does not return a value, its return_type is set to void.

- name represents the method name.

- parameter_list is a comma-separated sequence of type and identifier pairs. Parameters receive the values of the arguments passed to the method when it is called. If the method has no parameters, the parameter_list is empty.

Return Statement

The return statement in a method terminates the method execution and returns the program control to the caller. You can have any number of return statements in a method. The value returned by a method should match the return_type of the method.

Method Parameters

While calling methods, you can pass values to it to process on. The values passed to a method are called *arguments*, whereas the variables in a method (in parentheses) that receive the arguments passed to them are known as *formal parameters* or just *parameters*. The parameters appear in the form of variables inside the parentheses just after the method's name. The scope of the parameters is limited within the body of the method. (That is, they act as local variables of the method.)

To better understand the concept of defining and using methods in a class practically, you'll modify the RectArea class (refer to Listing 7.1). You will add two methods to the class; one method will initialize the data members, and the other method will compute the area of a rectangle through the data members and return the result. After adding the two methods, the RectArea class will appear, as shown in Listing 7.2.

Listing 7.2 Program Code in ClassDemo2.cs File

```
using System;
class RectArea {
    private int l,b;
    public void setData(int x, int y) {
        l=x;
        b=y;
    }
    public int getRect() {
        return l*b;
    }
}
class ClassDemo2 {
    static void Main() {
        RectArea rect = new RectArea();
        rect.setData(5,8);
        Console.WriteLine("Area of rectangle is {0}", rect.getRect());
    }
}
```

Output:

```
Area of rectangle is 40
```

You can see that an object of the RectArea class is created, named rect. The setData method is called on object rect, passing values 5 and 8 as arguments. The arguments 5 and 8 are assigned to the x and y parameters of the setData method, from which the values initialize the data members l and b. Thereafter, the getRect method is called on object rect that computes and returns the area of a rectangle.

Private Members

The ClassDemo2.cs explains defining of private members of a class. Recall that the private access specifier, when used with any class member, makes it inaccessible from outside the class body. The private data members can be accessed only in the class methods. If you try to access the private data members, l and b, directly in the Main method using the object rect as shown here:

```
rect.l=5;
```

you get this error:

```
'RectArea.l' is inaccessible due to its protection level
```

The ClassDemo2.cs program that you saw in Listing 7.2 contains a single class, RectArea, that you access from the main class, ClassDemo2. One thing you might be wondering is whether you can have only one class in a program. The answer is that you can have any number of classes in a program.

The RectTriang.cs program shown in Listing 7.3 contains two classes: RectArea and TriangArea. The RectArea class calculates the area of a rectangle, whereas the TriangArea class calculates the area of a triangle.

Listing 7.3 Program Code in RectTriang.cs File

```
using System;
class RectArea {
    private int l,b;
    public void setData(int x, int y) {
        l=x;
        b=y;
    }
    public int getRect() {
        return l*b;
    }
}
class TriangArea {
    private int b,h;
    public void setValues(int x, int y) {
        b=x;
        h=y;
    }
    public float getTriang() {
        return (float) 1/2*b*h;
    }
}
class RectTriang {
    static void Main() {
        RectArea rect = new RectArea();
        TriangArea trg = new TriangArea();
        rect.setData(5,8);
        trg.setValues(9,7);
        Console.WriteLine("Area of rectangle is {0}", rect.getRect());
        Console.WriteLine("Area of triangle is {0}", trg.getTriang());
    }
}
```

Output:

```
Area of rectangle is 40
Area of triangle is 31.5
```

You can see that objects of `RectArea` and `TriangArea` classes are created by name, `rect` and `trg`, respectively. The `setData` and `setValues` methods are called on objects `rect` and `trg` to initialize their respective data members. Finally, the `getRect` and `getTriang` methods are called on the two objects to compute the area of a rectangle and triangle, respectively.

In the previous chapter, we learned about the different types of parameters that can be sent to independent methods. The same types of parameters can also be sent to the methods defined in a class. What follows is an overview of the different types of parameters that can be sent to a class method.

Parameter Passing by Value and Reference

By default, value types, such as `int` and `char`, are passed by value to the method, which means the changes made to the parameters inside the method are not reflected in the actual arguments passed to the method.

By using the `ref` modifier, you can pass any value type by reference to a method. In other words, the `ref` modifier causes C# to create a call-by-reference rather than a call-by-value. It enables a method to alter the content of its arguments. The `ref` modifier is used both times, when the method is declared as well as when it is called.

Note

An argument passed by `ref` must be initialized to a value because the called method expects the `ref` argument to refer to a valid value.

The `PassByValueRef.cs` program shown in Listing 7.4 demonstrates passing of arguments to the method by value and by reference.

Listing 7.4 Program Code in PassByValueRef.cs File

```
using System;
class Passing {
    public void methodRef(ref int x) {
        x=x+5;
    }
    public void methodVal(int y) {
        y=y-10;
    }
}
class PassByValueRef {
    static void Main() {
        Passing p = new Passing();
```

```
        int a,b;
        a=b= 10;
        Console.WriteLine("Value of a before method call: {0}", a);
        p.methodRef(ref a);
        Console.WriteLine("Value of a after method call: {0}", a);
        a=b= 10;
        Console.WriteLine("Value of b before method call: {0}", b);
        p.methodVal(b);
        Console.WriteLine("Value of b after method call: {0}", b);
    }
}
```

Output:

```
Value of a before method call: 10
Value of a after method call: 15
Value of b before method call: 10
Value of b after method call: 10
```

You can see that an object of class Passing is created by name, p. Before calling the method methodRef, the initial value of the variable a is displayed (10). Then the variable a is passed by reference to the method methodRef. The argument a is assigned to the parameter x in the method. In the methodRef, the value of the parameter x is incremented by 5, so the value of the argument a is modified to a value of 15. The modified value of argument a is displayed on the screen.

Again, the initial value of variable b (10) is displayed on the screen. The variable b is passed to the methodVal method by value. (The copy of the value in argument b is passed to the method.) The value 10 is assigned to the parameter y. Because the argument is sent by value, any changes made in the parameter y in the method methodVal are limited to the method itself and, on returning to the caller, the argument b picks up its original value (10).

Output Parameters

The output parameter enables a method to return more than one value. For a method to return more than one value, it can use the traditional return statement to return a value and one or more output parameters to return more values to the caller. The output parameters are defined by using the out modifier. You don't need to initialize the output arguments before passing them to a method because it is the job of the called method to assign values to the output parameters. The values assigned to the output parameters in the method are received through the output arguments that are passed while calling the method.

Note

The output arguments and parameters are defined by the `out` modifier.

The `OutParameter.cs` program shown in Listing 7.5 demonstrates using output parameters in a method.

Listing 7.5 Program Code in OutParameter.cs File

```
using System;
class Passing {
    int a,b;
    public int AddMult(int x, int y, out int z) {
        a=x;
        b=y;
        z=a*b;
        return a+b;
    }
}
class OutParameter {
    static void Main() {
        Passing p = new Passing();
        int u,v,addn, mult;
        u=10;
        v=20;
        addn=p.AddMult(u,v, out mult);
        Console.WriteLine("The addition of the values {0} and {1} equals {2}, and the
multiplication of those values equals {3}", u,v,addn,mult);
    }
}
```

Output:

```
The addition of the values 10 and 20 equals 30, and the multiplication of those values
equals 200
```

You can see that an object of class `Passing` is created named p. Then the arguments
u, v, and `mult` are passed to the method `AddMult`, which in turn is assigned to the parameters x, y, and z, respectively. The argument `mult` is passed with the `out` modifier,
which means the value assigned to the parameter z in the `AddMult` is assigned to the
`mult` argument, too. The values in the parameters x and y are used to initialize the
data members a and b of the `Passing` class. To the output parameter z, the multiplication of the first two arguments is assigned. The value assigned to the parameter z is
assigned to the argument `mult`, too. When the program control returns to the caller,

the multiplication of the first two arguments, u and v, is displayed through the mult argument.

Method Overloading

Method overloading occurs when a class has two or more methods with the same name but with a different number and type of parameter (known as *signature*). The overloaded methods may have different return types, too. When an overloaded method is called, the number of parameters and their type are used to find and execute the matching method.

The MethodOverload1.cs program shown in Listing 7.6 demonstrates method overloading by computing the sum of different numbers and types of parameters.

Listing 7.6 Program Code in MethodOverload1.cs File

```
using System;
class AddVal {
    public void compute_sum(int x) {
        Console.WriteLine("Sum is {0}", x);
    }
    public void compute_sum(int x, int y) {
        Console.WriteLine("Sum is {0}", x+y);
    }
    public void compute_sum(int x, double y) {
        Console.WriteLine("Sum is {0}", x+y);
    }
    public void compute_sum(double x, double y) {
        Console.WriteLine("Sum is {0}", x+y);
    }
}
class MethodOverload1 {
    static void Main() {
        AddVal av = new AddVal();
        av.compute_sum(5);
        av.compute_sum(5,8);
        av.compute_sum(5, 9.17);
        av.compute_sum(3.782, 9.17);
    }
}
```

Output:

```
Sum is 5
Sum is 13
Sum is 14.17
Sum is 12.952
```

You can see that an object called `av` is created of the `AddVal` class. The `compute_sum` method of the class is overloaded. It is set to take the following:

- A single parameter of `int` type
- Two parameters of `int` type
- One parameter of `int` type and a second parameter of `double` type
- Both parameters of `double` type

Consequently, the `compute_sum` method is called on object `av` to compute and display the sum of parameters of different types. The method displays the sum of a single parameter of `int` type, two parameters of `int` type, one parameter of `int` type, the other of `double` type, and both parameters of `double` type.

ENCAPSULATION

Another important feature of OOP is *encapsulation*, which is the process of hiding data or encapsulating it from the outside world. It is only through the associated methods in the class that the data can be accessed and manipulated. The object defines all the operations via methods that are possible on the associated data. Therefore, data is accessed and updated by calling respective methods through the object. By encapsulating data, you make a class more secure and reliable. Encapsulation also simplifies the debugging and program maintenance task.

Encapsulation is ensured by implementing the following points:

- Defining the class data members as private, thereby making sure the data members of the class are not directly accessible from an object instance.

- Accessing the private data members through the class methods or by using properties. The properties use a pair of public accessor (`get`) and mutator (`set`) methods to manipulate private data members of a class.

The `ClassDemo3.cs` program shown in Listing 7.7 displays the code, name, and basic salary of a worker using classes. All three data members are defined as private to ensure encapsulation. You can access these data members through the class methods only, not directly by the instance. Also, the focus of this program is to make you understand how strings are passed to the class methods.

Listing 7.7 Program Code in ClassDemo3.cs File

```
using System;
class Worker {
    private int code,basicSalary;
    private string name;
```

```
    public void setWorker(int x, string y, int z) {
        code=x;
        name=y;
        basicSalary=z;
    }
    public void showWorker() {
        Console.WriteLine("Code: {0}, Name: {1}, Salary: {2}", code,name,basicSalary);
    }
}
class ClassDemo3 {
    static void Main() {
        Worker w = new Worker();
        w.setWorker(101, "Kelly", 5000);
        w.showWorker();
    }
}
```

Output:

```
Code: 101, Name: Kelly, Salary: 5000
```

You can see that an object of the Worker class is created named w. The setWorker method is called on object w passing the code, name, and basic salary of a worker. The arguments 101, Kelly, and 5000 passed to the setWorker method are assigned to the parameters x, y, and z, respectively. The parameters x, y, and z in the method setWorker in turn initialize the members code, name, and basicSalary of the Worker class. In other words, the values 101, Kelly, and 5000 are assigned to the members code, name, and basicSalary of the Worker class. Finally, the showWorker method is called on the object w to display information about the worker on the screen.

The next section explores a second way to implement encapsulation: accessing the private data members by using properties.

USE OF PROPERTIES

The property is a type of class member that is a combination of a field and methods. The property behaves like a field, allowing you to get and set its value. At the same time, the property acts like a method. Basically, a property consists of a name, along with get and set methods. The get and set methods (also known as accessors and mutators) are used to get and set the value of a field. The property name can be used in expressions and in assignments like a normal variable. After using a property name, the respective get and set methods are automatically invoked.

Here's the syntax of a property:

```
data_type property_name {
    get {
        // get accessor code
    }
    set {
        // set accessor code
    }
}
```

where data_type specifies the type of the property (whether it is of int, string, or some other data type). The property_name is the name of the property. After defining a property, whenever the property name is used in a program, its appropriate accessor is called. The set method (the mutator) automatically receives a parameter called value that contains the value to be assigned to the property.

The Property.cs program shown in Listing 7.8 defines a property called length that sets and gets the value of the data member l of the rect class.

Listing 7.8 Program Code in Property.cs File

```
using System;
class rect {
    private int l;
    public int length {
        get {
            return l;
        }
        set {
            l = value;
        }
    }
}
class Property {
    static void Main() {
        rect r = new rect();
        r.length = 5;
        Console.WriteLine("Length is {0}", r.length);
    }
}
```

Output:

```
Length is 5
```

In the preceding example, length is a property, and it has a get and a set method. While using the statement r.length=5, the set method is called, and the numerical value 5 is assigned to the parameter value, from which it is assigned to the data member 1. Similarly, after using r.length in the Console.WriteLine method, the get method is called, returning the value in the data member 1 of the class.

The Property1.cs program shown in Listing 7.9 demonstrates using two properties, length and breadth, to calculate the area of a rectangle. The properties ensure that only positive values of length and breadth are used for computing the area of a rectangle.

Listing 7.9 Program Code in Property1.cs File

```
using System;
class rect {
    private int l,b;
    public rect() { l = 0; b=0;}
    public int length {
        get {
            return l;
        }
        set {
            if(value >= 0) l = value;
        }
    }
    public int breadth {
        get {
            return b;
        }
        set {
            if(value >= 0) b = value;
        }
    }
}
class Property1 {
    static void Main() {
        rect r = new rect();
        Console.WriteLine("Initial values of length and breadth are {0} and {1}",
r.length, r.breadth);
        r.length = 5;
        r.breadth=8;
        Console.WriteLine("Length={0}, Breadth={1} and Area of rectangle is {2}",
r.length, r.breadth, r.length*r.breadth);
        r.length=-10;
```

```
        r.breadth=20;
        Console.WriteLine("Length={0}, Breadth={1} and Area of rectangle is {2}",
r.length, r.breadth, r.length*r.breadth);
    }
}
```

Output:

```
Initial values of length and breadth are 0 and 0
Length=5, Breadth=8 and Area of rectangle is 40
Length=5, Breadth=20 and Area of rectangle is 100
```

In the preceding example, an object r of rect class is created. The default constructor initializes the values of data members l and b to 0. Thereafter, using the length and breadth properties, values 5 and 8 are assigned to the data members l and b of the r object. Using the get accessors, the values in data members l and b are accessed and multiplied to calculate the area of a rectangle. While assigning the values to the data members l and b through the properties, the set method is invoked, which ensures that the values supplied are positive before initializing the data members. If a negative value is supplied, it is simply discarded.

The SetGet.cs program shown in Listing 7.10 is another one on Properties. The program defines a Worker class that uses properties to assign code, name, and basic salary to a worker object and uses respective accessors and mutators to display the data assigned to different data members of the class.

Listing 7.10 Program Code in SetGet.cs File

```
using System;
class Worker {
    private int code, basicSalary;
    private string name;
    public int Code{
        get{ return code;}
        set { code=value;}
    }
    public string Name{
        get{ return name;}
        set { name=value;}
    }
    public int Salary{
        get{ return basicSalary;}
        set { basicSalary=value;}
    }
```

```
    public void showWorker() {
        Console.WriteLine("Code: {0}, Name: {1}, Basic Salary: {2}", Code, Name,
Salary);
    }
}
class SetGet {
    static void Main() {
        Worker w = new Worker();
        w.Code=101;
        w.Name="Kelly";
        w.Salary=5000;
        w.showWorker();
    }
}
```

Output:

```
Code: 101, Name: Kelly, Basic Salary: 5000
```

An instance w of the Worker class is created. Three properties, Code, Name, and Salary, are defined with the respective accessors and mutators. Using the set method (mutator), the values 101, Kelly, and 5000 are assigned to the data members code, name, and basicSalary of the instance w. The showWorker method is invoked on the w object that invokes the accessors to fetch the data in the data members code, name, and basicSalary and display them on the screen.

THE THIS KEYWORD

The this keyword refers to the object, or. the current instance being referenced. For example, when you call a method of a class through its object, the reference to the object is automatically passed to the called method. The object reference that is passed to the called method is known as this. It is implicitly there.

The thisExample.cs program shown in Listing 7.11 demonstrates how this keyword represents the class instance being referenced. The program calculates the area of a rectangle.

Listing 7.11 Program Code in thisExample.cs File

```
using System;
class RectArea {
    private int l,b;
    public void setData(int l, int b) {
        this.l=l;
        this.b=b;
    }
```

```
    public int getRect() {
        return this.l*this.b;
    }
}
class thisExample {
    static void Main() {
        RectArea rect = new RectArea();
        rect.setData(5,8);
        Console.WriteLine("Area of rectangle is {0}", rect.getRect());
    }
}
```

Output:

```
Area of rectangle is 40
```

In the preceding code, you see that an object or instance of the class Rect is created named rect. The setData method on the rect object is invoked, passing the arguments 5 and 8 to it. Remember, while invoking the setData method, the object itself (rect) is also passed to the method. The rect object can be referenced and used in the setData method by using the this keyword. The passed arguments are assigned to the x and y parameters of the setData method. The statement this.l=x assigns the value in parameter x to the l data member of the rect object. Previous examples didn't use the this keyword because it is implicitly present. In other words, the statement l=x; also does the same thing: assigns the value in parameter x to the data member l of the object that invoked the method (of the rect object). The setData method therefore initializes the data members l and b of the rect object. Finally, the getRect method is invoked on the rect object to compute and return the area of a rectangle.

From the preceding discussion, it is clear that the following two statements are functionally the same:

```
l=x;
this.l=x;
```

The this keyword also helps to resolve ambiguity when the name of the data members and parameters match, as shown in the setData method:

```
class RectArea {
    private int l,b;
    public void setData(int l, int b) {
        l=l;
        b=b;
    }
}
```

You can see that the data members of the class and the names of the parameters match. The following statements result in ambiguity:

```
l=l;
b=b;
```

Warning messages appear, informing Assignment made to same variable (see Figure 7.1).

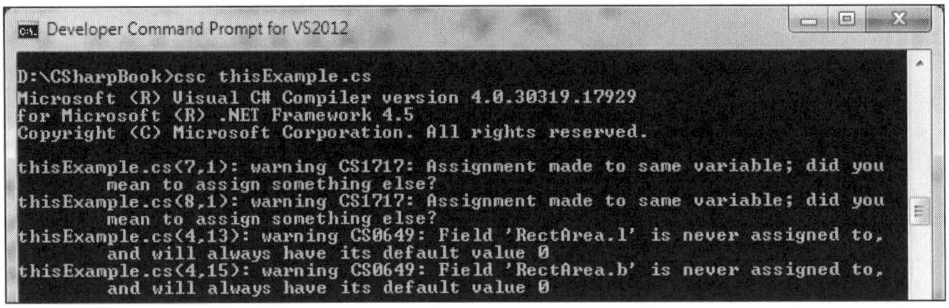

Figure 7.1
Warning appears when the class data member and parameter name matches.
Source: Visual Studio.

You can remove the ambiguity by using the this keyword, as shown in the setData method:

```
class RectArea {
    private int l,b;
    public void setData(int l, int b) {
        this.l=l;
        this.b=b;
    }
}
```

The statement this.l=l; in the preceding code indicates that the value in the parameter l has to be assigned to the object's data member l.

CONSTRUCTORS

You must initialize the instance variables, also called *data members*, of an object before using them in processing, or you get unexpected results. To ensure initialization of instance variables when an object is created, constructors are used. A *constructor* is a method that has the same name as that of the class and is automatically executed after an object is created. The constructor doesn't return anything.

Syntax:

```
access_specifier class_name(parameter_list) {
    // code to initialize object
}
```

The `access_specifier` of a constructor is usually set to public because it is called from outside the class. If the constructor is marked as private, it cannot be accessed outside the class and therefore will not help in initialization of data members. The constructors don't have a return type. Depending on the number of parameters passed, the constructors are categorized into the following two types:

- **Default constructors**—The constructors that have no parameters
- **Parameterized constructors**—The constructors with parameters

C# automatically provides a default constructor for all the objects that are created. The default constructor initializes the instance variables to the default value of zero. When you define your own default constructor, it overrides the one that C# provides.

The next section covers how default constructors are used to initialize the instance variables.

Default Constructors

As said earlier, the default constructors are the methods that have the same name as that of the class and have no parameters. The method is automatically executed after defining an object, and its main task is to initialize data members of the class. The `Constructor1.cs` program shown in Listing 7.12 demonstrates using the default constructor. The program defines a `RectArea` class to compute the area of a rectangle. The default constructor used in the class initializes the data members `l` and `b` of the `RectArea` class.

Listing 7.12 Program Code in Constructor1.cs File

```
using System;
class RectArea {
    private int l,b;
    public RectArea() {
        l=5;
        b=8;
    }
    public int getRect() {
        return l*b;
    }
}
```

```
class Constructor1 {
    static void Main() {
        RectArea rect = new RectArea();
        Console.WriteLine("Area of rectangle is {0}", rect.getRect());
    }
}
```

Output:

```
Area of rectangle is 40
```

You can see that the object rect is defined of the RectArea class. After defining the rect object, the default constructor, RectArea, is executed automatically. The default constructor initializes the data members l and b to the values 5 and 8, respectively. Then the getRect method is called on the rect object that multiplies the data members l and b to compute the area of the rectangle.

Here's one more quick example regarding the default constructor. The DefConstructWorker.cs file shown in Listing 7.13 displays information for a worker that includes code, name, basic salary, household allowance, child allowance, and gross salary. To represent the information data members, code, name, basicSalary, houseAllowance, childAllowance, and grossSalary are used and are initialized through the default constructor. Then the values of the rest of the three members are computed. houseAllowance is assumed to be 6% of basicSalary, childAllowance is assumed to be equal to $250, and grossSalary is calculated as per the following formula:

```
grossSalary = basicSalary + houseAllowance + childAllowance
```

Listing 7.13 Program Code in DefConstructWorker.cs File

```
using System;
class Worker {
    private int code,basicSalary;
    float houseAllowance,childAllowance,grossSalary;
    private string name;
    public Worker() {
        code=101;
        name="Kelly";
        basicSalary=5000;
    }
    public void computeSal() {
        houseAllowance=(float) basicSalary*6/100;
        childAllowance=250;
        grossSalary=basicSalary+houseAllowance+childAllowance;
    }
```

```
    public void showWorker() {
        Console.WriteLine("Code: {0}, Name: {1}, Basic Salary: {2}", code,name,
basicSalary);
        Console.WriteLine("Household allowance: {0}, Child allowance: {1}, Gross
Salary: {2}", houseAllowance,childAllowance,grossSalary);
    }
}
class DefConstructWorker {
    static void Main() {
        Worker w = new Worker();
        w.computeSal();
        w.showWorker();
    }
}
```

Output:

```
Code: 101, Name: Kelly, Basic Salary: 5000
Household allowance: 300, Child allowance: 250, Gross salary: 5550
```

You can see that the Worker class contains six data members: code for storing worker's code, name for storing worker's name, basicSalary for keeping basic salary, and houseAllowance, childAllowance, and grossSalary for storing household allowance, child allowance, and gross salary, respectively.

An object of the Worker class is created named w. After creating the object, the default constructor is automatically executed that initializes the members code, name, and basicSalary to values 101, Kelly, and 5000, respectively. Then the computeSal method on the w object is called to calculate the household allowance, child allowance, and gross salary. After computing the household allowance, child allowance, and gross salary, you call the showWorker method on object w to display the entire worker information.

In the preceding programs, you saw that, to invoke the default constructor, you need not pass any parameter while defining an object. The drawback of using the default constructor is that the data members of all the objects you define are initialized to the same default values. What if you want to initialize the data members of different objects to different values? That's where parameterized constructors come in handy.

Parameterized Constructors

As the name suggests, *parameterized constructors* are the class methods sharing the same name as that of the class and accepting parameters to initialize the instance variables of the object. Parameters are enclosed within the parentheses after the constructor name that accepts the arguments passed to it while creating an object. Like default constructors, parameterized constructors are automatically invoked while creating an object.

The `Constructor2.cs` program shown in Listing 7.14 demonstrates use of the parameterized constructor. The program defines a `RectArea` class to compute the area of a rectangle. Two objects are defined with different sets of parameters that invoke the parameterized constructor to initialize their respective data members, l and b. In other words, the program displays two areas of rectangles based on the supplied length and breadth values.

Listing 7.14 Program Code in Constructor2.cs File

```
using System;
class RectArea {
    private int l,b;
    public RectArea(int x, int y) {
        l=x;
        b=y;
    }
    public int getRect() {
        return l*b;
    }
}
class Constructor2 {
    static void Main() {
        RectArea rect1 = new RectArea(5, 8);
        RectArea rect2 = new RectArea(10, 20);
        Console.WriteLine("Area of first rectangle is {0}", rect1.getRect());
        Console.WriteLine("Area of second rectangle is {0}", rect2.getRect());
    }
}
```

Output:

```
Area of first rectangle is 40
Area of second rectangle is 200
```

You can see that two objects of the `RectArea` class are created, named rect1 and rect2. The parameters 5 and 8 that are passed while creating the object rect1 will invoke the parameterized constructor that in turn will initialize the data members l and b of the object. Similarly, the parameters 10 and 20 that passed while creating the object rect2 will invoke the parameterized constructor to initialize the data members l and b of object rect2. The method `getRect` called on the objects rect1 and rect2 will multiply the values in the data members of the two objects to calculate the area of a rectangle.

Here's one more example of a parameterized constructor. The DefConstructWorker.cs program that you saw in Listing 7.13 used a default constructor to display the code, name, basic salary, household allowance, child allowance, and gross salary of a worker. You'll now use the parameterized constructor to display the same information for two workers. The ParamConstructWorker.cs program shown in Listing 7.15 creates two worker objects and initializes their code, name, and basicSalary data members through the parameterized constructor.

Listing 7.15 Program Code in ParamConstructWorker.cs File

```
using System;
class Worker {
    private int code, basicSalary;
    float houseAllowance, childAllowance, grossSalary;
    private string name;
    public Worker(int x, string y, int z) {
        code=x;
        name=y;
        basicSalary=z;
    }
    public void computeSal() {
        houseAllowance=(float) basicSalary*6/100;
        childAllowance=250;
        grossSalary=basicSalary + houseAllowance + childAllowance;
    }
    public void showWorker() {
        Console.WriteLine("Code: {0}, Name: {1}, Basic Salary: {2}",
code,name,basicSalary);
        Console.WriteLine("Household allowance: {0}, Child allowance: {1}, Gross
Salary: {2}", houseAllowance,childAllowance,grossSalary);
    }
}
class ParamConstructWorker {
    static void Main() {
        Worker work1 = new Worker(101, "Kelly", 5000);
        Worker work2 = new Worker(102, "David", 6500);
        work1.computeSal();
        work2.computeSal();
        Console.WriteLine("Information of first worker Kelly is as under:");
work1.showWorker();
        Console.WriteLine("Information of second worker David is as under:");
work2.showWorker();
    }
}
```

Output:

```
Information of first worker Kelly is as under:
Code: 101, Name: Kelly, Basic Salary: 5000
Household allowance: 300, Child allowance: 250, Gross Salary: 5550
Information of second worker David is as under:
Code: 102, Name: David, Basic Salary: 6500
Household allowance: 390, Child allowance: 250, Gross Salary: 7140
```

You can see that the two objects, work1 and work2, are created for the Worker class. The values 101, Kelly, and 5000 passed with the work1 object invoke the parameterized constructor, thereby initializing its data members code, name, and basicSalary with the supplied parameters. Similarly, the values passed while creating the object rect2 invoke the parameterized constructor again to initialize its data members. The computeSal method is called on both objects to calculate the household allowance, child allowance, and gross salary based on the supplied formulas. Finally, the showWorker method is called on both objects to display values in the six data members code, name, basicSalary, houseAllowance, childAllowance, and grossSalary.

You can also use the this keyword that you used earlier with constructors. The thisKeyword.cs program shown in Listing 7.16 calculates the area of a rectangle for two objects. Recall that the this keyword used in the constructors and methods represents the invoking objects.

Listing 7.16 Program Code in thisKeyword.cs File

```
using System;
class RectArea {
    private int l,b;
    public RectArea(int x, int y) {
        this.l=x;
        this.b=y;
    }
    public int getRect() {
        return this.l*this.b;
    }
}
class thisKeyword {
    static void Main() {
        RectArea rect1 = new RectArea(5, 8);
        RectArea rect2 = new RectArea(10, 20);
        Console.WriteLine("Area of first rectangle is {0}", rect1.getRect());
        Console.WriteLine("Area of second rectangle is {0}", rect2.getRect());
    }
}
```

Output:

```
Area of first rectangle is 40
Area of second rectangle is 200
```

In the preceding code, you see that a parameterized constructor is called for both `rect1` and `rect2` to initialize their data members `1` and `b`, respectively. The `this` keyword found in the parameterized constructor as well as in the `getRect` method represents the invoking object (the object that invoked the constructor and the method).

Copy Constructors

A copy constructor creates a new object by copying data members from an existing object of the same type. For example, if you have a `Worker` class object named `work1` and you want to create another object, `work2`, with its data members initialized to the values in data member of `work1`, you can use the copy constructor to do so. What follows is a sample of the copy constructor:

```
public Worker(Worker wrkObject)
{
    code=wrkObject.code;
    name=wrkObject.name;
    basicSalary=wrkObject.basicSalary;
}
```

You can see that the data members `code`, `name`, and `basicSalary` of the object passed as a parameter to the constructor are copied into the newly created object.

A copy constructor is invoked by instantiating an object and passing it the name of the existing object (whose data members have to be copied):

```
Worker work2 = new Worker(work1);
```

In the preceding statement, the object `work2` is created with the same content as in the `work1` object. In other words, the values in data members of the `work1` object are copied into the data members of the `work2` object.

The `CopyConstructWorker.cs` program shown in Listing 7.17 demonstrates the copy constructor. It defines a class called `Worker` with three data members: `code`, `name`, and `basicSalary`. An object, `work1`, is created for the `Worker` class by using the parameterized constructor. Another object, `work2`, is created by copying the content of the object `work1`. In other words, using the copy constructor, the `work2` object is created from `work1`.

Listing 7.17 Program Code in CopyConstructWorker.cs File

```
using System;
class Worker {
    private int code, basicSalary;
    private string name;
    public Worker(int x, string y, int z) {
        code=x;
        name=y;
        basicSalary=z;
    }
    public Worker(Worker wrkObject)
    {
        code=wrkObject.code;
        name=wrkObject.name;
        basicSalary=wrkObject.basicSalary;
    }
    public void showWorker() {
        Console.WriteLine("Code: {0}, Name: {1}, Basic Salary: {2}",
code,name,basicSalary);
    }
}
class CopyConstructWorker {
    static void Main() {
        Worker work1 = new Worker(101, "Kelly", 5000);
        Worker work2 = new Worker(work1);
        Console.WriteLine("Information in the original work1 object is as under:");
        work1.showWorker();
        Console.WriteLine("\nInformation in the copied object, work2 is as under:");
        work2.showWorker();
    }
}
```

Output:

```
Information in the original work1 object is as under:
Code: 101, Name: Kelly, Basic Salary: 5000

Information in the copied object, work2 is as under:
Code: 101, Name: Kelly, Basic Salary: 5000
```

You can see that the work1 object is created by passing three values, 101, Kelly, and 5000, which initialize its data members code, name, and basicSalary. Then the work2 object is created from the object work1. The copy constructor is invoked, which copies the values 101, Kelly, and 5000 in data members code, name, and basicSalary of the work1 object into the respective data members of object work2.

Like method overloading, can constructors also be overloaded? Yes, they can. Read on for more.

Constructor Overloading

Constructor overloading means having more than one constructor in a class, each with a unique signature. Having a signature means the constructors may differ in number of parameters, their data types, or both. The ConstructorOverload.cs program shown in Listing 7.18 calculates the area of a rectangle for six different types of values. The RectArea class that is used in the program consists of two data members, l and b. The program uses the constructor overloading in accepting parameters of different numbers and types.

Listing 7.18 Program Code in ConstructorOverload.cs File

```
using System;
class RectArea {
    private int l,b;
    public RectArea() {
        l=3;
        b=6;
    }
    public RectArea(int x) {
        l=x;
        b=7;
    }
    public RectArea(int x, int y) {
        l=x;
        b=y;
    }
    public RectArea(float x, int y) {
        l=(int) x;
        b=y;
    }
    public RectArea(int x, float y) {
        l= x;
        b=(int) y;
    }
    public RectArea(float x, float y) {
        l= (int) x;
        b=(int) y;
    }
```

```
    public int getRect() {
        return l*b;
    }
}
class ConstructorOverload {
    static void Main() {
        RectArea rect1 = new RectArea();
        RectArea rect2 = new RectArea(2);
        RectArea rect3 = new RectArea(5, 8);
        RectArea rect4 = new RectArea(3.75f, 6);
        RectArea rect5 = new RectArea(4, 5.38f);
        RectArea rect6 = new RectArea(2.25f, 5.30f);
        Console.WriteLine("Area of first rectangle is {0}", rect1.getRect());
        Console.WriteLine("Area of second rectangle is {0}", rect2.getRect());
        Console.WriteLine("Area of third rectangle is {0}", rect3.getRect());
        Console.WriteLine("Area of fourth rectangle is {0}", rect4.getRect());
        Console.WriteLine("Area of fifth rectangle is {0}", rect5.getRect());
        Console.WriteLine("Area of sixth rectangle is {0}", rect6.getRect());

    }
}
```

Output:

```
Area of first rectangle is 18
Area of second rectangle is 14
Area of third rectangle is 40
Area of fourth rectangle is 18
Area of fifth rectangle is 20
Area of sixth rectangle is 10
```

While creating the objects, the compiler decides which constructor to call depending on the number and type of the parameters passed to the new operator. In this example, six objects of the RectArea class are created by passing different numbers of parameters and types. For example, the following statement:

```
RectArea rect1 = new RectArea();
```

contains no parameters, so the compiler invokes the default constructor for initializing the data members for this object.

Similarly, the following statement:

```
RectArea rect5 = new RectArea(4, 5.38f);
```

contains two parameters: int and float. So the parameterized constructor that matches the arguments (the one that has two parameters, first as int and the other as float) is invoked for initializing the parameters.

The ConstOverlodStudent.cs program shown in Listing 7.19 is another example of constructor overloading. The program contains a Student class that accepts a student's ID number, name, tuition fee, library fee, and boarding fee and displays the total fees. Constructor overloading is implemented by creating three constructors, each having a different number of parameters. The first constructor takes three parameters (ID, name, and tuitionFees amount), the second constructor takes one parameter extra for library fees, and the third constructor takes the parameter for boarding fees.

Listing 7.19 Program Code in ConstOverlodStudent.cs File

```
using System;
class Student {
    private int ID, tuitionFees;
    float totalFees;
    private string name;
    public Student(int u, string v, int w) {
        ID=u;
        name=v;
        tuitionFees=w;
        totalFees=w;
    }
    public Student(int u, string v, int w, int x) {
        //x parameter represents the library fees
        ID=u;
        name=v;
        tuitionFees=w;
        totalFees=w+x;
    }
    public Student(int u, string v, int w, int x, int y) {
        //y parameter represents the boarding fees
        ID=u;
        name=v;
        tuitionFees=w;
        totalFees=w+x+y;
    }
    public void showStudent() {
        Console.WriteLine("ID: {0}, Name: {1}, Tuition Fees: {2}, Total School Fees: {3}",
ID,name,tuitionFees, totalFees);
    }
}
class ConstOverlodStudent {
    static void Main() {
        Student stud1 = new Student(101, "Kelly", 1000);
```

```
        Student stud2 = new Student(102, "David", 1000, 200);
        Student stud3 = new Student(103, "Caroline", 1000, 200, 350);
        Console.WriteLine("Information of student Kelly is as under:");
        stud1.showStudent();
        Console.WriteLine("Information of student David is as under:");
        stud2.showStudent();
        Console.WriteLine("Information of student Caroline is as under:");
        stud3.showStudent();
    }
}
```

Output:

```
Information of student Kelly is as under:
ID: 101, Name: Kelly, Tuition Fees: 1000, Total School Fees: 1000
Information of student David is as under:
ID: 102, Name: David, Tuition Fees: 1000, Total School Fees: 1200
Information of student Caroline is as under:
ID: 103, Name: Caroline, Tuition Fees: 1000, Total School Fees: 1550
```

Three objects named stud1, stud2, and stud3 of the Student class are created. When creating the stud1 object, the ID, name, and tuition fee are passed in the form of values 101, Kelly, and 1000. The stud2 object has four parameters that represent the ID, name, tuition fee, and library fees. Similarly, the stud3 object uses five parameters that represent the ID, name, tuition fee, library fee, and boarding fee. Depending on the number of parameters used while defining the object, a respective constructor will be called. In addition to initializing the three data members ID, name, and tuitionFees, the constructor calculates the total fees, which is the sum of tuition fee, library fee, and boarding fee. The information for all three students is displayed by invoking the showStudent method on the respective objects.

Constructor Chaining

Constructor chaining is the process of calling one constructor from another. Look at the following example:

```
class Student {
    private int ID;
    private string name;
    public Student(int u) {
        ID=u;
        name="Kelly";
    }
```

```
    public Student(int u, string v) : this(u)          #1
    {
        name=v;
    }
    . . . . . . . . . . .
    . . . . . . . . . .
}
. . . . . . . . . .
. . . . . . . . . .
. . . . . . . . . .
static void Main() {
    Student stud1 = new Student(101);
    Student stud2 = new Student(102, "David");
}
```

In the preceding example, statement #1 defines a public Student(int u, string v) constructor that calls the public Student(int u) constructor. Basically, statement #1 instructs the compiler to execute the public Student(int u) constructor first, followed by the public Student(int u, string v) constructor. This way of calling a constructor from another constructor is called *initializer*.

Note

> You cannot explicitly call a constructor in C#. It is through the initializers that you can call one constructor from another.

Why is constructor chaining required? The answer is simple; it increases code efficiency.

With constructor overloading, some code is repeated in almost all constructors. Such code that is repeated in almost all constructors is cut from all the constructors, and a separate constructor is created from this code. All the rest of the constructors are then set to call this separate constructor through initializer. This technique avoids repetition of code and implements code reusability.

A constructor that calls an existing constructor is created by appending the constructor info (access specifier, constructor name, and parameters) with a colon (:). After the colon, the this keyword and the parameter list of the called constructor are supplied. The supplied parameter must match the parameter types of the called constructor. The called constructor is executed, followed by the caller constructor.

So that the concept of constructor chaining is clear, you'll rewrite the constructor overloading program ConstOverlodStudent.cs (refer to Listing 7.19) to implement constructor chaining. In other words, a constructor will call another constructor to initialize the data members and display student information. The modified program will appear as shown in Listing 7.20.

Listing 7.20 Program Code in CallingConstFromConst.cs File

```csharp
using System;
class Student {
    private int ID, tuitionFees;
    float totalFees;
    private string name;
    public Student(int u, string v, int w) {                        // #1
        ID=u;
        name=v;
        tuitionFees=w;
        totalFees=w;
    }
    public Student(int u, string v, int w, int x) : this(u,v,w)      // #2
    {
        //x parameter represents the library fees
        totalFees=w+x;                                              // #3
    }
    public Student(int u, string v, int w, int x, int y): this(u,v,w)  // #4
    {
        //y parameter represents the boarding fees
        totalFees=w+x+y;                                            // #5
    }
    public void showStudent() {
        Console.WriteLine("ID: {0}, Name: {1}, Tuition Fees: {2}, Total School Fees:
{3}", ID,name,tuitionFees, totalFees);
    }
}
class CallingConstFromConst {
    static void Main() {
        Student stud1 = new Student(101, "Kelly", 1000);            // #6
        Student stud2 = new Student(102, "David", 1000, 200);       // #7
        Student stud3 = new Student(103, "Caroline", 1000, 200, 350);  // #8
        Console.WriteLine("Information of student Kelly is as under:");
        stud1.showStudent();
        Console.WriteLine("Information of student David is as under:");
        stud2.showStudent();
        Console.WriteLine("Information of student Caroline is as under:");
        stud3.showStudent();
    }
}
```

Output:

```
Information of student Kelly is as under:
ID: 101, Name: Kelly, Tuition Fees: 1000, Total School Fees: 1000
Information of student David is as under:
ID: 102, Name: David, Tuition Fees: 1000, Total School Fees: 1200
Information of student Caroline is as under:
ID: 103, Name: Caroline, Tuition Fees: 1000, Total School Fees: 1550
```

Statement #6 results in invoking the constructor at statement #1. This constructor initializes the data members ID, name, tuitionFees, and totalFees. Statement #7 invokes the constructor at statement #2. This constructor calls the constructor at #1; therefore, the constructor at #1 is executed first, followed by the constructor at #2. After executing the constructor at #1, the execution resumes from statement #3. Similarly, statement #8 invokes the constructor at statement #4. This constructor again calls the constructor at #1, so the constructor at #1 is executed first, followed by the constructor at #4. After executing the constructor at #1, the execution resumes from statement #5.

GARBAGE COLLECTION

Garbage collection is a procedure initiated by the operating system to free up the memory or other resources used by an application that is no longer being used. When all the references to an object are complete and the object is not referenced anywhere in the program, it is assumed that it is no longer required, and the memory and other resources it uses are released for use by other objects. Garbage collection is initiated automatically by the operating system—usually when the free memory falls below a threshold.

Destructors, also called *finalizers*, are methods that are the opposite of constructors and usually contain code to release resources allocated to the object. Destructors take no parameters and are automatically called just before an object is destroyed or when an object is no longer referenced. Here's the syntax of a defining constructor:

```
~class_name( ) {
    // code to release resources
}
```

You can see that the name of the destructor resembles the constructor (that is, it has the same name as that of the class). To distinguish it from a constructor, it uses ~ (tilde) as the prefix. The destructors have no return type.

The Finalizer.cs program shown in Listing 7.21 demonstrates use of a finalizer in releasing allocated resources. The program defines a RectArea class to calculate the area of a rectangle. The class uses a constructor to initialize its data members. After the area of the rectangle is displayed, the finalizer is called by setting the instance to `null`. The finalizer, as expected, releases the allocated resources.

Listing 7.21 Program Code in Finalizer.cs File

```
using System;
class RectArea {
    private int l,b;
    public RectArea(int x, int y) {
        l=x;
        b=y;
        Console.WriteLine("Constructor is called");
    }
    public int getRect() {
        return l*b;
    }
    ~ RectArea() {
        Console.WriteLine("Finalizer is called");
    }
}
class Finalizer {
    static void Main() {
        RectArea rect = new RectArea(5, 8);
        Console.WriteLine("Area of first rectangle is {0}", rect.getRect());
        rect=null;
    }
}
```

Output:

```
Constructor is called
Area of first rectangle is 40
Finalizer is called
```

You can see that the finalizer has the same name as that of the constructor and is prefixed by ~ (tilde). The finalizer is invoked when the instance `rect` is set to `null`. The text message `Finalizer is called` appears on the screen to confirm that the finalizer is called.

STATIC CLASSES AND MEMBERS

From the programs created so far, you have learned that a standard procedure for working with the classes is to create their instance and access their members via instance. In other words, the members of a class were accessed through instance only. Static members are different in the following ways:

- Static members can be used by themselves without reference to a specific instance of the class. (In other words, static members of the class can be accessed without instantiating the class.)

- A static member cannot be accessed through an instance. Instead, to access a static member from outside the class, you need to specify the name of its class, followed by the dot operator, which is then followed by the static member that you want to access.

- Traditionally, when an instance of the class is created, a separate copy of data members is created for it. The static members are global variables, so when an instance of the class is created, no separate copy of a static variable is created for it. This means that the static data members can be shared by all instances of the class.

- A static data member is automatically initialized if it is not initialized explicitly. The static data member of `numeric` type is initialized to `zero`, `reference` type is initialized to `null`, and `Boolean` type is initialized to `false`.

Besides data members and methods, a complete class can be declared as static. A static class can only have static data members and methods. You get a compilation error if any nonstatic member is added to a static class. Also, a static class cannot be instantiated. A nonstatic class can have static as well as nonstatic members. A nonstatic class can be instantiated, but it cannot access static members via instance of the class. Remember that a static method can directly call only other static methods of its class, but it cannot directly call a nonstatic method of its class. Similarly, a static method can directly access only other static data members of its class, but not a nonstatic member of its class.

You will learn about static members (data members and methods) via the following methods:

- Creating a nonstatic class having static members
- Creating a static class having static members

The `StaticExample1.cs` program shown in Listing 7.22 is an example of a nonstatic class having static members. The program explains how the static members `x` and `y` of a nonstatic class `StaticMember` are accessed.

Listing 7.22 Program Code in StaticExample1.cs File

```
using System;
class StaticMember
{
    public static int x = 10;
    public static int y;
    public StaticMember(int a, int b)
    {
        x = a;
        y = b;
    }
    public static int Sum()
    {
        return x+y;
    }
    public int Addition()
    {
        return x+y;
    }
}
class StaticExample1
{
    public static void Main()
    {
        Console.WriteLine("Initial value of x is {0} and y is {1} ", StaticMember.x,
StaticMember.y);
        StaticMember s=new StaticMember(25,50);
        Console.WriteLine("New value of x is {0} and that of y is {1} ", StaticMember.x,
StaticMember.y);
        Console.WriteLine("Sum of the two values is {0}", StaticMember.Sum());
        Console.WriteLine("Sum of the two values is {0}", s.Addition());
    }
}
```

Output:

```
Initial value of x is 10 and y is 0
New value of x is 25 and that of y is 50
Sum of the two values is 75
Sum of the two values is 75
```

The nonstatic class just shown consists of static as well as nonstatic data members and methods. The static data members and methods are marked by the `static` keyword. The variables x and y are static data members of the class. The method `Sum` is a static method of the class. `StaticMember` is a nonstatic constructor, and `Addition` is a method of the class.

The static data member x is explicitly initialized to value 10, whereas the static data member y is automatically initialized to value 0. The program access displays the initial values of the static data member variables x and y through the class name. Also, an instance of the StaticMember class s is created, passing values 25 and 50 to its constructor. The constructor initializes the static data members x and y to values 25 and 50, respectively. The new values of the static data members are displayed. Also, the program calls the static and nonstatic methods Sum and Addition, respectively, through the class and instance of the class to display the addition of the static data members.

In the following example, you create a static class. Recall that a static class cannot be instantiated, and it cannot have a nonstatic data member or method. You will be using a static constructor in the example.

The benefit of using static classes is that the compiler prevents any instance members from being added to the class accidentally. Also, because the static class cannot be instantiated, the overhead of creating objects is removed, which improves program performance.

A static constructor is called automatically when the class is loaded, before any of its instance is created and before any instance constructor is called. A static constructor is used to initialize data members of the class as a whole. As with a normal instance constructor, a static constructor cannot have access modifiers and cannot be called directly by the program.

The StaticExample2.cs program shown in Listing 7.23 explains how the static members of the static class Rect are accessed.

Listing 7.23 Program Code in StaticExample2.cs File

```
using System;
static class Rect
{
    public static int l,b;
    static Rect()
    {
        l=5;
        b=8;
    }
    public static int GetArea()
    {
        return l * b;
    }
}
```

```
class StaticExample2
{
    public static void Main()
    {
        Console.WriteLine("Length is {0}, Breadth is {1}, Area of rectangle is {2}" ,
Rect.l, Rect.b, Rect.GetArea());
    }
}
```

Output:

```
Length is 5, Breadth is 8, Area of rectangle is 40
```

The program is simple to understand. The static data members l and b of the static class Rect are initialized to values 5 and 8, respectively, when the class is loaded. The program accesses and displays the static data members l and b through the class name Rect. Also, the static method GetArea is called using the class name to print the area of the rectangle. The GetArea method accesses the static data members l and b to compute the area of a rectangle.

NAMESPACE

A *namespace* provides a logical grouping to organize related classes, structures, delegates, enumerations, interfaces, and other types. A namespace serves two purposes:

- It provides a way to keep one set of names separate from another. Names declared in one namespace do not conflict with the same names declared in another. Without a namespace, the class names, method names, variable names, method names, and property names may conflict. For example, if you defined a class called Rectangle, it could conflict with another class named Rectangle defined in any library used in your program. But a namespace restricts the visibility of names declared within it, so it helps to resolve conflicts.

- A namespace, once defined, can be imported in any other program to readily use the classes, its methods, and its other content. That way, you can say that a namespace behaves like a library in which you define frequently used content once and import and use it in another program, thereby avoiding repetitive statements.

Note

A namespace can be nested.

Here's the syntax for defining a namespace:

```
namespace name {
    // members
}
```

where `name` is the name of the namespace, and members can be classes, structures, delegates, enumerations, interfaces, or another namespace.

The `custom_namespace.cs` program shown in Listing 7.24 creates a namespace, `custom_namespace`, that defines two classes: `MessageClass` and `PrintClass`. The `MessageClass` defines two methods, `disp` and `show`, and the `PrintClass` defines a `print` method.

Listing 7.24 Program Code in custom_namespace.cs File

```
using System;
namespace custom_namespace
{
    class MessageClass
    {
        public void disp()
        {
            Console.WriteLine("The disp method of MessageClass in custom_namespace");
        }
        public void show()
        {
            Console.WriteLine("The show method of MessageClass in custom_namespace");
        }
    }
    class PrintClass
    {
        public void print()
        {
            Console.WriteLine("The print method of PrintClass in custom_namespace");
        }
    }
}
```

A namespace declaration defines a scope. You can see that the two classes, `MessageClass` and `PrintClass`, are defined in the `custom_namespace` namespace. Namespaces can hold other types besides classes, including structures, interfaces, enumerations, and delegates.

The `UsingCustomNamespace.cs` program shown in Listing 7.25 explains how to use the classes defined in the namespace `custom_namespace` that you created in Listing 7.24.

Listing 7.25 Program Code in UsingCustomNamespace.cs File

```
class UsingCustomNamespace
{
    public static void Main()
    {
        custom_namespace.MessageClass m=new custom_namespace.MessageClass();
        custom_namespace.PrintClass p=new custom_namespace.PrintClass();
        m.disp();
        m.show();
        p.print();
    }
}
```

Because `MessageClass` and `PrintClass` are defined within the `custom_namespace`, you can see that, while creating their objects, the two classes are qualified with the namespace `custom_namespace`. If you don't qualify the class names with the namespace in which they are defined, the compiler cannot identify them. Once the objects of the two classes are created, you can use them and access their methods without namespace qualification.

To run the preceding program, you need to compile it along with the file that contains the namespace. In other words, you need to compile `UsingCustomNamespace.cs` and `custom_namespace.cs` together, as shown here:

```
C:\> csc UsingCustomNamespace.cs custom_namespace.cs
```

To run the program, you don't need to specify the namespace file:

```
C:\> UsingCustomeNamespace
```

Here's the output that you get:

```
The disp method of MessageClass in custom_namespace
The show method of MessageClass in custom_namespace
The print method of PrintClass in custom_namespace
```

Instead of having two separate files, you can combine the namespace and the class that uses that namespace into a single file, as shown in Listing 7.26.

Listing 7.26 Program Code in UsingCustomNamespace.cs File

```
using System;
namespace custom_namespace
{
    class MessageClass
    {
```

```
        public void disp()
        {
            Console.WriteLine("The disp method of MessageClass in custom_namespace");
        }
        public void show()
        {
            Console.WriteLine("The show method of MessageClass in custom_namespace");
        }
    }
    class PrintClass
    {
        public void print()
        {
            Console.WriteLine("The print method of PrintClass in custom_namespace");
        }
    }
}
class UsingCustomNamespace
{
    public static void Main()
    {
        custom_namespace.MessageClass m=new custom_namespace.MessageClass();
        custom_namespace.PrintClass p=new custom_namespace.PrintClass();
        m.disp();
        m.show();
        p.print();
    }
}
```

You can see that the class UsingCustomNamepspace that uses the namespace is defined below custom_namespace.

It is always preferable to keep namespace(s) in a separate file for readability and for easy maintenance. When the namespace is kept in a separate file, you can import it in the calling class through the using directive.

Namespace Importing

You can import a desired namespace in the calling class by using the using directive. The using directive not only imports the namespace, allowing you to access its members in the current class, but relieves you from calling methods without using their fully qualified name. For example, writing a statement using System in the program allows you to type only the method names of members of the System namespace without typing the word System in every statement.

Note

System is the namespace that the .NET Framework library uses.

The UsingCustomNamespace2.cs program shown in Listing 7.27 demonstrates importing the custom_namespace (that you created in Listing 7.24) in the current program.

Listing 7.27 Program Code in UsingCustomNamespace2.cs File

```
using custom_namespace;
class UsingCustomNamespace2
{
    public static void Main()
    {
        MessageClass m=new MessageClass();
        PrintClass p=new PrintClass();
        m.disp();
        m.show();
        p.print();
    }
}
```

Once it's imported, you can access the classes defined in that namespace. While compiling the program, you need to include the namespace file, as shown in the following command:

```
C:\>csc UsingCustomNamespace2.cs custom_namespace.cs
```

To run it, use the following command:

```
C:\>UsingCustomNamespace2
```

Output:

```
The disp method of MessageClass in custom_namespace
The show method of MessageClass in custom_namespace
The print method of PrintClass in custom_namespace
```

Note

If you are not using the using directive, you can call the methods defined in the namespace using the fully qualified names. In other words, you can call namespace members with fully qualified names. A fully qualified name includes every element from the namespace name up to the method call.

In the preceding program, you can see that, by using the `using` directive, you can access its class members, `MessageClass` and `PrintClass`, without using the fully qualified name.

You can also nest namespaces inside one another.

Namespace Nesting

Nesting of namespaces allows you to organize your code hierarchically. The outer namespace may represent a category, inner namespace may represent a subcategory, and so on. You can nest any number of namespaces. In the `custom_namespace.cs` program shown in Listing 7.28, the `inner_namespace` namespace is nested within the `custom_namespace` namespace.

Listing 7.28 Program Code in custom_namespace.cs File

```csharp
using System;
namespace custom_namespace
{
    namespace inner_namespace
    {
        class MessageClass
        {
            public void disp()
            {
                Console.WriteLine("The disp method of MessageClass in
custom_namespace.inner_namespace");
            }
            public void show()
            {
                Console.WriteLine("The show method of MessageClass in
custom_namespace.inner_namespace");
            }
        }
        class PrintClass
        {
            public void print()
            {
                Console.WriteLine("The print method of PrintClass in
custom_namespace.inner_namespace");
            }
        }
    }
}
```

You can see that the inner_namespace is nested inside the custom_namespace namespace. The nested namespace defines two classes: MessageClass and PrintClass. The MessageClass contains two methods, disp and show, and the PrintClass contains a single print method.

The UsingCustomNamespace2.cs program shown in Listing 7.29 imports the inner_namespace that is nested inside the custom_namespace and uses the classes defined in it.

Listing 7.29 Program Code in UsingCustomNamespace2.cs File

```
using custom_namespace.inner_namespace;
class UsingCustomNamespace2
{
    public static void Main()
    {
        MessageClass m=new MessageClass();
        PrintClass p=new PrintClass();
        m.disp();
        m.show();
        p.print();
    }
}
```

The program instantiates the MessageClass and PrintClass and invokes their respective methods.

Again, while compiling the program, you need to include the namespace file, as shown in the following command:

```
C:\> csc UsingCustomNamespace2.cs custom_namespace.cs
```

To run it, use the following command:

```
C:\> UsingCustomNamespace2
```

Output:

```
The disp method of MessageClass in custom_namespace.inner_namespace
The show method of MessageClass in custom_namespace.inner_namespace
The print method of PrintClass in custom_namespace.inner_namespace
```

Namespace Alias Creation

The namespace alias helps in renaming namespaces. You can shorten long namespaces by assigning a smaller alias to it. You create an alias for a namespace with the alias directive using the following syntax:

```
using alias = name_space;
```

Here, `alias` becomes another name for the namespace specified by `name_space`. Once `alias` has been created, you can use it in place of the original namespace.

For example, the following statement creates an alias `class1` for the `MessageClass` class defined in the `inner_namespace` namespace nested in the `custom_namespace` namespace:

`using class1=custom_namespace.inner_namespace.MessageClass;`

You can create an object of the `MessageClass` with the following statement:

`class1 m=new class1();`

The `UsingCustomNamespace3.cs` program shown in Listing 7.30 demonstrates using the namespace alias. The program creates two aliases, called `class1` and `class2`. `class1` and `class2` represent the `MessageClass` and `PrintClass` class of the `inner_namespace` that is nested inside the `custom_namespace`.

Listing 7.30 Program Code in UsingCustomNamespace3.cs File

```
using class1=custom_namespace.inner_namespace.MessageClass;
using class2=custom_namespace.inner_namespace.PrintClass;
class UsingCustomNamespace3
{
    public static void Main()
    {
        class1 m=new class1();
        class2 p=new class2();
        m.disp();
        m.show();
        p.print();
    }
}
```

To compile the program, you need to include the namespace file:

`C:\> csc UsingCustomNamespace3.cs custom_namespace.cs`

To run the program, use the following command:

`C:\> UsingCustomNamespace3`

Output:

```
The disp method of MessageClass in custom_namespace.inner_namespace
The show method of MessageClass in custom_namespace.inner_namespace
The print method of PrintClass in custom_namespace.inner_namespace
```

You can see that the objects of the MessageClass and PrintClass are created and named m and p from the defined aliases class1 and class2. Using the objects m and p, the methods disp, show, and print of the respective classes are invoked.

INTERNAL MODIFIER

The internal access specifier allows a class to expose its members to other methods and objects in the current assembly. As a result, any internal member can be accessed from any class or method defined within the application in which the member is defined. The protected internal access specifier makes members of a class accessible to the methods of the classes in the current assembly and to the methods of the inheriting class.

The program InternalSpecifierExample.cs shown in Listing 7.31 demonstrates use of the internal access specifier.

Listing 7.31 Program Code in InternalSpecifierExample.cs File

```
using System;
class RectArea {
    private int l,b;
    internal void setData(int x, int y) {
        l=x;
        b=y;
    }
    internal int getRect() {
        return l*b;
    }
}
class InternalSpecifierExample {
    static void Main() {
        RectArea rect = new RectArea();
        rect.setData(5,8);
        Console.WriteLine("Area of rectangle is {0}", rect.getRect());
    }
}
```

Output:

```
Area of rectangle is 40
```

In the preceding example, you see that the two methods of the RectArea class, setData and getRect, are declared as internal methods. In other words, any class in the same application or assembly can access them. The two methods are accessed by the object defined in the InternalSpecifierExample class.

Note

The internal access specifier hides its member variables and methods from other classes and objects that reside in other namespaces.

Summary

In this chapter, you used classes and the `new` operator and accessed public members. You discovered the difference between a `struct` and a `class` and the procedure to use methods in a class. Furthermore, you used the `return` statement and read about method parameters, private members, and implementation of passing parameters by value and reference to the methods in a class. You used output parameters and applied method overloading to the class methods. Later, you learned about encapsulation, properties, the `this` keyword, default constructors, parameterized constructors, copy constructors, constructor overloading, and constructor chaining. You realized the benefits of garbage collection, destructors/finalizers, and static classes and members. We learned to use, import, nest, and create namespaces and how to use the internal modifier.

The next chapter is focused on inheritance and polymorphism. You will learn to use single inheritance and protected members and call base class constructors. You will read about different types of inheritance, including multilevel, hierarchical, and hybrid. You will learn about method overriding, virtual methods, sealed class and methods, and method hiding. Finally, you will discover how to use abstract classes, abstract properties, and polymorphism.

Chapter 8

INHERITANCE AND POLYMORPHISM

This chapter's topics include the following:

- Types of inheritance
- Method overriding
- Sealed class and methods
- Method hiding
- Abstract classes
- Abstract properties
- Polymorphism

Inheritance is one of the principles of object-oriented programming that makes the existing classes act as building blocks to make larger applications. In other words, the method and instance variables of class(es) can be reused in some other class through inheritance. The inheriting class is known as a *derived class* or *subclass*, and the class that is being inherited is known as the *base class* or *superclass*, as shown in Figure 8.1.

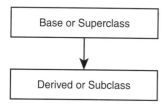

Figure 8.1
Block diagram showing single inheritance.
© 2015 Cengage Learning®.

The inheriting class can define its own instance variables and methods. Therefore, the object of the inheriting class can access the instance variables and methods of the base class as well as that of the inheriting class. The syntax for inheriting a class is given here:

```
class DerivedClass : BaseClass {
    . . .
}
```

DerivedClass, after inheriting BaseClass, has the right to access the public or protected methods of the base class. A class can inherit, at most, one base class. (In other words, a class cannot derive from two or more classes.) DerivedClass can be further inherited by another class until and unless DerivedClass is declared as sealed. You will learn more about sealed classes and methods later in this chapter. The inheritance can be public, private, or protected. By default, inheritance is always implicitly public.

Note

The System.Object class is the root class of all classes.

TYPES OF INHERITANCE

In C#, you can implement the following types of inheritance:

- **Single inheritance**—This is the simplest type of inheritance. Here, a single class is derived from a single base class (see Figure 8.1).

- **Hierarchical inheritance**—More than one class is derived from a single base class in this type of inheritance. Figure 8.2(a) demonstrates hierarchical inheritance, where classes B, C, and D are derived from a single base class, A.

- **Multilevel inheritance**—In this type of inheritance, a derived class is created from another derived class. Figure 8.2(b) shows an example of multilevel inheritance, where class C is derived from class B, which in turn is derived from class A.

- **Hybrid inheritance**—This type of inheritance is a combination of single, hierarchical, and multilevel inheritances. Figure 8.2(c) demonstrates hybrid inheritance, where classes C and D are derived from class B (hierarchical inheritance), and class B is derived from class A (single inheritance).

Note

In multiple inheritance, a class is derived from more than one base class. But multiple inheritance is not supported by C# using classes and can be implemented using interfaces.

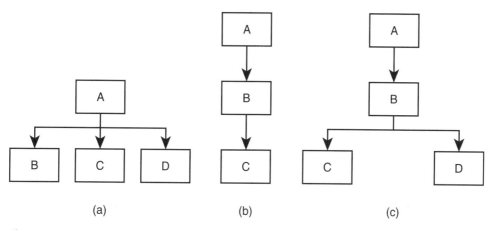

Figure 8.2
Block diagram showing (a) hierarchical inheritance, (b) multilevel inheritance, and (c) hybrid inheritance.
© 2015 Cengage Learning®.

Now you'll write programs for inheritance, starting with the simplest case: single inheritance.

Single Inheritance

The program `Inherit1.cs` shown in Listing 8.1 demonstrates single inheritance. The `RectArea` class, which is meant for calculating the area of a rectangle, is inherited by another class, `TrgArea`. The object of the `TrgArea` class, because it's able to access methods of the base class `RectArea` and of its own class, is used to calculate both the area of a rectangle and the area of a triangle.

Listing 8.1 Program Code in Inherit1.cs File

```
using System;
class RectArea {
    private int l,b,a;
    public void setRect(int x, int y) {
        l=x;
        b=y;
    }
    public int getRect() {
        a=l*b;
        return a;
    }
}
```

```
class TrgArea :RectArea {
    private int b,h;
    private float a;
    public void setTrg(int x, int y) {
        b=x;
        h=y;
    }
    public float getTrg() {
        a=(float)1/2*b*h;
        return a;
    }
}
class Inherit1 {
    static void Main() {
        TrgArea t = new TrgArea();
        t.setRect(5,8);
        t.setTrg(19,7);
        Console.WriteLine("Area of rectangle is {0}", t.getRect());
        Console.WriteLine("Area of triangle is {0}", t.getTrg());
    }
}
```

Output:

```
Area of rectangle is 40
Area of triangle is 66.5
```

The RectArea class consists of three data members—1, b, and a—and two member functions—setRect and getRect. The class TrgArea consists of three data members—b, h, and a—and two member functions: setTrg and getTrg. Because the class TrgArea inherits the class RectArea, its object has the right to access the public members of the RectArea class. Also, the object t of the TrgArea class can access methods of the RectArea class and its own class, TrgArea. Because the object t can access four methods—setRect, getRect, setTrg, and getTrg—it calculates and displays the area of a rectangle as well as the area of a triangle.

Again, the Inherit2.cs program shown in Listing 8.2 demonstrates simple inheritance. Two classes, Worker and Officer, are defined in the program. Assuming that an officer gets all privileges that a worker gets plus something more, the program shows reusability through inheritance. In this example, you can assume that the worker gets the basic salary and the officer gets the basic salary plus the household and child allowance. In the program, you define a class Worker with data members code, name, and basicSalary. The Officer class inherits the Worker class, so it is able to access all its methods. You don't need to redefine the data members code, name, and basicSalary in the Officer class because it accesses them through inheritance. Only two data members, `houseAllowance` and `childAllowance`, are defined in the `Officer` class to store the household and child allowance information.

Listing 8.2 Program Code in Inherit2.cs File

```
using System;
class Worker {
    private int code, basicSalary;
    private string name;
    public void setWorker(int x, string y, int z) {
        code=x;
        name=y;
        basicSalary=z;
    }
    public void showWorker() {
        Console.WriteLine("Code: {0}, Name: {1}, Salary: {2}", code, name, basicSalary);
    }
}
class Officer: Worker{
    private float houseAllowance, childAllowance;
    public void setOfficer(float u, float v) {
        houseAllowance=u;
        childAllowance=v;
    }
    public void showOfficer() {
        Console.WriteLine("Household allowance: {0}, Child allowance: {1}",
houseAllowance, childAllowance);
    }
}
class Inherit2 {
    static void Main() {
        Worker wkr = new Worker();
        Officer ofcr = new Officer();
        wkr.setWorker(101, "Kelly", 5000);
        ofcr.setWorker(102, "David", 7000);
        ofcr.setOfficer(400, 200);
        Console.WriteLine("Information of worker is as given below:");
        wkr.showWorker();
        Console.WriteLine("Information of officer is as given below:");
        ofcr.showWorker();
        ofcr.showOfficer();
    }
}
```

Output:

```
Information of worker is as given below:
Code: 101, Name: Kelly, Salary: 5000
Information of officer is as given below:
Code: 102, Name: David, Salary: 7000
Household allowance: 400, Child allowance: 200
```

Here's what's happening with the preceding program:

- The Worker class contains these data members—code, name, and basicSalary—and two member functions—setWorker and showWorker. The Officer class contains two data members—houseAllowance and childAllowance—and two member functions—setOfficer and getOfficer. Because the Officer class inherits the Worker class, the object of the Officer class can also access the public members setWorker and showWorker of the Worker class. In other words, the Officer class object ofcr can access methods of the Worker class and its own class.

- The Worker and Officer classes are instantiated by wkr and ofcr objects. The setWorker method is invoked on the wkr object to initialize its data members code, name, and basicSalary.

- The showWorker method is invoked on the wkr object to display the information assigned to the code, name, and basicSalary data members.

- The setWorker method is invoked on the ofcr object to initialize the data members code, name, and basicSalary.

- The setOfficer method is invoked on the ofcr object to initialize the data members houseAllowance and childAllowance.

- The showWorker method is invoked on the ofcr object to display the code, name, and basic salary that were assigned by invoking the setWorker method.

- The showOfficer method is invoked on the ofcr object to display the household and child allowance values.

- In the derived class, if you try to access the private variable of a base class, you get the following error:

```
error CS0122: 'Worker.basicSalary' is inaccessible due to its protection level
```

In both Inherit1.cs and Inherit2.cs, which you saw in Listings 8.1 and 8.2, although a class is derived by another class, the derived class is not able to access the data members of the base class. That is true because the data members of the base class are declared as private. To enable the derived class to access the data members of the base class, you need to change their access specifier from private to protected.

Using Protected Members

Recall from the previous chapter that protected members are those that members of the owner class and members of the inheriting class can access. You cannot access protected members from other parts of the program using the dot (.) operator. Obviously, the protected specifier implements security by ensuring that values of the data members are not accessed or modified accidently by other parts of the program but only by the base and inheriting class members.

The program ProtectedAccess.cs, shown in Listing 8.3, demonstrates how the protected data members of the base class are accessed in the derived class. The program defines two classes, Worker and Officer, where the Officer class inherits the Worker class. The program explains how the protected data member basicSalary of the Worker class is accessed in the Officer class to calculate the household allowance, which is assumed to be 6 percent of the basic salary.

Listing 8.3 Program Code in ProtectedAccess.cs File

```
using System;
class Worker {
    protected int code, basicSalary;
    protected string name;
    public void setWorker(int x, string y, int z) {
        code=x;
        name=y;
        basicSalary=z;
    }
    public void showWorker() {
        Console.WriteLine("Code: {0}, Name: {1}, Salary: {2}", code, name, basicSalary);
    }
}
class Officer: Worker{
    private float houseAllowance, childAllowance;
    public void setOfficer(int x, string y, int z) {
        setWorker(x,y,z);
        houseAllowance=(float) basicSalary*6/100;
        childAllowance= 250;
    }
    public void showOfficer() {
        showWorker();
        Console.WriteLine("Household allowance: {0}, Child allowance: {1}",
houseAllowance, childAllowance);
    }
}
```

```
class ProtectedAccess {
    static void Main() {
        Worker wkr = new Worker();
        Officer ofcr = new Officer();
        wkr.setWorker(101, "Kelly", 5000);
        ofcr.setOfficer(102, "David", 7000);
        Console.WriteLine("Information of worker is as given below:");
        wkr.showWorker();
        Console.WriteLine("Information of officer is as given below:");
        ofcr.showOfficer();
    }
}
```

Output:

```
Information of worker is as given below:
Code: 101, Name: Kelly, Salary: 5000
Information of officer is as given below:
Code: 102, Name: David, Salary: 7000
Household allowance: 420, Child allowance: 250
```

Here's what's happening with the preceding program:

■ The data members code, name, and basicSalary of the Worker class are declared protected, which means that the class methods and the derived class methods can access these data members.

■ The Officer class data members houseAllowance and childAllowance are declared as private because you want them to be accessed only by the Officer object.

■ The Officer class inherits the Worker class. Thus, the Officer class object can use five data members: two of its own (houseAllowance and childAllowance) and three of the Worker class (code, name, and basicSalary).

■ The Worker and Officer class are instantiated by the wkr and ofcr objects.

■ The setWorker and showWorker methods are invoked on the wkr object to initialize and display the information assigned to the data members code, name, and basicSalary.

■ The setOfficer method is invoked on the ofcr object with values 102, David, and 7000. The setOfficer method in turn invokes the setWorker method with the supplied values to initialize the data members code, name, and basicSalary. Remember, because these members are declared as protected, the Officer object is able to access these data members. The setOfficer method also calculates the household allowance, which is assumed to be 6 percent of the basic salary. Assuming the child allowance is $250, the method initializes the `childAllowance` member to value `250`.

- The `showOfficer` method is invoked on the `ofcr` object. The method in turn invokes the `showWorker` method to display the code, name, and basic salary that were assigned by invoking the `setWorker` method. The `showOfficer` method also displays the household and child allowance values through the `houseAllowance` and `childAllowance` data members.

Calling Base Class Constructors

After inheriting a class, the derived class gets all the public and protected members of the base class. To initialize data members of the base class, the derived class needs to call the base class constructor. From the constructor in the derived class, the constructor of the base class is called by specifying the base keyword followed by the arguments that need to be passed to the constructor, if any.

Note

If you don't explicitly call a base class constructor in a derived class constructor, the compiler automatically calls the base class's default constructor.

The program `CallBaseConst.cs`, shown in Listing 8.4, demonstrates calling of the base class constructor. The program has a base class called `Worker` and a derived class called `Officer`. The `Worker` class stores the code name and basic salary, whereas the `Officer` class contains members to store household and child allowance. The household allowance is assumed to be 6 percent of the basic salary, and the child allowance is assumed to be equal to $250. The program demonstrates calling of the `Worker` class constructor from the `Officer` class constructor.

Listing 8.4 Program Code in CallBaseConst.cs File

```
using System;
class Worker {
    protected int code, basicSalary;
    protected string name;
    public Worker(int x, string y, int z) {
        code=x;
        name=y;
        basicSalary=z;
    }
```

```
    public void showWorker() {
        Console.WriteLine("Code: {0}, Name: {1}, Salary: {2}", code, name, basicSalary);
    }
}
class Officer: Worker{
    private float houseAllowance, childAllowance;
    public Officer(int x, string y, int z) : base(x,y,z) {
        houseAllowance =(float) basicSalary *6/100;
        childAllowance =250;
    }
    public void showOfficer() {
        showWorker();
        Console.WriteLine("Household allowance: {0}, Child allowance: {1}",
houseAllowance, childAllowance);
    }
}
class CallBaseConst {
    static void Main() {
        Worker wkr = new Worker(101, "Kelly", 5000);
        Officer ofcr = new Officer(102, "David", 7000);
        Console.WriteLine("Information of worker is as given below:");
        wkr.showWorker();
        Console.WriteLine("Information of officer is as given below:");
        ofcr.showOfficer();
    }
}
```

Output:

```
Information of worker is as given below:
Code: 101, Name: Kelly, Salary: 5000
Information of officer is as given below:
Code: 102, Name: David, Salary: 7000
Household allowance: 420, Child allowance: 250
```

Here's what's happening with the preceding program:

- The Worker class has three protected data members: code, name, and basicSalary.

- The Officer class has two private data members—houseAllowance and childAllowance—to handle household and child allowance.

- The Officer class inherits the Worker class.

- The object wkr of the Worker class is created. The values 101, Kelly, and 5000 are passed while creating the object, so the parameterized constructor is called. This in turn initializes the data members code, name, and basicSalary of the object.

- Again, the `Officer` class object called `ofcr` is created. Values `102`, `David`, and `7000` are passed while creating the `ofcr` object, which results in invoking its parameterized constructor. From the `Officer` class's constructor, the `Worker` class (base class's constructor) is called and the parameters `102`, `David`, and `7000` are passed to it to initialize the data members `code`, `name`, and `basicSalary`.

- After executing the `Worker` class's constructor, the body of the `Officer` class's constructor is executed to calculate the household and child allowance. The household allowance is assumed to be 6 percent of the basic salary, and the child allowance is assumed to be $250.

- The `showWorker` method is invoked on the `wkr` object to display the code, name, and basic salary of the worker.

- The `showOfficer` method is invoked on the `ofcr` object. The method in turn invokes the `showWorker` method to display the code, name, and basic salary that were assigned by invoking the `Worker` class's constructor. The `showOfficer` method also displays the household and child allowance values.

Multilevel Inheritance

In multilevel inheritance, a class inherits a base class, and the derived class is in turn inherited by another class, and so on.

The program `MultiLevel.cs`, shown in Listing 8.5, demonstrates multilevel inheritance. The program has three classes: `Worker`, `Officer`, and `Manager`. The `Worker` class is inherited by the `Officer` class, which in turn is inherited by the `Manager` class. The following situation leads to multilevel inheritance:

- The `Worker` class deals with three data members: `code`, `name`, and `basicSalary`.

- The `Officer` class requires five data members to work with: `code`, `name`, `basicSalary`, `houseAllowance`, and `childAllownc`.

- The `Manager` class requires seven data members: `code`, `name`, `basicSalary`, `houseAllowance`, `childAllowance`, `expatAllownc`, and `carAllownc`.

- When the `Officer` class inherits the `Worker` class, it automatically gets access to its three protected data members: `code`, `name`, and `basicSalary`. Therefore, the class is required to define just two data members to handle household and child allowance. The household allowance is assumed to be 6 percent of the basic salary, and the child allowance is assumed to be equal to $250.

- When the `Manager` class inherits the `Officer` class, it gains access to the data members that are accessible by the `Officer` class (`code`, `name`, `basicSalary`, houseAllowance, and `childAllowance`). So the `Manager` class needs to define just two data members to calculate expatriation and car allowance, respectively. The expatriation allowance is assumed to be 16 percent of the basic salary. The car allowance is assumed to be equal to $150.

Multilevel inheritance is considered the best approach in such a situation. The `MultiLevel.cs` program (shown in Listing 8.5) creates a `Worker` class with three data members: `code`, `name`, and `basicSalary`. The `Officer` class inherits the `Worker` class and gains access to its three protected data members: `code`, `name`, and `basicSalary`. The `Officer` defines only two data members: `houseAllowance` and `childAllowance`. The `Manager` class inherits the `Officer` class and defines the remaining two data members: `expatAllowance` and `carAllowance`.

Listing 8.5 Program Code in MultiLevel.cs File

```
using System;
class Worker {
    protected int code,basicSalary;
    protected string name;
    public void setWorker(int x, string y, int z) {
        code=x;
        name=y;
        basicSalary=z;
    }
    public void showWorker() {
        Console.WriteLine("Code: {0}, Name: {1}, Salary: {2}", code, name, basicSalary);
    }
}
class Officer: Worker{
    private float houseAllowance, childAllowance;
    public void setOfficer(int x, string y, int z) {
        setWorker(x,y,z);
        houseAllowance =(float) basicSalary *6/100;
        childAllowance = 250;
    }
    public void showOfficer() {
        showWorker();
        Console.WriteLine("Household allowance: {0}, Child allowance: {1}",
    houseAllowance, childAllowance);
    }
}
class Manager: Officer{
    private float expatAllowance, carAllowance;
```

```
    public void setManager(int x, string y, int z) {
        setOfficer(x,y,z);
        expatAllowance =(float) basicSalary *16/100;
        carAllowance = 150;
    }
    public void showManager() {
        showOfficer();
        Console.WriteLine("Expatriation allowance: {0}, Car Allowance: {1}",
expatAllowance,carAllowance);
    }
}
class MultiLevel {
    static void Main() {
        Worker wkr = new Worker();
        Officer ofcr = new Officer();
        Manager mgr=new Manager();
        wkr.setWorker(101, "Kelly", 5000);
        ofcr.setOfficer(102, "David", 7000);
        mgr.setManager(103, "Caroline", 9000);
        Console.WriteLine("Information of worker is as given below:");
        wkr.showWorker();
        Console.WriteLine("\nInformation of officer is as given below:");
        ofcr.showOfficer();
        Console.WriteLine("\nInformation of manager is as given below:");
        mgr.showManager();
    }
}
```

Output:

```
Information of worker is as given below:
Code: 101, Name: Kelly, Salary: 5000

Information of officer is as given below:
Code: 102, Name: David, Salary: 7000
Household allowance: 420, Child allowance: 250

Information of manager is as given below:
Code: 103, Name: Caroline, Salary: 9000
Household allowance: 540, Child allowance: 250
Expatriation allowance: 1440, Car Allowance: 150
```

Here's what's happening with the preceding program:

- The data members code, name, and basicSalary of the Worker class are declared protected. (They can be accessed by the Worker class methods as well as by the derived class methods.)

- The Worker class is inherited by the Officer class.

- The Officer class is inherited by the Manager class.

- The Officer class data members houseAllowance and childAllowance are declared as private because they will not be accessed in the Manager class. You would have declared them protected if you expected to use them in the inheriting class.

- The Manager class data members expatAllowance and carAllowance are declared as private because they will not be accessed from any other class.

- The Worker, Officer, and Manager classes are instantiated by wkr, ofcr, and mgr objects, respectively.

- The setWorker and showWorker methods are invoked on the wkr object to initialize and display the information assigned to the data members code, name, and basicSalary.

- The setOfficer method is invoked on the ofcr object with the values 102, David, and 7000. The setOfficer method in turn invokes the setWorker method with the supplied values to initialize the data members code, name, and basicSalary. The setOfficer method also calculates the household allowance, which is assumed to be 6 percent of the basic salary. Assuming that the child allowance is $250, the method initializes the childAllowance member to value 250.

- The setManager method is invoked on the mgr object with the values 103, Caroline, and 9000. The setManager method invokes the setOfficer method, passing the supplied parameters to it. setOfficer, as you already know, invokes the setWorker method with the given parameters to initialize the data members code, name, and basicSalary. After returning from the setWorker method, the setOfficer method calculates household and child allowance. After returning from the setOfficer method, the setManager calculates the expatriation and car allowance. The expatriation allowance is assumed to be 16 percent of the basic salary. The car allowance is assumed to be equal to $150.

- The showOfficer method is invoked on the ofcr object. The method in turn invokes the showWorker method to display the code, name, and basic salary that were assigned by invoking the setWorker method. The showOfficer method also displays the household and child allowance values using the houseAllowance and childAllowance data members.

- The showManager method is invoked on the mgr object. The method in turn invokes the showOfficer method, which then invokes the showWorker method. The showWorker method displays the code, name, and basic salary, and the showOfficer method displays the household and child allowance values. After returning from the showOfficer method, the showManager method displays the expatriation and car allowance.

Hierarchical Inheritance

Hierarchical inheritance occurs when more than one class is derived from a single base class (see Figure 8.2(a)).

The program `HierarchInherit.cs`, shown in Listing 8.6, demonstrates hierarchical inheritance. The program has three classes: `Worker`, `Officer`, and `Manager`. Both `Officer` and `Manager` are derived from the `Worker` class. The `Worker` class deals with members code, name, and basic salary. The `Officer` class, besides code, name, and basic salary, requires two more fields to handle household and child allowance. The household allowance is assumed to be 6 percent of the basic salary, and the child allowance is assumed to be equal to $250. The `Manager` class also requires the code, name, and basic salary plus two data members more that can calculate expatriation and car allowance. The expatriation allowance is assumed to be 16 percent of the basic salary. The car allowance is assumed to be equal to $150.

Therefore, out of five data members required by the `Officer` and `Manager` class, three of them—code, name, and basic salary—are common. Hierarchical inheritance is the best approach to deal with such situations. The program creates a `Worker` class with three data members: `code`, `name`, and `basicSalary`. The `Officer` class inherits the `Worker` class and gains access to its three protected data members: `code`, `name`, and `basicSalary`. The `Officer` defines only two data members: `houseAllowance` and `childAllowance`. The `Manager` class also inherits the `Worker` class, so it can access its protected members `code`, `name`, and `basicSalary`. The class defines the remaining two data members: `expatAllowance` and `carAllowance`.

Listing 8.6 Program Code in HierarchInherit.cs File

```
using System;
class Worker {
    protected int code,basicSalary;
    protected string name;
    public void setWorker(int x, string y, int z) {
        code=x;
        name=y;
        basicSalary=z;
    }
    public void showWorker() {
        Console.WriteLine("Code: {0}, Name: {1}, Salary: {2}", code, name, basicSalary);
    }
}
class Officer: Worker{
    private float houseAllowance, childAllowance;
```

```
    public void setOfficer(int x, string y, int z) {
        setWorker(x,y,z);
        houseAllowance =(float) basicSalary *6/100;
        childAllowance =250;
    }
    public void showOfficer() {
        showWorker();
        Console.WriteLine("Household allowance: {0}, Child allowance: {1}",
houseAllowance, childAllowance);
    }
}
class Manager: Worker{
    private float expatAllowance, carAllowance;
    public void setManager(int x, string y, int z) {
        setWorker(x,y,z);
        expatAllowance =(float) basicSalary *16/100;
        carAllowance = 150;
    }
    public void showManager() {
        showWorker();
        Console.WriteLine("Expatriation allowance: {0}, Car Allowance: {1}",
expatAllowance,carAllowance);
    }
}
class HierarchInherit {
    static void Main() {
        Worker wkr = new Worker();
        Officer ofcr = new Officer();
        Manager mgr=new Manager();
        wkr.setWorker(101, "Kelly", 5000);
        ofcr.setOfficer(102, "David", 7000);
        mgr.setManager(103, "Caroline", 9000);
        Console.WriteLine("Information of worker is as given below:");
        wkr.showWorker();
        Console.WriteLine("\nInformation of officer is as given below:");
        ofcr.showOfficer();
        Console.WriteLine("\nInformation of manager is as given below:");
        mgr.showManager();
    }
}
```

Output:

```
Information of worker is as given below:
Code: 101, Name: Kelly, Salary: 5000
```

Information of officer is as given below:
Code: 102, Name: David, Salary: 7000
Household allowance: 420, Child allowance: 250

Information of manager is as given below:
Code: 103, Name: Caroline, Salary: 9000
Expatriation allowance: 1440, Car Allowance: 150

Here's what's happening with the preceding program:

- The data members code, name, and basicSalary of the Worker class are declared protected because you want them to be accessed by the Worker class methods as well as by the inheriting classes Officer and Manager.

- The Officer class inherits the Worker class.

- The Manager class also inherits the Worker class.

- The Officer class data members houseAllowance and childAllowance are declared as private because no other class will access them.

- The Manager class data members expatAllowance and carAllowance are declared as private because they will not be accessed from any other class.

- The Worker, Officer, and Manager classes are instantiated by wkr, ofcr, and mgr objects, respectively.

- The setWorker and showWorker methods are invoked on the wkr object to initialize and display the information assigned to the data members code, name, and basicSalary.

- The setOfficer method is invoked on the ofcr object, which in turn invokes the setWorker method to initialize the data members code, name, and basicSalary. The setOfficer method also calculates the household allowance and child allowance.

- The setManager method is invoked on the mgr object, which also invokes the setWorker method to initialize the data members code, name, and basicSalary. In addition, the setManager method calculates the expatriation and car allowance.

- The showOfficer method is invoked on the ofcr object, which in turn invokes the showWorker method to display the code, name, and basic salary. The showOfficer method also displays the household and child allowance values through the houseAllowance and childAllowance data members.

- The showManager method is invoked on the mgr object. The method in turn invokes the showWorker method to display the code, name, and basic salary. After returning from the showWorker method, the showManager method displays the expatriation and car allowance through the expatAllowance and carAllowance data members.

Hybrid Inheritance

Hybrid inheritance is a combination of single, hierarchical, and multilevel inheritances. Here, a class inherits a base class, and the inheriting class may be inherited by another class. This multilevel inheritance can be up to any number of levels. The final derived class is then inherited by two or more classes.

The program `Hybrid.cs`, shown in Listing 8.7, demonstrates hybrid inheritance. The program has four classes: `Worker`, `Officer`, `Manager`, and `Director`. The `Worker` class is inherited by the `Officer` class. The `Officer` class is inherited by the `Manager` and `Director` classes. The following circumstances have led to hybrid inheritance:

- The `Worker` class deals with three data members: `code`, `name`, and `basicSalary`.

- The `Officer` class requires five data members to work with: `code`, `name`, `basicSalary`, `houseAllowance`, and `childAllowance`. If the `Officer` class inherits the `Worker` class, it can access its three members. So the `Officer` class will be left to define only two members: `houseAllowance` and `childAllowance`.

- The `Manager` class requires seven data members: `code`, `name`, `basicSalary`, `houseAllowance`, `childAllowance`, `expatAllowance`, and `carAllowance`. Five of these members match with the `Officer` class. If the `Manager` class inherits the `Officer` class, it needs to define only two data members: `expatAllowance` and `carAllowance`.

- The `Director` class requires seven data members: `code`, `name`, `basicSalary`, `houseAllowance`, `childAllowance`, `medicAllowance`, and `cityAllowance`. Again, five of these members match with the `Officer` class. If the `Director` class inherits the `Officer` class, it needs to define only two data members: `medicAllowance` and `childAllowance`.

The `Hybrid.cs` program (Listing 8.7) defines a `Worker` class with three data members: `code`, `name`, and `basicSalary`. The `Officer` class inherits the `Worker` class and gains access to its three protected data members: `code`, `name`, and `basicSalary`. The `Officer` defines two data members: `houseAllowance` and `childAllowance`. The household allowance is assumed to be 6 percent of the basic salary, and the child allowance is assumed to be equal to $250.

The `Manager` class inherits the `Officer` class and gains access to the five data members that are accessible to the `Officer` class. The `Manager` class defines the remaining two data members: `expatAllowance` and `carAllowance`. The expatriation allowance is assumed to be 16 percent of the basic salary. The car allowance is assumed to be equal to $150.

The Director class also inherits the Officer class and gains access to its five data members. The Director class defines the remaining two data members—medicAllowance and cityAllowance—to represent medical and city allowance, respectively. The medical allowance is assumed to be 25 percent of the basic salary, and the car allowance is assumed to be equal to 10 percent of the basic salary.

Listing 8.7 Program Code in Hybrid.cs File

```
using System;
class Worker {
    protected int code,basicSalary;
    protected string name;
    public void setWorker(int x, string y, int z) {
        code=x;
        name=y;
        basicSalary=z;
    }
    public void showWorker() {
        Console.WriteLine("Code: {0}, Name: {1}, Salary: {2}", code, name, basicSalary);
    }
}
class Officer: Worker{
    private float houseAllowance, childAllowance;
    public void setOfficer(int x, string y, int z) {
        setWorker(x,y,z);
        houseAllowance =(float) basicSalary *6/100;
        childAllowance = 250;
    }
    public void showOfficer() {
        showWorker();
        Console.WriteLine("Household allowance: {0}, Child allowance: {1}",
houseAllowance, childAllowance);
    }
}
class Manager: Officer{
    private float expatAllowance, carAllowance;
    public void setManager(int x, string y, int z) {
        setOfficer(x,y,z);
        expatAllowance =(float) basicSalary *16/100;
        carAllowance = 150;
    }
    public void showManager() {
        showOfficer();
```

```
        Console.WriteLine("Expatriation allowance: {0}, Car Allowance: {1}",
expatAllowance,carAllowance);
    }
}
class Director: Officer{
    private float medicAllowance, cityAllowance;
    public void setDirector(int x, string y, int z) {
        setOfficer(x,y,z);
        medicAllowance =(float) basicSalary *25/100;
        cityAllowance = (float) basicSalary *10/100;
    }
    public void showDirector() {
        showOfficer();
        Console.WriteLine("Medical allowance: {0}, City Allowance: {1}",
medicAllowance,cityAllowance);
    }
}
class Hybrid {
    static void Main() {
        Worker wkr = new Worker();
        Officer ofcr = new Officer();
        Manager mgr=new Manager();
        Director dirc=new Director();
        wkr.setWorker(101, "Kelly", 5000);
        ofcr.setOfficer(102, "David", 7000);
        mgr.setManager(103, "Caroline", 9000);
        dirc.setDirector(104, "John", 9000);
        Console.WriteLine("Information of worker is as given below:");
        wkr.showWorker();
        Console.WriteLine("\nInformation of officer is as given below:");
        ofcr.showOfficer();
        Console.WriteLine("\nInformation of manager is as given below:");
        mgr.showManager();
        Console.WriteLine("\nInformation of director is as given below:");
        dirc.showDirector();
    }
}
```

Output:

```
Information of worker is as given below:
Code: 101, Name: Kelly, Salary: 5000

Information of officer is as given below:
Code: 102, Name: David, Salary: 7000
Household allowance: 420, Child allowance: 250
```

```
Information of manager is as given below:
Code: 103, Name: Caroline, Salary: 9000
Household allowance: 540, Child allowance: 250
Expatriation allowance: 1440, Car Allowance: 150

Information of director is as given below:
Code: 104, Name: John, Salary: 9000
Household allowance: 540, Child allowance: 250
Medical allowance: 2250, City Allowance: 900
```

Here's what's happening with the preceding program:

- The data members code, name, and basicSalary of the Worker class are declared as protected because you want them to be accessible by the Worker class's own methods as well as by other inheriting classes.

- The Officer class inherits the Worker class. Therefore, this class can access the three data members code, name, and basicSalary of the Worker class.

- The Officer class defines two private data members—houseAllowance and childAllowance—to calculate household and child allowance.

- The Manager class inherits the Officer class. Therefore, the class is able to access five data members that are accessible by the Officer class (code, name, basicSalary, houseAllowance, and childAllowance).

- The Manager class defines two data members—expatAllowance and carAllowance— to calculate the expatriation and car allowance.

- The Director class also inherits the Officer class. Like the Manager class, the Director class is able to access these five data members: code, name, basicSalary, houseAllowance, and childAllowance. The Director class defines two data members—medicAllowance and cityAllowance—to calculate the medical and city allowance.

- The Worker, Officer, Manager, and Director classes are instantiated by the wkr, ofcr, mgr, and dirc objects, respectively.

- The setWorker and showWorker methods are invoked on the wkr object to initialize and display the information assigned to the data members code, name, and basicSalary.

- The setOfficer method is invoked on the ofcr object, which in turn invokes the setWorker method to initialize the data members code, name, and basicSalary. The setOfficer method also calculates household and child allowance.

■ The `setManager` method is invoked on the `mgr` object, which invokes the `setOfficer` method. The `setOfficer` method, in turn, invokes the `setWorker` method to initialize the data members `code`, `name`, and `basicSalary`. In addition, the `setManager` method calculates the expatriation and car allowance.

■ The `setDirector` method is invoked on the `dirc` object, which invokes the `setOfficer` method. The `setOfficer` method, in turn, invokes the `setWorker` method to initialize the data members `code`, `name`, and `basicSalary`. In addition, the `setDirector` method calculates the medical and city allowance.

■ The `showOfficer` method is invoked on the `ofcr` object, which in turn invokes the `showWorker` method to display the code, name, and basic salary. The `showOfficer` method also displays the household and child allowance values through the `houseAllowance` and `childAllowance` data members.

■ The `showManager` method is invoked on the `mgr` object. The method in turn invokes the `showOfficer` method to display the code, name, basic salary, household allowance, and child allowance. The method also displays the expatriation and car allowance through the `expatAllowance` and `carAllowance` data members.

■ The `showDirector` method is invoked on the `dirc` object. The method in turn invokes the `showOfficer` method to display the code, name, basic salary, household allowance, and child allowance. The method also displays the medical and city allowance through the `medicAllowance` and `cityAllowance` data members.

METHOD OVERRIDING

When a class inherits another class, it gains access to the public and protected members of the base class. If the inheriting class is not happy with the definition of any of the methods of the base class and redefines it in its class body, the method of the base class is said to be overridden. For method overriding, the derived class needs to redefine the method with the same name, return type, and signature as that of the base class. The method that is to be overridden has to be declared as virtual in the base class. A method is declared as virtual by preceding its declaration with the keyword `virtual`. When a `virtual` method of the base class is overridden (redefined) in the derived class, the overriding method must be preceded by the `override` modifier.

Remember, only a virtual method can be overridden. If you override a nonvirtual method of the base class, a compilation error is generated. If the derived class redefines a method with the same signature as that of the base class's virtual method but doesn't declare it with the `override` modifier, a warning message is displayed asking to use either the `override` keyword for overriding the method or a `new` keyword for hiding the method.

To allow the derived class to override a method of the base class, C# provides two options: virtual methods and abstract methods.

If the derived class does not require any changes in the current definition of the base class method(s), it can access it right away. If the intent of the derived class is to define its own version, it can override the method, writing the desired code and prefixing the method with the keyword override. The overriding method must have the same signature as that of the base class's virtual method. (It must have the same name, number, and type of parameters. In addition, it must return the same type.) Virtual methods enable you to have a different implementation of the same method to serve classes' specific needs.

Note

You cannot declare a private method when using the virtual or override keyword. If you do, you get a compile-time error.

The VirtualMethod1.cs program shown in Listing 8.8 demonstrates method overriding. The program defines two classes—Rect and Triangle—where Triangle inherits the Rect class. The data members x and y of the base class Rect are declared protected to make them accessible in the derived class Triangle. The method Area in the Rect class calculates the area of a rectangle, which is x * y. The Triangle class cannot use the Area method of the Rect class because the formula for the area of a triangle is 1 / 2 * x * y. So the Triangle class defines its own Area method, thereby overriding that of the base class Rect. The object of the Triangle class invokes the Area method of the Triangle class instead of the Rect class.

Note

The base class Rect declares its Area method as virtual to inform the inheriting class(es) that the method is available to override.

Listing 8.8 Program Code in VirtualMethod1.cs File

```
using System;
class Rect
{
    protected float x,y;
    public void SetValues(float a, float b)
    {
```

```
        x=a;
        y=b;
    }
    public virtual float Area()
    {
        return x*y;
    }
}
class Triangle: Rect
{
    public void GetValues()
    {
        Console.Write("Enter base and height : ");
        x = float.Parse(Console.ReadLine());
        y = float.Parse(Console.ReadLine());
    }
    public override float Area()
    {
        return (float)1/2*x*y;
    }
}
class VirtualMethod1
{
    static void Main()
    {
        Rect r = new Rect();
        r.SetValues(5,8);
        Console.WriteLine("Area of rectangle is : {0}", r.Area());
        Triangle t = new Triangle();
        t.GetValues();
        Console.WriteLine("Area of triangle is : {0}", t.Area());
    }
}
```

Output:

```
Area of rectangle is : 40
Enter base and height : 13
17
Area of triangle is : 110.5
```

In the preceding program, there are two classes—Rect and Triangle—where Rect is the base class and Triangle is the derived class. The Rect class contains two methods: SetValues and Area. Out of these two methods, the Area method is declared as virtual, thereby allowing the inheriting class, Triangle, to override it. The Triangle class redefines the Area method in its own way. The Area method in the Triangle class is declared as override to report that it is overriding the Area method of the base class Rect.

The MethodOverriding.cs program shown in Listing 8.9 is another example of method overriding. The program defines two classes: Worker and Officer. The program calculates the household allowance for the worker and the officer. The formula for calculating the household allowance is assumed to be different for both. The household allowance of the worker is assumed to be 6 percent of the basic salary, and that of the officer is assumed to be 8 percent of the basic salary. Therefore, the householdAllowance method of the Worker class, which calculates 6 percent of the basic salary, is overridden in the Officer class to calculate the household allowance as 8 percent of the basic salary.

Listing 8.9 Program Code in MethodOverriding.cs File

```
using System;
class Worker {
    protected int code, basicSalary;
    protected string name;
    private float houseAllowance;
    public void setWorker(int x, string y, int z) {
        code=x;
        name=y;
        basicSalary=z;
    }
    public virtual void householdAllowance()
    {
        houseAllowance =(float) basicSalary *6/100;
        Console.WriteLine("Household allowance: {0}", houseAllowance);
    }
    public void showWorker() {
        Console.WriteLine("Code: {0}, Name: {1}, Salary: {2}", code, name, basicSalary);
    }
}
class Officer: Worker{
    private float houseAllowance;
    public void setOfficer(int x, string y, int z) {
        setWorker(x,y,z);
    }
    public override void householdAllowance()
    {
```

```
            houseAllowance =(float) basicSalary *8/100;
            Console.WriteLine("Household allowance: {0}", houseAllowance);
        }
        public void showOfficer() {
            showWorker();
        }
    }
    class MethodOverriding {
        static void Main() {
            Worker wkr = new Worker();
            Officer ofcr = new Officer();
            wkr.setWorker(101, "Kelly", 5000);
            ofcr.setOfficer(102, "David", 7000);
            Console.WriteLine("Information of worker is as given below:");
            wkr.showWorker();
            wkr.householdAllowance();
            Console.WriteLine("\nInformation of officer is as given below:");
            ofcr.showOfficer();
            ofcr.householdAllowance();
        }
    }
```

Output:

```
Information of worker is as given below:
Code: 101, Name: Kelly, Salary: 5000
Household allowance: 300

Information of officer is as given below:
Code: 102, Name: David, Salary: 7000
Household allowance: 560
```

Here's what's happening with the preceding program:

- The Worker and Officer classes are instantiated as the wkr and ofcr objects, respectively.

- The setWorker method on the wkr object is invoked to initialize the data members code, name, and basicSalary (for the wkr object).

- The setOfficer method on the ofcr object is invoked, which in turn invokes the setWorker method of the base class to initialize the data members code, name, and basicSalary (for the ofcr object).

- The householdAllowance method is invoked on the wkr object to calculate the household allowance for the worker, which is assumed to be 6 percent of the basic salary.

- The householdAllowance method is invoked on the ofcr object to calculate the household allowance for the officer, which is assumed to be 8 percent of the basic salary. The ofcr object finds two householdAllowance methods: one in the base class Worker, and the other in the derived class Officer. Because the householdAllowance method of the Officer class overrides that of the Worker class, the ofcr object invokes only the overriding method.

- The showWorker method on the wkr object is called to display the data assigned to the code, name, and basicSalary data members.

- The showOfficer method on the ofcr object is called, which in turn calls the showWorker method of the Worker class to display the data assigned to the code, name, and basicSalary data members.

The preceding program shows method overriding in single inheritance. You can also perform method overriding in multilevel inheritance. The MultiOverride.cs program shown in Listing 8.10 demonstrates method overriding in multilevel inheritance. The program defines three classes: Worker, Officer, and Manager. The Worker class defines four data members: code, name, basicSalary, and houseAllowance. The Worker class is inherited by the Officer class, which in turn is inherited by the Manager class. The household allowance for the worker is assumed to be 6 percent of the basic salary, whereas that of the officer and manager is assumed to be 8 percent and 10 percent of the basic salary, respectively. The householdAllowance method of the Worker class calculates the household allowance as 6 percent of its basic salary. The householdAllowance method is overridden in the Officer and Manager classes to calculate the household allowance as 8 percent and 10 percent of basic salary, respectively.

Listing 8.10 Program Code in MultiOverride.cs File

```
using System;
class Worker {
    protected int code, basicSalary;
    protected float houseAllowance;
    protected string name;
    public Worker(int x, string y, int z) {
        code=x;
        name=y;
        basicSalary=z;
    }
    public void showWorker() {
        Console.WriteLine("Code: {0}, Name: {1}, Salary: {2}", code, name, basicSalary);
    }
```

```
    public virtual void householdAllowance() {
        houseAllowance =(float) basicSalary *6/100;
        Console.WriteLine("Household allowance: {0}", houseAllowance);
    }
}
class Officer: Worker{
    public Officer(int x, string y, int z) :base(x,y,z) {}
    public override void householdAllowance() {
        houseAllowance =(float) basicSalary *8/100;
        Console.WriteLine("Household allowance: {0}", houseAllowance);
    }
}
class Manager: Officer{
    public Manager(int x, string y, int z) :base(x,y,z) {}
    public override void householdAllowance() {
        houseAllowance =(float) basicSalary *10/100;
        Console.WriteLine("Household allowance: {0}", houseAllowance);
    }
}
class MultiOverride{
    static void Main() {
        Worker wkr = new Worker(101, "Kelly", 5000);
        Officer ofcr = new Officer(102, "David", 7000);
        Manager mgr=new Manager(103, "Caroline", 9000);
        Console.WriteLine("Information of worker is as given below:");
        wkr.showWorker();
        wkr.householdAllowance();
        Console.WriteLine("\nInformation of officer is as given below:");
        ofcr.showWorker();
        ofcr.householdAllowance();
        Console.WriteLine("\nInformation of manager is as given below:");
        mgr.showWorker();
        mgr.householdAllowance();
    }
}
```

Output:

```
Information of worker is as given below:
Code: 101, Name: Kelly, Salary: 5000
Household allowance: 300

Information of officer is as given below:
Code: 102, Name: David, Salary: 7000
Household allowance: 560
```

```
Information of manager is as given below:
Code: 103, Name: Caroline, Salary: 9000
Household allowance: 900
```

You can see that the household allowance is calculated through the `householdAllowance` method that exists in each of the classes.

Is there any way to stop a class from inheriting a specific class? Or is there any way to stop a class from overriding any method of the base class? Yes! Read on.

SEALED CLASS AND METHODS

C# allows classes and methods to be declared as sealed. A sealed class cannot be inherited, whereas a sealed method cannot be overridden.

Example:

```
sealed class A
{
    // body of the class A
}
class B:A // A compilation error is generated
{
    // body of class B
}
```

In the preceding code sample, a compilation error generates when class `B` tries to inherit sealed class `A`.

The important classes or methods with essential and critical code that you don't want to be overridden or changed are marked as sealed.

```
class A
{
    public sealed override void ClassAMethod()
    {
        // body of method
    }
}
class B:A
{
    public override void ClassAMethod() // A compilation error is generated
    {
    }
}
```

If you want to use the sealed keyword on a method or property, it must override a base class method.

The SealedExample.cs program shown in Listing 8.11 demonstrates a sealed class and methods. The program consists of three classes: Worker, Officer, and Manager. It accepts the code, name, and basic salary of the worker, officer, and manager and displays them along with household allowance, which is assumed to be some percentage of the basic salary.

In the program, the Officer class is declared as sealed, making it nonderivable. Also, its householdAllowance method is declared as sealed, making it impossible to override.

Listing 8.11 Program Code in SealedExample.cs File

```
using System;
class Worker {
    protected int code, basicSalary;
    protected float houseAllowance;
    protected string name;
    public Worker(int x, string y, int z) {
        code=x;
        name=y;
        basicSalary=z;
    }
    public void showWorker() {
        Console.WriteLine("Code: {0}, Name: {1}, Salary: {2}", code, name, basicSalary);
    }
    public virtual void householdAllowance() {
        houseAllowance=(float) basicSalary *6/100;
        Console.WriteLine("Household allowance: {0}", houseAllowance);
    }
}
sealed class Officer: Worker{
    public Officer(int x, string y, int z) :base(x,y,z) {}
    public sealed override void householdAllowance() {
        houseAllowance =(float) basicSalary *8/100;
        Console.WriteLine("Household allowance: {0}", houseAllowance);
    }
}
class Manager: Worker{
    public Manager(int x, string y, int z) :base(x,y,z) {}
}
```

```
class SealedExample{
    static void Main() {
        Worker wkr = new Worker(101, "Kelly", 5000);
        Officer ofcr = new Officer(102, "David", 7000);
        Manager mgr =new Manager(103, "Caroline", 9000);
        Console.WriteLine("Information of worker is as given below:");
        wkr.showWorker();
        wkr.householdAllowance();
        Console.WriteLine("\nInformation of officer is as given below:");
        ofcr.showWorker();
        ofcr.householdAllowance();
        Console.WriteLine("\nInformation of manager is as given below:");
        mgr.showWorker();
        mgr.householdAllowance();
    }
}
```

Output:

```
Information of worker is as given below:
Code: 101, Name: Kelly, Salary: 5000
Household allowance: 300

Information of officer is as given below:
Code: 102, Name: David, Salary: 7000
Household allowance: 560

Information of manager is as given below:
Code: 103, Name: Caroline, Salary: 9000
Household allowance: 540
```

Because the Officer class is declared as sealed, the Manager class cannot derive it. Also, because the householdAllowance method of the Officer class is declared sealed, you get a compilation error if any class tries to override it. The Worker class defines four data members: code, name, basicSalary, and houseAllowance. The Worker class is inherited by the Officer class, which in turn is declared as sealed. The household allowance for the worker, officer, and manager is assumed to be 6 percent, 8 percent, and 6 percent of the basic salary, respectively. The Manager class inherits the Worker class instead of the Officer class because the Officer class is sealed and cannot be inherited.

METHOD HIDING

C# not only supports method overriding, but also method hiding. Method hiding involves hiding the base class methods behind the derived class methods that have the same signature as that of the base class. Method hiding is used if you expect some collision of method names (methods have the same name, return type, and signature) in a base and derived class and you want the methods of the derived class in that case. You must declare a hiding method using the new keyword.

You might be wondering about the difference between method overriding and method hiding. In *method overriding*, the parent class exposes its methods that can be overridden by declaring them as virtual. The derived class can override such virtual methods by using the override keyword. In *method hiding*, any of the base class's methods can be overridden in the derived class by using the new keyword. In other words, even if the base class method(s) is not declared as virtual, it can be overridden in the derived class through method hiding.

The MethodHiding.cs program shown in Listing 8.12 demonstrates method hiding by overriding the base class method. The program defines two classes: Worker and Officer. The classes take the code, name, and salary of the worker and officer and print the entered information along with the household allowance. The household allowance of the worker and officer is assumed to be 6 percent and 8 percent of the basic salary, respectively. The householdAllowance method in the base class Worker calculates the household allowance for the worker, and the method is overridden in the Officer class by using the new keyword.

Listing 8.12 Program Code in MethodHiding.cs File

```
using System;
class Worker {
    protected int code, basicSalary;
    protected string name;
    private float houseAllowance;
    public void setWorker(int x, string y, int z) {
        code=x;
        name=y;
        basicSalary=z;
    }
    public void householdAllowance()
    {
        houseAllowance =(float) basicSalary *6/100;
        Console.WriteLine("Household allowance: {0}", houseAllowance);
    }
    public void showWorker() {
        Console.WriteLine("Code: {0}, Name: {1}, Salary: {2}", code, name, basicSalary);
    }
}
```

```
class Officer: Worker{
    private float houseAllowance;
    public void setOfficer(int x, string y, int z) {
        setWorker(x,y,z);
    }
    public new void householdAllowance()
    {
        houseAllowance =(float) basicSalary *8/100;
        Console.WriteLine("Household allowance: {0}", houseAllowance);
    }
    public void showOfficer() {
        showWorker();
    }
}
class MethodHiding {
    static void Main() {
        Worker wkr = new Worker();
        Officer ofcr = new Officer();
        wkr.setWorker(101, "Kelly", 5000);
        ofcr.setOfficer(102, "David", 7000);
        Console.WriteLine("Information of worker is as given below:");
        wkr.showWorker();
        wkr.householdAllowance();
        Console.WriteLine("\nInformation of officer is as given below:");
        ofcr.showOfficer();
        ofcr.householdAllowance();
    }
}
```

Output:

```
Information of worker is as given below:
Code: 101, Name: Kelly, Salary: 5000
Household allowance: 300

Information of officer is as given below:
Code: 102, Name: David, Salary: 7000
Household allowance: 560
```

You can see that, by using the new keyword, the householdAllowance method of the base class is hidden from the derived class Officer object, ofcr. The ofcr object consequently invokes the householdAllowance method defined in the Officer object. The output of this program is the same as that of the MethodOverriding.cs program (see Listing 8.9).

Abstract Classes

In C#, you can define abstract classes as well as abstract methods. An *abstract class* is a base class that cannot be instantiated and is provided just to offer an outline for subclasses. An abstract class can be used only through overriding. The abstract methods are declared inside an abstract class and are used to dictate to the subclass the type of members it must contain. The abstract members in the abstract class are just declared, not implemented. The abstract members are implemented in the derived class. A class that derives an abstract class and does not implement the abstract methods results in a compilation error. A class containing even a single abstract method is considered an abstract class. An abstract class can also contain methods with complete implementation (nonabstract methods), besides abstract methods.

Example:

```
abstract class Shape
{
    protected float x,y;
    public void SetValues(float a, float b)
    {
        x=a;
        y=b;
    }
    public abstract float Area();
}
```

In the preceding example, the abstract class Shape is defined, which contains a single abstract method, Area. The class that derives the Shape class must define the Area method. The constraint is not applicable to the nonabstract method of the class SetValues. The deriving class can readily use the SetValues method. You can see in the preceding example that the abstract classes are declared using the abstract modifier in the class declaration. Also, the abstract member functions and properties are declared using the abstract keyword.

An abstract class may not contain even a single abstract member. Also, you can have an abstract class only with nonabstract members, as shown in the following example:

```
abstract class Shape
{
    protected float x,y;
    public void SetValues(float a, float b)
    {
        x=a;
        y=b;
    }
}
```

Note

When implementing abstract members in a derived class, you must use the `override` modifier.

The `AbstractExample.cs` file shown in Listing 8.13 demonstrates how an abstract method of an abstract class is implemented in the derived classes. The program defines the abstract class `Shape`, which contains the abstract method `Area`. The `Shape` class is inherited by two classes: `Rect` and `Triangle`. `Rect` and `Triangle` implement the abstract method `Area` of the `Shape` class.

Listing 8.13 Program Code in AbstractExample.cs File

```
using System;
abstract class Shape
{
    protected float x,y;
    public void SetValues(float a, float b)
    {
        x=a;
        y=b;
    }
    public abstract float Area();
}
class Rect: Shape
{
    public void GetRect(float a, float b)
    {
        SetValues(a,b);
    }
    public override float Area()
    {
        return (float) x*y;
    }
}
class Triangle: Shape
{
    public void GetTrig()
    {
        Console.Write("Enter base and height : ");
        x = float.Parse(Console.ReadLine());
        y = float.Parse(Console.ReadLine());
    }
```

```
    public override float Area()
    {
        return (float)1/2*x*y;
    }
}
class AbstractExample
{
    static void Main()
    {
        Rect r=new Rect();
        Triangle t=new Triangle();
        r.GetRect(5,8);
        t.GetTrig();
        Console.WriteLine("Area of rectangle is : {0}", r.Area());
        Console.WriteLine("Area of triangle is : {0}", t.Area());
    }
}
```

Output:

```
Enter base and height : 17
13
Area of rectangle is : 40
Area of triangle is : 110.5
```

In the preceding example, you see that the abstract class Shape contains two methods: SetValues and Area. SetValues is a nonabstract method, so it is defined (implemented); Area is an abstract method that does not contain implementation.

Two classes, Rect and Triangle, are derived from the Shape class, and the Area method is implemented in these classes. Both Rect and Triangle can implement the Area method as per their requirement. Within the Main method, Rect and Triangle are instantiated to create objects r and t, respectively. The GetRect method is called on object r, passing values 5 and 8 to it as parameters. The GetRect method in turn invokes the nonabstract method SetValues of the Shape class to initialize data members x and y. Similarly, the GetTrig method is called on object r that prompts the user to enter values for the data members x and y. Finally, the Area method is called on objects r and t to calculate the area of a rectangle and triangle, respectively.

ABSTRACT PROPERTIES

Not only can you have abstract methods in an abstract class, but you can have abstract properties, too. As with abstract methods, the abstract properties must be implemented by the deriving class. The AbstractProperties.cs program shown in Listing 8.14

demonstrates use of abstract properties. The program defines an abstract class called Shape that contains the abstract properties length and breadth. The classes Rect and Triangle inherit the Shape class and therefore implement the two abstract properties: length and breadth.

Listing 8.14 Program Code in AbstractProperties.cs File

```
using System;
abstract class Shape
{
   protected float l,b;
   public abstract float length
   {
      get;
      set;
   }
   public abstract float breadth
   {
      get;
      set;
   }
}
class Rect:Shape
{
   public override float length
   {
      get
      {
         return l;
      }
      set
      {
         l = value;
      }
   }
   public override float breadth
   {
      get
      {
         return b;
      }
```

```
        set
        {
            b = value;
        }
    }
    public float Area()
    {
        return l*b;
    }
}
class Triangle:Shape
{
    public override float length
    {
        get
        {
            return l;
        }
        set
        {
            l = value;
        }
    }
    public override float breadth
    {
        get
        {
            return b;
        }
        set
        {
            b = value;
        }
    }
    public float Area()
    {
        return (float) 1/2*l*b;
    }
}
class AbstractProperties
{
    static void Main()
    {
        Rect r=new Rect();
        Triangle t=new Triangle();
```

```
        r.length=5;
        r.breadth=8;
        t.length=5;
        t.breadth=8;
        Console.WriteLine("Area of rectangle is : {0}", r.Area());
        Console.WriteLine("Area of triangle is : {0}", t.Area());
    }
}
```

Output:

```
Area of rectangle is : 40
Area of triangle is : 20
```

You can see that the get/set properties for the data members l and b are defined in the derived classes Rect and Triangle. The difference between abstract and virtual members is that the abstract member is not implemented in the base class and must be implemented in derived classes. In contrast, a member defined as virtual must be implemented in the base class and may be overridden in the derived class if you prefer a different action.

POLYMORPHISM

One of the fundamental concepts of object-oriented programming is polymorphism. The term *polymorphism* means having multiple forms (determining which version of the method to call depending on the type of object being referred by the reference at runtime). It is the virtual methods that enable calling of different versions of the same method depending on the context; therefore, to implement polymorphism, virtual methods are used. Specifically, polymorphism falls in two categories:

- **Compile time polymorphism**—Compile time polymorphism is also known as *early binding* and *static polymorphism*. Method overloading and operator overloading are two techniques of implementing compile time polymorphism. Recall from Chapter 7, "Classes and Objects," that method overloading involves defining more than one method with the same name but a different signature. Such methods perform a different task on the various input parameters. You will be learning about operator overloading in Chapter 10, "Operator Overloading."

Note

Compile time polymorphism is known as *early binding* because the compiler has the knowledge of different overloaded method names at compile time. The compiler also knows beforehand which method must be executed when called.

■ **Runtime polymorphism**—Runtime polymorphism is also known as *late binding* and *dynamic polymorphism*. Abstract classes and virtual functions (method overriding) are the two techniques of implementing runtime polymorphism. You read about abstract classes and method overriding earlier in this chapter. You saw how a derived class overrides a base class method to suit its needs. Recall that the methods of the base class that are supposed to be overridden are declared as virtual methods. The virtual methods, therefore, can be implemented in different ways in the derived classes. The call to these functions is decided at runtime.

The program `Polymorph.cs`, shown in Listing 8.15, demonstrates polymorphism. The program defines a class A that has a virtual method called `disp`. The virtual method is overridden by the inheriting classes B, C, and D. Each class implements the `disp` method in its own way.

Listing 8.15 Program Code in Polymorph.cs File

```
using System;
class A
{
    public virtual void disp() { Console.WriteLine("A::disp()"); }
}
class B : A
{
    public override void disp() { Console.WriteLine("B::disp()"); }
}
class C : A
{
    public override void disp() { Console.WriteLine("C::disp()"); }
}
class D : A
{
    public void show() { Console.WriteLine("D::show()"); }
}
class Polymorph
{
    static void Main(string[] args)
    {
        A a = new A();
        B b = new B();
        C c = new C();
        D d = new D();
        a.disp();
        b.disp();
```

```
            c.disp();
            d.show();
            a=b;
            a.disp();
            a=c;
            a.disp();
            a=d;
            a.disp();
        }
    }
```

Output:

```
A::disp()
B::disp()
C::disp()
D::show()
B::disp()
C::disp()
A::disp()
```

You can see in the preceding program that class A is inherited by classes B, C, and D. Class A declares the virtual method disp, which is overridden by classes B and C. Class D does not define the disp method. The first four outputs, A::disp(), B::disp(), C::disp(), and D::show(), appear after calling the disp method on objects a, b, and c and the show method on object d. Thereafter, you see that object a is set to refer to object b. Object a is allowed to refer to object b without complaints from the compiler because class B inherits class A. The statement a.disp() makes the runtime to call the disp method of class B for the simple reason that it is declared as a virtual method in the base class A, displaying B::disp() on the screen. Again, the object a is set to refer to object c and calls the c.disp() method. The runtime finds the overriding method in class C, so it invokes it, displaying C::disp() on the screen. Finally, object a is set to refer to object d. But because class D does not define the method disp, the disp method that is defined in class A is called, displaying A::disp() on the screen.

To conclude, C# determines the version of the method to call based on the type of the object being referred to by the reference at runtime. The type of the object being referred to, not the type of the reference, determines the version of the virtual method to be executed. Therefore, different versions of the virtual method can be executed by setting the base class reference to refer at different derived objects.

SUMMARY

In this chapter, you learned to use single inheritance and protected members and how to call base class constructors. You read about the different types of inheritance, including multilevel, hierarchical, and hybrid. You also read about method overriding, virtual methods, sealed class, and method hiding. You saw how to use abstract classes and abstract properties and implement polymorphism.

The next chapter is focused on interfaces. You will learn to define, extend, and implement an interface. You will also learn to implement an explicit interface.

CHAPTER 9

INTERFACES

This chapter's topics include the following:

- Invoking interface members at the object level
- Implementing multiple interfaces
- Handling ambiguity when implementing multiple interfaces
- Implementing an interface explicitly
- Verifying interface implementation
- Implementing a multilevel interface
- Implementing interface properties
- Understanding how a structure implements an interface
- Passing an interface as a parameter
- Returning an interface

An interface appears like a class that contains only declarations of methods, properties, indexers, and events. It doesn't contain data members—only the signatures of its members. It cannot declare modifiers for its members. The class(es) that inherit the interface must implement each of the declared interface members. Therefore, an interface simply defines a behavior that the inheriting class or structure can support.

You might be wondering what the difference is between interface types and abstract classes. An *abstract class*, in addition to the abstract methods, can define nonabstract methods, any number of constructors, data members, and so on. An *interface*, on the other hand, can contain only abstract member definitions. Following are the characteristics of interfaces:

- Interfaces are defined using the C# interface keyword.

- Interfaces never specify a base class.

- Access specifiers are not used for interface members because all interface members are implicitly public and abstract.

- Interfaces cannot have data members or constructors.

- An interface can't be instantiated directly. Any class or struct that implements an interface must define the method(s) with the matching signatures, as specified in the interface. Also, the defined method(s) must be declared public and nonstatic.

- A class or struct that implements an interface must provide an implementation for all the interface members.

- If a base class implements an interface, all the derived classes inherit that implementation. However, the derived class can reimplement the interface members instead of using the base class implementation.

- A class can inherit only one base class. In other words, multiple inheritance is not allowed in C#. But a class can inherit any number of discrete interfaces. A common naming convention is to prefix all interface names with a capital *I*.

Note

When a class inherits from one or more interfaces, the class is *implementing* those interfaces.

INVOKING INTERFACE MEMBERS AT THE OBJECT LEVEL

When a class supports an interface, you can invoke the members directly from the object level. The Interface1.cs program shown in Listing 9.1 demonstrates how an interface is implemented and how the implemented methods are invoked through the class objects. The program defines an interface called ICalcArea that declares two methods: setVal and getArea. The rect class implements the ICalcArea interface and therefore defines the two methods.

Listing 9.1 Program Code in Interface1.cs File

```
interface ICalcArea
{
    void setVal(float x, float y);
    float getArea();
}
```

```
class rect : ICalcArea
{
    float l,b;
    public void setVal(float x, float y)
    {
        l=x;
        b=y;
    }
    public float getArea()
    {
        return l*b;
    }
    public static void Main()
    {
        rect r = new rect();
        r.setVal(10.0f, 20.0f);
        System.Console.WriteLine("Area of rectangle is {0}", r.getArea());
    }
}
```

Output:

```
Area of rectangle is 200
```

Interfaces ensure that the deriving classes implement the methods and properties declared in the interface. ICalcArea in the preceding code has a single method named getArea. Because the interface specifies only the signature of methods, the getArea method does not have an implementation but ends with a semicolon(;). The inheriting class rect implements the getArea method. The rect class is instantiated by creating an object named r. The implemented setVal method is called through the object r to initialize the data members l and b. Finally, the getArea method is called on object r to display the area of a rectangle.

The method implementation must have the same signature, parameters, and method name as defined in the ICalcArea interface; otherwise, you get a compiler error.

Note

The class or struct that inherits an interface must implement all the interface members, or it results in a compiler error.

Here's one quick example of implementing of interface. The SingleInterface.cs program shown in Listing 9.2 demonstrates a single interface implementation. *Single interface* here means that there is a single interface (and no inheritance is applied on this interface). The interface is named IRectInterface, and it declares a single method, dispArea.

Listing 9.2 Program Code in SingleInterface.cs File

```
interface IRectInterface
{
  void dispArea();
}
class SingleInterface : IRectInterface
{
    public void dispArea()
    {
        System.Console.WriteLine("Method implemented of IRectInterface");
    }
    public static void Main()
    {
        SingleInterface singint = new SingleInterface();
        singint.dispArea();
    }
}
```

Output:

```
Method implemented of IRectInterface
```

You can see that the class SingleInterface implements the IRectInterface interface and defines the dispArea method. An object of the SingleInterface class is created named singint, and the dispArea method is invoked on the singint object to display the message Method implemented of IRectInterface.

As mentioned at the beginning of the chapter, C# does not support multiple inheritance, but it does support multiple interfaces.

IMPLEMENTING MULTIPLE INTERFACES

You can force a class to support different behaviors by making it implement more than one interface. Just as in the case of a single interface, in a multiple interface, the implementing class must implement all the members of the interfaces.

The MultipleInterface.cs program shown in Listing 9.3 demonstrates implementation of multiple interfaces. The program defines two interfaces: IRectInterface and ITriangleInterface. The IRectInterface interface declares a method called dispArea, and the ITriangleInterface interface declares a method called dispTrg. The MultipleInterface class implements both interfaces and therefore implements both dispArea and dispTrg.

Listing 9.3 Program Code in MultipleInterface.cs File

```
interface IRectInterface
{
    void dispArea();
}
interface ITriangleInterface
{
    void dispTrg();
}
class MultipleInterface : IRectInterface, ITriangleInterface
{
    public void dispArea()
    {
        System.Console.WriteLine("Method implemented of IRectInterface");
    }
    public void dispTrg()
    {
        System.Console.WriteLine("Method implemented of ITriangleInterface");
    }
    public static void Main()
    {
      MultipleInterface multint = new MultipleInterface();
      multint.dispArea();
      multint.dispTrg();
    }
}
```

Output:

```
Method implemented of IRectInterface
Method implemented of ITriangleInterface
```

MultipleInterface is instantiated by creating an object called multint. The two methods—dispArea and dispTrg—that the class implements are invoked through the multint object to display the respective messages.

HANDLING AMBIGUITY WHEN IMPLEMENTING MULTIPLE INTERFACES

While implementing multiple interfaces, ambiguity might occur if an interface declares method(s) that have the same signatures as existing class members or other interface members. The MultiInterfaceAmbig.cs program shown in Listing 9.4 demonstrates the situation that leads to ambiguity while implementing multiple interfaces. The program defines two interfaces: IRectInterface and ITriangleInterface. Both interfaces declare a method, dispArea, with the matching signature. The MultiInterfaceAmbig class implements both interfaces. Because the interfaces declare the method with the same method name, an ambiguity arises: the MultiInterfaceAmbig class has two methods with the same name and signature to implement. The MultiInterfaceAmbig class can implement only one method, not two.

Listing 9.4 Program Code in MultiInterfaceAmbig.cs File

```
interface IRectInterface
{
    void dispArea();
}
interface ITriangleInterface
{
    void dispArea();
}
class MultiInterfaceAmbig : IRectInterface, ITriangleInterface
{
    public void dispArea()
    {
        System.Console.WriteLine("Method implemented of IRectInterface");
    }
    public static void Main()
    {
        MultiInterfaceAmbig multint = new MultiInterfaceAmbig();
        multint.dispArea();
    }
}
```

Output:

```
Method implemented of IRectInterface
```

You can see that the MultiInterfaceAmbig class implements the dispArea method only once. (In other words, it implements the member of both interfaces by this single implementation.) Remember, you can invoke the dispArea method shown earlier through either interface or through the `MultiInterfaceAmbig` class. The implementation of the `dispArea` method shown earlier works fine if you want both interfaces to display the same result or output. To display different results from the two `dispArea` methods, you need to resolve the ambiguity first.

One solution to resolve the ambiguity in implementing multiple interfaces is explicit interface implementation. A class that implements an interface can explicitly implement a member of that interface. Read on to learn how.

IMPLEMENTING AN INTERFACE EXPLICITLY

Explicit interface implementation enables a class to implement multiple interfaces that have the same method names and signatures. It avoids any ambiguity that might arise while implementing the similar methods. To explicitly implement an interface member, just use its fully qualified name in the declaration. A fully qualified interface name has the following format:

```
InterfaceName.MemberName
```

When an interface method is explicitly implemented, it is no longer visible as a public member of the class. The explicit implementation of a method hides it from the class. The only way to access such methods is through the interface.

The `MultiInterfaceExplicit.cs` program shown in Listing 9.5 demonstrates implementing of the interface members explicitly. The program defines two interfaces: `IRectInterface` and `ITriangleInterface`. Both interfaces declare a method, `dispArea`, with the same signature. The `MultiInterfaceExplicit` class implements both `IRectInterface` and `ITriangleInterface`. To avoid ambiguity, one of the `dispArea` methods is explicitly implemented from the `IRectInterface` interface.

Listing 9.5 Program Code in MultiInterfaceExplicit.cs File

```
interface IRectInterface
{
    void dispArea();
}
interface ITriangleInterface
{
    void dispArea();
}
class MultiInterfaceExplicit : IRectInterface, ITriangleInterface
{
    void IRectInterface.dispArea()
    {
```

```
            System.Console.WriteLine("Method implemented of IRectInterface");
    }
    public void dispArea()
    {
            System.Console.WriteLine("Method implemented of ITriangleInterface");
    }
    public static void Main()
    {
      MultiInterfaceExplicit multint = new MultiInterfaceExplicit();
      IRectInterface rectint = (IRectInterface)multint;
      ITriangleInterface trgint = (ITriangleInterface)multint;
      rectint.dispArea();
      trgint.dispArea();
      multint.dispArea();
    }
}
```

Output:

```
Method implemented of IRectInterface
Method implemented of ITriangleInterface
Method implemented of ITriangleInterface
```

You can see that the class `MultiInterfaceExplicit` explicitly implements the interface member `dispArea`. For explicit implementation, the `dispArea` method is defined with its fully qualified name (in `InterfaceName.MemberName` syntax). The explicitly implemented method, `dispArea`, is accessed through the interface instance `rectint`. On the other hand, the `dispArea` method that is implemented without using the fully qualified name can be accessed through the `ITriangleInterface` interface as well as through the object of the `MultiInterfaceExplicit` class.

Note

An interface member that is explicitly implemented can be accessed only through an instance of the interface, not from a class instance.

In the preceding program, out of the two methods, one was explicitly implemented and the other was not. Now you'll modify the preceding program to implement methods of both interfaces explicitly. The `MultipleInterfaceExp.cs` program shown in Listing 9.6 demonstrates explicit implementation of methods for two interfaces. The program defines two interfaces called `IRectInterface` and `ITriangleInterface`. Both interfaces declare a method called `dispArea`. The `MultipleInterfaceExp` class implements both interfaces. The class defines two float data members: `length` and `breadth`. To initialize the data members, a parameterized constructor is defined in the class.

Both methods are explicitly implemented. One dispArea method is explicitly implemented from the IRectInterface interface, and the other is explicitly implemented from the ITriangleInterface interface.

Listing 9.6 Program Code in MultipleInterfaceExp.cs File

```
interface IRectInterface
{
    void dispArea();
}
interface ITriangleInterface
{
    void dispArea();
}
class MultipleInterfaceExp : IRectInterface, ITriangleInterface
{
    float length, breadth;
    MultipleInterfaceExp(float l, float b)
    {
        length=l;
        breadth=b;
    }
    void IRectInterface.dispArea()
    {
        System.Console.WriteLine("Area of rectangle is {0}",length*breadth);
    }
    void ITriangleInterface.dispArea()
    {
        System.Console.WriteLine("Area of triangle is {0}",
(float)1/2*length*breadth);
    }
    public static void Main()
    {
        MultipleInterfaceExp multint = new MultipleInterfaceExp(10.0f, 20.0f);
        IRectInterface rectint = (IRectInterface)multint;
        ITriangleInterface trgint = (ITriangleInterface)multint;
        rectint.dispArea();
        trgint.dispArea();
    }
}
```

Output:

```
Area of rectangle is 200
Area of triangle is 100
```

Because both interface methods are implemented explicitly, they will not be publicly visible to the class and therefore cannot be invoked from the class object but through interfaces. Instances of the IRectInterface and ITriangleInterface interfaces are created and named rectint and trgint. The explicitly implemented method dispArea is invoked through the two interface instances rectint and trgint to calculate and display the area of a rectangle and triangle, respectively.

VERIFYING INTERFACE IMPLEMENTATION

While calling an interface's method through an object, how can you be sure that the class implements the interface? If the class has implemented the interface method, it is fine; otherwise, you get exceptions. There are two ways to ensure that the class supports the said interfaces. The first is by using the as keyword, and the second is by using the is keyword.

Using the as Keyword

You can use the as keyword to determine if the given class supports the given interface. If the object can be treated as the specified interface, a valid reference to the interface is returned, or you get a null reference. The following statements make it clearer:

```
ClassName class_object = new ClassName();
Interface1 interfceObj = class_object as Interface1;
if(interfceObj != null)
  interfceObj.methodName();
```

In the preceding statements, you see that class_object is an object of the ClassName class. If the ClassName has implemented Interface1, the as keyword returns a valid reference to the interface. If the reference to the interface is not null, it is verified that the ClassName has implemented Interface1, and you can go ahead and access the implemented method, methodName.

Using the is Keyword

You can use the is keyword for an implemented interface. The keyword returns false if the class is not compatible with the specified interface. Look at the following example:

```
ClassName class_object = new ClassName();
if(class_object is Interface1)
  class_object.methodName();
```

In the preceding statements, you see that class_object is an object of the ClassName class. If ClassName has implemented Interface1, the is keyword returns true. The true value from the is keyword confirms that ClassName has implemented Interface1, and you can go ahead and access the implemented method, methodName.

The CheckSupport.cs program shown in Listing 9.7 demonstrates how to ensure whether a class implements the said interfaces. The program defines two interfaces: IRectInterface and ITriangleInterface. IRectInterface declares the dispArea method. Similarly, ITriangleInterface declares the dispTrg method. The CheckSupport class implements both interfaces. In other words, the class implements both methods that are declared in the interfaces dispArea and dispTrg. Using the as and is keywords, a confirmation is made whether the class implements the interfaces. Once confirmed that the class implements the said interfaces, the implemented methods are invoked.

Listing 9.7 Program Code in CheckSupport.cs File

```
interface IRectInterface
{
    void dispArea();
}
interface ITriangleInterface
{
    void dispTrg();
}
class CheckSupport : IRectInterface, ITriangleInterface
{
    float length, breadth;
    CheckSupport(float l, float b)
    {
        length=l;
        breadth=b;
    }
    public void dispArea()
    {
        System.Console.WriteLine("Area of rectangle is {0}",length*breadth);
    }
    public void dispTrg()
    {
        System.Console.WriteLine("Area of triangle is {0}", (float)1/2
*length*breadth);
    }
    public static void Main()
    {
```

```
         CheckSupport chksprt = new CheckSupport(10.0f, 20.0f);
         IRectInterface rectint = chksprt as IRectInterface;
         if(rectint != null)
            rectint.dispArea();
         if(chksprt is ITriangleInterface)
            chksprt.dispTrg();
      }
}
```

Output:

```
Area of rectangle is 200
Area of triangle is 100
```

You can see that the CheckSupport class is instantiated by creating the chksprt object. Values 10.0f and 20.0f that are passed while creating the chksprt object initialize the object's data members length and breadth. Because the CheckSupport class implements both IRectInterface and ITriangleInterface, the as keyword returns a valid reference to the IRectInterface interface. Using the IRectInterface reference, the dispArea method is called to display the area of the rectangle.

Similarly, the is keyword returns true to confirm that the CheckSupport class supports the ITriangleInterface interface. Using the chksprt object, the dispTrg method is called to display the area of the triangle.

IMPLEMENTING A MULTILEVEL INTERFACE

Interfaces can also inherit other interfaces. The main thing to remember is that if an interface inherits another interface, any implementing class or struct must implement every interface member in the entire inheritance chain. The MultilevelInterface.cs program shown in Listing 9.8 demonstrates implementing a multilevel interface. The program defines two interfaces—IRectInterface and ITriangleInterface—where the later interface inherits the former interface. Each interface declares a single method. IRectInterface declares a method called dispArea, and ITriangleInterface declares the dispTrg method. The class MultilevelInterface implements ITriangleInterface. Consequently, the MultilevelInterface class is compelled to implement methods of both base interface IRectInterface and derived interface ITriangleInterface.

Listing 9.8 Program Code in MultilevelInterface.cs File

```
interface IRectInterface
{
   void dispArea();
}
```

```
interface ITriangleInterface :   IRectInterface
{
    void dispTrg();
}
class MultilevelInterface : ITriangleInterface
{
    float length, breadth;
    MultilevelInterface(float l, float b)
    {
        length=l;
        breadth=b;
    }
    public void dispArea()
    {
        System.Console.WriteLine("Area of rectangle is {0}",length*breadth);
    }
    public void dispTrg()
    {
        System.Console.WriteLine("Area of triangle is {0}",
(float)1/2*length*breadth);
    }
    public static void Main()
    {
        MultilevelInterface multlevelint = new MultilevelInterface(10.0f, 20.0f);
        multlevelint.dispArea();
        multlevelint.dispTrg();
    }
}
```

Output:

```
Area of rectangle is 200
Area of triangle is 100
```

Because the MultilevelInterface class inherits from ITriangleInterface, it also inherits IRectInterface. Therefore, the MultilevelInterface class implements the dispArea method specified in the IRectInterface interface and the dispTrg method specified in the ITriangleInterface interface.

An object of the MultilevelInterface class is created named multlevelint. The values 10.0f and 20.0f passed while creating the multlevelint object initialize the data members length and breadth, respectively. The implemented dispArea and dispTrg methods calculate and display the area of a rectangle and triangle, respectively.

IMPLEMENTING INTERFACE PROPERTIES

Besides methods, the interfaces can declare any number of properties. A read-write property can be declared in an interface using the following syntax:

```
retType PropName { get; set; }
```

Following is the syntax for declaring a write-only property in an interface:

```
retType PropName { set; }
```

A read-only property is declared in an interface through the following syntax:

```
retType PropName { get; }
```

The InterfaceProperty.cs program shown in Listing 9.9 demonstrates interface properties. The program defines an interface called IUserInfo that declares read-write properties called Name and EmailAdd. The IUserInfo interface is implemented by the Users class, which defines the two properties. The Users class is instantiated by creating its object called usr that uses the Name and EmailAdd properties to assign and access the user's name and email address.

Listing 9.9 Program Code in InterfaceProperty.cs File

```
interface IUserInfo
{
    string Name
    {
        get; set;
    }
    string EmailAdd
    {
        get; set;
    }
}
public class Users : IUserInfo
{
    private string name, emailadd;
    public string Name
    {
        get
        {
            return name;
        }
        set
        {
            name = value;
        }
    }
```

```
    public string EmailAdd
    {
        get
        {
            return emailadd;
        }
        set
        {
            emailadd = value;
        }
    }
}
class InterfaceProperty
{
    static void Main()
    {
        Users usr = new Users();
        System.Console.Write("Enter your name: ");
        usr.Name = System.Console.ReadLine();
        System.Console.Write("Enter your email address: ");
        usr.EmailAdd = System.Console.ReadLine();
        System.Console.WriteLine("The user's name is {0} and email address is
{1}",usr.Name, usr.EmailAdd);
    }
}
```

Output:

```
Enter your name: bintu
Enter your email address: bintu@yahoo.com
The user's name is bintu and email address is bintu@yahoo.com
```

You can see that the Users class implements the IUserInfo interface. The Users class implements the two properties Name and EmailAdd that are declared in the IUserInfo interface. An object of the Users class is created, named usr. The program asks the user to enter the name and email address that are assigned to the Name and EmailAdd properties, respectively, through the mutators. Similarly, the respective accessors of the two properties are invoked to access and display the user's name and email address.

You have seen enough examples of an interface being implemented by classes. Now you'll learn how a structure implements an interface.

UNDERSTANDING HOW A STRUCTURE IMPLEMENTS AN INTERFACE

Similar to classes, structs can implement interfaces. Besides defining the fields, the structs can implement the method(s) declared in the specific interface. Recall that the struct type is a value type that defines certain members or fields. It can contain constructors, methods, properties, and so on.

The `StructInterface.cs` shown in Listing 9.10 demonstrates how a struct implements an interface. The program defines an interface called `Allowance` that declares a single method, `houseAllownc`. The method is supposed to calculate household allowance. The program also defines a struct called `Worker` that contains the members `code`, `name`, and `basicSalary` of type `int`, `string`, and `int`, respectively. The `Worker` struct is defined to store information about a worker. The `struct` implements the `Allowance` interface. Assuming the household allowance of a worker is 6 percent of basic salary, the `Worker` struct implements the `houseAllownc` method to calculate the household allowance.

Listing 9.10 Program Code in StructInterface.cs File

```
using System;
interface Allowance
{
    float houseAllownc(int s);
}
struct Worker : Allowance
{
    public int code;
    public string name;
    public int basicSalary;
    public Worker(int c, string n, int s) {
        code=c;
        name = n;
        basicSalary= s;
    }
    public float houseAllownc(int s)
    {
        return (float) basicSalary*6/100;
    }
}
class StructInterface {
    static void Main() {
    Worker wkr=new Worker(101, "Kelly", 5000);
```

```
      Console.WriteLine("Information of Worker - Code: {0}, Name: {1}, Salary:
{2}, Household Allowance: {3}", wkr.code, wkr.name, wkr.basicSalary,
wkr.houseAllownc(wkr.basicSalary));
   }
}
```

Output:

Information of Worker - Code: 101, Name: Kelly, Salary: 5000, Household Allowance: 300

You can see that the variable wkr of the Worker type is created and, using the constructor, its fields code, name, and basicSalary are initialized to 101, Kelly, and 5000, respectively. The information in the three fields is displayed, along with the household allowance that is calculated by invoking the implemented method named houseAllownc.

Now you'll read how an interface is passed as a parameter to a method.

PASSING AN INTERFACE AS A PARAMETER

Like any data type, the interface can be passed as a parameter to a method. The InterfaceParameter.cs program shown in Listing 9.11 demonstrates how to do so. The program defines an interface called IRectInterface that declared a method, dispArea. A class called A implements the IRectInterface interface and therefore defines the dispArea method. In the main class of the program, InterfaceParameter, a static method called XYZMethod is defined that takes a parameter of the IRectInterface type. The method invokes the dispArea method of the interface through the supplied parameter.

Listing 9.11 Program Code in InterfaceParameter.cs File

```
interface IRectInterface
{
   void dispArea();
}
 class A : IRectInterface
{
   public void dispArea()
   {
       System.Console.WriteLine("Method implemented of IRectInterface");
   }
}
class InterfaceParameter
{
   static void XYZMethod( IRectInterface AObj )
```

```
    {
        AObj.dispArea();
    }
    static void Main()
    {
        A AObject=new A();
        XYZMethod(AObject );
    }
}
```

Output:

```
Method implemented of IRectInterface
```

You can see that in the Main method, an object of class A is defined named AObject. Class A has implemented the dispArea method of the IRectInterface interface. The static method XYZMethod is invoked, and class A object AObject is passed to it. In the XYZMethod, the parameter is received in the AObj parameter of the IRectInterface type. Using the AObj parameter, the dispArea method is invoked that displays the message Method implemented of IRectInterface.

Now that you understand how to send an interface as a parameter, you'll learn how a method can return an interface.

RETURNING AN INTERFACE

As with any data type, you can make a method return an interface. The InterfaceReturn.cs program shown in Listing 9.12 shows how a method can return an interface. The program defines an interface called IRectInterface that declares a method called dispArea. The program also defines three classes named A, B, and C. Out of these three classes, only class B implements the IRectInterface interface. A static method called FindInterface is defined in the main class of the program, InterfaceReturn. The FindReturn method accepts an array of objects as a parameter. The method iterates through each object and checks whether any of the objects implements the IRectInterface interface. The method returns the object that implements the IRectInterface interface.

Listing 9.12 Program Code in InterfaceReturn.cs File

```
interface IRectInterface
{
    void dispArea();
}
class A
```

```
    {

    }
    class B : IRectInterface
    {
        public void dispArea()
        {
            System.Console.WriteLine("Method implemented of IRectInterface");
        }
    }
    class C
    {

    }
    class InterfaceReturn
    {
      static IRectInterface FindInterface(object[] classObjects)
      {
        IRectInterface rectInterface=null;
        foreach (object classObj in classObjects)
        {
            if (classObj is IRectInterface)
            {
                rectInterface = (IRectInterface)classObj;
                break;
            }
        }
        return rectInterface;
      }
      public static void Main()
      {
          A AObject=new A();
          B BObject=new B();
          C CObject=new C();
          IRectInterface   rectint = FindInterface(new object[] {AObject, BObject,
CObject});
          rectint.dispArea();
      }
    }
```

Output:

```
Method implemented of IRectInterface
```

You can see that in the Main method of the main class, InterfaceReturn, the objects of classes A, B, and C are defined by the names AObject, BObject, and CObject, respectively.

The three objects AObject, BObject, and CObject are sent to the FindInterface method in the form of an object array. The FindInterface method returns the first interface method (or it could return an array (or List) of interfaces of the objects) that contain the interface so that all objects can be executed.

SUMMARY

In this chapter, you learned about interfaces. You saw how the interface members are invoked at the object level and how multiple interfaces are implemented. You also learned about an ambiguous situation that might arise while implementing multiple interfaces and removing ambiguity through explicit interface implementation. You verified interface implementation, implemented a multilevel interface, and implemented interface properties. You also saw how structures implement interfaces, how an interface can be passed as a parameter, and how an interface can be returned from a method.

The next chapter is focused on operator overloading. You will learn about different overloadable operators and the need for operator overloading. You will learn to overload unary operators, binary operators, and comparison operators.

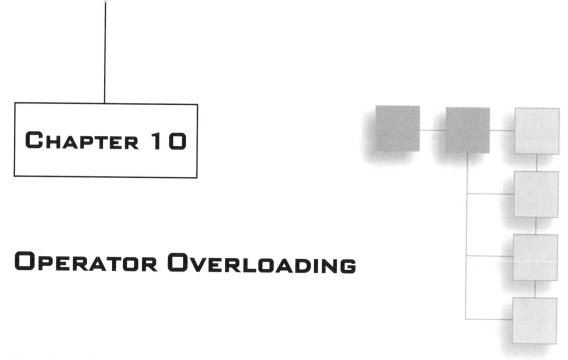

CHAPTER 10

OPERATOR OVERLOADING

This chapter's topics include the following:

- Binary operator overloading
- Unary operator overloading
- true and false operator overloading
- Comparison operators overloading
- Conversion operators overloading

Operator overloading involves extending the task of the operators to perform operations on objects. In other words, through operator overloading, you can make the operators do jobs they wouldn't ordinarily do. For example, the + (plus) operator's intended use is for adding numerical data types (int, long, float, double, and so on). If, in addition to adding the numerical data types, the plus operator is set to add objects and structs, you'd say the operator is overloaded. After loading an operator, it continues to perform its original task and, along with it, it extends its capability to complete similar tasks on objects of classes. Therefore, operator overloading enables you to execute mathematical/logical operations on class objects, structs, and other types using the usual operators. Also, operator overloading enables you to convert data of one type to another.

C# allows overloading of almost all operators. Table 10.1 displays the operators that can be overloaded and those that cannot.

Table 10.1 Overloadable and Nonoverloadable Operators

Operators	Description
+, -, !, ~, ++, --, true, false	These unary operators can be overloaded.
+, -, *, /, %, &, |, ^, <<, >>	These binary operators can be overloaded.
==, !=, <, >, <=, >=	These comparison operators can be overloaded.
&&, ||	These conditional logical operators cannot be overloaded.
+=, -=, *=, /=, %=,&=, |=, ^=, <<=,>>=	These assignment operators cannot be overloaded.
=, ., ?:, ->, new, is, sizeof, typeof	These operators cannot be overloaded.

© 2015 Cengage Learning®.

Note

The comparison operators must be overloaded in pairs. In other words, if the == operator is overloaded, the != operator must also be overloaded. Similarly, if the < operator is overloaded, the > operator must also be overloaded.

To overload an operator, you define a static member function using the operator keyword. This static member function then defines the action of the operator. You can overload binary, unary, comparison, and other operators. Binary operator overloading is covered first.

BINARY OPERATOR OVERLOADING

Binary operators take two arguments. The following operators can be overloaded:

+, -, *, /, %, &, |, ^, <<, >>

You'll begin with the + operator, which normally adds two arguments together.

The following example adds two int values:

```
int a = 10;
int b = 20;
int c = a + b;
```

The + operator adds the two integers and assigns the result of addition to variable c.

Adding int, float, and strings is fine, but can you use the + operator to add structs or class objects? Yes! You can do this through binary operator overloading. The syntax for overloading binary operators follows:

```
public static return_type operator op(param_type1 operand1, param_type2 operand2)
{
   // code
}
```

where op refers to the operators such as +, -, /, and * that you want to overload. The return_type indicates the type of value returned by the specified operation. It can be anything except for void. The operands refer to the items on which you want to perform operations. For binary operators, at least one of the operands must be of the same type as the class.

The OperatorOvr1.cs program shown in Listing 10.1 demonstrates binary operator overloading by adding two Product objects. The program defines a Product class that consists of two data members, qty and price, where qty is of int type and price is of double type. Two objects of the Product class are created and named p1 and p2. Their data members qty and price are initialized through the parameterized constructor. The two objects p1 and p2 are added through binary operator overloading, and the resultant sum is stored in a third Project object, p3. Finally, the content of the three objects is displayed on the screen.

Listing 10.1 Program Code in OperatorOvr1.cs File

```
using System;
class Product {
   int qty;
   double price;
   public Product() {
      qty=0;
      price=0;
   }
   public Product(int x, double y)
   {
      qty=x;
      price=y;
   }
   public static Product operator +(Product op1, Product op2)
   {
      Product addedProd = new Product();
      addedProd.qty = op1.qty + op2.qty;
```

```
        addedProd.price = op1.price + op2.price;
        return addedProd;
    }
    public void Show()
    {
        Console.WriteLine("Quantity: {0}, Price: {1}", qty, price);
    }
}
class OperatorOvr1 {
    static void Main() {
        Product p1 = new Product(10, 15.13);
        Product p2 = new Product(50, 100.85);
        Product p3 = new Product();
        Console.Write("First Product: ");
        p1.Show();
        Console.Write("Second Product: ");
        p2.Show();
        p3=p1+p2;
        Console.Write("Addition of two products: ");
        p3.Show();
    }
}
```

Output:

```
First Product: Quantity: 10, Price: 15.13
Second Product: Quantity: 50, Price: 100.85
Addition of two products: Quantity: 60, Price: 115.98
```

You can see that the values 10 and 15.13 that are passed as parameters while creating the first Product object p1 invoke the parameterized constructor to initialize its data members qty and price. Similarly, the qty and price members of another object, p2, are initialized to 50 and 100.85, respectively. The statement p3=p1+p2 invokes the overloaded + operator method, passing the objects p1 and p2 to it, which are assigned to its parameters op1 and op2. In the overloaded + operator method, a Product object is created called addedProd. The qty and price members of the addedProd object are initialized to the sum of qty and price members of the objects op1 and op2, respectively. In other words, the qty and price members of the two objects are added together and assigned to the respective members of the newly created object. Finally, the addedProd object is returned and assigned to the object p3 in the Main method. Data members qty and price of p1, p2, and p3 are displayed to verify the addition.

In binary operator overloading, out of the two operands that have been added, one has to be of the same type as the class, and the other operand can be of any type.

The second operand can even be a constant. Read on to learn how to add a constant value to an object using binary operator overloading.

Adding a Constant to an Object

While overloading the + operator, not only can you add two objects, but you can add an integer or another data type to an object.

The OperatorOvrConst.cs program shown in Listing 10.2 demonstrates adding an integer value to a Product object using binary operator overloading. The program defines a Product class composed of two data members, qty and price, of type int and double, respectively. The program explains adding an integer to an object as well as adding an object to an integer. Confused? Keep reading.

The following two statements give the same result but need to be implemented separately:

```
p2=p1+5;
p2=5 + p1;
```

The first statement needs to overload the + operator that contains the Product object as the first parameter and an int type as the second parameter. In contrast, the second statement requires the parameters to be placed in reverse order. (It requires the first parameter to be of int type and the other to be of Product type.) Therefore, the + operator is overloaded twice in the program. A Product object is created called p1, and its data members qty and price are initialized to values 10 and 15.13 through the parameterized constructor. An integer value 5 is added to the object p1, and the result is stored into another object, p2. Similarly, int value 10 is added to the object p1, and the result of addition is stored in the third object, p3. The content of the three objects is displayed on the screen by invoking the Show method.

Listing 10.2 Program Code in OperatorOvrConst.cs File

```
using System;
class Product {
  int qty;
  double price;
  public Product() {
    qty=0;
    price=0;
  }
  public Product(int x, double y)
  {
    qty=x;
    price=y;
  }
```

```csharp
    public static Product operator +(Product op1, int z)
    {
       Product addedProd = new Product();
       addedProd.qty = op1.qty + z;
       addedProd.price = op1.price + z;
       return addedProd;
    }
    public static Product operator +(int z, Product op1)
    {
       Product addedProd = new Product();
       addedProd.qty = op1.qty + z;
       addedProd.price = op1.price + z;
       return addedProd;
    }
    public void Show()
    {
       Console.WriteLine("Quantity: {0}, Price: {1}", qty, price);
    }
}
class OperatorOvrConst {
    static void Main() {
       Product p1 = new Product(10, 15.13);
       Product p2 = new Product();
       Product p3 = new Product();
       Console.Write("Original Product: ");
       p1.Show();
       p2=p1+5;
       Console.Write("Product after adding value 5: ");
       p2.Show();
       p3=10+p1;
       Console.Write("Product after adding value 10: ");
       p3.Show();
    }
}
```

Output:

```
Original Product: Quantity: 10, Price: 15.13
Product after adding value 5: Quantity: 15, Price: 20.13
Product after adding value 10: Quantity: 20, Price: 25.13
```

You can see in the preceding program that two methods are used for binary operator overloading. The first method has the first parameter as the Product object and the other as an `int` type. The second method has the first parameter as an `int` type and the other as the `Product` object. Both methods enable you to add the `int` data to each data member of the `Product` class. The statement `p2=p1+5;` invokes the first binary operator overloading method and passes the `Product` object p1 and integer 5 to it. Similarly, the statement `p3=10+p1;` invokes the second binary operator overloading method and passes integer 10 and `Product` object p1 to it.

Note

When overloading a binary operator, one of the operands must be of the same type as that of the class. The other operand can be of any other type.

Adding Two Complex Numbers

You can use the concept of binary operator overloading to add two complex numbers. Complex numbers are those composed of two parts: real and imaginary. The imaginary part is suffixed with i, called *iota*. For example, the following complex number consists of 2 and 3 as real and imaginary parts, respectively:

2 + 3i

The `AddingComplexNumb.cs` program shown in Listing 10.3 demonstrates adding of two complex numbers by overloading the + operator. The program defines a `Complex` class composed of two data members of `int` type: `real` and `imaginary`. The program overloads the + operator that takes two `Complex` objects as parameters. In the overloaded + operator method, the `real` and `imaginary` values of the two `Complex` objects are added. The added `real` and `imaginary` values are wrapped in a `Complex` object and returned. The program overrides the `ToString` method to display the complex numbers in the following format:

real_value + imaginary_value i

Listing 10.3 Program Code in AddingComplexNumb.cs File

```
using System;
class Complex
{
    private int real, imaginary;
    public Complex(int real, int imaginary)
    {
        this.real = real;
        this.imaginary = imaginary;
    }
```

```
    public static Complex operator +(Complex c1, Complex c2)
    {
        return new Complex(c1.real + c2.real, c1.imaginary + c2.imaginary);
    }
    public override string ToString()
    {
        return (String.Format("{0} + {1}i", real, imaginary));
    }
}
class AddingComplexNumb
{
    static void Main()
    {
        Complex comp1 = new Complex(2, 3);
        Complex comp2 = new Complex(3, 4);
        Complex sum = comp1 + comp2;
        System.Console.WriteLine("First complex number is {0}", comp1);
        System.Console.WriteLine("Second complex number is {0}", comp2);
        System.Console.WriteLine("The sum of the two complex numbers is {0}", sum);
    }
}
```

Output:

```
First complex number is 2 + 3i
Second complex number is 3 + 4i
The sum of the two complex numbers is 5 + 7i
```

You can see that two Complex objects are created called comp1 and comp2. The real and imaginary members of the first Complex object, comp1, are initialized to 2 and 3, respectively. Similarly, the members of the second Complex object, comp2, are initialized to 3 and 4, respectively. The overloaded + operator method is invoked after adding the two objects. The two objects being involved in addition are passed to the overloaded + operator method, where their respective real and imaginary values are added. The added real and imaginary values of the two Complex objects are returned in the form of a Complex object. The returned Complex object is assigned to the Complex object sum. Finally, comp1, comp2, and sum are displayed by overriding the ToString() method.

UNARY OPERATOR OVERLOADING

Unary operators are those that require only a single operand/parameter for the operation. The following operators can be overloaded:

+, -, !, ~, ++, --, true, false

The syntax for overloading unary operators follows:

```
public static return_type operator op(param_type operand)
{
  //code
}
```

where `op` refers to the operators such as +, -, /, and * that you want to overload. `return_type` indicates the type of value that the specified operation will return, and `operand` refers to the item on which you want to perform operations. For unary operators, `operand` and `return_type` must be of the same type as the class for which the operator is being defined.

The following rules apply when overloading unary operators:

- In ++ or -- operators, `operand` and `return_type` must be of the defining type (of the same type as the class for which the operator is being overloaded).

- In +, -, !, or ~ operators, `operand` must be of the defining type, and `return_type` can be of any type.

- In `true` or `false` operators, `operand` must be of the defining type, and `return_type` must be of the `bool` type.

Now you'll come to understand the concept of unary operator overloading by overloading the ++ operator.

The `OperatorOvr2.cs` program shown in Listing 10.4 demonstrates overloading of the ++ operator for incrementing values of class object data members. The program defines a `Product` class composed of two data members, `qty` and `price`, of `int` and `double` type, respectively. The program overloads the ++ operator to increment the values of the `qty` and `price` data members by 1.

Listing 10.4 Program Code in OperatorOvr2.cs File

```
using System;
class Product {
  int qty;
  double price;
  public Product() {
    qty=0;
    price=0;
  }
  public Product(int x, double y)
  {
    qty=x;
```

```
      price=y;
   }
   public static Product operator ++(Product op)
   {
      op.qty++;
      op.price++;
      return op;
   }
   public void Show()
   {
      Console.WriteLine("Quantity: {0}, Price: {1}", qty, price);
   }
}
class OperatorOvr2 {
   static void Main() {
      Product p = new Product(10, 15.13);
      Console.Write("Original Product: ");
      p.Show();
      p++;
      Console.Write("Product after incrementing by 1: ");
      p.Show();
   }
}
```

Output:

```
Original Product: Quantity: 10, Price: 15.13
Product after incrementing by 1: Quantity: 11, Price: 16.13
```

You can see that a `Project` object p is created, and its data members qty and price are initialized to values 10 and 15.13, respectively. The initial values of the members are displayed using the Show method. Thereafter, the overloaded ++ operator method is called by invoking the following statement:

```
p++;
```

In the overloaded ++ operator method, the values of both qty and price of the invoking object are incremented by 1. After incrementing the values of the data members, the object is returned. The Show method is called again to verify that the increment took place successfully.

Note

The ++ and -- unary operators apply on the same instance and return the same instance. They do not apply on the new instance.

TRUE AND FALSE OPERATOR OVERLOADING

By overloading true and false operators, you can use the objects of the class in conditional branching. In other words, the object(s) are compared and return true or false based on some expression. In true and false operator overloading, the return type will be bool. The returned bool value can be used in decision-making.

Note

The true and false operators must be overloaded in pairs.

The TrueFalseOvr.cs program shown in Listing 10.5 demonstrates overloading of true and false operators. The program defines a Product class composed of a single data member, qty, of int type. The program overloads the true operator that returns the bool value true if the value of the data member qty of the invoking object is not equal to 0. Because the true and false operators need to be overloaded in pairs, the program overloads the false operator, too. The overloaded false operator method returns the bool value true if the qty member of the invoking object is equal to 0.

Listing 10.5 Program Code in TrueFalseOvr.cs File

```
class Product
{
  public int qty;
  public Product(int x)
  {
    qty = x;
  }
  public static bool operator true(Product p) {
    return (p.qty != 0);
  }
  public static bool operator false(Product p) {
    return (p.qty == 0);
  }
}
class TrueFalseOvr
{
  static void Main()
  {
    Product p = new Product(10);
    if (p) System.Console.WriteLine("Product quantity is nonzero");
    else    System.Console.WriteLine("Product quantity is zero");
  }
}
```

Output:

```
Product quantity is nonzero
```

You can see that a `Project` object called p is defined, and its data member `qty` is initialized to value 10. The overloaded `bool` operator methods are invoked. Because the value of the `qty` member of the object p is not equal to 0, the overloaded `true` operator method returns `true`, thereby displaying the message `Product quantity is nonzero` on the screen.

COMPARISON OPERATORS OVERLOADING

Comparison operators take two arguments, and as the name suggests, these operators are used in making expressions that evaluate to a `bool` value of `true` or `false`. The following operators can be overloaded: ==, !=, <, >, <=, and >=. The comparison operators must be implemented in pairs. In other words, if the == operator is overloaded, the != operator must also be overloaded. Similarly, if the < operator is overloaded, the > operator must also be overloaded.

Depending on the expression, the comparison operators return a `bool` value that might be used in conditional branching or looping.

The `OperatorOvr3.cs` program shown in Listing 10.6 demonstrates comparison operator overloading by comparing two objects. The program defines a `Product` class composed of the single data member `qty` of `int` type. Two objects, p1 and p2, of the `Product` class are created in the program. The comparison operator < (less than) is overloaded to compare the two objects. In the overloaded < operator method, the values of the data member `qty` of the two comparing objects are compared and, accordingly, the `bool` value is returned.

Listing 10.6 Program Code in OperatorOvr3.cs File

```
using System;
class Product {
  int qty;
  public Product() {
    qty=0;
  }
  public Product(int x)
  {
    qty=x;
  }
  public static bool operator < (Product op1, Product op2)
  {
```

```
      if( op1.qty < op2.qty) return true;
      else return false;
   }
   public static bool operator > (Product op1, Product op2)
   {
      if( op1.qty > op2.qty) return true;
      else return false;
   }
   public int getQuantity()
   {
      return qty;
   }
}
class OperatorOvr3 {
   static void Main() {
      Product p1 = new Product(10);
      Product p2 = new Product(50);
      if(p1 <p2)
         Console.Write("Product p1 is smaller than p2 i.e. {0} is smaller than
{1}", p1.getQuantity(), p2.getQuantity());
      else
         Console.Write("Product p2 is smaller than p1 i.e. {0} is smaller than {1}",
p2.getQuantity(), p1.getQuantity());
   }
}
```

Output:

```
Product p1 is smaller than p2 i.e. 10 is smaller than 50
```

You can see that the Product class is instantiated by creating two objects: p1 and p2. While creating the two objects, values 10 and 50 are passed to invoke the respective parameterized constructor that in turn initializes the data member qty of the two objects to values 10 and 50, respectively. The overloaded < operator method is invoked when the p1 object is compared to object p2 (p1 < p2). The objects p1 and p2 are passed as parameters to the overloaded < operator method. In the overloaded < operator method, the values in the qty members of the two objects p1 and p2 are compared. Because the qty member of object p1 is less than that of object p2, the overloaded < operator method returns the bool value true to the Main method. Consequently, the if block is executed, displaying the message Product p1 is smaller than p2 i.e. 10 is smaller than 50 on the screen.

Note

Although you are not invoking the overloaded > operator method in the Main method, you are still defining it in the program because comparison operators are overloaded in pairs.

The objects of a class are of reference type, so the method of comparing objects is different from that of comparing value types. System.Object defines the following three methods for comparing objects for equality:

- **The ReferenceEquals() method**—This is a static method that checks whether two references refer to the same instance of a class (that is, if the two references contain the same address in memory). The method returns true if it's supplied with two references that refer to the same object instance; otherwise, it returns false.

```
RectArea rect1 = new RectArea();
RectArea rect2 = new RectArea();
RectArea rect3=rect1;
if (ReferenceEquals(rect1, rect2)) // will return false as both rect1 and rect2
refer to different objects
if (ReferenceEquals(rect1, rect3)) // will return true as rect1 and rect3 refer to
the same object
if(ReferenceEquals(null, null)); // returns true as null is equal to null
if(ReferenceEquals(null,rect1); // returns false as object rect1 cannot be equal
to null
```

- **The virtual Equals() method**—The System.Object implementation of the virtual version of Equals() also works by comparing references. However, because this method is virtual, you can override it in your own classes to compare objects by value.

- **The static Equals() method**—The static version of Equals() actually does the same thing as the virtual instance version. The difference is that the static version takes two parameters and compares them for equality. The method first checks whether the references it has been passed are null. If both are null, the method returns true. If just one of them is null, the method returns false. If both references actually refer to some object, the method calls the virtual instance version of Equals().

The ClassCompare.cs program shown in Listing 10.7 checks whether the specified objects refer to the same object of the class. The program defines a RectArea class composed of two integer data members: l and b. The class defines two member methods, setdata and getrect, to assign values to the data members l and b and to return the result of calculation, respectively.

Listing 10.7 Program Code in ClassCompare.cs File

```
using System;
class RectArea {
  private int l,b;
  public void setdata(int x, int y) {
    l=x;
    b=y;
  }
  public int getrect() {
    return l*b;
  }
}
class ClassCompare {
  static void Main() {
    RectArea rect1 = new RectArea();
    RectArea rect2 = new RectArea();
    RectArea rect3=rect1;
    if (ReferenceEquals(rect1, rect2))
      Console.WriteLine("The objects rect1 and rect2 refer to the same object of the
class");
    else
      Console.WriteLine("The objects rect1 and rect2 do not refer to the same object of
the class");
    if (ReferenceEquals(rect1, rect3))
      Console.WriteLine("The objects rect1 and rect3 refer to the same object of the
class");
    else
      Console.WriteLine("The objects rect1 and rect3 do not refer to the same object of
the class");
  }
}
```

Output:

```
The objects rect1 and rect2 do not refer to the same object of the class
The objects rect1 and rect3 refer to the same object of the class
```

You can see that two objects of the RectArea class are created and named rect1 and rect2.
One more object, rect3, is set to refer to the object rect1. Through the if statement, it is
checked whether the rect1 and rect2 objects refer to the same object. Because rect1 and
rect2 refer to a different object, the message The objects rect1 and rect2 do not refer to
the same object of the class is displayed on the screen. Similarly, objects rect1 and rect3
are checked. Because rect1 and rect3 refer to the same object, the message The objects
rect1 and rect3 refer to the same object of the class is displayed on the screen.

The OverloadEqualOpr.cs program shown in Listing 10.8 explains overloading of == and != operators to check whether the two specified objects are equal or unequal. The program defines a Product class consisting of a data member of int type called qty. Two objects of the Product class are created, named p1 and p2. The qty members of the two objects p1 and p2 are initialized to values 10 and 50 through the parameterized constructor. An overloaded == operator method is defined that returns the value true if the qty members of the invoking objects are equal; otherwise, the method returns false. Also, an overloaded != operator method is defined that returns the bool value true if the qty members of the two invoking objects are unequal; otherwise, the method returns false.

Listing 10.8 Program Code in OverloadEqualOpr.cs File

```
using System;
class Product {
   int qty;
   public Product() {
      qty=0;
   }
   public Product(int x) {
      qty=x;
   }
   public static bool operator == (Product op1, Product op2) {
      if( op1.qty == op2.qty) return true;
      else return false;
   }
   public static bool operator != (Product op1, Product op2){
      return !(op1==op2);
   }
   public int getQuantity(){
      return qty;
   }
}
class OverloadEqualOpr {
   static void Main() {
      Product p1 = new Product(10);
      Product p2 = new Product(50);
      if(p1 ==p2)
        Console.Write("Product p1 is equal to p2 i.e. {0} is equal to {1}",
   p1.getQuantity(), p2.getQuantity());
      else
        Console.Write("Product p1 is not equal to p2 i.e. {0} is not equal to {1}",
   p1.getQuantity(), p2.getQuantity());
   }
}
```

After compiling the preceding program, you get the following warning messages:

```
OverloadEqualOpr.cs(3,7): warning CS0660: 'Product' defines operator == or operator !=
but does not override Object.Equals(object o)
OverloadEqualOpr.cs(3,7): warning CS0661: 'Product' defines operator == or operator !=
but does not override Object.GetHashCode()
```

You can see that the compiler is asking to override the `Object.Equals` and `Object.GetHashCode` methods.

The .NET Framework class library `System.Object` defines the following methods:

- `Equals(object)` **method**—Determines whether the invoking object refers to the same object as the one referred to by the argument. It returns `true` if the objects are the same, and `false` otherwise. You can override this method in classes to compare the content of two objects for equality. The `Equals(object, object)` method invokes `Equals(object)` to compute its result.

- `GetHashCode( )` **method**—Returns a hash code associated with the invoking object. This hash code can be used with any algorithm that employs hashing as a means of accessing stored objects.

If you overload the `==` operator, you need to override `Equals(object)` and `GetHashCode( )` because the `==` operator and the `Equals(object)` method function the same. When `Equals( )` is overridden, you also need to override `GetHashCode( )` for compatibility.

After adding the `Equals` and `GetHashCode` methods to `OverloadEqualOpr.cs` (shown in Listing 10.8), the program appears as shown in Listing 10.9. Only the code in bold is newly added; the rest is the same as in Listing 10.8.

Listing 10.9 Program Code in OverloadEqualOpr.cs File

```
using System;
class Product {
  int qty;
  public Product() {
    qty=0;
  }
  public Product(int x)
  {
    qty=x;
  }
  public static bool operator == (Product op1, Product op2)
  {
    if( op1.qty == op2.qty) return true;
    else return false;
```

```
  }
  public static bool operator != (Product op1, Product op2)
  {
    return !(op1==op2);
  }
  public override bool Equals(Object obj) {
    if (obj == null || GetType() != obj.GetType()) return false;
    Product p = (Product)obj;
    return qty.Equals(p.qty);
  }
  public override int GetHashCode() {
    return qty.GetHashCode();
  }
  public int getQuantity()
  {
    return qty;
  }
}
class OverloadEqualOpr {
  static void Main() {
  Product p1 = new Product(10);
  Product p2 = new Product(50);
  if(p1 ==p2)
    Console.Write("Product p1 is equal to p2 i.e. {0} is equal to {1}",
p1.getQuantity(), p2.getQuantity());
  else
    Console.Write("Product p1 is not equal to p2 i.e. {0} is not equal to {1}",
p1.getQuantity(), p2.getQuantity());
  }
}
```

Output:

Product p1 is not equal to p2 i.e. 10 is not equal to 50

You can see that the value of the qty member of Product object p1 is set to 10, and the value of the Product object p2 is set to 50. After you encounter the statement p1==p2, the overloaded == operator method is called, and objects p1 and p2 are passed to it as parameters. In the method, the values of the qty members of the passed objects are compared. Because the values 10 and 50 (assigned to the respective qty members) are not equal, the method returns the bool value false. Consequently, the message Product p1 is not equal to p2 i.e. 10 is not equal to 50 is displayed on the screen.

CONVERSION OPERATORS OVERLOADING

Casting means converting a value of one type to another data type so that it can be used in a calculation or further processing. The conversion of data types provided by casting can be either implicit or explicit.

Implicit casting means automatic casting from one data type to another when the two data types are compatible. This type of casting occurs while assigning data of one type to another.

The following example casts an `int` to a `double` type:

```
int i = 10;
double d = i;
```

Implicit casting takes place in the preceding statement. `int` is converted to `double` because the `double` data type can accommodate the `int` type. The compiler automatically performs implicit casting. Implicit casting is invisible to the user. It is used when there is no risk of data loss or when there's an exception. Casting from a smaller type to a larger one can be through implicit casting because there are no chances of data loss.

Similarly, the following example implicitly converts an `int` type to a `long` type:

```
int n = 10;
long l;
l =n;
```

Explicit casting, on the other hand, does not occur automatically but is done by the user to ensure that casting is valid and no exception or error will occur. If the conversions for the two data types are not entirely compatible, may cause exceptions, or may result in loss of data, they are handled explicitly. For casting a type explicitly, a `cast` operator is prefixed on the source type. The `cast` operator is the desired data type enclosed in parentheses ().

The following example explicitly converts a `float` type to an `int` type:

```
float k = 10.5f;
int n = (int) k;
```

Here, `(int)` is doing explicit casting that converts the variable `k` (`float` type value) into an `int` type.

Explicit casting is visible. (The user knows that a conversion of type is taking place.) This casting helps ensure that no exception or data loss occurs during conversion. While converting from a large to a small type, there is a risk of losing data or sign (when a negative value is converted to 0), so explicit casting is appropriate in such situations.

Sometimes you cannot create conversion operators. You cannot create operators that convert a class to the object data type, convert a class to a defined interface, or convert from a base class to a derived class.

Creating an Implicit Conversion Operator

The implicit and explicit cast operators are unary operators. The following syntax is for the implicit conversion operator:

```
public static implicit operator target-type(source-type object)
```

where `target-type` is the data type where you want the object in `source-type` to be converted. One of the two data types (`source-` or `target-type`) must be the same as the class in which the declaration is made.

Example:

```
public static implicit operator int(Inches inchObject)
```

The preceding line is a method declaration that converts the `Inches` object `inchObject` into an `int` type.

Assuming that `inch` is a data member of the `Inches` class, the following code implicitly converts value 24 inches (contained in the `Inches` object) into feet. (The `Inches` type is implicitly converted to the `int` type.)

The `Main` method shows the code as demonstrated here:

```
static void Main()
{
    Inches inc=new Inches(24);
    int feet1=inc;
}
```

Creating an Explicit Conversion Operator

The syntax for creating an explicit conversion operator is shown here:

```
public static explicit operator target-type(source-type object)
```

The following example explicitly converts or casts an `int` type to an `Inches` type (into an `Inches` object). In other words, it converts the feet value into inches:

```
public static explicit operator Inches(int x)
{
    Inches inchObj = new Inches();
    inchObj.inch = x * 12;
    return inchObj;
}
```

You can see that an `Inches` object is created named `inchObj`. The supplied feet value in the `int` type is multiplied by 12 to convert it to inches. The result in inches is assigned to the `inch` member of the `Inches` class, and the `inchObj` is returned. The following code in the `Main` method explicitly converts feet into inches:

```
int feet2=5;
Inches inchObj = (Inches) feet2;
Console.WriteLine("{0} feet becomes {1} in inches", feet2,inchObj.ToString());
```

The `(Inches)` operator used in the preceding code declares that explicit casting is taking place.

The `ConversionOvrload.cs` program shown in Listing 10.10 demonstrates implicit and explicit conversion. The program defines a class called `Inches` that contains a data member `inch` of type `int`. The program converts inches into feet. A foot consists of 12 inches. When an `Inches` object is assigned to a variable of type `int`, the inches value stored in the `Inches` object (in `inch` data member) is implicitly converted into feet. (The value will be divided by 12 and returned.)

Similarly, an `int` type data can be explicitly converted into an `Inches` object. In other words, any feet value (in an `int` variable) can be explicitly converted to an `Inches` object. (The feet value is divided by 12 and assigned to an `inch` member of the `Inches` object.)

Listing 10.10 Program Code in ConversionOvrload.cs File

```
using System;
class Inches
{
  private int inch;
  public Inches()
  {
  }
  public Inches(int n)
  {
    inch = n;
  }
  public static explicit operator Inches(int x)
  {
    Inches inchObj = new Inches();
    inchObj.inch = x * 12;
    return inchObj;
  }
}
```

```
   public static implicit operator int(Inches inchObject)
   {
     return inchObject.inch/12;
   }
   public override string ToString()
   {
     return (this.inch.ToString());
   }
}
class ConversionOvrload
{
   public static void Main()
   {
     Inches inc=new Inches(24);
     int feet1=inc;
     Console.WriteLine("Inches in feet becomes {0} ",feet1);
     int feet2=5;
     Inches inchObj = (Inches) feet2;
     Console.WriteLine("{0} feet becomes {1} in inches", feet2,inchObj.ToString());
   }
}
```

Output:

```
Inches in feet becomes 2
5 feet becomes 60 in inches
```

You can see that an Inches object is created named inc. Value 24 is assigned to the inch member of the Inches object inc. The inc object is assigned to the int variable feet1, resulting in calling the implicit conversion operator method. The implicit conversion operator method divides the values in the inch member by 12 and returns the result.

An int variable named feet2 is defined and is initialized to value 5. The int value is explicitly converted into an Inches object by calling the explicit conversion operator method. In the explicit conversion operator method, an Inches object is created called inchObj. The supplied parameter in feet is multiplied by 12 and assigned to the inch member of the inchObj object. The inchObj object is returned to the Main method, where feet and inches values are displayed.

Here's one more quick example of explicit and implicit conversion. The ConversionOvr.cs program shown in Listing 10.11 explains implicit and explicit conversion. The program defines a class named BookInfo that contains two data members, qty and rate, where qty is of int type and rate is of double type. The qty and rate represent the quantity and price of the book, respectively. The BookInfo object, when assigned to a `float` variable, implicitly converts the object content into `float`. In other words, the program returns the total amount of the books by multiplying the quantity and rate members of the object. The `BookInfo` object will be implicitly converted into `float` by simply multiplying `qty` and `rate` members and returning the result.

Similarly, a `float` type value can be explicitly converted into a `BookInfo` object. The `float` value is assigned to the rate member of the `BookInfo` object, and the `qty` member is set to default value 10. Assuming that the `qty` (quantity) of the new `BookInfo` object is 10, the `float` value can be explicitly converted to the `BookInfo` object (assigned to the rate member of the `BookInfo` object).

Listing 10.11 Program Code in ConversionOv.cs File

```
using System;
class BookInfo
{
    int qty;
    float rate;
    public BookInfo()
    {
    }
    public BookInfo(int q,float r)
    {
        this.qty = q;
        this.rate = r;
    }
    public static implicit operator float(BookInfo bk)
    {
        return bk.qty * bk.rate;
    }
    public static explicit operator BookInfo(float value)
    {
        BookInfo bkinf= new BookInfo();
        bkinf.qty = 10;        //assuming default quantity
        bkinf.rate =value;
        return bkinf;
    }
    public override string ToString()
    {
        return string.Format("Quantity={0} and Rate={1}", this.qty, this.rate);
    }
}
class ConversionOv
{
```

```
public static void Main(string[] args)
{
   BookInfo book = new BookInfo(10, 12.99f);
   float amt = book;
   Console.WriteLine("Total amount of the books is {0} ",amt);
   float price = 15.25f;
   BookInfo bkinfo = (BookInfo)price;
   Console.WriteLine(bkinfo.ToString());
}
}
```

Output:

```
Total amount of the books is 129.9
Quantity=10 and Rate=15.25
```

You can see that a `BookInfo` object is created named `book`. Values 10 and 12.99 are assigned to the members `qty` and `rate` of the `BookInfo` object `book`. The `book` object is assigned to the `float` variable `amt`, thereby resulting in calling the implicit conversion operator method. The implicit conversion operator method multiplies the values in the `qty` and `rate` members and returns the total amount for the books.

A `float` variable named `price` is defined and initialized to value 15.25. The `float` value is explicitly converted into the `BookInfo` object by calling the explicit conversion operator method. In the explicit conversion operator method, a `BookInfo` object is created called `bkinf`. The float value is assigned to the rate member of the `bkinf` object. The `qty` member of the object is set to default value 10. After assigning values to the `qty` and `rate` members, the `bkinf` object is returned to the `Main` method, where quantity and rate values are displayed.

SUMMARY

In this chapter, you saw how operator overloading enables you to use operators in your custom types (structs and classes) the way you use them in normal data types. You learned to implement binary operator overloading when adding two objects, add constants to objects, and add two complex numbers. You discovered how to implement unary operator overloading, implement `true` and `false` operator overloading, implement comparison operator overloading, and compare objects for equality. Finally, you learned to implement conversion operator overloading, create an implicit conversion operator, and create an explicit conversion operator.

The next chapter focuses on delegates and events. You will learn to use delegates, delegate methods, delegate instantiation, and delegate invocation. You will also learn to use unicast and multicast delegates. Finally, you will learn to handle events.

CHAPTER 11

DELEGATES AND EVENTS

This chapter's topics include the following:

- Delegates introduction
- Multicast delegates
- Covariance and contravariance
- Generic delegate types
- Anonymous method
- Difference between delegates and interfaces
- Event handling

DELEGATES INTRODUCTION

A *delegate* is a .NET class that encapsulates a method and stores the address or reference to a method. It defines the kind of method that delegate instances can call. It also defines the method's signature (the method's return type, number of parameters, and their types). The first step to working with delegates is to declare them.

Declaring Delegates

Delegate declaration determines the methods that can be referenced by a delegate. Delegates are declared in a class or a namespace by using the `delegate` keyword and by specifying the signature of the method it will call. Here's the syntax for declaring a delegate:

```
delegate <return type> <delegate-name> <parameter list>
```

The following statement declares a delegate named Calculate that references a method returning an int type and accepts two parameters of that type:

```
delegate int Calculate (int x, int y);
```

The access modifiers public, private, and protected can be applied to the delegates to control their visibility. After you've declared a delegate, you can instantiate it to encapsulate a method of that signature. Then you can invoke the method through the delegate in the same way that you invoke it through a normal instance.

After declaring a delegate, you need to create its instance.

Instantiating Delegates

A delegate object is created with the new keyword and is associated with the method that it is supposed to point or refer to. Assigning or associating a method to a delegate variable creates a delegate instance. For example, both of the following statements create an instance of the Calculate delegate named r:

```
Calculate r = Rect;
Calculate r = new Calculate(Rect);
```

An instance called r is created of the Delegate class and set to refer to the Rect method. Remember, the method signature of the Rect method must match the delegate's method signature. (The method must have the same return type, the same number of parameters, and the same data type for each parameter as the delegate.)

If you have a method that accepts a single string parameter and another method that accepts two string parameters, you need to declare a separate delegate type for each method.

Note

A method signature represents its return type, the number of parameters it has, and the data type of each parameter.

The method to which the delegate is referring can be invoked through the delegate instance.

Invoking the Referenced Method

Assume that the Rect method that your delegate instance r is pointing to is as follows:

```
static int Rect (int x, int y)
{
    return x *y;
}
```

You can see that the Rect method matches the delegate's method signature. It takes two parameters of int types. The following statement invokes the Rect method through the delegate instance r:

```
r(5,8);
```

The preceding statement is really the same as r.Rect(5,8);

You can see that the delegate instances are called just like simple methods.

Here are the characteristics of delegates:

- Delegates allow you to reference a method and enable you to implement any desired functionality at runtime.

- Each delegate type describes the number and the types of the arguments and the type of the return value of methods that it can encapsulate.

- Once a delegate type has been declared, a delegate object must be created and associated with a particular method.

- Defining a delegate is like defining a new class. Delegates are implemented as classes derived from the class System.MulticastDelegate, which is derived from the base class System.Delegate.

- A delegate can call any method as long as its signature matches the delegates. This makes delegates ideal for anonymous invocation.

- Delegates are object oriented, type safe, and secure. While defining the delegate, you need to specify the complete signature of the methods that it is going to point to.

- For static methods, a delegate object encapsulates the method to be called. A delegate object encapsulates both an instance and a method on the instance.

- A delegate variable is assigned a method at runtime. This is useful for writing plug-in methods.

The Delegate1.cs program shown in Listing 11.1 demonstrates use of the delegate type. The program declares a delegate called Calculate that can reference any method that returns the int type and takes two parameters of the int type. The program shows how a delegate instance is created, refers to the desired method, and invokes the referenced method.

Listing 11.1 Program Code in Delegate1.cs File

```
using System;
delegate int Calculate (int x, int y);
class Delegate1
{
    static int Rect (int x, int y)
    {
        return x *y;
    }
    static void Main()
    {
        Calculate r = Rect; //same as Calculate r = new Calculate(Rect);
        Console.WriteLine ("Area of rectangle is "+ r(5,8));
    }
}
```

Output:

```
Area of rectangle is 400
```

You can see that a delegate called Calculate is declared that takes two integer arguments and returns data of type int. A method called Rect is defined that accepts two parameters of int type and returns int type. In the Main() method, an instance of the delegate Calculate is created named r. The delegate instance r invokes the Rect method, passing two arguments, 5 and 8, to it. The result returned by the Rect method is displayed on the screen.

As mentioned before, a delegate can point to or reference any method as long as its signature matches that of the delegate. The Delegate2.cs program shown in Listing 11.2 explains how a delegate can be set to point to two methods. The program declares a delegate called FunDelegate that can reference any method that returns an int type and takes two parameters of int type. Two static methods AddNum and MultNum are defined that return the sum and the product of the supplied parameters, respectively. Both methods have the same signature as the delegate. (Both take two parameters of int type and return an int type.)

Listing 11.2 Program Code in Delegate2.cs File

```
using System;
delegate int FuncDelegate(int m, int n);
```

```
class Delegate2
{
    public static int AddNum(int p, int q)
    {
        return p+q;
    }
    public static int MultNum(int p, int q)
    {
        return p*q;
    }
    static void Main(string[] args)
    {
        FuncDelegate delegvar1 = new FuncDelegate(AddNum);
        FuncDelegate delegvar2 = new FuncDelegate(MultNum);
        Console.WriteLine("Sum of 10 and 20 is {0}", delegvar1(10,20));
        Console.WriteLine("Multiplication of 10 and 20 is {0}", delegvar2(10,20));
    }
}
```

Output:

```
Sum of 10 and 20 is 30
Multiplication of 10 and 20 is 200
```

You can see that the FuncDelegate is instantiated by creating two instances, called delegvar1 and delegvar2. The delegvar1 and delegvar2 instances are set to reference the AddNum and MultNum methods, respectively. The AddNum method is invoked through the delegate instance delegvar1, and parameters 10 and 20 are passed to it. Similarly, the MultNum method is invoked through the delegvar2 instance, and parameters 10 and 20 are passed to it. The values returned by the two methods are displayed on the screen.

The delegate types are incompatible with each other, even if their signatures are the same. The following snippet results in a compiler error:

```
delegate int FuncDelegate1(int m, int n);
delegate int FuncDelegate2(int m, int n);
FuncDelegate1 delegvar1 =AddNum;
FuncDelegate2 delegvar2 =delegvar1;
```

In the preceding statements, the delegate instance delegvar1 is set to reference the AddNum method. The delegate instance delegvar2 cannot be assigned to another instance delegvar2 because the delegates are incompatible.

Delegate instances are considered equal if they have the same method targets. In the following code snippet, the two delegate instances delegvar1 and delegvar2 are considered equal because they refer to the same method: AddNum.

```
delegate int FuncDelegate(int m, int n);
FuncDelegate delegvar1 =AddNum;
FuncDelegate delegvar2 =AddNum;
if (delegvar1 == delegvar2);
{
    ...........
}
```

In the preceding code snippet, the statement(s) in the if block execute because the delegate instances delegvar1 and delegvar2 are equal.

Instance Versus Static Method Targets

When an instance method is assigned to a delegate object, the object maintains a reference to the method as well as to the instance to which the method belongs. The System.Delegate class's Target property represents this instance. The System.Delegate class's Target property is set to null for a delegate referencing a static method. The Target property is explained later in this chapter.

The Delegate2b.cs program shown in Listing 11.3 demonstrates pointing at the instance method. The program declares a delegate called Calculate that can reference any method that returns an int and takes two parameters of int type. A class called Shapes is defined that includes a method called Rect. The signature of the Rect method is set to match the Calculate delegate. An instance of the Shape class called shp is created. An instance of the Calculate delegate is created named r, and it is set to reference the Rect method of the shp instance. Finally, the instance method Rect is invoked through the delegate instance r.

Listing 11.3 Program Code in Delegate2b.cs File

```
using System;
delegate int Calculate (int x, int y);
class Shapes
{
    public int Rect (int x, int y)
    {
        return x *y;
    }
}
class Delegate2b
```

```
{
    static void Main()
    {
        Shapes shp=new Shapes();
        Calculate r = new Calculate(shp.Rect);
        if(r.Target == shp)
        {
            Console.WriteLine ("Method been reference is: {0}",r.Method);
            Console.WriteLine ("Area of rectangle is "+ r(5,8));
        }
    }
}
```

Output:

```
Method been reference is: Int32 Rect(Int32, Int32)
Area of rectangle is 40
```

You can see that the instance of the Calculate delegate r is set to reference the Rect method of the Shape class's instance shp. Because the delegate is pointing at the instance method (and not the static method), the Target property of the delegate instance represents the shp instance. The if statement ensures that the delegate's Target property represents the shp instance. The Method property of the delegate instance is used to display the method name that the delegate instance points to. The instance method Rect is invoked through the delegate instance r, and the result returned by the instance method is displayed on the screen.

MULTICAST DELEGATES

A *multicast delegate* represents a delegate that can invoke more than one method at once. All delegate instances have multicast capability. In other words, a delegate instance can reference not just a single method, but a list of methods. A multicast delegate also represents a list of the assigned delegates. Delegates of the same type can be combined. A multicast delegate is basically a list of delegates or a list of methods with the same signature. The benefit of using a multicast delegate is that it can call a collection of methods instead of only a single method.

You can use the + and += operators to add a reference of the specified method to a delegate instance. You can also use these operators to combine delegate instances. For example, the following statements make the Calculate delegate instance r reference at the Rect and Sum methods:

```
Calculate r = Rect
r+=Sum;
```

Invoking the delegate instance, r now calls both the Rect and the Sum methods. The methods are invoked in the order they are added to the delegate instance. Remember, if either of the methods throws an exception, the delegate call immediately stops, and no other methods in the list are called.

Like the += operator, you can use the -= operator to remove the specified delegate operand or method from the specified delegate instance. The following example removes the Rect method from the delegate instance:

```
r -= Rect;
```

Invoking the instance r causes only Sum to be invoked. If the method being removed is the last method, the delegate instance becomes null. Remember, calling a null delegate results in a runtime error.

Note

MulticastDelegate is implemented as a linked list of delegates, and additions and removals are done at the end of the list.

The Delegate3.cs program shown in Listing 11.4 demonstrates multicast delegates. The program declares a delegate called FunDelegate that can reference any method that returns an int and that takes two parameters of int type. Two static methods that match the delegate's signature are defined, named AddNum and MultNum. The AddNum and MultNum methods return the addition and multiplication of the supplied parameters, respectively. An instance of the delegate FuncDelegate is defined named delegvar. The delegvar instance implements multicasting by referencing both AddNum and MultNum.

Note

If a multicast delegate has a nonvoid return type, the caller receives the return value of the last invoked method. The preceding methods are called, but their return values are discarded. To process every return value, iterate the delegate list and invoke each delegate individually.

Listing 11.4 Program Code in Delegate3.cs File

```
using System;
delegate int FuncDelegate(int m, int n);
class Delegate3
{
    public static int AddNum(int p, int q)
    {
        return p+q;
    }
```

```
    public static int MultNum(int p, int q)
    {
        return p*q;
    }
    static void Main(string[] args)
    {
        FuncDelegate delegvar =AddNum;
        delegvar+=MultNum;
        Console.WriteLine("Multiplication of 10 and 20 is {0}", delegvar(10,20));
        delegvar-=MultNum;
        Console.WriteLine("Addition of 10 and 20 is {0}", delegvar(10,20));
        delegvar-=AddNum;
        if(delegvar !=null)
            Console.WriteLine("Result of the method that is invoked by the delegate is
{0}", delegvar(10,20));
        else
            Console.WriteLine("Delegate is not pointing to any method");
    }
}
```

Output:

```
Multiplication of 10 and 20 is 200
Addition of 10 and 20 is 30
Delegate is not pointing to any method
```

In the preceding program, you see that the FuncDelegate instance delegvar is set to reference at AddNum. Then the reference of the MultNum method is added to the delegvar instance, implementing multicast delegates. Both methods are invoked through the delegvar instance. The methods are called in the order they are added to the delegvar instance. (AddNum is called, followed by MultNum.) As expected, the return value of the AddNum method is discarded, and only the return value of the MultNum method is displayed on the screen.

Thereafter, the MultNum method is removed from the invocation list, leaving the delegvar instance to refer only at the AddNum method. The delegvar instance is used again to invoke the AddNum method for displaying the addition of the supplied parameters. After you remove the AddNum reference from the delegvar instance, it becomes null, thereby displaying the message Delegate is not pointing to any method on the screen.

Note

Delegates are immutable. When you call += or −=, a new delegate instance is created to represent a new list of targets or methods and assigned to the existing variable.

Recall that all delegate types implicitly derive from `System.MulticastDelegate`, which inherits from `System.Delegate`. This means that when you create a delegate type, you indirectly declare a class type that derives from `System.MulticastDelegate`. This class, besides certain methods, provides an invocation list that contains the addresses or pointers of the methods to be invoked by the delegate object. The methods that `System.MulticastDelegate` (or `System.Delegate`) provides can be used to interact with the invocation list. Some of the methods are described in Table 11.1.

Table 11.1 Methods of the System.MulticastDelegate Class

Method	Description
`Method`	Returns a `System.Reflection.MethodInfo` object that represents details of a static method maintained by the delegate.
`Target`	If the method being called is an instance method (not a static method), `Target` returns an object that represents the method maintained by the delegate. If the method being called is static, `Target` equals `null`.
`Combine()`	Adds a method to the list maintained by the delegate. The method can be invoked by using the overloaded += operator.
`GetInvocationList()`	Returns an array of `System.Delegate` objects, each representing a particular method that may be invoked.
`Remove()/RemoveAll()`	Removes a method (or all methods) from the delegate's invocation list. The method can be invoked by using the overloaded −= operator.

© 2015 Cengage Learning®.

Multicast delegates also involve combining of delegates. When the combination is called, all methods pointed by the individual delegates are called. Remember, only delegates of the same type can be combined.

The `DelegateCompose.cs` program shown in Listing 11.5 demonstrates combining of two delegate instances. The program declares a delegate `FuncDelegate` that can point to any method that takes two parameters of int type and returns nothing. Two static methods, AddNum and MultNum, are defined that match the delegate's signature. The methods take two parameters of int type and display their addition and multiplication, respectively. The delegate FuncDelegate is instantiated by creating its two instances named delegvar1 and delegvar2, respectively. The delegvar1 instance is set to reference at the AddNum method, and delegvar2 instance is set to reference at the MultNum method. The two delegate instances, delegvar1 and delegvar2, are combined to create the third delegate, delegvar3.

Listing 11.5 Program Code in DelegateCompose.cs File

```
using System;
delegate void FuncDelegate(int m, int n);
class DelegateCompose
{
    public static void AddNum(int p, int q)
    {
        Console.WriteLine("Sum of {0} and {1} is {2}", p,q,p+q);
    }
    public static void MultNum(int p, int q)
    {
        Console.WriteLine("Multiplication of {0} and {1} is {2}", p,q,p*q);
    }
    static void Main(string[] args)
    {
        FuncDelegate delegvar1 = new FuncDelegate(AddNum);
        FuncDelegate delegvar2 = new FuncDelegate(MultNum);
        FuncDelegate delegvar3=delegvar1 + delegvar2;
        delegvar3(10,20);
    }
}
```

Output:

```
Sum of 10 and 20 is 30
Multiplication of 10 and 20 is 200
```

You can see that the delegate instance delegvar3 is composed from the combination of delegate instances delegvar1 and delegvar2. After calling the delegate instance delegvar3, the methods pointed to by the two delegate instances are called in sequential order. Therefore, the result of the sum and multiplication operations on the parameters 10 and 20 is displayed on the screen.

The two delegate instances are combined using the addition operator. Similarly, the delegate instances are subtracted using the subtraction operator. If the delegate instance being subtracted from the combination is not found, you get the original combination. After you delete the last delegate instance, the empty list (combination) is represented by null.

Note

Multicast delegates are considered equal if they reference the same methods in the same order.

The Delegate3b.cs program shown in Listing 11.6 demonstrates use of the methods of the System.MulticastDelegate class in creating multicast delegates, iterating through the invocation list, and combining and removing the delegates from the invocation list. The program declares a delegate called FunDelegate that can reference to any method that takes two parameters of int type but returns nothing. Two static methods that match the delegate's signature are defined, named AddNum and MultNum. The AddNum and MultNum methods display the addition and multiplication of the supplied parameters, respectively. The delegate FuncDelegate is instantiated by creating its two instances named delegvar1 and delegvar2, respectively. The delegvar1 instance is set to reference at the AddNum method, and the delegvar2 instance is set to reference at the MultNum method. Using the Combine method, the two delegate instances, delegvar1 and delegvar2, are combined to create the third delegate, delegvar3. The GetInvocationList () method is called on the delegvar3 instance to get the array of delegates composed in it. Using the foreach loop, each of the delegates in delegvar3 is accessed and assigned to the temporary delegate delsingle that is invoked to call the associated methods.

Listing 11.6 Program Code in Delegate3b.cs File

```
using System;
delegate void FuncDelegate(int m, int n);
class Delegate3b
{
    public static void AddNum(int p, int q)
    {
        Console.WriteLine("Addition of {0} and {1} is {2}", p,q,p+q);
    }
    public static void MultNum(int p, int q)
    {
        Console.WriteLine("Multiplication of {0} and {1} is {2}", p,q,p*q);
    }
    static void Main(string[] args)
    {
```

```
FuncDelegate delegvar1 = new FuncDelegate(AddNum);
FuncDelegate delegvar2 = new FuncDelegate(MultNum);
FuncDelegate delegvar3=(FuncDelegate) Delegate.Combine(delegvar1, delegvar2);
if( delegvar3 != null )
{
    foreach( FuncDelegate delgsingle in delegvar3.GetInvocationList() )
    {
        try
        {
            delgsingle(10,20);
        }
        catch{ }
    }
}
delegvar3 = (FuncDelegate) Delegate.Remove(delegvar3, delegvar2);
delegvar3(10,20);
delegvar3= (FuncDelegate) Delegate.RemoveAll(delegvar3, delegvar3);
if(delegvar3 !=null)
    delegvar3(10,20);
else
    Console.WriteLine("Delegate is not pointing to any method");
    }
}
```

Output:

```
Addition of 10 and 20 is 30
Multiplication of 10 and 20 is 200
Addition of 10 and 20 is 30
Delegate is not pointing to any method
```

You can see that the delegate instances delegvar1 and delegvar2 are combined to create the delegvar3 instance. Each delegate (delegvar1 and delegvar2) is accessed by iterating through the invocation list and invoked to call the referenced method. In other words, the AddNum and MultNum methods that are referenced by the delegate instances delegvar1 and delegvar2 are called to display the sum and multiplication of the passed parameters, respectively. The Remove method is called on delegvar3 to remove delegvar2 from the combination. Recall that the methods are removed from the combination in reverse order. (The instance that is added last is removed first.) The delegate that is left in delegvar3's invocation list is delegvar1. The delegvar3 instance is invoked to call the AddNum method that is referenced by the delegvar1 instance. Finally, the RemoveAll method is called on delegvar3 to remove all the delegate instances (delegvar1) from the delegvar3 instance, making its value null.

The `RemoveAll` method is called with the following syntax:

```
new_delegate_instance=(target_delegate_casting) Delegate.RemoveAll
(source_delegate, delegates_to_remove)
```

The delegates in the `delegates_to_remove` invocation list are removed from the `source_delegate` invocation list and assigned to the `new_delegate_instance`. Before assigning the left-out delegates to the `new_delegate_instance`, you need to cast them into the desired delegate type.

COVARIANCE AND CONTRAVARIANCE

You know that a method's argument types and return type should match the delegate's argument types and return types. However, this condition can be relaxed through application of covariance and contravariance.

In *covariance*, a method can be encapsulated whose return type is directly or indirectly derived from the return type of a delegate. In other words, the return value of a method that is referenced by the delegate can have a different return type if the return type of the method is a subclass of the return type of the delegate.

Assume that there is a base class, `RectArea`, with a method named `returnRectAreaObj()` and a derived class, `TrgArea`, with a method called `returnTrgAreaObj()`. The name of the method suggests what it can return. For example, the `returnRectAreaObj()` method returns the `RectArea` object, and the `returnTrgAreaObj()` method returns the `TrgArea` object.

The following example declares a covariant delegate called `CovDelg` with return type `RectArea`:

```
public delegate RectArea CovDelg( );
```

Because the return type of the `CovDelg` is `RectArea`, it can encapsulate the methods that have the return type `RectArea` or `TrgArea`. Specifically, the methods `returnRectAreaObj()` and `returnTrgAreaObj()` can be encapsulated by the `CovDelg` delegate because these methods return objects of `RectArea` and `TrgArea`, respectively.

In *contravariance*, a method can take a parameter that is a base of the delegate's parameter type. In other words, the contravariance deals with the parameters rather than the return types.

To understand the concept of contravariance, assume that there are two methods, `PassRectArea` and `PassTrgArea`, that take the parameters of type `RectArea` and `TrgArea` object, respectively.

The following statement declares a contravariant delegate called `ContDelg` that takes a parameter of type `TrgArea` object:

```
public delegate void ContDelg(TrgArea objTrgArea);
```

Because the `TrgArea` class derives from the `RectArea` class, the `ContDelg` delegate, in addition to encapsulating the method `PassTrgArea`, can encapsulate the method `PassRectArea`. The `PassTrgArea` method takes the `TrgArea` object as a parameter, and the `PassRectArea` method takes the `RectArea` object as a parameter. If a delegate takes a parameter of a derived type, the contravariance allows it to be used to reference a method that takes a base class type as a parameter. That enables you to call both methods: one with a base-type parameter, and the other with a derived-type parameter.

Assuming that `t` is the `trgArea` object, the following statements invoke the `PassRectArea` method that takes the `RectArea` object as a parameter:

```
ContDelg contDelg = new ContDelg(PassRectArea);
contDelg(t);
```

Similarly, the following statement invokes the `PassTrgArea` method that takes the `TrgArea` object as a parameter:

```
contDelg = new ContDelg(PassTrgArea);
contDelg(t);
```

The contravariance delegate `contDelg` can reference the two methods that take parameters of the `RectArea` class and the derived class `TrgArea`.

The `CoVariance.cs` program shown in Listing 11.7 demonstrates covariance (how a delegate can encapsulate methods whose return type is directly or indirectly derived from the return type of a delegate). The program defines two classes, `RectArea` and `TrgArea`, where the `TrgArea` class inherits the `RectArea` class. The `RectArea` class defines a method, `returnRectAreaObj`, that returns the `RectArea` object. Similarly, the `trgArea` class defines a method, `returnTrgAreaObj`, that returns the `TrgArea` object.

A covariant delegate called `CovDelg` is declared with the return type `RectArea`. As a covariant delegate, it can encapsulate the methods `returnRectAreaObj` and `returnTrgAreaObj`, which have the return type `RectArea` or its derived class `TrgArea`.

Listing 11.7 Program Code in CoVariance.cs File

```
using System;
class RectArea {
   public RectArea returnRectAreaObj( )
   {
      Console.WriteLine ("Returning the RectArea object");
```

```
            return this;
        }
    }
    class TrgArea:RectArea {
        public TrgArea returnTrgAreaObj( )
        {
            Console.WriteLine ("Returning the TrgArea object");
            return this;
        }
    }
    class CoVariance
    {
        public delegate RectArea CovDelg( );
        static void Main()
        {
            RectArea r = new RectArea( );
            TrgArea t = new TrgArea( );
            CovDelg covDelg = new CovDelg(r.returnRectAreaObj);
            covDelg( );
            covDelg = new CovDelg(t.returnTrgAreaObj);
            covDelg( );
        }
    }
```

Output:

```
Returning the RectArea object
Returning the TrgArea object
```

You can see that the covariant delegate CovDelg is set to reference at returnRectAreaObj and returnTrgAreaObj methods of the RectArea and TrgArea classes, respectively. The delegate is invoked to call the two methods that display the messages Returning the RectArea object and Returning the TrgArea object, respectively.

Now that you've gotten some background, you'll write a program that demonstrates contravariance.

The CoVarianceApp.cs program shown in Listing 11.8 demonstrates contravariance and covariance. The program explains how a method can take a parameter that is a base of the delegate's parameter type. Also, the program explains how a delegate can encapsulate methods whose return type is derived from a return type of delegate.

The program defines two classes, RectArea and TrgArea, where the TrgArea class inherits the RectArea class. The RectArea class defines two private data members: 1 and b. The class defines two methods, returnRectAreaObj and getRect, that return the RectArea object and the area of a rectangle (1 * b), respectively. The trgArea class defines two data members: b and h. The class defines two methods, returnTrgAreaObj and getTrg, that return the TrgArea object and the area of a triangle (1/2*b*h), respectively.

The program also defines two static methods, PassRectArea and PassTrgArea, that take the RectArea and TrgArea objects as parameters, respectively.

A covariant delegate is declared named CovDelg, with return type RectArea. Also, a contravariant delegate is declared named ContDelg, which takes a parameter of type TrgArea object. As per their definition, the covariant delegate CovDelg can encapsulate the methods returnRectAreaObj and returnTrgAreaObj. Similarly, the contravariant delegate can encapsulate the two methods PassTrgArea and PassRectArea. The program shows how the covariant and contravariant delegates call their referenced methods to calculate the area of a rectangle and triangle, respectively.

Listing 11.8 Program Code in CoVarianceApp.cs File

```
using System;
class RectArea
{
    int l, b;
    public RectArea returnRectAreaObj( )
    {
        l=5;
        b=8;
        return this;
    }
    public int getRect( ) {
        return l*b;
    }
}
class TrgArea : RectArea
{
    int b,h;
    public TrgArea returnTrgAreaObj( )
    {
        b=5;
        h=8;
        return this;
    }
    public float getTrg( ) {
        return (float)1/2*b*h;
    }
}
```

```
class CoVarianceApp
{
    public delegate RectArea CovDelg( );
    public delegate void ContDelg(TrgArea objTrgArea);
    private static void PassRectArea(RectArea objRectArea)
    {
        Console.WriteLine ("Object of RectArea class is passed as parameter to this
method");
    }
    private static void PassTrgArea(TrgArea objTrgArea)
    {
        Console.WriteLine ("TrgArea object is passed to this method. Area of triangle is
{0}", objTrgArea.getTrg());
    }
    static void Main(string[] args)
    {
        RectArea r = new RectArea();
        TrgArea t = new TrgArea();
        CovDelg covDelg = new CovDelg(r.returnRectAreaObj);
        covDelg();
        Console.WriteLine ("Area of rectangle is {0}", covDelg().getRect());
        covDelg = new CovDelg(t.returnTrgAreaObj);
        covDelg();
        ContDelg contDelg = new ContDelg(PassRectArea);
        contDelg(t);
        contDelg = new ContDelg(PassTrgArea);
        contDelg(t);
    }
}
```

Output:

```
Area of rectangle is 40
Object of RectArea class is passed as parameter to this method
TrgArea object is passed to this method. Area of triangle is 20
```

You can see that the RectArea and TrgArea classes are instantiated by creating the objects r and t, respectively. An instance of the CovDelg delegate is created named covDelg, which references the instance method returnRectAreaObj of the RectArea class. The delegate instance is invoked to call the returnRectAreaObj method, which initializes the values of the data members l and b and returns the RectArea object. The getRect method is called through the RectArea object that is returned by the delegate. The getRect method displays the area of a rectangle by multiplying the values of the data members 1 and b.

After displaying the area of a rectangle, the covariance delegate instance covDelg is set to reference at the returnTrgAreaObj method of the TrgArea class. The delegate instance is invoked to call the returnTrgAreaObj method that in turn initializes the data members b and h and returns the TrgArea object. An instance of the contravariant delegate ContDelg is created called contDelg, which references the PassRectArea method. The contDelg delegate is invoked passing the TrgArea object t to it, which calls the PassRectArea method. The PassRectArea method simply displays the text message Object of RectArea class is passed as parameter to this method to indicate that the method has been successfully called. Then the contDelg delegate is set to reference at the PassTrgArea method. The contDelg instance is invoked, passing the TrgArea object to it that calls the PassTrgArea method. The PassTrgArea method uses the TrgArea object that is passed to it to call the getTrg method to display the area of a triangle.

GENERIC DELEGATE TYPES

Suppose that you want to define a delegate type that can reference a method of any type; whether the method returns int, float, or any other type, the delegate must be able to reference it. Similarly, assume that you have certain methods that take a single parameter but of different types. In other words, one method takes a parameter of int type, the other takes a parameter of float type, and so on. If you want a single delegate that can reference such methods, you need to use generic delegates.

Generic delegates are not bound to any specific type. These delegates can reference methods that return different types and take parameters of different types. The flexible delegates that can be set to point at the methods that return a desired type and take parameters of a desired type are known as *generic delegates*. An example of a generic delegate is shown here:

```
public delegate T DispMessage<T>(T arg);
```

The preceding statement declares a generic delegate called DispMessage that can point to any method whose return type is T and that takes a single parameter of T type. The character T can be substituted by the data type of the method that the delegate wants to point to. For example, if T is substituted by int, this delegate can point to any method that returns an int type and takes a single parameter of int type. Similarly, if T is replaced by the float type, the same delegate can point to any method that returns a float type and that takes a single parameter of the float type.

Therefore, at the time of defining the delegate instance, you need to specify the return and parameter types of the method to reference. You specify the return and parameter types by substituting the <T>, as shown in the following example:

The following statement registers the delegate for the desired target:

```
DispMessage<string> delg =new DispMessage<string>(Show);
```

The preceding statement creates a delegate instance called delg that is set to point at the Show method, which returns a string type and takes a parameter of the string type. You can use the same delegate to create a delegate instance that returns a float type and takes a single parameter of the float type, as shown here:

```
DispMessage<float> delgvar =new DispMessage<float>(Commission);
```

The preceding statement creates a delegate instance called delgvar that points at the Commission method, which then returns the float type and takes a single parameter of it.

From the preceding examples, you might wonder if the return type and the type of parameters need to be the same. The answer is no. The return type of the method that is pointed to by the generic delegate can be different from the parameter types. Also, if there are multiple parameters in a method, they can be of different types. The following example of generic delegates can reference methods whose return type is different from its parameter types:

```
public delegate T2 DispMessage<T1,T2>(T1 arg);
```

In the preceding example, you can see that two types are used. T1 represents the parameter types, and T2 represents the return type of the method. While defining the delegate instance, you need to supply two types to substitute for T1 and T2. For example, the following statement creates a delegate instance called delg that is set to point at the Show method that returns the float type and that takes a parameter of the int type:

```
DispMessage<int, float> delg =new DispMessage<int, float>(Show);
```

Observe that <T1, T2> used in delegate declaration are replaced by the desired return and parameter types.

The GenericDelegate.cs program shown in Listing 11.9 demonstrates creation and invoking of *generic delegates*—the delegates that are not bound to a specific type. The program declares a generic delegate called Calculate that returns a T type and takes two parameters of T type. To demonstrate how the generic delegates invoke methods of different types, the program defines two static methods named Rect and Triangle. The Rect method returns the int type and takes two parameters of that type.

The `Triangle` method, on the other hand, returns the `float` type and takes two parameters of that type. The delegate points at both the methods and invokes them.

Listing 11.9 Program Code in GenericDelegate.cs File

```
using System;
public delegate T Calculate<T>(T arg1, T arg2);
class GenericDelegate
{
    static void Main(string[] args)
    {
        Calculate<int> r =new Calculate<int>(Rect);
        Console.WriteLine ("Area of rectangle is " + r(5,8));
        Calculate<float> t =new Calculate<float>(Triangle);
        Console.WriteLine ("Area of triangle is "+ t(5,8));
    }
    static float Triangle (float x, float y)
    {
        return (float)1/2*x *y;
    }
    static int Rect (int x, int y)
    {
        return x *y;
    }
}
```

Output:

```
Area of rectangle is 40
Area of triangle is 20
```

The generic delegate is instantiated twice by creating two objects named `r` and `t`, where instance `r` is set to reference at the `Rect` method (which returns `int` and takes a single parameter of `int` type). The instance `t` is set to reference at the `Triangle` method, which returns a `float` type and takes a single parameter of that type. The two delegate instances `r` and `t` are invoked to call the two methods `Rect` and `Triangle`, respectively. Values 5 and 8 are passed as parameters while invoking the two methods to display the area of a rectangle and a triangle.

What if you want a small change in the preceding program? You want the `Triangle` method to accept parameters of the `int` type but return a result in the `float` type. (You want the return and parameter types to be different in the `Triangle` method.)

To create that change, modify the preceding GenericDelegate.cs program (see Listing 11.9) to appear as shown in Listing 11.10. Only the statements in bold are modified. The rest is the same as in Listing 11.9.

Listing 11.10 Program Code in GenericDelegate.cs File

```
using System;
public delegate T2 Calculate<T1, T2>(T1 arg1, T1 arg2);
class GenericDelegate
{
    static void Main(string[] args)
    {
        Calculate<int, int> r =new Calculate<int, int>(Rect);
        Console.WriteLine ("Area of rectangle is "+ r(5,8));
        Calculate<int, float> t =new Calculate<int, float>(Triangle);
        Console.WriteLine ("Area of triangle is "+ t(5,8));
    }
    static float Triangle (int x, int y)
    {
        return (float)1/2*x *y;
    }
    static int Rect (int x, int y)
    {
        return x *y;
    }
}
```

Output:

```
Area of rectangle is 40
Area of triangle is 20
```

You can see that the Triangle method is modified to accept parameters of the int type and return a result of the float type. Also, in the code, you see that two types, T1 and T2, are specified while declaring the Calculate delegate. While you're making the delegate instance r to reference at the Rect method, both the return and the parameter types are supplied as int. Obviously, this is because the return and parameter types in the Rect method are of the int type.

While defining the delegate instance t, the types supplied are int and float because the Triangle method takes parameters of the int type and returns the result of the float type. Both delegate instances r and t are invoked to call their respective referenced methods, Rect and Triangle.

ANONYMOUS METHOD

Besides using named methods, C# enables you to use anonymous methods to work with delegates. Anonymous methods allow declaration of inline methods, which use the keyword delegate instead of a method name followed by the body of the method enclosed in parentheses. If the delegate has parameters, you pass them to the anonymous method, enclosing them in parentheses following the keyword delegate. If the delegate has no parameters, use the keyword delegate followed either by empty parentheses or no parentheses at all.

The Anonymous1.cs program shown in Listing 11.11 demonstrates invoking of the anonymous method.

Listing 11.11 Program Code in Anonymous1.cs File

```
using System;
public delegate void AddVal(int x, int y);
class Anonymous1 {
    static void Main() {
        AddVal addvalues = delegate(int a, int b) {
            Console.Write("Addition is {0}", a+b);
        };
        addvalues(10,20);
    }
}
```

Output:

```
Addition is 30
```

You can see in the preceding program that a delegate AddVal is declared that has two int parameters and returns void (nothing). In the Main() function, an instance of the AddVal delegate is created named addvalues, and a block of code is passed via the anonymous method to it following the delegate keyword and the enclosed parameters. The block of code passed to the addvalues delegate is the anonymous method that will be called when the addvalues() method is called. A semicolon (;) reports termination of the anonymous method definition. The anonymous method is called with the addvalues() method. The arguments 10 and 20 are used while calling the addvalues() method and then assigned to the parameters a and b of the anonymous method. The addition of the parameters is then displayed on the screen.

The Anonymous2.cs program shown in Listing 11.12 demonstrates an anonymous method returning a value. As expected, you only need to take care of the fact that the type of value returned by the anonymous method must be compatible with the return type specified by the delegate.

Listing 11.12 Program Code in Anonymous2.cs File

```
using System;
public delegate int AddVal(int x, int y);
class Anonymous2 {
    static void Main() {
        int k;
        AddVal addvalues = delegate(int a, int b) {
            return a+b;
        };
        k=addvalues(10,20);
        Console.Write("Addition of 10 and 20 is {0}", k);
    }
}
```

Output:

```
Addition of 10 and 20 is 30
```

After using the preceding examples on delegates, you might be thinking that delegates and interfaces are the same. They're actually quite different. Read on.

DIFFERENCE BETWEEN DELEGATES AND INTERFACES

A task that can be performed with a delegate can also be performed with an interface. For example, the Delegate1.cs program shown in Listing 11.1 can be written in terms of an interface, as shown in Listing 11.13.

Listing 11.13 Program Code in InterfaceApp.cs File

```
interface Calculate
{
    int Rect();
}
class InterfaceApp : Calculate
{
    int l,b;
    public InterfaceApp(int x, int y)
    {
        l=x;
        b=y;
    }
    public int Rect()
```

```
    {
        return l*b;
    }
    public static void Main()
    {
        InterfaceApp r = new InterfaceApp(5,8);
        System.Console.WriteLine("Area of rectangle is {0}", r.Rect());
    }
}
```

Output:

```
Area of rectangle is 40
```

Although both delegates and interfaces include only the declaration, there is a considerable difference between them. The characteristics of delegates and interfaces clearly differentiate among the two.

Here are the characteristics of delegates:

- Delegates only have a declaration. No implementation is provided for delegates. They are just safe callbacks or function pointers.

- Delegates can reference any method of the class, provided the argument and return types match that of their own. Therefore, delegates help in "anonymous" invocation.

- Delegates are preferred when a class may need more than one implementation of the method.

Here are the characteristics of interfaces:

- Interfaces contains only the declaration of the method, not the definition or implementation code. Implementation of the method is done in the class.

- Interfaces allow you to extend some objects' functionality or behavior.

- Interfaces can be inherited. In fact, interfaces are used to simulate multiple inheritance in C#.

- Interface calls are faster than delegate calls.

- Instances of interface can be created.

- Interface calls are faster than delegate calls. Calling of a method through a delegate is indirect.

- Method pointers are accessed, and then the concerned method is called. An interface reference is a reference to an instance of an object that implements the interface. It's faster to call a method through an interface reference.

- Interfaces are preferred when a class needs only one implementation of the method.

EVENT HANDLING

Events are usually task initiaters. Pressing Enter or clicking a mouse are the common events that you create or that occur while you're working with any application or program. A C# *event* is a class member that is fired whenever a specific designated event (action) takes place. If you want to be notified when an event occurs, you need to register for that event. When an event occurs, registered methods are automatically invoked. Registration of methods is done through delegates that specify the signature of the methods that are registered for it. The methods that are invoked when an event occurs are known as *event handlers*. The code that you want to run when an event occurs is enclosed in an event handler. An event can have many handlers, so defining an event is a two-step process. First, you need to define a delegate type that specifies the methods to be called when the event is fired. Second, you need to declare an event using the C# event keyword to indicate the related delegate type. To try out events practically, you must learn to declare them.

Declaring an Event

To declare an event, you must declare a delegate to which the event is supposed to be associated. For example, the following statement declares a delegate called Calculate that can reference a method that takes two parameters of int type and returns nothing:

```
delegate void Calculate (int x, int y);
```

After you declare a delegate, you declare an event using the following syntax:

```
public event delegate_name event_name
```

For example, the following statement defines a delegate named Calculate and an event named EventToCalculate, which invokes the delegate when the event is fired:

```
public static event Calculate EventToCalculate;
```

In other words, events can hold delegates, and they can be used to invoke methods whose signature matches the associated delegates. Instead of invoking the methods directly using the delegate, the event is invoked or fired, and then it invokes the delegate, which then calls the referenced method.

You can add delegates to an event using the += operator. The syntax for adding a delegate instance to an event is given here:

```
event_name+= delegate_instance;
```

To invoke the event and the event handler (the method referenced by the delegate), you need to specify the event name along with any required parameters (as defined by the associated delegate).

The EventDemo.cs program shown in Listing 11.14 demonstrates how an event is fired and how an event handler that is associated to the event is invoked. The program declares a delegate called Calculate that can reference a method that takes two parameters of int type and returns nothing. An event called EventToCalculate is declared that invokes the Calculate delegate if the event occurs or is fired.

Listing 11.14 Program Code in EventDemo.cs File

```
using System;
delegate void Calculate (int x, int y);
class EventDemo
{
    public static event Calculate EventToCalculate;
    static void Rect (int x, int y)
    {
        Console.WriteLine("Area of rectangle is {0}", x *y);
    }
    static void Main()
    {
        EventToCalculate+=new Calculate(Rect);
        EventToCalculate(5,8);
    }
}
```

Output:

```
Area of rectangle is 40
```

You can see that a static method, Rect, is defined that takes two int parameters to calculate the area of a rectangle. The Rect method simply displays the calculated area of the rectangle and does not return anything. An instance of the Calculate delegate is created that references the Rect method. Using the += operator, the delegate instance is added to the event EventToCalculate. The EventToCalculate is fired passing two int arguments: 5 and 8. As expected, the EventToCalculate event invokes the Calculate delegate, which in turn invokes the referenced method, Rect. The values 5 and 8 are assigned to the Rect method's parameters, thereby displaying the area of a rectangle on the screen.

Note

The Rect method that is invoked in the preceding program on occurrence of the event is also known as the *event handler.*

You can have more than one event handler associated to an event. The EventProg.cs program shown in Listing 11.15 demonstrates how you can invoke several event handlers when a single event occurs. The program declares a delegate called EventHandler that can reference a method that takes no parameter and returns nothing. An event called dispMessage is declared that invokes the EventHandler delegate when the event occurs.

Listing 11.15 Program Code in EventProg.cs File

```
using System;
public delegate void EventHandler();
class EventProg
{
    public static event EventHandler dispMessage;
    static void Main()
    {
        dispMessage += new EventHandler(handler1);
        dispMessage += new EventHandler(handler2);
        dispMessage += new EventHandler(handler3);
        dispMessage.Invoke();
    }
    static void handler1()
    {
        Console.WriteLine("This is event handler 1");
    }
    static void handler2()
    {
        Console.WriteLine("This is event handler 2");
    }
    static void handler3()
    {
        Console.WriteLine("This is event handler 3");
    }
}
```

```
This is event handler 1
This is event handler 2
This is event handler 3
```

You can see that three static methods, handler1, handler2, and handler3, are defined that take no parameters and simply display a text message. The three handler methods are added to the event (to its invocation list) using the += operator. In other words, three instances of the EventHandler delegate are created that reference the respective handler method. All three delegate instances are then added to the dispMessage event. The Invoke method is called on the event to fire it. Consequently, all three handler methods are invoked sequentially—in the order they were added to the invocation list, thereby displaying the respective text messages.

In the previous two programs, you learned to invoke the static methods when an event occurred. The EventDelg.cs program shown in Listing 11.16 demonstrates invoking of a class method when an event occurred. The program declares a delegate called ProductDelegate that can reference a method that takes no parameter and returns nothing. A class named Product is defined that contains a data member named qty. The class also contains a parameterized constructor that initializes the data member qty. Besides the constructor, the class defines two member methods: RaiseEvent and Display. An event called ProductEvent is declared that invokes the ProductDelegate delegate when the event occurs.

Listing 11.16 Program Code in EventDelg.cs File

```
using System;
public delegate void ProductDelegate();
public class Product
{
    public event ProductDelegate ProductEvent;
    int qty;
    public Product(int v)
    {
        qty=v;
    }
    public void RaiseEvent()
    {
        ProductEvent();
    }
    public void Display()
    {
        Console.WriteLine("Product quantity is {0}", qty);
```

```
        }
}
class EventDelg
{
    static void Main()
    {
        Product p = new Product(10);
        p.ProductEvent += new ProductDelegate(p.Display);
        p.RaiseEvent();
    }
}
```

Output:

```
Product quantity is 10
```

An instance of the Product class is created named p. The data member qty of instance p is initialized to value 10 through the parameterized constructor. An instance of the ProductDelegate delegate is created that references the Display method of the Product instance p. The delegate instance is then added to the ProductEvent event using the += operator. In other words, the Display method of the Product instance is added to the event's invocation list. The RaiseEvent method is called on instance p that in turn fires the ProductEvent. As expected, the ProductEvent invokes the ProductDelegate delegate, which in turn calls the p instance's Display method. The Display method displays the value of the data member qty on the screen.

In all the event programs discussed earlier, the event was fired manually. But you can also make the event fire automatically based on some action. The EventApp.cs program shown in Listing 11.17 demonstrates how an event is fired automatically. The program defines a Product class that contains a data member named qty. The program defines a ProductEvent that invokes the ProductDelegate when the event is fired. In the program, the event is automatically fired when the user changes the value of the data member qty.

Listing 11.17 Program Code in EventApp.cs File

```
using System;
public delegate void ProductDelegate();
public class Product
{
    public event ProductDelegate ProductEvent;
    int qty;
    public Product(int v)
    {
        qty=v;
    }
```

```
    public int Qty
    {
        get { return qty; }
        set
        {
            if (qty == value) return;
            if (ProductEvent != null)
            {
                qty = value;
                ProductEvent();
            }
        }
    }
    public void Display()
    {
        Console.WriteLine("Product quantity is {0}", qty);
    }
}
class EventApp
{
    static void Main()
    {
        Product p = new Product(10);
        p.Display();
        p.ProductEvent += new ProductDelegate(p.Display);
        p.Qty=10;
        p.Qty=20;
    }
}
```

Output:

```
Product quantity is 10
Product quantity is 20
```

You can see that an instance of the Product class is created named p, and its data member qty is initialized to value 10. The Display method on instance p is called to display the initial value of the data member qty. An instance of the ProductDelegate delegate is created that references the Display method of the Product instance p. The delegate instance is then added to the ProductEvent event. Also, when the ProductEvent is fired, the Display method of the Product instance is invoked. Using the Qty property, the value of the data member qty is modified. In the setter method, the new value that is assigned to the `qty` member is compared to its current value. If the new and current values are the same, nothing will happen, but if the new value is different from the `qty`'s current value, the new value is assigned to the `qty` member and the `ProductEvent` is fired. The `ProductEvent` invokes the `ProductDelegate` delegate, which in turn calls the `p` instance's `Display` method to display the new value that is assigned to the data member `qty`.

Event Accessors

You can easily add events to classes to enable objects to implement event handling when an event occurs. When you add an event to the class through the `+=` operator, the compiler automatically generates two event accessors. The event accessors are basically two methods that are named `add` and `remove` and are similar to the `get` and `set` accessors used with properties. The `add` accessor registers a new subscription to an event, and the `remove` accessor unregisters an existing one.

You can override the `add` and `remove` methods for an event to run additional code while implementing the events.

Event accessors can be explicitly declared as follows:

```
class MyClass
{
    private event delegate_name private_event;
    public event delegate_name event_name
    {
        add
        {
            private_event += value;
        }
        remove
        {
            private_event -= value;
        }
    }
}
```

When you use the `+=` operator on an event, it calls the `add` accessor. Similarly, after calling the `-=` operator, the `remove` accessor is invoked. Each accessor receives a variable named `value` that holds the details of the subscriber. The `add` accessor adds the value to the event, and the `remove` accessor unregisters the subscriber. You can add desired code in the accessors, like checking some condition before registering or unregistering the subscriber.

The `EventAccessor.cs` program shown in Listing 11.18 demonstrates invoking of `event` accessors. The program explains how `add` and `remove` accessors can be overridden while implementing the events. The program declares a delegate called `Calculate` that can reference a method that takes no parameters and returns nothing. A class named `Rect` is defined that is meant to calculate the area of a rectangle. The class contains two data members, `l` and `b` (for length and breadth), a parameterized constructor, and two member methods called `RaiseEvent` and `Display`. An event called `RectEvent` is declared that invokes the `Calculate` delegate on occurrence of the event. The class also defines an event called `CalculateEvent`, along with its `add` and `remove` methods (or accessors). The `add` and `remove` accessors are invoked after using the `+=` and `-=` operators, respectively.

Listing 11.18 Program Code in EventAccessor.cs File

```
using System;
public delegate void Calculate();
public class Rect
{
    int l,b;
    private Calculate RectEvent;
    public Rect(int x, int y)
    {
        l=x;
        b=y;
    }
    public event Calculate CalculateEvent
    {
        add
        {
            Console.WriteLine("Attaching the {0} delegate to the RectEvent", value);
            RectEvent += value;
        }
        remove
        {
            Console.WriteLine("Detaching the {0} delegate from the RectEvent", value);
            RectEvent -= value;
        }
    }
    public void RaiseEvent()
    {
        RectEvent();
    }
```

```
    public void Display()
    {
        Console.WriteLine("Area of rectangle is {0}", l*b);
    }
}
class EventAccessor
{
    static void Main()
    {
        Rect p = new Rect(5,8);
        p.CalculateEvent+=new Calculate(p.Display);
        p.RaiseEvent();
        p.CalculateEvent-=new Calculate(p.Display);
    }
}
```

Output:

```
Attaching the Calculate delegate to the RectEvent
Area of rectangle is 40
Detaching the Calculate delegate from the RectEvent
```

You can see that an instance of the Rect class is created named p, and its data members l and b are initialized to values 5 and 8, respectively. An instance of the Calculate delegate is created that references the Display method of the Rect instance p. The delegate instance is then added to the p instance's CalculateEvent event by using the += operator. After using the += operator, the add accessor is invoked, which adds the supplied delegate instance to the RectEvent event. Then the RaiseEvent method is called on the p instance that fires the RectEvent. The RectEvent invokes the Calculate delegate, which in turn calls the p instance's Display method to display the area of the rectangle by multiplying the length and breadth data members. After printing the area of a rectangle, the delegate instance is removed from the p instance's CalculateEvent event using the -= operator. Consequently, the remove accessor is invoked, which removes the supplied delegate instance from the RectEvent event.

Note

> You can set both accessors to execute their code within a lock statement to ensure thread safety. Thread safety is an essential requirement in multithreaded applications. In multithreaded applications, a resource might be accessed by one or more threads simultaneously, so to maintain consistency, you must synchronize the threads. The resource is updated by only one thread at a time so that the resource is not left in an invalid state.

SUMMARY

In this chapter, you learned to use delegates. You saw how delegates are declared, instantiated, and invoked. You also discovered how to invoke the referenced methods and how to use the multicast delegates. You distinguished between covariance and contravariance and learned about generic delegate types, anonymous methods, and the basic difference between delegates and interfaces. Finally, you learned to declare events and to use event accessors in C# programs.

The next chapter is focused on collections. You will learn to store and manage collections of objects. You will use lists, linked lists, dictionaries, and arrays. You will learn about standard as well as generic collections.

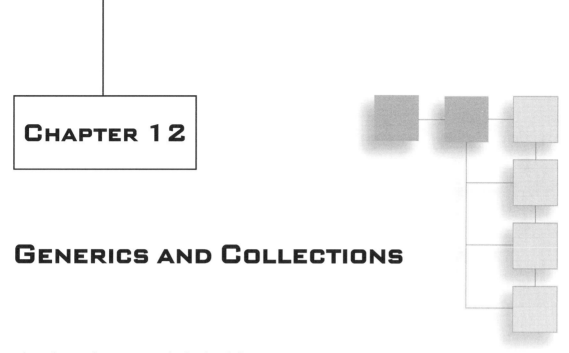

CHAPTER 12

GENERICS AND COLLECTIONS

This chapter's topics include the following:

- Collections
- Standard interfaces
- IEnumerators
- Hashtable
- SortedList
- BitArray
- Stack
- Queue
- Generics
- Generic collections
- SortedSet
- LinkedList<T>

COLLECTIONS

Collections, as the name suggests, refer to a group of objects. The .NET Framework provides a standard set of types for storing and managing collections of objects. These include lists, linked lists, dictionaries, and arrays. Unlike arrays, where the size is fixed, collections can dynamically grow and shrink to accommodate objects. With the exception of arrays, all collections are classes, so their instances are created to use them. There are two types of collections:

- Standard collections that are found under the System.Collections namespace
- Generic collections that are found under the System.Collections.Generic namespace

Following are the commonly used classes of the System.Collections namespace:

- **ArrayList**—Represents an ordered collection of an object. Unlike with an array, an ArrayList size is not static; it resizes automatically when new items are dynamically added or removed. Also, you can add and remove items from the specified index location in an ArrayList.

- **Hashtable**—Stores key/value pairs. A key is associated with each element or value in the collection. A value can be accessed from a hashtable by specifying its key.

- **SortedList**—Stores key/value pairs, where the values are sorted by the key values. Any element or value can be accessed by specifying its key or index value. In that way, a sorted list is considered a combination of an ArrayList and a hashtable.

- **BitArray**—Represents an array that stores the binary digits in the form of Boolean values. In other words, it stores Boolean values true and false, where true indicates bit 1 and false indicates bit 0. You can access elements from the BitArray using an integer index that begins from 0. In C#, Boolean values are represented by the bool data type.

- **Stack**—Represents a last in, first out (LIFO) collection of objects. It uses push and pop operations to insert and remove objects from the stack. The object that is added last is removed first.

- **Queue**—Represents a first in, first out (FIFO) collection of objects. It uses enqueue and dequeue operations to add and remove objects from the queue. The object that is added first is the one that is removed first.

The collection's functionality, such as accessing and managing collection elements, is available through interfaces. Following are the interfaces available in the System.Collections namespace:

- **IEnumerable**—Enables you to loop through elements in a collection.

- **ICollection**—Enables you to determine the number of elements in a collection and copy them in a simple array type.

- **IList**—Provides a list of elements for a collection, along with the capabilities for accessing and managing them.

■ `IDictionary`—Provides a list of elements that are accessible via a key value, rather than an index. The `IDictionary` interface is implemented by classes that support collections of associated keys and values.

The `Object` class is the base class of every type in .NET. All the collections implement the `IEnumerable` interface, which is extended by the `ICollection` interface. The `IDictionary` and `IList` interfaces are derived from `ICollection`, as shown in Figure 12.1.

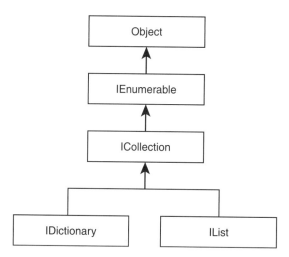

Figure 12.1
Hierarchy of interfaces.
© 2015 Cengage Learning®.

STANDARD INTERFACES

The .NET Framework provides standard interfaces for enumerating, comparing, and creating collections. Following is the list of standard interfaces:

■ `IEnumerator` **interface**—The `IEnumerator` interface provides iterative capability for a collection. It requires implementation of three methods: `MoveNext`, `Reset`, and `Current`.

■ `IEnumerable` **interface**—This provides support for the `foreach` iteration. The `IEnumerable` interface includes one public method called `GetEnumerator`. So, for implementing the `IEnumerable` interface, you need to implement the `GetEnumerator` method. However, the `GetEnumerator` method returns an `IEnumerator` interface. Therefore, to implement `IEnumerable`, you must also implement `IEnumerator`, or you cannot cast the return value from the `GetEnumerator` method to the

`IEnumerator` interface. In short, the use of `IEnumerable` requires that the class implement `IEnumerator`.

Note

The `IEnumerable` interface enables you to use custom objects in the form of a collection. In other words, it makes the user-defined classes appear as a collection.

IENUMERATORS

The `IEnumerator` interface provides the basis of traversal in a `foreach` loop. Without this interface, you could not traverse the elements of a collection in a `foreach` loop. The `foreach` loop cannot work without the `GetEnumerator` operation. Therefore, all the collections implement the interface `IEnumerable` and hereby provide the operation `GetEnumerator`.

Enumerators allow you to traverse the contents of a collection. Because a collection might contain data of different data structures, interfaces like `IEnumerable` and `IEnumerator` are used to implement a common traversal mechanism. Remember, enumerators can be used to read the elements in the collection, but they cannot be used to modify them.

The `IEnumerator` interface declaration follows:

```
public interface IEnumerator
{
    bool MoveNext();
    object Current { get; }
    void Reset();
}
```

`IEnumerator` requires implementation of the following three methods:

- **MoveNext**—Advances the current element to the next position. The method returns `false` if there are no more elements in the collection. The method is always called before retrieving the first element. The initial index is 0, and each `MoveNext` method increments the index by 1.

- **Current**—Returns the element at the current position. If the last call to `MoveNext` returned `false`, `Current` is undefined. Also, you cannot set `Current` to the first element of the collection.

- **Reset**—Moves back to the start. You can enumerate the collection again after calling this method.

Note

Collections do not implement enumerators; instead, they provide enumerators via the IEnumerable interface.

Using Iterator

An *iterator* is a method, property, or indexer that supplies all the values to be used in a foreach block in sequence. It contains one or more yield statements and is usually named GetEnumerator, but you can assign it any name. An iterator returns either IEnumerable or IEnumerator. The IEnumerableSimpleApp.cs file shown in Listing 12.1 demonstrates using an iterator to return the IEnumerable interface type.

Listing 12.1 Program Code in IEnumerableSimpleApp.cs File

```
using System;
using System.Collections;
class IEnumerableSimpleApp
{
    static IEnumerable IteratorBlock()
    {
        for (int i=0; i < 5; i++)
        {
            yield return i.ToString();
        }
        yield return "Numbers Over";
    }
    static void Main()
    {
        foreach (string str in IteratorBlock())
        {
            Console.WriteLine(str);
        }
    }
}
```

Output:

```
0
1
2
3
4
Numbers Over
```

In the preceding code, the static method `IteratorBlock()` is an iterator whose return type is an `IEnumerable` interface. The method uses the `yield` keyword to supply five numerical values to the `foreach` block for displaying them on the screen. The `yield` statement returns object type values. Because the object is the base class for all types, the `yield` statements can return any type.

The `IEnumeratorSimpleApp.cs` file shown in Listing 12.2 demonstrates using an iterator in returning the `IEnumerator` interface type.

Listing 12.2 Program Code in IEnumeratorSimpleApp.cs File

```
using System;
using System.Collections;

class IEnumeratorSimpleApp
{
    static void Main()
    {
    string   [] numbers = new string[5] {"0","1" , "2" ,"3", "4"};
    IEnumerator enums = numbers.GetEnumerator();
        System.Console.WriteLine("The numbers from 0 to 4 are:");
    while(enums.MoveNext())
        System.Console.WriteLine(enums.Current);
enums.Reset();
        System.Console.WriteLine("\nRepeating again – the numbers from 0 to 4
are:");
    while(enums.MoveNext())
        System.Console.WriteLine(enums.Current);
    }
}
```

Output:

```
The numbers from 0 to 4 are:
0
1
2
3
4

Repeating again – the numbers from 0 to 4 are:
0
1
2
3
4
```

Enumerating the Generic Collection Classes

Later in this chapter, you learn about generic collection classes. These classes implement generic interfaces, like IEnumerable<T>. You can enumerate over a generic collection.

The IEnumerableApp.cs file shown in Listing 12.3 demonstrates how a generic interface, IEnumerable<T>, is returned by an iterator.

Listing 12.3 Program Code in IEnumerableApp.cs File

```
using System;
using System.Collections.Generic;
class IEnumerableApp
{
    static IEnumerable<string> GetDemoEnumerable()
    {
        for (int i=0; i < 5; i++)
        {
            yield return i.ToString();
        }
        yield return "Numbers Over";
    }
    static void Main()
    {
        foreach (string str in GetDemoEnumerable())
        {
            Console.WriteLine(str);
        }
    }
}
```

Output:

```
0
1
2
3
4
Numbers Over
```

You can see that IEnumerable of string type is returned by the GetDemoEnumerable() iterator. Remember, while using the yield return statement, the function should return an IEnumerable and should be called from an iteration block (foreach statement).

The ArrayEnumerator file shown in Listing 12.4 demonstrates implementing IEnumerable and IEnumerator interfaces.

Listing 12.4 Program Code in ArrayEnumerator File

```
using System;
using System.Collections;

public class SingleDim : IEnumerable
{
    private int[] array;
    SingleDim(int[] arr)
    {
        array = arr;
    }
    public IEnumerator GetEnumerator()
    {
        return new ArrayEnumerator(this);
    }
    private class ArrayEnumerator : IEnumerator
    {
        private int loc = -1;
        private SingleDim a;
        public ArrayEnumerator(SingleDim a)
        {
            this.a = a;
        }
        public bool MoveNext()
        {
            if (loc < a.array.Length - 1)
            {
                loc++;
                return true;
            }
            else
            {
                return false;
            }
        }
        public void Reset()
        {
            loc = -1;
        }
        public object Current
        {
            get
```

```
        {
            return a.array[loc];
        }
    }
}
static void Main()
{
    int[] data = { 1, 2, 3,4,5 };
    SingleDim arry = new SingleDim(data);
    Console.WriteLine("Array elements are: ");
    foreach (int item in arry)
    {
        Console.WriteLine(item);
    }
}
}
```

Output:

```
Array elements are:
1
2
3
4
5
```

Because the ArrayEnumerator class implements the IEnumerator interface, it defines the MoveNext, Reset, and Current methods. The three methods return the next array element, reset the array index, and return the current array index value, respectively. The GetEnumerator() iterator returns the ArrayEnumerator object that implements the IEnumerator interface, which in turn is used for iterating through the array values.

In addition to being used with built-in types int and string, enumerators can be used to iterate through objects. The ObjectsCollection.cs file shown in Listing 12.5 demonstrates how to iterate through the array of objects. An Employee class stores the code, name, and basic salary of employees. Using the IEnumerable interface, you iterate through the employee information.

Listing 12.5 Program Code in ObjectsCollection.cs File

```
using System;
using System.Collections;

public class Employee
{
```

```
    int Code;
    string Name;
    int BasicSalary;
    public Employee(){}
    public Employee(int c, string name, int basicsal)
    {
        this.Code = c;
        this.Name =name;
        this.BasicSalary = basicsal;
    }
    public override string ToString()
    {
        return String.Format("Code: {0}, Name: {1} and Basic Salary: {2}", Code, Name,
BasicSalary);
    }
}
public class EmployeesCollection : IEnumerable
{
    ArrayList employeesList = new ArrayList();
    public EmployeesCollection() { }
    public void AddEmployee(Employee emp)
    {
        employeesList.Add(emp);
    }
    public Employee GetEmployee(int index)
    {
        return (Employee)employeesList[index];
    }
    IEnumerator IEnumerable.GetEnumerator()
    {
        return employeesList.GetEnumerator();
    }
}
class ObjectsCollection
{
    static void Main()
    {
        Employee e1=new Employee(101, "John", 5000);
        Employee e2=new Employee(102, "Caroline",6500);
        EmployeesCollection empList=new EmployeesCollection();
        empList.AddEmployee(e1);
        empList.AddEmployee(e2);
        Console.WriteLine("The Employee information at index location 1 is
"+empList.GetEmployee(1));
```

```
        Console.WriteLine("The information of all employees is as follows:");
        foreach (Employee emp in empList)
        {
            Console.WriteLine(emp);
        }
    }
}
```

Output:

```
The Employee information at index location 1 is Code: 102, Name: Caroline and Basic
Salary: 6500
The information of all employees is as follows:
Code: 101, Name: John and Basic Salary: 5000
Code: 102, Name: Caroline and Basic Salary: 6500
```

Information about two employees named John and Caroline is added to the ArrayList. Using the GetEnumerator() iterator, the information about these employees is accessed or iterated and displayed on the screen.

HASHTABLE

A hashtable, as the name suggests, stores elements and uses a hash code to find elements quickly. The hash code here means a unique key that is used to store and access information or values in the hashtable.

The HashtableDemo.cs file shown in Listing 12.6 demonstrates using a hashtable in storing and accessing the prices of certain food items.

Listing 12.6 Program Code in HashtableDemo.cs File

```
using System;
using System.Collections;

class HashtableDemo
{
    static void Main()
    {
        Hashtable htable = new Hashtable();
        htable["Pizza"] = 15;
        htable["Hot Dog"] = 2;
        htable.Add ("Noodles", 6);
        htable.Add ("Burger", 5);
        Console.WriteLine("Price of Pizza is {0}", htable["Pizza"]);
        ICollection htKeys = htable.Keys;    //Use htable.Values for fetching only values
        Console.WriteLine("\nFood items available are:");
        foreach (string str in htKeys)
```

```
        {
            Console.WriteLine("{0}", str);
        }
        Console.WriteLine("\nPrice of different food items:");
        foreach (DictionaryEntry de in htable)
        {
            Console.WriteLine("Price of {0} is {1}", de.Key, de.Value);
        }
        htable.Remove("Hot Dog");
        Console.WriteLine("\nPrice of food items except Hot Dog:");
        foreach (DictionaryEntry de in htable)
        {
            Console.WriteLine("Price of {0} is {1}", de.Key, de.Value);
        }
    }
}
```

Output:

```
Price of Pizza is 15

Food items available are:
Pizza
Noodles
Burger
Hot Dog

Price of different food items:
Price of Pizza is 15
Price of Noodles is 6
Price of Burger is 5
Price of Hot Dog is 2

Price of food items except Hot Dog:
Price of Pizza is 15
Price of Noodles is 6
Price of Burger is 5
```

By specifying the key or hash code, you can access its associated value. The Keys property of the hashtable returns all the keys or hash codes in the hashtable. Using the foreach loop, all the keys (food items) in the hashtable are accessed and displayed on the screen. The DictionaryEntry is used to access the key as well as the value properties of a hashtable. The DictionaryEntry is used in the foreach loop to display the food items and their respective prices on the screen. The Remove method is used to remove the key Hot Dog from the hashtable.

SORTEDLIST

A SortedList represents a collection where information is kept in terms of key-value pairs. The values are sorted in terms of keys. The information or value can be accessed by specifying the respective key or index. In that way, the SortedList is a combination of an array and a hashtable.

Following are a few of the SortedList properties:

- Capacity—Gets or sets the capacity of the SortedList.
- Count—Gets the count of the number of elements in the SortedList.
- Item—Gets and sets the value associated with a specific key in the SortedList.
- Keys—Fetches the keys in the SortedList.
- Values—Fetches the values in the SortedList.

Following are few of the methods of the SortedList:

- void Add(object key, object value)—Adds an element with the specified key and value into the SortedList.
- void Clear()—Removes all elements from the SortedList.
- bool ContainsKey(object key)—Returns Boolean value true if the SortedList contains a specific key.
- bool ContainsValue(object value)—Returns Boolean value true if the SortedList contains a specific value.
- object GetByIndex(int index)—Returns the value at the specified index.
- object GetKey(int index)—Returns the key at the specified index.
- IList GetKeyList()—Returns all the keys in the SortedList.
- void Remove(object key)—Removes the element with the specified key from the SortedList.
- void RemoveAt(int index)—Removes the element at the specified index of the SortedList.

The SortedListDemo.cs file shown in Listing 12.7 demonstrates using SortedList in storing and accessing the prices of certain food items.

Listing 12.7 Program Code in SortedListDemo.cs File

```
using System;
using System.Collections;

class SortedListDemo
{
    static void Main()
    {
        SortedList sortedList = new SortedList();
        sortedList.Add("Pizza", 15);
        sortedList.Add("Hot Dog", 2);
        sortedList.Add ("Noodles", 6);
        sortedList.Add ("Burger", 5);
        Console.WriteLine("Price of Pizza is {0}", sortedList["Pizza"]);
        Console.WriteLine("\nList of food items available:");
        for (int i = 0; i < sortedList.Count; i++)
        {
            Console.WriteLine("Price of {0} is {1}", sortedList.GetKey(i),
                sortedList.GetByIndex(i));
        }
    }
}
```

Output:

```
Price of Pizza is 15

List of food items available:
Price of Burger is 5
Price of Hot Dog is 2
Price of Noodles is 6
Price of Pizza is 15
```

You can see that certain food items are added to the SortedList using their respective keys through the Add method. The value or price of a food item is accessed by specifying its key. The key or the name of each food item is accessed and displayed through the GetKey method. Similarly, the value or price of each food item is accessed by invoking the GetByIndex method.

BITARRAY

BitArray is a compact and easy-to-use array of bit values that represent Boolean values true and false. The true value indicates that the bit is on, and the false value indicates that the bit is off. The array can be used in bitwise operations.

The BitArrayDemo.cs file shown in Listing 12.8 demonstrates using BitArray in keeping Boolean values.

Listing 12.8 Program Code in BitArrayDemo.cs File

```csharp
using System;
using System.Collections;

class BitArrayDemo
{
    static void Main()
    {
        BitArray bitArray = new BitArray(4);
        bitArray[0]= false;
        bitArray[1]=true;
        bitArray[2]= true;
        bitArray[3]=false;
        Console.WriteLine("Boolean values in the bit array are:");
        for (int i = 0; i < bitArray.Count; i++)
            Console.WriteLine("{0}", bitArray[i]);
        Console.WriteLine("\nBoolean values in the bit array are:");
        IEnumerator ienum;
        ienum = bitArray.GetEnumerator();
        while (ienum.MoveNext())
            Console.WriteLine(ienum.Current);
        Console.WriteLine("\nOutput in binary form:");
        for (int i = 0; i < bitArray.Count; i++)
            Console.Write(bitArray.Get(i) ? 1 : 0);
    }
}
```

Output:

```
Boolean values in the bit array are:
False
True
True
False

Boolean values in the bit array are:
False
True
True
False

Output in binary form:
0110
```

You can see that a BitArray is created and certain Boolean values are stored in its first four indices. The Boolean values true and false in the BitArray are displayed on the screen using its indices. Also, the Boolean values are displayed using the IEnumerator interface. Finally, the Boolean values in the `BitArray` are displayed in the form of values 1 and 0. The Boolean value `true` is represented by 1, and `false` is represented by 0.

STACK

A *stack* is a simple collection that represents a LIFO collection of instances. The item that is added last to the stack is removed first. The following example defines a stack collection called `stack`:

```
Stack stack = new Stack();
```

After you create a stack collection, you can use its `Push` and `Pop` methods to add to and remove items from it. Also, you can use its `Peek` method to display the item at its top. Remember, the `Peek` method just displays the item; it doesn't remove it. You will learn about `Stack <T>` generic collection later in this chapter.

The `StackCollection.cs` file shown in Listing 12.9 demonstrates how the items are pushed, popped, and peeked in a stack.

Listing 12.9 Program Code in StackCollection.cs File

```
using System;
using System.Collections;

class StackCollection{
    static void Main() {
        Stack stack = new Stack();
        stack.Push("John");
        stack.Push("Caroline");
        stack.Push("Kelly");
        Console.WriteLine("The element popped from the stack is {0}", stack.Pop());
        Console.WriteLine("The element at the top of the stack is {0}", stack.Peek());
        Console.WriteLine("The element popped from the stack is {0}", stack.Pop());
        Console.WriteLine("The number of elements in the stack is {0}", stack.Count);
    }
}
```

Output:

```
The element popped from the stack is Kelly
The element at the top of the stack is Caroline
The element popped from the stack is Caroline
The number of elements in the stack is 1
```

You can see that three names—John, Caroline, and Kelly—are pushed into the stack. The name on the top—Kelly—is popped. Thereafter, the name Caroline is peeked (displayed). Then Caroline is popped and the count of the items left in the stack is displayed on the screen.

QUEUE

A *queue* is a collection that represents a FIFO collection of objects. The item that is added first is removed first. The following example defines a queue collection called queue:

```
Queue queue = new Queue();
```

You can use the following methods of a queue collection to manage its content:

- **Enqueue**—Adds an item to the queue
- **Dequeue**—Removes an item from the queue
- **Peek**—Displays the first item in the queue
- **Count**—Returns the count of the elements in the queue

The QueueCollection.cs file shown in Listing 12.10 demonstrates how the items are enqueued, dequeued, and peeked in a queue.

Listing 12.10 Program Code in QueueCollection.cs File

```
using System;
using System.Collections;

class QueueCollection{
    static void Main() {
        Queue queue = new Queue();
        queue.Enqueue("John");
        queue.Enqueue("Caroline");
        queue.Enqueue("Kelly");
        Console.WriteLine("The first element removed from the queue is {0}",
queue.Dequeue());
        Console.WriteLine("The element at the beginning of the queue is {0}",
queue.Peek());
        Console.WriteLine("The number of elements in the queue is {0}", queue.Count);
    }
}
```

Output:

```
The first element removed from the queue is John
The element at the beginning of the queue is Caroline
The number of elements in the queue is 2
```

You can see that the names John, Caroline, and Kelly are added or enqueued in the queue. The name in the front, John, is dequeued and displayed on the screen. Thereafter, the name Caroline is peeked (just displayed). The count of the items left in the queue is displayed on the screen.

GENERICS

Generics make the code reusable across different types by creating a template that contains placeholder types. The type can then be substituted by the desired data type. Generics enable you to specify the data types of the programming elements when they are actually used in the program. Therefore, you can create a class or method that can work with any data type. In addition to classes and methods, you can create your own generic interfaces, events, and delegates. Generics also increase type safety and reduce casting and boxing.

The .NET Framework class library contains several generic collection classes in the System.Collections.Generic namespace.

A generic type declares type parameters. A *type parameter* is a placeholder that is passed to a generic method/class/interface/delegate and is filled in by the required data type. It is supplied immediately after the name of the method/class/interface/ delegate and is enclosed within angle brackets (<Type>). A generic method may appear in the following syntax:

```
access_specifier return_type method_name<T>(T parameter)
{
    ...
    ...
}
```

It can be any identifier, but T is primarily used to represent the type parameter.

Following is the syntax to define multiple type parameters:

```
access_specifier return_type method_name<T1, T2>(T1 parameter1, T2 parameter2 )
{
    ...
    ...
}
```

The preceding example defines two type parameters. The first method parameter is assumed to be of type T1, and the second is assumed to be of type T2. These two types are then provided when calling the method.

Generic refers to the classes and other structures that operate on a parameterized type (on different types of data). Using generics, you can create collections like linked lists, hashtables, stacks, queues, and trees that operate on items of any data type, thereby resulting in increasing reusability of the code. In addition, generics allow you to define type-safe classes without compromising performance.

The GenericMethod.cs file shown in Listing 12.11 demonstrates the generic method. Parameters of different types are passed to the method to swap.

Listing 12.11 Program Code in GenericMethod.cs File

```
using System;
using System.Collections.Generic;

class GenericMethod
{
    static void Swap<T>(ref T x, ref T y)
    {
        T temp;
        temp =x;
        x = y;
        y = temp;
    }
    static void Main(string[] args)
    {
        int a, b;
        string p, q;
        a = 5;
        b = 10;
        Console.WriteLine("Before Swap, a={0} and b={1}",a,b);
        Swap<int>(ref a, ref b);
        Console.WriteLine("After Swap, a={0} and b={1}", a, b);
        p = "Hello";
        q = "World";
        Console.WriteLine("Before Swap, p={0} and q={1}",p,q);
        Swap<string>(ref p, ref q);
        Console.WriteLine("After Swap, p={0} and q={1}", p,q);
    }
}
```

Output:

```
Before Swap, a=5 and b=10
After Swap, a=10 and b=5
Before Swap, p=Hello and q=World
After Swap, p=World and q=Hello
```

Besides int, a string type can be swapped by a single generic method. Now that you understand how a generic method works, you can learn to create a generic class. As expected, a generic class is one whose data members and methods do not operate only on a specific data type, but with different types of data.

The Generics1.cs file shown in Listing 12.12 demonstrates a generic class. A generic class called DummyList is created that maintains an array of data of different types. The class defines methods for the Add, Remove, and RemoveFromEnd methods that add an element to the array, removing an element from the specified index, and removing an element from the end. Elements of different types can be handled through this class.

Listing 12.12 Program Code in Generics1.cs File

```
using System;
public class DummyList<T>
{
    int size;
    int indx=-1;
    T[] items;
    public DummyList():this(10)
    {}
    public DummyList(int x)
    {
        size = x;
        items = new T[size];
    }
    public void Add(T item)
    {
        indx++;
        if(indx >= size) throw new IndexOutOfRangeException();
            items[indx] = item;
    }
    public T RemoveFromEnd()
    {
        if(indx >= 0)
        {
            return items[indx--];
        }
        else throw new InvalidOperationException("The list is empty");
    }
    public T Remove(int x)
    {
```

```
        if(indx >= 0)
        {
            T item;
            item=items[x];
            for (int i=x;i<indx;i++) items[i]=items[i+1];
                indx--;
            return item;
        }
        else throw new InvalidOperationException("The list is empty");
    }
}
class Generics1
{
    static void Main(string[] args)
    {
        DummyList<int> mylist = new DummyList<int>();
        mylist.Add(10);
        mylist.Add(20);
        Console.WriteLine(mylist.Remove(0));
        Console.WriteLine(mylist.RemoveFromEnd());
        mylist.Add(30);
        mylist.Add(40);
        Console.WriteLine(mylist.Remove(1));
        Console.WriteLine(mylist.RemoveFromEnd());
    }
}
```

Output:

```
10
20
40
30
```

In the first line of the preceding code, in the public class DummyList<T>, T is the name of a type parameter enclosed within the angle brackets (<>). The <T> acts as a placeholder for the actual type that will be supplied at the time of object creation. The DummyList class is the generic class, and the parameter stored within angle brackets is the generic type parameter.

Note

You can use any character, not just T, although it is traditional to use T. You can also use any descriptive name for the type parameter.

Observe the following statement for creating an object of the DummyList class:

```
DummyList<int> mylist = new DummyList<int>();
```

The actual type of the object, mylist, is determined by the type to which the generic type parameter T is bound at the time of creating the object. Because the int type is specified for T, the object of the DummyList class, mylist will deal with the int type. In other words, a version of the DummyList class is created in which all occurrences of generic type parameter T are replaced with the int type. Similarly, if the string is specified for T, at the time of creating the object, the object will deal with the string type.

DummyList<T> is basically an abstract and is known as an open constructed type because T does not refer to an actual type. In contrast, DummyList<int> is a closed constructed type because it results in creation of the class specific to a data type.

Here's one more example of a generic class. The GenericArrayApp.cs file shown in Listing 12.13 demonstrates creation of a generic class that manages values of different types in its array.

Listing 12.13 Program Code in GenericArrayApp.cs File

```
using System;
using System.Collections.Generic;
public class CustomGenericArray<T>
{
    private T[] arr;
    public CustomGenericArray(int size)
    {
        arr = new T[size + 1];
    }
    public T getValue(int index)
    {
        return arr[index];
    }
    public void setValue(int index, T value)
    {
        arr[index] = value;
    }
    public int getCount()
    {
        return arr.Length -1;
    }
}
```

```
class GenericArrayApp
{
    static void Main(string[] args)
    {
        CustomGenericArray<int> intArray = new CustomGenericArray<int>(5);
        intArray.setValue(0, 7);
        intArray.setValue(1, 3);
        intArray.setValue(2, 8);
        intArray.setValue(3, 5);
        intArray.setValue(4, 1);
        Console.WriteLine("Integer elements in the array are: ");
        for (int i = 0; i < intArray.getCount(); i++)
        {
            Console.WriteLine(intArray.getValue(i));
        }
        Console.WriteLine();
        CustomGenericArray<float> floatArray = new CustomGenericArray<float>(3);
        floatArray.setValue(0, 7.5f);
        floatArray.setValue(1, 10.99f);
        floatArray.setValue(2, 13.25f);
        Console.WriteLine("Float elements in the array are: ");
        for (int i = 0; i < floatArray.getCount(); i++)
        {
            Console.WriteLine(floatArray.getValue(i));
        }
    }
}
```

Output:

```
Integer elements in the array are:
7
3
8
5
1

Float elements in the array are:
7.5
10.99
13.25
```

You can see that the CustomGenericArray class is created, which stores values of different data types in its array. The class defines methods to assign values of different types, access values, and return the count of values in its array. The program shows how `int` and `float` values are managed through the generic class.

GENERIC COLLECTIONS

Generic collections are the generic equivalents for the `System.Collections` classes found in the `System.Collections.Generic` space. They avoid creation of custom collections for each type in the application, thereby resolving problems of the boxing and unboxing operations. They are type safe, and they are compatible with the `System.Collections`. The following generic collections are found in `System.Collections.Generic`:

- `List<T>`
- `Dictionary<K, V>`
- `Queue<T>`
- `Stack<T>`

The placeholder `T` can be replaced by the type of the data that will be stored in the collection.

Generic List<T>

The `Generic List <T>` collection provides an efficient and dynamically allocated array. It is usually used to store a list of identical objects. The advantage of using the `List<T>` class is that it can grow and shrink with the number of objects that are stored in it. The class is contained within the `System.Collections.Generic` namespace. The syntax for creating a `List<T>` collection follows:

```
List<T> name = new List<T>();
```

where `T` represents any data type.

The following example creates a list object called `lst` that can store five strings:

```
List<string> lst = new List<string>(5);
```

You can instantiate and populate a list object simultaneously, as shown in the next statement:

```
List<int> lst = new List<int> {1, 2, 3};
```

The methods that are used with the list collection are briefly described in Table 12.1.

Table 12.1 Methods of List Collection

Method	Description

Add	After creating a list object, you can items to it using the Add method. The following statement adds a string, Apple, to the lst object:
	
	`lst.Add("Apple");`
	
	Remember, the Add method adds elements to the end of a list. The elements stored in a list object can be accessed using the index value. The index value is enclosed within the square brackets after the list object name. The first item in a list object is stored at index 0, the second item at index 1, and so on. The following example displays the first item in the list object:
	
	`Console.WriteLine (lst[0]);`
	
	You can assign or modify the elements in a list object through the index value. For example, the following statement assigns or modifies the element at index location 1 in the list object:
	
	`lst[1] = "Mango";`

Remove	This method is used to remove the specified element from a list object. The following statement deletes or removes the Mango string from the lst object: `lst.Remove("Mango");` If there are duplicate elements in the list object, the Remove method only removes the first matching instance.
Insert	This method inserts a new element at the desired index location in a list. The method takes two arguments. The first argument is an integer representing the index location where you want to insert the element, and the second argument is the element itself. For example, the following example inserts the element Grapes at index location 1 in the list object lst: `lst.Insert(1, "Grapes");`
Sort	This method sorts the elements in the specified list object. The following example sorts or arranges the elements in the list object lst: `lst.Sort();`
Contains	This method searches for the specified element in the specified list object. The method returns true if the specified element is found in the list, or false if it is not.

(Continued)

Table 12.1 Methods of List Collection (*Continued*)

Method	Description
IndexOf	This method searches for the specified element in the specified list object and returns its index value if it is found. The method returns a value of −1 if the item is not found in the list object. For example, the following statement displays the index location of the Mango string in the list object lst: `Console.WriteLine(lst.IndexOf("Mango"));`
LastIndexOf	This method returns the index value of the last element that matches the specified item. It is used when a list contains duplicate elements.
Clear	This method removes all the elements from the specified list object and sets the Count property to 0. The following example removes all the elements in the list object lst: `lst.Clear();`

© 2015 Cengage Learning®.

Following are the two commonly used list properties:

- **Capacity**—Indicates the size of the specified list object. It returns the count of the elements that can be stored in a list object.

- **Count**—Indicates the count of the items that are currently stored in the list.

Note

The Capacity property remains unchanged after using the Clear method because the property represents the count of the elements that a list object can store and not the count of currently stored elements. To remove the capacity of a list object, follow the Clear() method with the TrimExcess() method.

The ListCollection.cs file shown in Listing 12.14 demonstrates using the List<T> collection. Certain fruits are stored in the list. The Add and Remove methods are used to add and remove items from the list. New fruit is inserted using the Insert method. Also, the program explains how to search a specific fruit in the list.

Listing 12.14 Program Code in ListCollection.cs File

```
using System;
using System.Collections.Generic;

class ListCollection{
    static void Main() {
        List<string> lst = new List<string>(5);
        string str;
        lst.Add("Apple");
        lst.Add("Mango");
        lst.Add("Orange");
        lst.Add("Banana");
        Console.WriteLine("\nThe capacity of List is {0} elements", lst.Capacity);
        Console.WriteLine("\nThe List contains {0} elements as shown below:",
lst.Count);
        foreach (string f in lst)
        {
            Console.WriteLine(f);
        }
        Console.WriteLine("\nFollowing are the {0} elements in the list:", lst.Count);
        for(int i=0;i<lst.Count;i++)
        {
            Console.WriteLine(lst[i]);
        }
        lst.Remove("Orange");
        Console.WriteLine("\nThe List after removing an item now contains {0} elements
as shown below:", lst.Count);
        foreach (string f in lst)
        {
            Console.WriteLine(f);
        }
        lst.Insert(2,"Grapes");
        Console.WriteLine("\nThe List after inserting an item at index location 2 now
contains {0} elements as shown below:", lst.Count);
        foreach (string f in lst)
        {
            Console.WriteLine(f);
        }
        lst.Sort();
```

The List after inserting an item at index location 2 now contains 4 elements as shown

be   Console.WriteLine("\nThe List after sorting all its elements appears as shown
below:");
```
        foreach (string f in lst)
```

```
        {
            Console.WriteLine(f);
        }
        Console.Write("Enter a fruit name to search: ");
        str = Console.ReadLine();
        int m=lst.IndexOf(str);
        if(m!=-1) Console.WriteLine("The fruit {0} is found in the List at position {1} ",
str,m+1);
        else Console.WriteLine("The fruit {0} is not found in the List", str);
        lst.Clear();
        Console.WriteLine("\nThe List is cleared. Now it has {0} elements", lst.Count);
    }
}
```

Output:

The capacity of List is 5 elements

The List contains 4 elements as shown below:
Apple
Mango
Orange
Banana

Following are the 4 elements in the list:
Apple
Mango
Orange
Banana

The List after removing an item now contains 3 elements as shown below:
Apple
Mango
Banana

The List after inserting an item at index location 2 now contains 4 elements as shown
below:
Apple
Mango
Grapes
Banana

The List after sorting all its elements appears as shown below:
Apple
Banana
Grapes
Mango
Enter a fruit name to search: Banana
The fruit Banana is found in our List at position 2

The List is cleared. Now it has 0 elements

Besides the usual data types, a list can be used to store a collection of objects. The program shown in Listing 12.15 shows how a list of Employee objects is created. In the program, you are going to use the following three methods:

- Foreach, which accesses each item in the list
- FindAll, which searches the objects in the list that meet the given criteria
- Sort, which sorts the objects in the list on the specified object field

Listing 12.15 Program Code in ListOfObjects.cs File

```
using System;
using System.Collections.Generic;

public class Employee
{
    public int Code, BasicSalary;
    public string Name;
    public Employee(int c, string name, int basicsal)
    {
        this.Code = c;
        this.Name = name;
        this.BasicSalary = basicsal;
    }
}
class ListOfObjects
{
    static void Main(string[] args)
    {
        List<Employee> empList = new List<Employee>();
        empList.Add(new Employee(101, "John", 5000));
        empList.Add(new Employee(102, "Kelly", 6500));
        empList.Add(new Employee(103, "Laura", 4000));
        Console.WriteLine("Unsorted list of employees:");
        Console.WriteLine("Code\tName\tBasic Salary");
        foreach(Employee e in empList) {
            Console.WriteLine("{0}\t{1}\t{2}",e.Code, e.Name, e.BasicSalary);
        };
        List<Employee> filteredEmp = empList.FindAll(delegate(Employee e) { return
e.BasicSalary < 6000; });
        Console.WriteLine("\nEmployees with salary less than $6000");
        filteredEmp.ForEach(delegate(Employee e) {
            Console.WriteLine(String.Format("Code: {0}, Name: {1} and Basic Salary:
{2}", e.Code, e.Name, e.BasicSalary)); });
```

```
        empList.Sort(delegate(Employee e1, Employee e2) { return
e1.Name.CompareTo(e2.Name); });
        Console.WriteLine("\nSorted list by employee name: ");
        Console.WriteLine("Code\tName\tBasic Salary");
        foreach(Employee e in empList) {
            Console.WriteLine("{0}\t{1}\t{2}",e.Code, e.Name, e.BasicSalary);
        };
    }
}
```

Output:

```
Unsorted list of employees:
Code....Name....Basic Salary
101....John....5000
102....Kelly....6500
103....Laura....4000

Employees with salary less than $6000
Code:  101,  Name:  John and Basic Salary:  5000
Code:  103,  Name:  Laura and Basic Salary:  4000

Sorted list by employee name:
Code Name Basic Salary
101  John   5000
102  Kelly  6500
103  Laura  4000
```

You can see that a class called Employee is created composed of three data members: Code, Name, and BasicSalary. The class includes a parameterized constructor to initialize its data members.

A list of Employee objects is created named empList. Using the Add method, three Employee objects are added to the empList. Thereafter, using the FindAll method, all the employees that have salary < $6000 are filtered out and stored in another list object: filteredEmp. The Foreach method is used to access each object in the list and display the content in its data members. Finally, the empList object is sorted in alphabetical order of the employee names.

Queue<T>

Queue<T> is a generic collection that represents a FIFO collection of objects. The item that is added first is removed first. The following example defines a generic queue collection called intQueue of size five elements:

```
Queue<int> intQueue = new Queue<int>(5);
```

The intQueue collection defined above can store elements of int type.

Following are the methods that can be used with the Queue<T> generic collection:

- **Enqueue**—Adds an element to the end of the queue. The following example adds the value 5 to the intQueue collection:

```
intQueue.Enqueue(5);
```

- **Peek**—Returns the element at the beginning of the queue without removing it. The following example returns the element at the beginning of the queue intQueue:

```
int value = intQueue.Peek();
```

- **Dequeue**—Removes and returns the value at the beginning of the queue. The following example removes and returns the element at the beginning of the queue intQueue:

```
int value = intQueue.Dequeue();
```

The GenericQueue.cs file shown in Listing 12.16 demonstrates using the Queue<T> collection in adding, removing, and displaying int values.

Listing 12.16 Program Code in GenericQueue.cs File

```
using System;
using System.Collections.Generic;

class GenericQueue{
    static void Main() {
        Queue<int> intQueue = new Queue<int>(5);
        intQueue.Enqueue(5);
        intQueue.Enqueue(10);
        intQueue.Enqueue(15);
        Console.WriteLine("The element removed from the queue is {0}",
intQueue.Dequeue());
        Console.WriteLine("The element at the beginning of the queue is {0}",
intQueue.Peek());
        Console.WriteLine("The number of elements in the queue is {0}",
intQueue.Count);
    }
}
```

Output:

```
The element removed from the queue is 5
The element at the beginning of the queue is 10
The number of elements in the queue is 2
```

Stack<T>

Stack<T> is a generic collection that represents a LIFO collection of instances. The item that is added last to the stack is removed first. The following example defines a generic stack collection called intStack of size five elements:

```
Stack<int> intStack = new Stack<int>(5);
```

The intStack collection defined here can store elements of int type.

Following are the methods that can be used with Stack<T> generic collection:

- **Push**—Adds an element at the top of the stack. The following example adds an integer value 5 at the top of the stack intStack:

  ```
  intStack.Push(5);
  ```

- **Peek**—Returns an element at the top of the stack without removing it. The following example displays a value that is at the top of the stack intStack without removing it:

  ```
  int value = intStack.Peek();
  ```

- **Pop**—Removes and returns the value at the top of the stack. The following example removes and returns the integer value at the top of the stack intStack:

  ```
  int value = intStack.Pop();
  ```

The GenericStack.cs file shown in Listing 12.17 demonstrates use of the Stack<T> collection in adding, removing, and displaying int values.

Listing 12.17 Program Code in GenericStack.cs File

```
using System;
using System.Collections.Generic;
class GenericStack{
    static void Main() {
        Stack<int> intStack = new Stack<int>(5);
        intStack.Push(5);
        intStack.Push(10);
        intStack.Push(15);
        Console.WriteLine("The element popped from the stack is {0}", intStack.Pop());
        Console.WriteLine("The element at the top of the stack is {0}",
intStack.Peek());
        Console.WriteLine("The element popped from the stack is {0}", intStack.Pop());
        Console.WriteLine("The number of elements in the stack are {0}",
intStack.Count);
    }
}
```

Output:

```
The element popped from the stack is 15
The element at the top of the stack is 10
The element popped from the stack is 10
The number of elements in the stack are 1
```

Recall that the `Count` property returns the count of the values found in the stack.

SORTEDSET

`SortedSet` is an ordered set collection that is part of the `System.Collections.Generic` namespace. The collection stores elements in a sorted order and eliminates the duplicate values from the collection. The methods of the `SortedSet` are briefly described in Table 12.2.

Table 12.2 Methods of SortedSet

Method	Description
Add	The `Add` method is called to add new elements to the `SortedSet`. The method returns a Boolean value to indicate whether the new element is successfully added. The method returns `true` if the new element is successfully added; otherwise, it returns `false`. Note: An element is not added to the `SortedSet` if it already exists. No exceptions are thrown if the element already exists.
UnionWith	This method returns the union of two collections. All elements are added to one collection. Assuming that `foodItems` and `foodList` are the two collections, the following statement creates a union of the two into `foodItems`: `foodItems.UnionWith(foodList);`
RemoveWhere	This method is used to remove all the elements from the `SortedSet` that match a certain criteria. The following statement removes all the elements from the `SortedSet` `foodItem` that begin with character N: `foodItems.RemoveWhere(item => item.StartsWith("N"));` You can see that the `RemoveWhere` method is called with a lambda function that is used as a predicate condition. The method removes all the elements for which the method returns `true`.
IntersectWith	`IntersectWith` modifies the `SortedSet` instance so that it contains only the elements that were common in the

(Continued)

Table 12.2 Methods of SortedSet (Continued)

Method	Description
	SortedSet instance and the selected collection. In other words, the method returns the intersection of the two collections.
SymmetricExceptWith	The SymmetricExceptWith method returns all the elements in the two collections that are found in only one collection and not both collections. In other words, it displays the unique items in both collections.
ExceptWith	The ExceptWith method removes all the elements found in the selected collection from the SortedSet instance. The resulting SortedSet contains the unique elements. Only the elements that don't match the selected collection will be left; the rest will be deleted.
Overlaps	The Overlaps method returns a Boolean value indicating whether the selected collection has any elements in common with the SortedSet. The method returns true if even a single element is common in the selected collection and the SortedSet. The method returns false if no elements are in common.
IsSubsetOf	Returns true if the invoking SortedSet is the subset of the specified set.
IsSupersetOf	Returns true if the invoking SortedSet is the superset of the specified set.
IsProperSubsetOf	Returns true if the invoking SortedSet is the proper subset of the specified set. A proper subset means the two sets cannot have the same number of elements.
IsProperSupersetOf	Returns true if the invoking SortedSet is the proper superset of the specified set. Again, a proper superset means the two sets cannot have the same number of elements.

The SortedSet supports the following two properties:

- Min—Displays the lowest element value in the SortedSet
- Max—Displays the highest element value in the SortedSet

The SortedSetCollect.cs file shown in Listing 12.18 demonstrates use of the SortedSet collection. The program creates a new, empty SortedSet instance called foodItems upon the managed heap. Using the Add method, the program adds four elements to the set. The program also demonstrates removal of the elements from the sorted set using the Remove and RemoveWhere methods.

Listing 12.18 Program Code in SortedSetCollect.cs File

```
using System;
using System.Collections.Generic;
class SortedSetCollect
{
    static void Main()
    {
        SortedSet<string> foodItems = new SortedSet<string>();
        List<string> foodList = new List<string>();
        foodItems.Add("Pizza");
        foodItems.Add("Hot Dog");
        foodItems.Add("Burger");
        foodItems.Add("Noodles");
        foodItems.Add("Hot Dog");
        Console.WriteLine("{0} Food Items in sorted order are:", foodItems.Count);
        foreach (string item in foodItems)
        {
            Console.WriteLine(item);
        }
        foodItems.Remove("Burger");
        foodItems.RemoveWhere(item => item.StartsWith("N"));
        Console.WriteLine("Rest of the food items in sorted order are");
        foreach (string item in foodItems)
        {
            Console.WriteLine(item);
        }
        foodList.Add("Hot Dog");
        foodList.Add("Taco");
        foodList.Add("French Fries");
        foodList.Add("Pizza");
        foodItems.UnionWith(foodList);
        Console.WriteLine("After union, there are {0} food items in the sorted set",
foodItems.Count);
        foreach (string item in foodItems)
        {
            Console.WriteLine(item);
        }
        foodItems.Clear();
        Console.WriteLine("The number of food items left is {0}", foodItems.Count);
    }
}
```

```
4 Food Items in sorted order are:
Burger
Hot Dog
Noodles
Pizza
Rest of the food items in sorted order are
Hot Dog
Pizza
After union, there are 4 food items in the sorted set
French Fries
Hot Dog
Pizza
Taco
The number of food items left is 0
```

You can see that the `foreach` loop construct is used to loop through and to display all the elements in the `SortedSet` instance.

You can also create a `SortedSet` instance from the elements in another collection, such as an array or list. To do so, the `SortedSet` constructor is called, passing the original collection reference to it.

The `SortedSetFromList.cs` file shown in Listing 12.19 demonstrates creation of `SortedSet` from the list collection.

Listing 12.19 Program Code in SortedSetFromList.cs File

```
using System;
using System.Collections.Generic;

class SortedSetFromList
{
    static void Main()
    {
        List<string> lst = new List<string>(5);
        lst.Add("Apple");
        lst.Add("Mango");
        lst.Add("Banana");
        lst.Add("Orange");
        lst.Add("Banana");
        SortedSet<string> fruits = new SortedSet<string>(lst);
        Console.WriteLine("{0} Fruits in sorted order are:", fruits.Count);
        foreach (string item in fruits)
        {
            Console.WriteLine(item);
        }
```

```
        Console.WriteLine("The minimum value in the SortedSet is {0}", fruits.Min);
      Console.WriteLine("The maximum value in the SortedSet is {0}",fruits.Max);
    }
}
```

Output:

```
4 Fruits in sorted order are:
Apple
Banana
Mango
Orange
The minimum value in the SortedSet is Apple
The maximum value in the SortedSet is Orange
```

Although Banana appears twice in the list, the duplicate is removed from the SortedSet so that the Banana element appears only once.

The SuperSubSortedSetCompare.cs file shown in Listing 12.20 demonstrates the concept of subset, superset, proper subset, and proper superset, respectively.

Listing 12.20 Program Code in SuperSubSortedSetCompare.cs File

```
using System;
using System.Collections.Generic;

class SuperSubSortedSetCompare
{
    static void Main()
    {
        SortedSet<string> foods = new SortedSet<string>();
        SortedSet<string> foodItems = new SortedSet<string>();
        SortedSet<string> allfoodItems = new SortedSet<string>();
        SortedSet<string> fewfoodItems = new SortedSet<string>();
        foods.Add("Pizza");
        foods.Add("Hot Dog");
        foods.Add("Burger");
        foods.Add("Noodles");
        foodItems.Add("Pizza");
        foodItems.Add("Hot Dog");
        foodItems.Add("Burger");
        foodItems.Add("Noodles");
        Console.WriteLine("foods is proper subset of foodItems: {0}",
foods.IsProperSubsetOf(foodItems));
        Console.WriteLine("foods is subset of foodItems:{0}",
foods.IsSubsetOf(foodItems));
        allfoodItems.Add("Pizza");
```

```
        allfoodItems.Add("Hot Dog");
        allfoodItems.Add("Burger");
        allfoodItems.Add("Noodles");
        allfoodItems.Add("French Fries");
        allfoodItems.Add("Ginger Bread");
        Console.WriteLine("foods is proper subset of foodItems: {0}",
    foods.IsProperSubsetOf(allfoodItems));
        Console.WriteLine("foods is subset of allfoodItems: {0}",
    foods.IsSubsetOf(allfoodItems));
        fewfoodItems.Add("Pizza");
        fewfoodItems.Add("Hot Dog");
        Console.WriteLine("foods is proper superset of fewfoodItems: {0}",
    foods.IsProperSupersetOf(fewfoodItems));
        Console.WriteLine("foods is superset of fewfoodItems: {0}",
    foods.IsSupersetOf(fewfoodItems));
    }
}
```

Output:

```
foods is proper subset of foodItems: False
foods is subset of foodItems:True
foods is proper subset of foodItems: True
foods is subset of allfoodItems: True
foods is proper superset of fewfoodItems: True
foods is superset of fewfoodItems: True
```

The SortedSetCompare.cs file shown in Listing 12.21 demonstrates the concept of finding the common and unique items in the SortedSets.

Listing 12.21 Program Code in SortedSetCompare.cs File

```
using System;
using System.Collections.Generic;

class SortedSetCompare
{
    static void Main()
    {
        SortedSet<string> foodItems = new SortedSet<string>();
        List<string> fruitList = new List<string>();
        foodItems.Add("Pizza");
        foodItems.Add("Hot Dog");
        foodItems.Add("Orange");
        foodItems.Add("Noodles");
        fruitList.Add("Apple");
        fruitList.Add("Mango");
```

```
        fruitList.Add("Hot Dog");
        fruitList.Add("Orange");
        foodItems.SymmetricExceptWith(fruitList);
        Console.WriteLine("Number of items that are unique in the two SortedSets is {0}",
    foodItems.Count);
        foreach (string item in foodItems)
        {
            Console.WriteLine(item);
        }
        foodItems.ExceptWith(fruitList);
        Console.WriteLine("\nNumber of food items that are left in foodItems after
    removing its elements that are common or match with fruitList is {0}", foodItems.Count);
        foreach (string item in foodItems)
        {
            Console.WriteLine(item);
        }
        foodItems.Add("Hot Dog");
        foodItems.Add("Orange");
        Console.WriteLine("\nThe foodItems and fruitList have at least one element in
    common: {0}", foodItems.Overlaps(fruitList));
        foodItems.IntersectWith(fruitList);
        Console.WriteLine("\nNumber of food items that are common with fruitList is {0}",
    foodItems.Count);
        foreach (string item in foodItems)
        {
            Console.WriteLine(item);
        }
    }
}
```

Output:

```
Number of items that are unique in the two SortedSets is 4
Apple
Mango
Noodles
Pizza

Number of food items that are left in foodItems after removing its elements that are
common or match with fruitList is 2
Noodles
Pizza

The foodItems and fruitList have at least one element in common: True

Number of food items that are common with fruitList is 2
Hot Dog
Orange
```

The SortedSet foodItems is compared to the list collection to find the unique and the common items between them.

Dictionary

A dictionary is an associative array that represents a collection of keys and values. Basically, it is an implementation of a hashtable. Thus, elements in a dictionary can be quickly searched through keys. Because each value has an associated key, dictionaries consume more memory.

Dictionary<K, V> is a generic collection that contains data in key/value pairs. For example, the following statement defines a dictionary called priceList that stores integer keys and string values:

```
Dictionary<string, int> priceList = new Dictionary<string, int>();
```

Following are the methods that you can use with the Dictionary<K, V> generic collection:

- **Add**—Adds the specified key and value to the dictionary. For example, the following statement adds the value 15 to the dictionary priceList under the key Pizza:

  ```
  priceList.Add("Pizza", 15);
  ```

- **Remove**—Removes the value with the specified key from the dictionary. The following example removes the value that is associated with the key Pizza from the dictionary priceList:

  ```
  priceList.Remove("Pizza");
  ```

- **Count**—Returns the count of the key/value pairs contained in the dictionary. The following statement counts the number of key/value pairs in the dictionary priceList:

  ```
  int c = priceList.Count;
  ```

Note

The dictionary type is usually used when you want to assign a unique identifier to the items stored in a collection.

The DictionaryCollection.cs file shown in Listing 12.22 demonstrates use of the Dictionary collection in storing prices of certain food items. The food items and their prices are stored in the form of key/value pairs. The program demonstrates how you can access the value of a food item by specifying the respective key. The Keys property of the Dictionary collection is used to access all the keys or food items in the collection.

Listing 12.22 Program Code in DictionaryCollection.cs File

```
using System;
using System.Collections.Generic;

class DictionaryCollection
{
    static void Main()
    {
        Dictionary<string, int> priceList = new Dictionary<string, int>();
        priceList.Add("Pizza", 15);
        priceList.Add("Hot Dog", 2);
        priceList.Add("Burger", 5);
        priceList.Add("Noodles", 6);
        Console.WriteLine("There are {0} items", priceList.Count);
        Console.WriteLine("Price of Pizza is {0}",priceList["Pizza"]);
        Console.Write("Enter food item name whose price you want to see ");
        string str = Console.ReadLine();
        if (priceList.ContainsKey(str))
            Console.WriteLine("Price of {0} is {1}",str, priceList[str]);
        else
            Console.WriteLine("Sorry, {0} not found",str);
        List<string> foodList = new List<string>(priceList.Keys);
        Console.WriteLine("Below is the list of available food items");
        foreach (string items in foodList)
        {
            Console.WriteLine("{0}",items);
        }
        Console.WriteLine("Below is the complete price list");
        foreach (KeyValuePair<string, int> pair in priceList)
        {
            Console.WriteLine("Price of {0} is {1}",pair.Key,pair.Value);
        }
        priceList.Remove("Pizza");
        Console.WriteLine("Number of items left is {0}", priceList.Count);
    }
}
```

Output:

```
There are 4 items
Price of Pizza is 15
Enter food item name whose price you want to see Hot Dog
```

```
Price of Hot Dog is 2
Below is the list of available food items
Pizza
Hot Dog
Burger
Noodles
Below is the complete price list
Price of Pizza is 15
Price of Hot Dog is 2
Price of Burger is 5
Price of Noodles is 6
Number of items left is 3
```

The priceList variable is declared as a Dictionary<string int>, which means the priceList is declared as a dictionary where the key is a string and the value is type int. Recall that a value is associated with a key in a dictionary. Four values, 15, 2, 5, and 6, are added to the priceList dictionary under the keys Pizza, Hot Dog, Burger, and Noodles, respectively. In other words, the price of Pizza is assumed to be $15, the price of Hot Dog is assumed to be $2, and so on.

Using the Count property of the dictionary, the count of the number of items (food items) in the dictionary is displayed. Using the ContainsKey method, the food item entered by the user is searched in the dictionary and, if it is found, its value (the price of the food item) is displayed on the screen.

LINKEDLIST<T>

LinkedList<T> is a doubly linked list, where each element references the next and the previous element. In other words, each element in a linked list has two references: Next and Previous. The Next reference keeps the reference of the next element, and the Previous reference keeps the reference of the previous element. Consequently, a linked list can be traversed in forward as well as in backward direction. To traverse a linked list forward, the Next reference of each element is used. In contrast, to traverse a linked list backward, the Previous reference is used. Inserting an element between a linked list is quite easy; it simply requires setting the Next reference of the previous item and the Previous reference of the next item to reference the newly inserted item. The disadvantage of linked lists is that the elements can be accessed sequentially only (one after the other); you cannot access linked list elements randomly.

Note

Because linked lists need extra storage for Next and Previous references, they are usually not used for small data items.

The `LinkedListCollection.cs` file shown in Listing 12.23 demonstrates use of the `LinkedList` collection to store and access certain `int` values.

Listing 12.23 Program Code in LinkedListCollection.cs File

```
using System;
using System.Collections.Generic;
public class LinkedListCollection
{
    static void Main()
    {
        LinkedList<int> lnklst = new LinkedList<int>();
        lnklst.AddLast(10);
        lnklst.AddLast(20);
        lnklst.AddLast(30);
        Console.WriteLine("Elements in a linked list:");
        foreach(int n in lnklst)
        {
          Console.WriteLine(n);
        }
        lnklst.AddFirst(8);
        lnklst.AddFirst(3);
        Console.WriteLine("\nAfter adding two elements in the beginning:");
        foreach(int n in lnklst)
        {
          Console.WriteLine(n);
        }
        LinkedListNode<int> node = lnklst.Find(20);
        lnklst.AddBefore(node, 15);
        Console.WriteLine("\nAfter adding an element, 15, before 20:");
        foreach(int n in lnklst)
        {
          Console.WriteLine(n);
        }
        lnklst.AddLast(80);
        Console.WriteLine("\nAfter adding an element, 80, at the end:");
        foreach(int n in lnklst)
        {
          Console.WriteLine(n);
        }
    }
}
```

Output:

```
Elements in a linked list:
10
20
30

After adding two elements in the beginning:
3
8
10
20
30

After adding an element, 15, before 20:
3
8
10
15
20
30

After adding an element, 80, at the end:
3
8
10
15
20
30
80
```

You can see that a linked list is created in which three int values are stored. The values in the linked list are displayed on the screen. Using AddLast and AddFirst, values are added at the end and at the beginning of the linked list. The Find method is used to find a particular item in the linked list. The AddBefore method is used to add or insert a value before the specified value.

SUMMARY

In this chapter, you learned to use collections. You learned about simple and generic collections. You also saw different interfaces that are used to iterate through the collections.

The next chapter is focused on types of errors. You will learn to use exceptions. You will learn to use the try, catch, and final statements in exception handling to detect bugs in the programs.

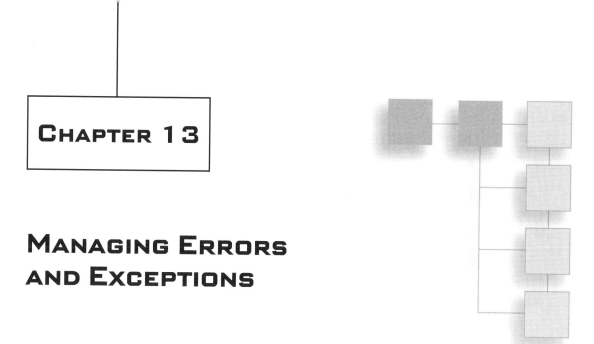

CHAPTER 13

MANAGING ERRORS AND EXCEPTIONS

This chapter's topics include the following:

- Introducing errors and exceptions
- Using multiple try blocks
- Using multiple catch blocks
- Throwing an exception
- Nesting try blocks
- Creating your own exception
- Using the checked/unchecked operator

You'll begin your journey by learning about types of errors.

INTRODUCING ERRORS AND EXCEPTIONS

Errors are the mistakes you make while writing programs. You need to remove these mistakes to enable the program to compile and deliver the desired results. Broadly, errors fall under the following types:

- **Syntax errors**—Also known as *compile-time errors*, *syntax errors* occur when some code does not match the grammar of the programming language being used. For example, you might type a reserved key in uppercase (C# is case sensitive), omit a semicolon (;), or use a variable that is not yet declared. The built-in Code Editor of Microsoft Visual Studio helps you avoid syntax errors.

While you're typing the code, IntelliSense starts building a list of words that match the character typed and displays the suggestions to choose from. Also, it underlines a mistyped keyword to indicate the possibility of error.

■ **Logic errors**—*Logic errors* occur when the program has no syntax errors and executes to give output, but the output that it produces is either wrong or unpredictable. Besides yielding wrong results, logical errors might result in hanging a computer or crashing the system. Removal of logical errors requires detailed analysis of code and application of proper debugging steps.

Logic errors appear after you run a program. In addition to logic errors, there is one more type of runtime error, known as an exception. An *exception* is an unforeseen error that might exist in a program. A good program should contain code to detect and handle such an error.

Exception handling is a mechanism that handles runtime errors. It relieves you from checking code manually, because whenever an exception occurs, the exception handler comes into play, executing the remedy code. In other words, exceptions help you avoid application crashes and display reasons for the error in understandable format.

Note

If you do not handle exceptions, the .NET runtime environment provides a default mechanism that terminates the program.

Following are some common reasons for exceptions:

■ **Errors in code**—These errors include omitting null checks, passing invalid arguments to a method, and applying conversions on wrong types.

■ **Runtime error**—These errors include insufficient memory or a stack overflow, an error in accessing files, a configuration file not being available, failure to connect to a database, or failure of an external component.

The Exception Hierarchy

In C#, exceptions are represented by classes. All exception classes are derived from the built-in exception class Exception, which is part of the System namespace. Thus, all exceptions are subclasses of Exception.

There are two types of exceptions:

■ ApplicationException—A user program generates these exceptions.

■ SystemException—The Common Language Runtime (CLR) generates these exceptions.

System.Exception is a class at the top of the standard exceptions hierarchy. It's where the C# runtime system generates all exceptions.

Here are a few of the standard exceptions:

- System.ArithmeticException—A base class for exceptions that occur during arithmetic operations, such as System.DivideByZeroException and System.OverflowException

- System.DivideByZeroException—Thrown when an integer is divided by 0

- System.OverflowException—Thrown when overflow occurs in a checked operation

- System.ArgumentException—Thrown when any argument to a method is invalid

- System.ArgumentNullException—Thrown when a null argument is passed to a method

- System.ArgumentOutOfRangeException—Thrown when an argument value is out of range

- System.ArrayTypeMismatchException—Thrown when an element of incompatible type attempts storage in an array

- System.IndexOutOfRangeException—Thrown when you attempt to index an array through an index that is either less than 0 or beyond its boundaries

- System.InvalidCastException—Thrown when an explicit conversion from a base type or interface to a derived type fails

- System.NullReferenceException—Thrown when a null reference is used (when you refer to a nonexisting object)

- System.OutOfMemoryException—Thrown when available memory becomes too low to satisfy a memory allocation request

- System.StackOverflowException—Thrown when the execution stack is exhausted by having too many pending method calls

Keywords Used in Exception Handling

C# exception handling is managed via four keywords: try, catch, throw, and finally.

- try—The code that you want to check for occurrence of any exception is enclosed in a try block. If an exception occurs within the try block, it is thrown.

- catch—The exception that is thrown on occurrence of exception in a try block is caught via code mentioned in a catch block. In other words, the catch provides code to handle respective exceptions. A try block can throw multiple exceptions. To handle multiple exceptions, you can have multiple catch blocks.

- **throw**—The runtime system automatically throws exceptions, but sometimes you want to throw an exception manually. The throw block is used to manually throw an exception.

- **finally**—Usually the program terminates and exits on occurrence of an exception. The code that you want to run always—whether an exception occurs or not—is written within the finally block. You cannot transfer control out of a finally block by using break, continue, return, or goto.

If any exception occurs inside the try block, the control transfers to the appropriate catch block and later to the finally block. Both catch and finally blocks are optional. The try block can exist with one or more catch blocks or a finally block or with both catch and finally blocks. If there is no exception inside the try block, the control directly transfers to the finally block.

Note

The try and catch blocks work together. There cannot be a catch without a try.

Here's the syntax of try-catch-finally blocks:

```
Try
{
    // Code that can cause exception(s)
}
Catch(Excep_Type1 Excep_Obj)
{
    // Code to handle the exception
}
Catch(Excep_Type2 Excep_Obj)
{
    // Code to handle the exception
}
::::::::::::::::::::::::::::::::::
[Finally
{
    // Any cleanup code
} ]
```

The code that can cause an exception is enclosed in a try block. When the Excep_Type1 exception occurs, it is thrown and caught by the corresponding catch block, which executes the remedy action. There can be more than one catch block associated with a try, each handling one type of exception. If an exception occurs for which there is no catch block, the .NET runtime environment executes its default mechanism for handling an exception: it terminates program execution. In other words, the code defined in the catch block is executed, and all other catch blocks are bypassed. When an exception is caught, the exception object Excep_Obj receives its information. If you are not using the Except_Obj in the catch block, you don't need to specify the exception object Excep_Obj in the catch block.

If no exception is thrown, a try block is executed completely, all its catch blocks are bypassed, and the program resumes execution from the finally block (if it is there). The finally block contains the code that you want to execute whether an exception occurs or not.

Note

A catch block is executed only if an exception is thrown.

To grasp exception handling and its practical use, you'll write a program that commits mistakes but does not implement exception handling. The code shown in Listing 13.1 demonstrates a program without exception handling.

Listing 13.1 Program Code in TryCatch1.cs File

```
using System;
class TryCatch1
{
    static void Main()
    {
        int x = 10,y=0,z ;
        z = x/y;
        Console.WriteLine("Result of dividing {0} by {1} is {2}", x,y,z);
    }
}
```

The preceding program compiles but shows an error during execution. The division by zero is a runtime error. Because no exception handling is implemented in this code, the program terminates abnormally with the following error message:

```
Unhandled Exception: System.DivideByZeroException: Attempted to divide by zero. At
TryCatch1.Main()
```

Recall that if any exception is not caught through a suitable catch block, the default mechanism of the .NET runtime terminates the execution of the entire program.

If the user is using Windows 7, the exception throws a Windows error screen. The program shows the exception in the console window, but Windows tries to send the problem to Microsoft to resolve it.

Now you'll modify the program by enclosing the code that might create a runtime error within the try block. Also, you'll learn to handle the divide by zero error by catching the DivideByZeroException. The program with a try and catch block applied appears as shown in Listing 13.2. The code in bold is added; the rest is the same as in Listing 13.1.

Listing 13.2 Program Code in TryCatch1.cs File

```
using System;
class TryCatch1
{
    static void Main()
    {
        int x = 10,y=0,z =0;
        try{
            z = x/y;
            Console.WriteLine("Result of dividing {0} by {1} is {2}", x,y,z);
        }
        catch(DivideByZeroException ex)
        {
            Console.WriteLine("Exception has occurred", ex);
        }
    }
}
```

Output:

```
Exception has occurred
```

Because you have handled the exception DivideByZeroException, the program will not terminate unexpectedly as it did earlier. Instead, after an exception, the program control jumps from the try block to the catch block (terminating the try block in between) that defines the respective exception, DivideByZeroException. After handling the exception (executing the statements inside the catch block), the program resumes its execution following the catch block.

If a finally block is present, the code inside the finally block also is executed. Therefore, the exception handling enables your program to respond to runtime errors and continue executing code.

Note

If a try block doesn't throw an exception, no catch will be executed, and program control will resume after the catch.

What if you believe that your program might have errors in two places? Can you have more than one try block in a program handle exceptions in different parts of the program? Yes, you can. Read on.

USING MULTIPLE TRY BLOCKS

You can have multiple try blocks in a program to check different parts. In the program shown in Listing 13.3, you check two blocks of codes for runtime errors by enclosing them in two different try blocks and handle their respective exceptions through catch blocks. Only the code in bold is new; the rest is the same as shown in Listing 13.2.

Listing 13.3 Program Code in TryCatch1.cs File

```csharp
using System;
class TryCatch1
{
    static void Main()
    {
        int x = 10,y=0,z =0;
        int[] p=new int[3];
        try{
            z = x/y;
            Console.WriteLine("Result of dividing {0} by {1} is {2}", x,y,z);
        }
        catch(DivideByZeroException ex)
        {
            Console.WriteLine("Exception has occurred - divide by zero", ex);
        }
        try
        {
            p[3]=23;
            Console.WriteLine("Array element is {0}", p[0]);
        }
        catch(System.IndexOutOfRangeException ex)
        {
            Console.WriteLine("Exception has occurred - index out of range", ex);
        }
        finally
        {
            Console.WriteLine("This is the finally block");
        }
    }
}
```

Output:

```
Exception has occurred - divide by zero
Exception has occurred - index out of range
This is the finally block
```

In the preceding program, you check for the following two errors:

- Whether any numeral is divided by 0
- Whether an index value that is used by an array is within the prescribed range

Because variable x is divided by y, which is 0, the DivideByZeroException occurs. The program jumps from the try block to the catch block displaying the message Exception has occurred - divide by zero. After executing the catch block, the program resumes its execution following the catch block.

Also, an int array, p is defined of size 3 elements. Therefore, the valid index values of the array p are 0, 1, and 2. If you access any index in the range 0 to 2, the program runs successfully, but if you attempt to index the array beyond its boundaries, such as trying to use index value 3 or more on your array p, the exception IndexOutOfRangeException is thrown. The preceding program throws the exception IndexOutOfRangeException, which is caught by the catch block, thereby displaying the message Exception has occurred - index out of range on the screen. Whether the exception occurs or not, the code in the finally block always executes. So the program also displays the message This is the finally block on the screen.

If you don't handle the exception IndexOutOfRangeException, the program terminates, displaying the following error message:

```
Unhandled Exception: System. IndexOutOfRangeException: Index was outside the bounds of
the array. At TryCatch1.Main()
```

In the program shown in Listing 13.4, you see how to catch one more exception: FormatException. You want to convert a string to an integer through the Convert.ToInt32 function. You can convert a string into an integer only when it contains numeric content. If you try to convert nonnumeric content to an integer, the exception FormatException is thrown. Only the code in bold is new; the rest is identical to Listing 13.3.

Listing 13.4 Program Code in TryCatch1.cs File

```csharp
using System;
class TryCatch1
{
    static void Main()
    {
        int x = 10,y=0,z =0,n=0;
        int[] p=new int[3];
        String str;
        try{
            z = x/y;
            Console.WriteLine("Result of dividing {0} by {1} is {2}", x,y,z);
        }
        catch(DivideByZeroException ex)
        {
            Console.WriteLine("Exception has occurred - divide by zero", ex);
        }
        try
        {
            p[3]=23;
            Console.WriteLine("Array element is {0}", p[0]);
        }
        catch(System.IndexOutOfRangeException ex)
        {
            Console.WriteLine("Exception has occurred - index out of range", ex);
        }
        try
        {
            str="John";
            n=Convert.ToInt32(str);
            Console.WriteLine("Value in variable n is {0}", n);
        }
        catch(FormatException ex)
        {
            Console.WriteLine("Exception has occurred - format exception", ex);
        }
        finally
        {
            Console.WriteLine("This is the finally block");
        }
    }
}
```

Output:

```
Exception has occurred - divide by zero
Exception has occurred - index out of range
Exception has occurred - format exception
This is the finally block
```

In the programs `DivideByZeroException` and `IndexOutOfRangeException`, exceptions are thrown that are caught by their respective `catch` blocks. The `catch` blocks display the messages `Exception has occurred - divide by zero` and `Exception has occurred - index out of range`. Also, because the program tries to convert a string `John` to an integer by using the `Convert.ToInt32` function, which is not possible, the `FormatException` exception is also thrown. The `FormatException` exception is caught by the corresponding `catch` block, so the message `Exception has occurred - format exception` is displayed on the screen. In the last line, the `finally` block executes and displays the message `This is the finally block`.

Not only can a program have multiple `try` blocks, but a single `try` block can have multiple `catch` blocks.

USING MULTIPLE CATCH BLOCKS

You can associate more than one `catch` block with a single `try` block. Each `catch` block must catch a different type of exception. All the code that is expected to contain an error is enclosed within the `try` block. When any statement in the `try` block throws an exception, it is caught or held by the corresponding `catch` block. If any `catch` block handles the exception, the code in that `catch` block is executed, and the program resumes execution following the `catch` block. The `TryCatch2.cs` file shown in Listing 13.5 catches three exceptions: array-boundary, divide-by-zero errors, and format.

Listing 13.5 Program Code in TryCatch2.cs File

```
using System;
class TryCatch2
{
    static void Main()
    {
        int x = 10,y=0,z =0,n=0;
        int[] p=new int[3];
        String str;
        try{
            z = x/y;
            Console.WriteLine("Result of dividing {0} by {1} is {2}", x,y,z);
            p[3]=23;
```

```
            Console.WriteLine("Array element is {0}", p[0]);
            str="John";
            n=Convert.ToInt32(str);
            Console.WriteLine("Value in variable n is {0}", n);
        }
        catch(DivideByZeroException ex)
        {
            Console.WriteLine("Exception has occurred – divide by zero", ex);
        }
        catch(System.IndexOutOfRangeException ex)
        {
            Console.WriteLine("Exception has occurred – index out of range", ex);
        }
        catch(FormatException ex)
        {
            Console.WriteLine("Exception has occurred – format exception", ex);
        }
    }
}
```

Output:

```
Exception has occurred – divide by zero
```

The variable x is divided by y, which is 0, hence the `DivideByZeroException` exception is thrown which is caught by the corresponding `catch` block. The message `Exception has occurred - divide by zero` is displayed by the exception handling the `catch` block. The rest of the statements in the `try` block that follow the statement that caused the `DivideByZeroException` exception do not execute at all.

To catch all types of exceptions, you define a `catch` block with no exception type. This makes the `catch` block execute regardless of what type of exception occurs. The following syntax handles all the exceptions that might occur in a `try` block.

```
try
{
    // code that can cause exception(s)
}
catch
{
    // Code to handle the exception
}
```

Even though you can use a `catch` block with an `Exception` type parameter to catch all exceptions that might occur in the `try` block, all exceptions are directly or indirectly inherited from the `Exception` class.

The CatchAll.cs file shown in Listing 13.6 demonstrates a catch block that can handle or catch all types of exceptions. The program contains three try blocks that contain the code that throws DivideByZeroException, IndexOutOfRangeException, and FormatException, respectively. The three exceptions are caught by three catch blocks, where each catch block is enabled to catch all exceptions.

Listing 13.6 Program Code in CatchAll.cs File

```
using System;
class CatchAll
{
    static void Main()
    {
        int x = 10,y=0,z =0,n=0;
        int[] p=new int[3];
        String str;
        try{
            z = x/y;
            Console.WriteLine("Result of dividing {0} by {1} is {2}", x,y,z);
        }
        catch(Exception ex)
        {
            Console.WriteLine("Exception has occurred - "+ex.ToString());
        }
        try{
            p[3]=23;
            Console.WriteLine("Array element is {0}", p[0]);
        }
        catch(Exception ex)
        {
            Console.WriteLine("Exception has occurred - "+ex.ToString());
        }
        try{
            str="John";
            n=Convert.ToInt32(str);
            Console.WriteLine("Value in variable n is {0}", n);
        }
        catch(Exception ex)
        {
            Console.WriteLine("Exception has occurred - "+ex.ToString());
        }
    }
}
```

Output:

```
Exception has occurred — System.DivideByZeroException: Attempted to divide by zero.
    at CatchAll.Main()
Exception has occurred — System.IndexOutOfRangeException: Index was outside the bounds
of the array.
    at CatchAll.Main()
Exception has occurred — System.FormatException: Input string was not in a correct
format.
    at System.Number.StringToNumber(String str, NumberStyles options, NumberBuffer&
number, NumberFormatInfo info, Boolean parseDecimal)
    at System.Number.ParseInt32(String s, NumberStyles style, NumberFormatInfo info)
    at CatchAll.Main()
```

You can see that whatever type of exception is thrown by a try block, it is handled by the catch blocks, and each catch block contains an exception-type parameter. Because all exceptions inherit from the Exception class, each catch block can handle any exception.

THROWING AN EXCEPTION

Up until now you have been catching the exceptions that are generated automatically by the runtime system. You can also manually throw an exception by using the throw statement.

Syntax:

```
throw exceptObj;
```

Here, exceptObj must be an instance of a class that is derived from the Exception class.

The ThrowException.cs file shown in Listing 13.7 demonstrates how the exception DivideByZeroException is thrown manually.

Listing 13.7 Program Code in ThrowException.cs File

```csharp
using System;
class ThrowException
{
    static void Main()
    {
        int x = 10,y=5,z =0;
        try{
            z = x/y;
            Console.WriteLine("Result of dividing {0} by {1} is {2}", x,y,z);
            throw new DivideByZeroException();
        }
```

```
        catch(DivideByZeroException ex)
        {
            Console.WriteLine("Exception has occurred", ex);
        }
    }
}
```

Output:

```
Result of dividing 10 by 5 is 2
Exception has occurred
```

You can see that `DivideByZeroException` is created using the `new` operator in the `throw` statement. The `new` operator creates a new object. But why you are creating an object? It's simple. The `throw` block throws an object, so you must create an object for it to throw.

An exception caught by one `catch` block can be rethrown so that it can be caught by another `catch` block. The idea is to check whether the respective exception handlers are handling the exceptions properly. To rethrow the same exception, simply write a `throw` without specifying the exception name in the `catch` block.

The `ThrowException.cs` file shown in Listing 13.8 demonstrates how a manually thrown exception is caught by a `catch` block and how the `catch` block rethrows another exception that in turn is caught by another `catch` block. The `DivideByZeroException` is thrown by using the `throw` statement in a `try` block. `DivideByZeroException` is caught by the `catch` block which, after displaying a desired message, throws another exception: `IndexOutOfRangeException`. `IndexOutOfRangeException` is caught by the `catch` block defined in the `Main` method.

Listing 13.8 Program Code in ThrowException.cs File

```
using System;
class ThrowException
{
    static void disp(string str)
    {
        int x = 10,y=5,z =0;
        try{
            z = x/y;
            Console.WriteLine("Hello {0}!",str);
            Console.WriteLine("Result of dividing {0} by {1} is {2}", x,y,z);
            throw new DivideByZeroException();
        }
        catch(DivideByZeroException ex)
```

```
        {
            Console.WriteLine("Exception has occurred – divide by zero", ex);
            throw new IndexOutOfRangeException("Exception thrown by disp method ",
ex);
        }
    }
    static void Main()
    {
        try{
            disp("John");
        }
        catch(System.IndexOutOfRangeException ex)
        {
            Console.WriteLine("Exception has occurred in Main block – index out of
range. Message: {0}", ex.Message);
            Console.WriteLine ("Inner Exception is {0}",ex.InnerException);
        }
    }
}
```

Output:

```
Hello John!
Result of dividing 10 by 5 is 2
Exception has occurred – divide by zero
Exception has occurred in Main block – index out of range. Message: Exception thrown by
disp method
Inner Exception is System.DivideByZeroException: Attempted to divide by zero.
   at ThrowException.disp(String str)
```

You can see that the disp function is called from within the try block. A string John is passed while calling the disp function. In the disp function, the message Hello John! is displayed. Also, DivideByZeroException is thrown using the throw statement within the try block. DivideByZeroException is caught by the catch block that displays the message Exception has occurred - divide by zero on the screen. In the catch block, another exception, IndexOutOfRangeException, is thrown, which is thereafter caught by the catch block defined in the Main method. The catch block in the Main method displays the message Exception has occurred - index out of range on the screen. To display messages from all inner exceptions of the generated exception, use the InnerException property. The InnerException property holds a reference to the inner exceptions (the history of all exceptions that are thrown).

NESTING TRY BLOCKS

You can nest one `try` block within another. If an exception is generated within the inner `try` block and is not caught by its `catch` block(s), it passes on to the outer `try` block.

Syntax of nested `try` blocks:

```
try      // Outer try block
{

    . . . . . . . . . . . . . .
    . . . . . . . . . . . . . .
try      // Inner try block
{
    // Code that can cause exception(s)
}
catch(Excep_Type1 Excep_Obj)          // Inner catch block
{
    // Code to handle the exception
}
[finally                              // Inner finally block
{
    // Any cleanup code
} ]
}
catch(Excep_Type1 Excep_Obj)          // Outer catch block
{
    // Code to handle the exception
}
[finally                              // Outer finally block
{
    // Any cleanup code
} ]
```

The following circumstances might occur while using nested `try` blocks:

- If an exception is thrown inside the outer `try` block but outside the inner `try` block, the exception is caught by the outer `catch` block and the outer `finally` block, if there is one, is executed.

- If an exception is thrown in the inner `try` block, it is caught by the inner `catch` block and the `finally` block (if one exists) is executed. Execution resumes inside the outer `try` block from the statement following the `catch` block.

- If an exception is thrown in the inner `try` block and there is no corresponding `catch` block to handle it, the inner `finally` block (if any exists) is executed. Also, the outer `catch` blocks are searched to see if they can handle that exception. If available, the outer `catch` block handles that exception, and the outer `finally` block (if one exists) is executed.

The `NestedTry.cs` file shown in Listing 13.9 demonstrates nested `try` blocks. The inner `try` block throws `IndexOutOfRangeException` that is caught by the inner `catch` block. After executing the statements in the inner `catch` block, the inner `finally` block is executed. The program resumes execution following the `finally` block (in the outer `try` block). The outer `try` block throws `DivideByZeroException` that is caught by the outer `catch` block. After executing the outer `catch` block, the outer `finally` block is executed.

Listing 13.9 Program Code in NestedTry.cs File

```
using System;
class NestedTry {
    static void Main() {
        int x = 10,y=0,z =0;
        int[] p=new int[3];
        try{
            try{
                p[3]=23;
                Console.WriteLine("Array element is {0}", p[0]);
            }
            catch(IndexOutOfRangeException ex)
            {
                Console.WriteLine("Exception has occurred, index out of range - "+
                    ex.ToString());
            }
            finally
            {
                Console.WriteLine("This is the inner finally block");
            }
            z = x/y;
        }
        catch(DivideByZeroException ex)
        {
            Console.WriteLine("Exception has occurred - divide by zero", ex);
        }
        finally
        {
            Console.WriteLine("This is the outer finally block");
        }
    }
}
```

Output:

```
Exception has occurred, index out of range - System.IndexOutOfRangeException: Index was
outside the bounds of the array.
    at NestedTry.Main()
This is the inner finally block
Exception has occurred – divide by zero
This is the outer finally block
```

The message `Exception has occurred, index out of range` is displayed when the inner `catch` block handles `IndexOutOfRangeException`, which is thrown by the inner `try` block. Then the `This is the inner finally block` message is displayed upon execution of the inner `finally` block. The `Exception has occurred - divide by zero` message is displayed by the outer `catch` block when the `DivideByZeroException` exception is thrown by the outer `try` block. The message `This is the outer finally block` is displayed upon execution of the outer `finally` block.

CREATING YOUR OWN EXCEPTION

Although the .NET Framework contains all kinds of exception types that are sufficient to handle most of the errors, it also provides a facility to create your own custom exceptions. Custom exceptions help to simplify code and improve error handling. The custom exceptions must inherit from either the `System.Exception` class or one of its standard derived classes, like `SystemException` or `ApplicationException`. `SystemException` is meant for those exceptions defined by the CLR, whereas `ApplicationException` is thrown by a user program. It is recommended that the new exception classes you define derive from the `Exception` class. In its simplest form, a custom exception class just needs to have a name, as shown here:

```
public class CustomException: Exception
{
}
```

You can see that a basic custom exception named `CustomException` is created by deriving from the `Exception` class. After adding a constructor, the custom exception appears as shown here:

```
public class CustomException: Exception
{
    public CustomException()
    {
    }
    public CustomException(string str): base(str)
    {
    }
}
```

With the preceding code format, your custom exception acts like other standard exceptions. You can throw an instance of CustomException and pass a string that describes the cause of the error.

The CustomException.cs file shown in Listing 13.10 demonstrates creation of a custom exception named CustomException. The program defines a CustomException, throws the exception manually, and catches it with the required catch block.

Listing 13.10 Program Code in CustomException.cs File

```
using System;
class CustomException : Exception
{
    public CustomException()
    {
        Console.WriteLine("My own exception");
    }
    public CustomException(string str): base(str)
    {
    }
}
class CreateException
{
    public static void Main()
    {
        try
        {
            throw new CustomException("Hello!");
        }
        catch(Exception ex)
        {
            Console.WriteLine("The CustomException is caught - " + ex.ToString());
        }
    }
}
```

Output:

```
The CustomException is caught - CustomException: Hello!
   at CreateException.Main()
```

You can see that your CustomException is thrown manually using the throw function in the try block. The message passed while throwing the exception is Hello, but it could be any text that explains the cause of the error. The parameterized constructor of CustomException is invoked, which in turn invokes the constructor of the base class (the Exception class). The thrown CustomException is handled by the catch block defined in the Main method. The catch block displays the message that caused the exception.

Now you'll read about checked and unchecked operators, which are quite useful in performing long arithmetic calculations.

USING THE CHECKED/UNCHECKED OPERATOR

The checked and unchecked operators determine whether to throw an exception or not in case of overflow. You have to decide whether you want the overflow error to be detected or whether you want it to be ignored.

■ The checked operator enforces overflow checking by throwing an exception if an overflow occurs. If a block of code is marked as checked, the CLR checks for occurrence of overflow and throws OverflowException if overflow occurs.

■ The unchecked operator doesn't throw an exception if an overflow occurs. It simply suppresses overflow checking in the code, thereby losing data in the code that is marked as unchecked.

Note

unchecked is the default in C#.

The CheckedExample.cs file shown in Listing 13.11 demonstrates application of checked and unchecked operators in detecting overflow conditions.

Listing 13.11 Program Code in CheckedExample.cs File

```
using System;
class CheckedExample
{
    static void Main()
    {
        int a;
        byte b;
        a=Int32.MaxValue;
        b=byte.MaxValue;
        Console.WriteLine ("The maximum value of Int32 is {0}", a);
        Console.WriteLine ("The maximum value of byte is {0}", b);
        try{
            checked
```

```
        {
            a++;
            b++;
        }
    }
    catch(Exception ex)
    {
        Console.WriteLine(ex.Message.ToString());
    }
    Console.WriteLine ("Exception will be thrown. The Int32 will not be
incremented. Value remains {0}", a);
    Console.WriteLine ("Exception will be thrown. The byte will not be incremented.
Value remains {0}", b);
    try{
        unchecked
        {
            a++;
            b++;
        }
    }
    catch(Exception ex)
    {
        Console.WriteLine(ex.Message.ToString());
    }
    Console.WriteLine ("The Int32 after incrementing by 1 becomes {0}", a);
    Console.WriteLine ("The byte type after incrementing by 1 becomes {0}", b);
    }
}
```

Output:

```
The maximum value of Int32 is 2147483647
The maximum value of byte is 255
Arithmetic operation resulted in an overflow.
Exception will be thrown. The Int32 will not be incremented. Value remains 2147483647
Exception will be thrown. The byte will not be incremented. Value remains 255
The Int32 after incrementing by 1 becomes -2147483648
The byte type after incrementing by 1 becomes 0
```

A byte can hold values in the range 0 to 255, and an Int32 can hold values in the range 0 to 2147483647. Incrementing either byte or Int32 will result in an overflow. After marking the code as checked, the CLR enforces overflow checking. It throws OverflowException upon incrementing the value of byte or Int32, displaying the message Arithmetic operation resulted in an overflow.

The benefit is that you don't get wrong results after marking the code checked. After marking the code as unchecked, you suppress overflow checking, thereby losing data. The byte type is unable to hold a value of 256, and the overflowing bits are discarded, assigning value 0 to the byte variable b. The same happens with Int32; it cannot hold the value 2147483648, so it assigns value -2147483648 (wrong value) to the Int32 variable a.

Summary

In this chapter, you learned about different types of errors, the role of exceptions, and various keywords that are required in exception handling. You learned to use try-catch-finally blocks, multiple try blocks, multiple catch clocks, and CatchAll exceptions. You also saw how to throw any exception manually and how to rethrow an exception. You learned to nest try blocks, create your own custom exceptions, and apply checked and unchecked operators in checking overflows in numerical computations.

The next chapter is focused on threads. You will learn how to use them in multitasking and how to employ thread synchronization. You will also learn about thread properties, thread management, and interruption and termination of threads.

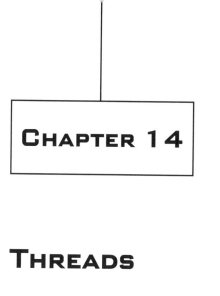

CHAPTER 14

THREADS

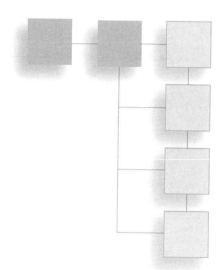

This chapter's topics include the following:

- Introduction to threads
- Life cycle of a thread
- Multithreading

INTRODUCTION TO THREADS

A *thread* is an independent execution unit containing a piece of code. Don't confuse threads with processes, because they're different. An application consists of several processes, and each process includes the memory, resources, and threads to execute the application. When an application is launched, the operating system starts a unique process dedicated to that application. All threads within a process share the same state and memory space and communicate with each other to perform different tasks.

When a process begins, a main thread is started. From the main thread, child threads are generated to perform concurrent tasks. .NET supports the multithreading operation; in other words, more than one thread can run simultaneously in an application to implement concurrency and increase efficiency of hardware used. When multiple threads are running in a single process, each thread is given the CPU's attention for a time slice. (The CPU switches from one thread to another, serving each thread for a specific time slice.) Remember, each thread is associated with a specific process and is an independent execution unit having its own code to run.

Note

The class that is used for working with threads in C# is System.Threading.Thread. The threads are created by extending the Thread class, which allows creating and accessing of individual threads in a multithreaded application.

Using the Main Thread

The first thread that is executed in a process is called the main thread. The threads created using the Thread class are called the *child threads* of the main thread. The MainThreadProg.cs file shown in Listing 14.1 demonstrates that the main thread is automatically created when a program executes.

Listing 14.1 Program Code in MainThreadProg.cs File

```
using System;
using System.Threading;

    class MainThreadProg
    {
        static void Main(string[] args)
        {
            Thread thread = Thread.CurrentThread;
            thread.Name = "Main Thread";
            Console.WriteLine("The current thread is {0}", thread.Name);
        }
    }
```

Output:

```
The current thread is Main Thread
```

Using the CurrentThread property of the Thread class, you create a thread object that points at the currently running thread (the main thread that is automatically created upon execution of the program). The thread object is assigned the name Main Thread through the Name property. The name assigned to the main thread is then displayed on the screen.

Creating Child Threads

Threads are created using the Thread class and are considered child threads of the main thread (because the main thread is automatically created when running the program). To create a child thread, first create a delegate object, passing a callback method to it as a parameter. The callback method contains the code that you want to execute when the thread runs. A new Thread object is created, and the delegate object is used to initialize the `Thread` object. The `Start` method on the `Thread` object is called to run the thread. Soon, the constructor of the `Thread` class is overloaded to accept a delegate parameter of type `ThreadStart` or `ParameterizedThreadStart`. The `ThreadStart` delegate defines a callback method that contains the code to execute when the thread runs.

Here are the steps for creating a thread:

1. **Create a System.Threading.Thread object**—The `Thread` object creates a managed thread in the .NET environment. The `Thread` class has a constructor that takes a `ThreadStart` delegate as a parameter. The `ThreadStart` delegate represents the thread's callback method, which is called after starting the thread.

2. **Creating the thread's callback function**—The thread's callback method is invoked after starting the thread and is used to create the `ThreadStart` delegate. The callback method may be an instance function or a static function. If the callback method is an instance function, you need to create an object of the class before creating the `ThreadStart` delegate. On the other hand, if the callback function is a static function, you can directly use the function name to instantiate the delegate.

Note

The thread's callback function should have `void` as both the return type and a parameter.

3. **Starting the thread**—The newly created thread is started using the `Thread` class's `Start` method. The operating system starts the current thread when the `Start` method is invoked.

All three steps are shown in the following code snippet:

```
public class ClassName
{
    static void Main()
    {
        ThreadStart deligobj = new ThreadStart(threadCallbackFunction);
        Thread threadObject = new Thread(deligobj);
        threadObject.Start();
        .......
    }
    static void threadCallbackFunction()
    {
        .......
    }
}
```

The `threadCallbackFunction` method in the preceding code snippet represents the code to execute when the thread runs. `delegateObject` is the delegate object that is created and initialized to the thread method `threadCallbackFunction`. The `Thread` object `threadObject` is created and initialized to the delegate object. Finally, the `threadObject` object is set to run by calling its `Start` method.

The `ThreadSample.cs` file shown in Listing 14.2 demonstrates creation of a child thread.

Listing 14.2 Program Code in ThreadSample.cs File

```
using System;
using System.Threading;

public class ThreadSample
{
    static void Main()
    {
        ThreadStart deligobj = new ThreadStart(ThreadCode);
        Thread childThread = new Thread(deligobj);
        Console.WriteLine("This is the main thread");
        childThread.Start();
    }
    static void ThreadCode()
    {
        Console.WriteLine ("This is the child thread");
    }
}
```

Output:

```
This is the main thread
This is the child thread
```

When the program begins its execution, the main thread is automatically created, and the message `This is the main thread` appears on the screen. Then a `Thread` object called `childThread` is created and initialized to the delegate object `deligobj`. The delegate object `deligobj` is in turn initialized to the thread method `ThreadCode`, ensuring that it will run when the thread starts. After starting the thread object `childThread`, the `ThreadCode` method executes and displays the message `This is the child thread` on the screen.

You want your child thread to do something more. You'll modify your `ThreadSample.cs` file such that the child thread created in it prints the sequence numbers from 0 to 10. You need to add a loop in the callback method `ThreadCode` (shown in bold in the listing).

Listing 14.3 Program Code in ThreadSample.cs File

```csharp
using System;
using System.Threading;

public class ThreadSample
{
    static void Main()
    {
        ThreadStart deligobj = new ThreadStart(ThreadCode);
        Thread childThread = new Thread(deligobj);
        Console.WriteLine("This is the main thread");
        childThread.Start();
    }
    static void ThreadCode()
    {
        for (int i=0; i <= 10; i++)
        {
            Console.WriteLine ("This is the child thread: {0}", i);
            Thread.Sleep(500);
        }
    }
}
```

Output:

```
This is the main thread
Child Thread : 0
Child Thread : 1
Child Thread : 2
Child Thread : 3
Child Thread : 4
Child Thread : 5
Child Thread : 6
Child Thread : 7
Child Thread : 8
Child Thread : 9
Child Thread : 10
```

The Sleep method, when called on the Thread class, makes the thread sleep or suspend for 500ms, so the sequence numbers appear after an interval of 500ms. You will learn about other methods and properties of the Thread class later in this chapter.

Instead of keeping all code in the main class, you can create a separate class dedicated to threads. In this custom class, you can keep callback methods and other code related to the threads. You can create the child thread in Listing 14.3 using a separate custom class, as shown in Listing 14.4.

Listing 14.4 Program Code in ThreadThroughClass.cs File

```
using System;
using System.Threading;
public class MyThread
{
    public void ThreadCode()
    {
        for (int i=0; i <= 10; i++)
        {
            Console.WriteLine ("This is the child thread: {0}", i);
            Thread.Sleep(500);
        }
    }
}
public class ThreadThroughClass
{
    static void Main()
    {
        MyThread threadObj = new MyThread();
        ThreadStart deligobj = new ThreadStart(threadObj.ThreadCode);
        Thread childThread = new Thread(deligobj);
        Console.WriteLine("This is the main thread");
        childThread.Start();
    }
}
```

The output of this program will be the same as that of Listing 14.3. In Listing 14.4, you create a separate class named `MyThread` and define the method `ThreadCode` in it. An object of the `MyThread` class is defined named `threadObj`. The delegate object `deligobj` is initialized to the thread method `ThreadCode` through the object `threadObj`. A Thread object called `childThread` is created and initialized to the delegate object `deligobj`. The `childThread` is started by calling the `Start` method, thereby invoking the `Thread` code method of the custom class `MyThread`.

To see how the CPU time switches between two threads, you'll assign some task to the main thread. Modify the `ThreadSample.cs` file so that the main thread does some task. The `ThreadSample.cs` file shown in Listing 14.5 prints the sequence numbers from 1 to 10 using the child thread. The program also prints sequence numbers from 0 to 5 using the main thread. The code in bold is new; the rest is the same as in Listing 14.3.

Listing 14.5 Program Code in ThreadSample.cs File

```
using System;
using System.Threading;

public class ThreadSample
{
    static void Main()
    {
        ThreadStart deligobj = new ThreadStart(ThreadCode);
        Thread childThread = new Thread(deligobj);
        childThread.Start();
        for (int i=0; i <= 5; i++)
        {
            Console.WriteLine ("This is the main thread: {0}", i);
            Thread.Sleep(1000);
        }
    }
    static void ThreadCode()
    {
        for (int i=0; i <= 10; i++)
        {
            Console.WriteLine ("This is the child thread: {0}", i);
            Thread.Sleep(500);
        }
    }
}
```

Output:

```
Main thread: 0
Thread1 : 0
Thread1 : 1
Main thread: 1
Thread1 : 2
Thread1 : 3
Main thread: 2
Thread1 : 4
Thread1 : 5
Main thread: 3
Thread1 : 6
Thread1 : 7
Thread1 : 8
Main thread: 4
Thread1 : 9
Main thread: 5
Thread1 : 10
```

The main thread is automatically created in the program. The thread object childThread is created and initialized to the delegate object deligobj. The Start method, when called on the thread object childThread, invokes the callback method ThreadCode. A for loop in the main method executes and displays the sequence numbers from 0 to 5. After every value displayed through the main thread, the main thread is suspended for 1000ms (for one second). When the main thread is suspended, the CPU time is assigned to the child thread childThread. The callback method ThreadCode executes. In the ThreadCode method, a for loop executes to display sequence numbers from 0 to 10. After every number displayed through the childThread, the childThread is suspended for 500ms. (Sequence numbers appear in intervals of 500ms.) To ensure that the childThread object finishes its code before the main thread terminates, the sleep time of the main thread is set to double (1000ms) that of the childThread object (500ms).

Note

When two or more threads are running in a program, you cannot be assured of the output because the operating system schedules threads. (The thread that comes first can be different each time.) Also, there's no guarantee that the sleeping thread will start running as soon as the sleep time is over because another thread may be currently running. So the thread whose sleep time is complete needs to wait until the currently running thread is either suspended or terminated.

You can control a thread in different ways: pause it, resume it, destroy it, or control its execution speed. Next, you'll learn some states that a thread undergoes during its life cycle.

LIFE CYCLE OF A THREAD

Here's the life cycle of a thread:

1. A new thread begins its life cycle in the Unstarted state.

2. The thread remains in the Unstarted state until the Thread method Start is called, which places the thread in the Started (also known as Ready or Runnable) state.

3. The highest priority started thread enters the Running state. (The CPU time is assigned to it.)

4. A Running thread enters the Stopped state when its job or task is over. Also, a Running thread can be forced to the Stopped state by calling the Abort method. The Abort method throws a ThreadAbortException in the thread, normally causing the thread to terminate.

5. A thread enters the Blocked state when the thread issues an input/output (I/O) request. In other words, the operating system blocks the thread to perform the I/O operations. The CPU time is not assigned to a Blocked thread.

6. After I/O operations are complete, the Blocked thread returns to the Started state so it can resume execution.

7. A Running thread may enter the WaitSleepJoin state either when it is asked to sleep for the specified number of milliseconds or when the Monitor method Wait is called. From the WaitSleepJoin state, a thread returns to the Started state when another thread invokes the Monitor method Pulse or PulseAll. The Pulse method moves the next waiting thread back to the Started state. The PulseAll method moves all waiting threads back to the Started state.

8. A sleeping thread returns to the Started state when the specified sleep duration expires.

9. Any thread in the WaitSleepJoin state can return to the Started state if the sleeping or waiting thread's Interrupt method is called by another thread in the program.

10. If a thread cannot continue executing unless another thread terminates, it calls the other thread's Join method to join the two threads. When two threads are joined, the waiting thread leaves the WaitSleepJoin state when the other thread completes execution.

Figure 14.1 demonstrates different states of a thread through a block diagram.

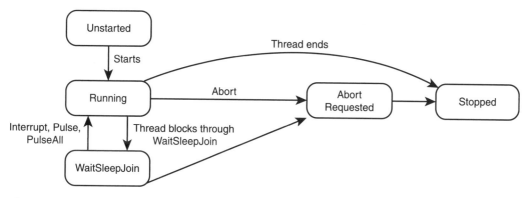

Figure 14.1
Block diagram of a thread's life cycle.
© 2015 Cengage Learning®.

To conclude, a thread can be in any of the states shown in Table 14.1.

Table 14.1 Thread States

State	Description
Unstarted	A thread is created within the Common Language Runtime (CLR) but not started.
Ready	A thread is ready to run and is waiting for the CPU time.
Running	A thread is in running mode after its Start method is invoked.
WaitSleepJoin	A running thread is suspended temporarily by invoking either the Sleep method or the monitor's Wait method.
Started	A suspended thread resumes to Started state when the conditions for which it was suspended are no longer valid.
Blocked	A thread is blocked when it's waiting for a resource or for I/O operations.
Stopped	A thread has finished its task.

© 2015 Cengage Learning®.

You can check the current state of a thread using its ThreadState property. The ThreadStates.cs file shown in Listing 14.6 demonstrates different states of a thread during its life cycle.

Listing 14.6 Program Code in ThreadStates.cs File

```
using System;
using System.Threading;

class ThreadStates
{
    public static Thread childThread;
    public static void ThreadCode()
    {
        try
        {
            Console.WriteLine("Thread starts");
            Console.WriteLine("Child thread paused for 2 seconds" );
            Thread.Sleep(2000);
            Console.WriteLine("Child thread resumes" );
            Console.WriteLine("Child thread is in WaitSleepJoin state : "+
(childThread.ThreadState == ThreadState.WaitSleepJoin));
```

```
            Thread.Sleep(1000);
            Console.WriteLine("Child thread completed");
        }
        catch (ThreadAbortException e)
        {
            Console.WriteLine("Child Thread Abort Exception");
        }
        finally
        {
            Console.WriteLine("Finally block");
        }
    }
    static void Main(string[] args)
    {
        ThreadStart deligobj = new ThreadStart(ThreadCode);
        Console.WriteLine("In Main: Creating the Child thread");
        childThread = new Thread(deligobj);
        childThread.Start();
        Thread.Sleep(3000);
        Console.WriteLine("Aborting the Child Thread");
        childThread.Abort();
    }
}
```

Output:

```
In Main: Creating the Child thread
Thread starts
Child thread paused for 2 seconds
Child thread resumes
Child thread is in WaitSleepJoin state : False
Aborting the Child Thread
Child Thread Abort Exception
Finally block
```

You can see different states of the child thread: how it starts, suspends, resumes, and terminates. When a thread is aborted, the ThreadAbortException is thrown, which can be caught but is automatically rethrown at the end of the catch block. Because the exception keeps throwing, the thread terminates. To stop the exception from being rethrown at the end of a catch block, you can call the Thread.ResetAbort method.

The Thread class provides several properties and methods to access information about the thread and to configure it as required. Table 14.2 shows a brief description of some of the most commonly used properties and methods of the Thread class.

Table 14.2 Properties and Methods of the Thread Class

Property	Description
CurrentContext	Gets the current context in which the thread is executing.
CurrentCulture	Gets or sets the culture for the current thread.
CurrentThread	Returns the currently running thread.
ExecutionContext	Gets an ExecutionContext object that contains information about the various contexts of the current thread.
IsAlive	Returns a Boolean value indicating the execution status of the current thread.
IsBackground	Gets or sets a value indicating whether or not a thread is a background thread.
IsThreadPoolThread	Gets a value indicating whether or not a thread belongs to the managed thread pool.
ManagedThreadId	Gets a unique identifier for the current managed thread.
Name	Gets or sets the name of the thread.
Priority	Gets or sets a value representing the priority of a thread.
ThreadState	Gets a value containing the states of the current thread.

© 2015 Cengage Learning®.

The ThreadProperties.cs file shown in Listing 14.7 displays the kind of thread information that can be accessed using different thread properties and methods.

Listing 14.7 Program Code in ThreadProperties.cs File

```
using System;
using System.Threading;

class ThreadProperties
{
    static void Main(string[] args)
    {
        Thread thread = Thread.CurrentThread;
        thread.Name = "Main Thread";
        Console.WriteLine("Information of Current Thread");
        Console.WriteLine("Thread Name: {0}", thread.Name);
        Console.WriteLine("Thread Status: {0}", thread.IsAlive);
        Console.WriteLine("Priority: {0}", thread.Priority);
        Console.WriteLine("Context ID: {0}", Thread.CurrentContext.ContextID);
```

```
        Console.WriteLine("Managed Thread ID: {0}",
Thread.CurrentThread.ManagedThreadId);
        Console.WriteLine("Current application domain: {0}",
Thread.GetDomain().FriendlyName);
    }
}
```

Output:

```
Information of Current Thread
Thread Name: Main Thread
Thread Status: True
Priority: Normal
Context ID: 0
Managed Thread ID: 1
Current application domain: ThreadProperties.exe
```

The program displays information about a currently running thread. Recall that the
CurrentThread property of the Thread class refers to the currently running thread. The
valid priority levels of a thread are Highest, AboveNormal, Normal, and BelowNormal.

Table 14.3 shows some of the most commonly used methods of the Thread class.

Table 14.3 Most Common Methods of the Thread Class

Method Name	Description
public void Abort()	Raises a ThreadAbortException in the thread on which it is invoked to begin the process of terminating the thread. Calling this method usually terminates the thread.
public static void BeginCriticalRegion()	Indicates that execution is about to enter a critical region of code.
public static void EndCriticalRegion()	Indicates that execution is about to reach the code where the critical region ends.
public void Interrupt()	Interrupts a thread that is in the WaitSleepJoin thread state.
public void Join()	Blocks the calling thread until a thread terminates (that is, it makes the calling thread wait, allowing other threads to finish their execution).
public static void ResetAbort()	Cancels an abort requested for the current thread.
public void Start()	Starts a thread.

(Continued)

Table 14.3 Most Common Methods of the Thread Class (*Continued*)

Method Name	Description
`public static void Sleep(int milliseconds)`	Makes the thread pause for the specified number of milliseconds.
`public static void SpinWait(int iterations)`	Causes a thread to wait the number of times defined by the `iterations` parameter.
`public static bool Yield()`	Causes the calling thread to yield execution to another thread that is ready to run on the current processor.

© 2015 Cengage Learning®.

Up until now, you have been creating a single child in the main thread. You need to be careful about thread safety while working with multiple threads.

MULTITHREADING

For concurrent execution, an application contains more than one thread, and each thread runs independently performing its specific task. In multithreading, the CPU is assigned to each thread for a time slice before moving onto the next thread. In other words, the CPU serves each thread or a given time interval in a round-robin fashion. Through multithreading, the efficiency of the program increases when CPU idle time in I/O operations can be utilized in executing another thread. But the problem occurs when two or more threads try to access the same resources at the same time. For example, if two or more threads access and alter a variable at the same time, changes made by only one thread will be visible; changes made by the other threads will be overwritten.

Now you'll create a program that implements multithreading. The `MultiThread.cs` file shown in Listing 14.8 demonstrates how two child threads access a common resource (a variable n). The program contains a static variable n and two child threads to try to increment its value by 1. The main thread then displays the new value of the variable n.

Listing 14.8 Program Code in MultiThread.cs File

```
using System;
using System.Threading;

class MultiThread
{
    static int n=10;
```

```
    static void Main()
    {
        Console.WriteLine ("Main thread starting");
        ThreadStart deligobj = new ThreadStart(ThreadCode);
        Thread childThread1 = new Thread(deligobj);
        childThread1.Name = "ChildThread1";
        Thread childThread2 = new Thread(deligobj);
        childThread2.Name = "ChildThread2";
        childThread1.Start();
        childThread2.Start();
        Console.WriteLine ("Value of n is {0}", n);
    }
    static void ThreadCode()
    {
        Console.WriteLine (Thread.CurrentThread.Name + " running");
        n++;
    }
}
```

Output:

```
Main thread starting
Value of n is 10
ChildThread1 running
ChildThread2 running
```

In this case, the value of variable n returns 10 because the main thread displays the variable's value before either of the thread finishes its callback method ThreadCode. After running the program for the second time, you might get a different output, as shown here:

```
Main thread starting
ChildThread1 running
Value of n is 11
ChildThread2 running
```

Again, you are getting an incorrect result because the main thread doesn't wait for the second thread to finish its callback method ThreadCode. To make the main thread wait until the two child threads finish their task, you must use the Join method. The Thread.Join method pauses the main thread until the other threads complete their task.

Now you'll modify the MultiThread.cs file such that the main thread does not exist but waits for the two child threads to finish their task of incrementing the value of the variable n. The modified code is shown in Listing 14.9. Only the code in bold is new; the rest is the same as in Listing 14.8.

Listing 14.9 Program Code in MultiThread.cs File

```
using System;
using System.Threading;

class MultiThread
{
    static int n=10;

    static void Main()
    {
        Console.WriteLine ("Main thread starting");
        ThreadStart deligobj = new ThreadStart(ThreadCode);
        Thread childThread1 = new Thread(deligobj);
        childThread1.Name = "ChildThread1";
        Thread childThread2 = new Thread(deligobj);
        childThread2.Name = "ChildThread2";
        childThread1.Start();
        childThread2.Start();
        childThread1.Join();
        childThread2.Join();
        Console.WriteLine ("Value of n is {0}", n);
    }
    static void ThreadCode()
    {
        Console.WriteLine (Thread.CurrentThread.Name + " running");
        n++;
    }
}
```

Output:

```
Main thread starting
ChildThread1 running
ChildThread2 running
Value of n is 12
```

In the preceding code, the main thread waits until both child threads complete their execution. Although you get the correct result from the preceding program, there's a chance results might be inconsistent because both threads execute simultaneously. The second child thread might read the old value of n (10 instead of 11, which was written by child thread 1). The condition of two or more threads accessing the same resource simultaneously for manipulation is known as *race condition*.

Ensuring Exclusive Operations Using Monitors

For consistent results, you need to ensure only one thread is operating on the shared resources. To enable only one thread to operate on the shared resources, you use the Monitor class. Monitor is a theoretical property that a thread can acquire or enter if no other thread has acquired it. After acquiring Monitor, a thread can access and update the shared resources and, when done, release or exit Monitor for other threads to acquire. Because only one thread is able to acquire Monitor at a time, two or more threads cannot update the same resources simultaneously. A thread can acquire and release Monitor several times. Monitor is only available to other threads once it is released or exited as many times as it was acquired or entered. A thread is asked to wait if it tries to acquire a Monitor class that is acquired by another thread until it is released.

Monitor requires you to specify the token (an object reference) that a thread must acquire to enter within the lock scope. To use Monitor, you need to create or determine an object that needs to be exclusively locked. One thread locks on the object's Monitor at a time, and until it exits or releases Monitor, all other threads wait to gain lock on the object's Monitor. Thus, only one thread can access and update the resource(s).

You can place Monitor locks directly on the shared resource or on a new object that you can then use to control the access to a collection of shared resources.

Note

> Monitor locks help to synchronize threads. They apply thread safety when multiple threads share some resources simultaneously. Monitor locks enable only one thread to access and update the resources; they block other threads from accessing the resources until they are unlocked by the locking thread. The shared resources are also known as *critical sections*. Monitor locks restrict the critical section to a single thread at a time. Remember, the Enter and Exit calls on Monitor should be balanced, or the same.

The MultiThread.cs file shown in Listing 14.10 demonstrates using Monitor in implementing thread safety. The program shows how only one child thread at a time can access and update a resource and therefore display consistent results.

Listing 14.10 Program Code in MultiThread.cs File

```
using System;
using System.Threading;

class MultiThread
{
    static int n=10;
    static object resourceLock = new object();
```

```
static void Main()
{
    Console.WriteLine ("Main thread starting");
    ThreadStart deligobj = new ThreadStart(ThreadCode);
    Thread childThread1 = new Thread(deligobj);
    childThread1.Name = "ChildThread1";
    Thread childThread2 = new Thread(deligobj);
    childThread2.Name = "ChildThread2";
    childThread1.Start();
    childThread2.Start();
    childThread1.Join();
    childThread2.Join();
    Console.WriteLine ("Value of n is {0}", n);
}
static void ThreadCode()
{
    Monitor.Enter(resourceLock);
    try{
        Console.WriteLine (Thread.CurrentThread.Name + " running");
        n++;
    }
    finally
    {
        Monitor.Exit(resourceLock);
    }
}
}
```

Output:

```
Main thread starting
ChildThread1 running
ChildThread2 running
Value of n is 12
```

The keyword lock provides help in synchronizing the thread operation. It ensures that only one thread can access a method at a time, thereby avoiding inconsistencies. Once a thread enters the callback method, a lock is applied, stopping any other thread from accessing the method. When the thread finishes the method, the lock is released so that other threads can access the method.

Observe that all code (critical section) is wrapped within a try block. The corresponding finally block ensures that the lock is released via the Monitor.Exit method, regardless of any exception that might occur. Critical section refers to that shareable code that you want to be accessed by only one thread at a time. Such shareable code being accessed by two threads simultaneously leads to inconsistency.

Using the Lock Statement

The `lock` statement acts as a shorthand notation for working with the `System.Threading.Monitor` class. However, `Monitor` provides necessary control and flexibility. A `lock` statement blocks or suspends the threads that try to get a lock on some resources until the resources are released. The `Monitor` class, on the other hand, provides the methods like `Monitor.Pulse` and `PulseAll` to inform the waiting threads that it has completed. With `Monitor`, if a thread tries for the lock and can't get it, the thread can execute alternate logic.

Note

In a multithreading environment, the term *thread safety* applies when only one thread is allowed to access and modify a certain critical section of code.

The `lock` statement automatically calls `Monitor.Enter` and `Monitor.Exit` with a try/finally block. Implementing thread synchronization with a `lock` statement is easy because you don't need to balance the `Enter` and `Exit` calls on `Monitor`. The code shown in Listing 14.11 shows thread synchronization through the `lock` statement.

Listing 14.11 Program Code in MultiThreadLock.cs File

```
using System;
using System.Threading;
class MultiThreadLock
{
    static int n=10;
    static object resourceLock = new object();
    static void Main()
    {
        Console.WriteLine ("Main thread starting");
        ThreadStart deligobj = new ThreadStart(ThreadCode);
        Thread childThread1 = new Thread(deligobj);
        childThread1.Name = "ChildThread1";
        Thread childThread2 = new Thread(deligobj);
        childThread2.Name = "ChildThread2";
        childThread1.Start();
        childThread2.Start();
        childThread1.Join();
        childThread2.Join();
```

```
        Console.WriteLine ("Value of n is {0}", n);
    }
    static void ThreadCode()
    {
        lock(resourceLock)
        {
            Console.WriteLine (Thread.CurrentThread.Name + " running");
            n++;
        }
    }
}
```

Interrupting a Thread

To interrupt a thread, call the Thread.Interrupt method. If the thread is in the WaitSleepJoin state, Thread.Interrupt causes the ThreadInterruptedException exception to be thrown. If the thread is not in the WaitSleepJoin state, the ThreadInterruptedException is thrown whenever the thread enters the WaitSleepJoin state the next time. Unlike ThreadAbortException, ThreadInterruptedException doesn't get rethrown automatically at the end in the catch block.

The ThreadInterruptProg.cs file shown in Listing 14.12 demonstrates how a thread in the WaitSleepJoin state is interrupted.

Listing 14.12 Program Code in ThreadInterruptProg.cs File

```
using System;
using System.Threading;

class ThreadInterruptProg
{
    public static Thread childThread1;
    public static Thread childThread2;

    public static void Main(string[] args)
    {
        Console.WriteLine("Main thread starting");
        childThread1 = new Thread(new ThreadStart(ThreadCode1));
        childThread2 = new Thread(new ThreadStart(ThreadCode2));
        childThread1.Start();
        childThread2.Start();
        childThread1.Join();
        childThread2.Join();
        Console.WriteLine("Exiting Main method");
    }
```

```
    private static void ThreadCode1()
    {
        Console.WriteLine ("Child1 thread is running");
        try
        {
            Console.WriteLine("Child1 thread 1 going to sleep");
            Thread.Sleep(20);
        }
        catch (ThreadInterruptedException e)
        {
            Console.WriteLine("Child thread 1 is interrupted ");
        }
        Console.WriteLine("Exiting Child thread1");
    }
    private static void ThreadCode2()
    {
        Console.WriteLine("Child thread 1 is in WaitSleepJoin state : "+
          (childThread1.ThreadState == ThreadState.WaitSleepJoin));
        Console.WriteLine("Interrupting Child thread1");
        childThread1.Interrupt();
    }
}
```

Output:

```
Main thread starting
Child1 thread is running
Child1 thread 1 going to sleep
Child thread 1 is in WaitSleepJoin state : True
Interrupting Child thread1
Child thread 1 is interrupted
Exiting Child thread1
Exiting Main method
```

You can see that the two child threads—childThread1 and childThread2—are started. In the childThread1's callback method, ThreadCode1, childThread1 is set to sleep for 20ms, thus switching from the Running state to the WaitSleepJoin state. When childThread1 goes to sleep, the childThread2's callback method ThreadCode2 executes. In the ThreadCode2 method, childThread1 is interrupted, thereby throwing ThreadInterruptedException.

Summary

In this chapter, you learned about how threads are different from processes, what role the main thread plays, and how child threads are created. You also saw different states in the life cycle of a thread and saw the role of different methods and properties of the Thread class. In addition, you learned what problems might occur while accessing common resources by multiple threads simultaneously. Finally, you saw how Monitor and lock statements ensure that common resources are used by only one thread at a time.

The next chapter is focused on data streams, streams, readers, and writers. You will also learn about different file I/O operations.

CHAPTER 15

STREAMS

This chapter's topics include the following:

- Introducing streams
- Handling files
- Reading a file randomly
- Reading and writing primitive types in binary format
- Performing character-based file I/O
- Reading an entire file
- Holding data temporarily using MemoryStream
- Managing a directory using DirectoryInfo

Because memory is volatile, the data that you want to save for future use is stored in files. Files store data on the secondary storage device, which you can retrieve whenever you want. Every file has a name composed of two parts: primary name and secondary name (also known as *extension*). The primary name and extension are separated by a period (.). A filename can also contain multiple periods. The .NET framework provides several classes for creating, reading, and writing to files. These classes are located in the System.IO namespace.

Before you learn how a file is opened and the data is written to it, you should know that the data in a file is stored in the form of a sequence of bytes called a *stream*. A stream is used to retrieve or store data.

INTRODUCING STREAMS

A stream represents a source that provides a sequence of bytes, such as a file, an input/output (I/O) device, an interprocess communication pipe, or a TCP/IP socket. Streams act as a communication path for transferring data from a source to a destination. In other words, data can be read from the streams, written into the streams, and searched in the streams. In addition to transferring data, streams can manipulate data. Streams can be read-only, write-only, or read-write.

There are two types of streams:

- **Output streams**—Data can be written into the output streams. The output streams can be a disk file, a printer, a remote server location, and so on.

- **Input streams**—Data can be read from the input streams and assigned to the memory variables in the program to process on. The input stream can be a file or any source. The most commonly used input stream is a keyboard.

All classes that represent streams inherit from the Stream class, which is an abstract class. The .NET Framework provides several classes derived from the Stream class. More specifically, the System.IO namespace contains almost all the classes to read and write data to and from streams. The main classes that are used to perform I/O operations are shown in Table 15.1.

Table 15.1   Classes Used to Perform I/O Operations

I/O Class	Description
Directory	Helps in manipulating a directory structure.
File	Helps in manipulating files.
Path	Performs operations on path information.
DriveInfo	Provides information for the drives.
FileInfo	Derived from the abstract FileSystemInfo class, this class performs operations on files.
DirectoryInfo	Derived from the abstract FileSystemInfo class, this class performs operations on directories.
BinaryReader	Reads primitive data from a binary stream.

BinaryWriter	Writes primitive data in binary format.
MarshalByRefObject	Used to establish communication among objects in different application domains. An application domain is a location in an operating system where one or more applications reside. Objects within an application domain can communicate directly, but to enable objects from different application domains to communicate, the MarshalByRefObject class is required.
Stream	An abstract base class for all streams. Represents a source of bytes.
FileStream	Used to read from and write to any location in a file.
MemoryStream	Used for random access to streamed data stored in memory.
BufferedStream	A temporary storage for a stream of bytes.
StreamReader	Used for reading characters from a byte stream.
StringReader	Used for reading from a string buffer.
StreamWriter	Used for writing characters to a stream.
StringWriter	Used for writing into a string buffer.

The .NET framework provides several classes for creating, reading, and writing to files on the secondary storage. These classes are located in the System.IO namespace. Specifically, C# provides FileStream, StreamReader, and StreamWriter classes to read from and write to a byte stream. To access the binary data, you use the BinaryReader and BinaryWriter classes. The hierarchy of the I/O class can be represented in the form of a block diagram, as shown in Figure 15.1.

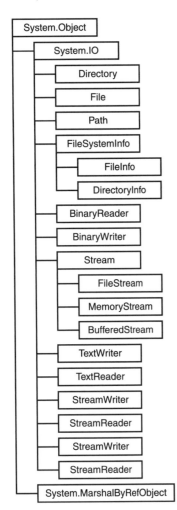

Figure 15.1
Block diagram showing hierarchy of I/O classes.
© 2015 Cengage Learning®.

You can see that the Directory, File, Path, FileSystemInfo, BinaryReader, and BinaryWriter classes are derived from System.Object. FileInfo and DirectoryInfo are derived from the FileSystemInfo class. System.MarshalByRefObject inherits from the System.Object class. The TextWriter, TextReader, and Stream classes inherit from the System.MarshalByRefObject class. The FileStream, MemoryStream, and BufferedStream classes are derived from the Stream class. StreamWriter and StringWriter implement the TextWriter class. StreamReader and StringReader implement the TextReader class.

The next section covers file handling in detail.

HANDLING FILES

The I/O system has classes that allow you to read and write files. All files are byte oriented, meaning that data is read and written into the files in terms of bytes. To create a byte-oriented stream attached to a file, use the `FileStream` class, which is derived from the `Stream` class. All the stream classes, including `FileStream`, are defined in the System.IO namespace.

Note

The System.IO needs to be included in all programs that deal with streams.

To create a byte stream linked to a file, create a `FileStream` object. `FileStream` defines several constructors. The most commonly used is shown here:

`FileStream(string filename, FileMode mode)`

Here, `filename` specifies the name of the file to open, and `mode` specifies the purpose for opening the file. In other words, through the `mode` parameter, you specify how the file needs to be opened. The valid options are listed here:

- **FileMode.Append**—For appending content to the end of a file.
- **FileMode.Create**—For creating a new output file. If a file already exists, it is overwritten.
- **FileMode.CreateNew**—For creating a new output file. The file must not already exist.
- **FileMode.Open**—Opens an existing file.
- **FileMode.OpenOrCreate**—Opens a file if it already exists and creates it if it does not.
- **FileMode.Truncate**—Opens an existing file and truncates its existing content.

By default, the `FileStream` constructor opens a file for read/write access.

To restrict access to just reading or just writing, use the following `FileStream` constructor:

`FileStream(string filename, FileMode mode, FileAccess type_access)`

where `filename` refers to the name of the file to open, and `mode` determines how the file will be opened. The `type_access` determines the way the file will be accessed. The valid options are `FileAccess.Read`, `FileAccess.Write`, and `FileAccess.ReadWrite`.

Example:

```
FileStream fp = new FileStream("letter.txt", FileMode.Open, FileAccess.Read);
```

The preceding command opens an existing file, letter.txt, for the purpose of reading. If some failure occurs while attempting to open the file, an exception is thrown. The exceptions are of various types and are thrown on occurrence of a specific type of error or failure. A few of the exception types are shown in Table 15.2.

Table 15.2   A Few of the File-Related Exceptions

Exception Type	Description
FileNotFoundException	Thrown if the file does not exist.
IOException	Thrown if the file cannot be opened because of some type of I/O error.
ArgumentNullException	Thrown if the filename is null.
ArgumentException	Thrown if the filename is invalid.
ArgumentOutOfRangeException	Thrown if the mode is invalid.
SecurityException	Thrown if the user does not have access rights.
PathTooLongException	Thrown if the filename or path is too long.
DirectoryNotFoundException	Thrown if the specified directory is invalid.

© 2015 Cengage Learning®.

Table 15.3 describes different methods defined by the FileStream class to perform read and write operations on files.

Table 15.3   Methods of the FileStream Class

Method	Description
ReadByte( )	Reads a single byte from a file and returns it as an integer value. It returns −1 when the end of the file is reached. It throws the exception NotSupportedException if the stream is not opened for input and throws the exception ObjectDisposedException if the stream is closed. Syntax: int ReadByte( )
Read( )	Reads the specified number of bytes from a file into an array. Syntax:

	`int Read(byte[ ] buf, int offset, int num)`
	Reads up to `num` number of bytes into the array, `buf` starting at offset, `buf [offset]`. The method returns the number of bytes successfully read. An `IOException` is thrown if an I/O error occurs.
`WriteByte()`	Writes the specified byte into the file.
	Syntax:
	`void WriteByte(byte b)`
	The exception `NotSupportedException` is thrown if the stream is not opened for output, and the exception `ObjectDisposedException` is thrown if the stream is closed.
`Write()`	Writes an array of bytes to a file.
	Syntax:
	`int Write(byte[ ] buf, int offset, int num)`
	The `num` number of bytes from the byte array `buf`, beginning at `buf[offset]`, is written into the file. The number of bytes written is returned. If an error occurs during writing, an `IOException` is thrown. If the underlying stream is not opened for output, a `NotSupportedException` is thrown.
`Flush()`	Immediately writes the data into the file, whether the buffer is full or not. Remember, after invoking different `write` methods on the files, the content may not be immediately written to the file and may be buffered by the operating system. This is done for efficiency reasons, and the buffered content is either periodically, or when it reaches some specific size, written into the physical file.
	Syntax:
	`void Flush( )`
	An `IOException` is thrown upon failure. If the stream was closed at the time of the call, `ObjectDisposedException` is thrown.
`void Close( )`	Closing the file releasing the system resources allocated to it.
	Syntax:
	`FileStream_object.Close()`
	It is a good practice to close an output file because it flushes out the buffered content into the physical file on disk before closing the file.

The CreateByteFile.cs file shown in Listing 15.1 demonstrates creation of a binary file. The program asks a user to enter a few numerical values that are then stored in the file in byte format. The user passes the filename through command-line arguments.

Listing 15.1 Program Code in CreateByteFile.cs File

```
using System;
using System.IO;
class CreateByteFile {
    static void Main(string[] args) {
        int i,n,k;
        FileStream fp=null;
        try {
            fp = new FileStream(args[0], FileMode.Create);
        } catch(IOException ex) {
            Console.WriteLine(ex.Message);
        }
        Console.Write("How many numbers do you want to store in the file? ");
        n = Convert.ToInt32(Console.ReadLine());
        Console.WriteLine("Enter {0} numbers ", n);
        try {
            for(i=1;i<=n;i++)
            {
                k = Convert.ToInt32(Console.ReadLine());
                fp.WriteByte((byte)k);
            }
        } catch(IOException ex) {
            Console.WriteLine(ex.Message);
        }
        fp.Close();
    }
}
```

Output:

```
CreateByteFile bytefile
How many numbers do you want to store in the file? 5
Enter 5 numbers
6
2
0
9
1
```

In Listing 15.1, the filename passed as a command-line argument is opened in `create` mode, overwriting its content if it already exists. A loop asks the user to enter a few numerical values that are stored in the file in byte format. When the writing operation is done, the file is closed. If, while running the program, you pass the filename as `bytefile`, it is opened in `write` mode, and data the user enters is stored in it.

The `ReadByteFile.cs` file shown in Listing 15.2 opens the file that is specified through command-line arguments in `read` mode and displays its content on the screen.

Listing 15.2 Program Code in ReadByteFile.cs File

```
using System;
using System.IO;
class ReadByteFile {
    static void Main(string[] args) {
        int i;
        FileStream fpin=null;
        try {
            fpin = new FileStream(args[0], FileMode.Open);
        } catch(IOException ex) {
            Console.WriteLine(ex.Message);
        }
        Console.WriteLine("The data in the byte file is: ");
        try {
            do {
                i = fpin.ReadByte();
                if(i !=-1) Console.WriteLine((byte)i);
            } while(i !=-1);
        } catch(IOException ex) {
            Console.WriteLine(ex.Message);
        }
        fpin.Close();
    }
}
```

Output:

```
ReadByteFile bytefile
The data in the byte file is:
6
2
0
9
1
```

You will get an exception if you don't provide the filename while running the `ReadByteFile` program. You can see that a `FileStream` object is created named `fpin`. This object opens the file whose name is passed through the command-line argument. Using the `ReadByte` method in a loop, each byte from the file is read and displayed on the screen. The `ReadByte` method returns –1 when the end of the file is reached, so the loop is set to terminate when the `ReadByte` method returns –1.

READING A FILE RANDOMLY

Up until now, you have been accessing the files in the traditional sequential method. But sometimes you don't want to fetch the content of a file in any particular order but randomly. To access a file randomly, position the file pointer inside the file at the required location. A file pointer determines the location of the next read/write operation to take place on the file. The method used to relocate the file pointer in the file is `Seek`.

The `Seek` method defined by `FileStream` allows you to set the file position indicator or the file pointer to the desired location in the file.

Syntax:

```
long Seek(long n, SeekOrigin location)
```

where `n` specifies the number of bytes that the file pointer needs to be positioned at (from the position specified by the `location` parameter). The `location` may be any of the following:

- **Begin**—Represents the beginning of the file
- **Current**—Represents the current location of the file pointer
- **End**—Represents the end of the file

After a call to the `Seek` method, the next `read` or `write` operation will occur from the new file pointer position. If any error occurs while seeking, an `IOException` is thrown. If the underlying stream does not support position requests, a `NotSupportedException` is thrown.

To set or get the position of the file pointer in a stream, you use the `Stream` class's `Position` property. Besides `Position`, a few more `Stream` properties are frequently used in programming. Table 15.4 shows a brief description of the most commonly used properties of the `Stream` class.

Table 15.4 A Few Stream Class Properties

Property	Description
bool CanRead	This property is true if the stream can be read.
bool CanSeek	This property is true if the stream supports position requests.
bool CanTimeout	This property is true if the stream can time out.
bool CanWrite	This property is true if the stream can be written.
long Length	This contains the length of the stream.
long Position	This represents the current position in the stream.
int ReadTimeout	This represents the time before a timeout will occur for read operations.
int WriteTimeout	This represents the time before a timeout will occur for write operations.

The ReadRandomFile.cs file shown in Listing 15.3 demonstrates reading a file content randomly. The filename is supplied through the command-line argument. The program reads a couple of bytes from the file randomly and displays the entire contents of the file in reverse order.

Listing 15.3 Program Code in ReadRandomFile.cs File

```
using System;
using System.IO;
class ReadRandomFile {
    static void Main(string[] args) {
        int i;
        FileStream fpin=null;
        try {
            fpin = new FileStream(args[0], FileMode.Open);
        } catch(IOException ex) {
            Console.WriteLine(ex.Message);
        }
        Console.WriteLine("The randomly accessed content of the file is as follows: ");
        try {
            fpin.Seek(0, SeekOrigin.Begin);
            i = fpin.ReadByte();
            if(i !=-1) Console.WriteLine("The first byte of the file is "+(byte)i);
            fpin.Seek(3, SeekOrigin.Begin);
```

```
                i = fpin.ReadByte();
                if(i !=-1) Console.WriteLine("The fourth byte of the file is "+(byte)i);
                Console.WriteLine("The data in the byte file in reverse order is: ");
                fpin.Seek(-1, SeekOrigin.End);
                try {
                    while (i!=-1) {
                        i = fpin.ReadByte();
                        if(i !=-1) Console.WriteLine((byte)i);
                        if(fpin.Position !=1)fpin.Seek(-2, SeekOrigin.Current);
                        else break;
                    };
                } catch(IOException ex) {
                    Console.WriteLine(ex.Message);
                }
            } catch(IOException ex) {
                Console.WriteLine(ex.Message);
            }
            fpin.Close();
        }
    }
}
```

Output:

```
C:\>ReadRandomFile bytefile
The randomly accessed content of the file is as follows:
The first byte of the file is 6
The fourth byte of the file is 9
The data in the byte file in reverse order is:
1
9
0
2
6
```

You can see that a FileStream object is created named fpin. It opens an existing file whose name is supplied through command-line arguments. Initially, the file pointer fpin is located at the beginning (at the 0th byte position of the file). The first byte in the file is read and displayed on the screen. Then, using the Seek method, the fpin is positioned at the 4th byte location in the file. The ReadByte method, therefore, reads the fourth byte in the file and displays it on the screen. Thereafter, the fpin is positioned at the end of the file. Using the ReadByte and Seek methods, a byte in the file is accessed from the fpin's current position, fpin is moved one byte back (toward the beginning of the file), and the accessed byte is displayed on the screen. The procedure is repeated until fpin reaches the beginning of the file.

READING AND WRITING PRIMITIVE TYPES IN BINARY FORMAT

To make the task of writing and reading primitive data types, strings, and arrays easier, you can use `BinaryReader` and `BinaryWriter` classes. The `BinaryReader` and `BinaryWriter` classes encapsulate a stream and, as the name suggests, these classes are meant to deal with binary files. (They manipulate the primitive types in binary form.) Continue reading to learn more about these classes.

Using BinaryWriter

Available in the System.IO namespace, the `BinaryWriter` class is used to write primitive data types, like `int`, `decimal`, `float`, and `double`, to a stream. The class also helps in writing arrays and strings into a stream in binary format. Because the data is written in binary format, it is not human readable.

A `BinaryWriter` object is created by passing a `FileStream` object to its constructor. Therefore, to create a `BinaryWriter` object, you have to first create a `FileStream` object and then pass it to the `BinaryWriter`'s constructor as shown here:

```
FileStream fpout = new FileStream ("example.binary", FileMode.CreateNew);
BinaryWriter binWriter = new BinaryWriter(fpout);
```

The preceding code creates a `BinaryWriter` object called `binWriter` that refers to the file `example.binary` for writing primitive data.

The `BinaryWriterApp.cs` file shown in Listing 15.4 demonstrates creating a binary file using the `BinaryWriter` class. The program creates a file whose name is passed through the command-line argument. The user is asked to enter a few numerical values, which are then stored in the file.

Listing 15.4 Program Code in BinaryWriterApp.cs File

```
using System;
using System.IO;
class BinaryWriterApp
{
    public static void Main(String[] args)
    {
        int k;
        string s;
        if (File.Exists(args[0]))
        {
            Console.WriteLine("{0} already exists!",args[0]);
            return;
        }
```

```
FileStream fpout = new FileStream (args[0], FileMode.CreateNew);
BinaryWriter binWriter = new BinaryWriter(fpout);
Console.WriteLine("Enter some numerical into the file. Write quit to stop");
do {
     s = Console.ReadLine();
     if(s != "quit") {
          try {
               k = Convert.ToInt32(s);
               binWriter.Write(k);
          } catch(IOException ex) {
               Console.WriteLine(ex.Message);
          }
     }
} while(s != "quit");
binWriter.Close();
fpout.Close();
   }
}
```

Output:

```
D:\>BinaryWriterApp doc.binary
Enter some numerical into the file. Write quit to stop
23
9
0
105
7
quit
```

You can see that the file doc.binary is created and the BinaryWriter object binWriter is set to refer to it. If the file doc.binary already exists, the program terminates, displaying the message file already exists! The user is then asked to enter some numerical values that are stored in the file using the Write method. After that, the user types quit and presses the Enter key to exit the loop.

Using BinaryReader

As the name suggests, the BinaryReader class is used to read binary data from a given stream. The class provides several methods to read all primitive types from the specified stream. These methods are in the format ReadX, where X represents the primitive type, like Boolean, Byte, Char, Double, Int16, Int32, and so on, that you want to read. A BinaryReader object is created by passing a FileStream object to its constructor. So to create a `BinaryReader` object, you have to create a `FileStream` object and then pass it to the `BinaryReader`'s constructor, as shown here:

```
FileStream fpin = new FileStream ("example.binary", FileMode.Open);
BinaryReader binReader = new BinaryReader(fpin);
```

The preceding code creates a `BinaryReader` object called `binReader` that refers to the file `example.binary` for reading primitive data.

The `BinaryReaderApp.cs` file shown in Listing 15.5 demonstrates reading of a primitive data type from a binary file using the `BinaryReader` class. The program reads the binary file `doc.binary` that you created in Listing 15.4. The program accesses all the integer values in the file and displays them on the screen.

Listing 15.5 Program Code in BinaryReaderApp.cs File

```
using System;
using System.IO;

class BinaryReaderApp
{
    public static void Main(String[] args)
    {
        if (!File.Exists(args[0]))
        {
            Console.WriteLine("{0} does not exist",args[0]);
            return;
        }
        FileStream fpin = new FileStream (args[0], FileMode.Open);
        BinaryReader binReader = new BinaryReader(fpin);
        Console.WriteLine("Numerical data in the file is :");
        while (binReader.PeekChar() != -1)
        {
            try
            {
                int k = binReader.ReadInt32();
                Console.WriteLine(k);
            } catch(IOException ex) {
                Console.WriteLine(ex.Message);
            }
        }
        binReader.Close();
        fpin.Close();
    }
}
```

Output:

```
D:\CSharpBook>BinaryReaderApp doc.binary
Numerical data in the file is :
23
9
0
105
7
```

You can see that the `doc.binary` is opened and the `BinaryReader` object `binReader` is set to refer to it. If the file does not exist, the program terminates, displaying the message `file does not exist`. Calling the `ReadInt32` method on the `BinaryReader` object in a loop, all the `int` values in the file are accessed and displayed on the screen. You invoke the `PeekChar` method so you know when you've reached the end of the file; that way you can terminate the loop and close the file.

Performing Character-Based File I/O

To perform a character-based file for managing text files, you use character streams to read and write into the file. Because, internally, each file consists of bytes, the `FileStream` is wrapped inside either a `StreamReader` or a `StreamWriter`. These classes automatically convert a byte stream into a character stream, and vice versa.

Using StreamWriter

`StreamWriter` writes characters to a stream in a particular encoding. To create a character-based output stream, you need to wrap a byte stream inside a `StreamWriter`. `StreamWriter` defines several constructors. One is shown here:

```
StreamWriter(Stream stream)
```

where `stream` is the name of an open stream. This constructor throws an `ArgumentException` if the specified `stream` is not opened for output and an `ArgumentNullException` if `stream` is `null`. You can also open a file directly using `StreamWriter` with the following constructors:

```
StreamWriter(string filename)
StreamWriter(string filename, bool append_flag)
```

where `filename` specifies the name of the file to open. The file is created if it does not already exist. The `append_flag`, if set to `true`, appends the content to the end of an existing file, or the content overwrites the earlier data in the file. An `IOException` exception is thrown if an I/O error occurs.

Note

The StreamWriter class actually inherits from the TextWriter class, which is abstract. The StreamWriter implements the TextWriter class. By default, StreamWriter writes the content in UTF-8 encoding.

Following are a few of the most common methods of StreamWriter:

- **Close( )**—Closes the file
- **Flush( )**—Immediately saves the file content from buffer to memory
- **Write( )**—Writes into the specified file using the File stream class
- **WriteLine( )**—Writes into a file (line by line)

The CreateCharacterFile.cs file shown in Listing 15.6 demonstrates using StreamWriter to create a text file. In other words, instead of binary format, data is written into the file in human-readable (character-based) format. The program asks the user to enter some text, which is then written into the file. When finished, the user types quit to exit the program.

Listing 15.6 Program Code in CreateCharacterFile.cs File

```
using System;
using System.IO;
class CreateCharacterFile {
    static void Main(string[] args) {
        string s;
        StreamWriter fstream_out =null;
        FileStream fp=null;                                    // #1
        try {
            fp = new FileStream(args[0], FileMode.Create);    // #2
            fstream_out = new StreamWriter(fp);               // #3
        }
        catch(IOException ex) {
            Console.WriteLine(ex.Message);
        }
        Console.WriteLine("Enter text to write into the file. Write quit to stop");
        try {
            do {
                s = Console.ReadLine();
                if(s != "quit") {
                    fstream_out.WriteLine(s);
                }
            } while(s != "quit");
```

```
        } catch(IOException ex) {
            Console.WriteLine(ex.Message);
        }
         finally
        {
            fstream_out.Dispose();
        }
    }
}
```

Output:

```
D:\>CreateCharacterFile characterfile.txt
Enter text to write into the file. Write quit to stop
I am fine
How are you?
Today is Monday
quit
```

You can see that the file named characterfile.txt is created. To store data in character format, the byte stream (the FileStream object fp) is wrapped inside a StreamWriter. The statement creates and initializes the FileStream object fp to null. Statement #2 creates the file whose name is passed through the command-line argument. Statement #3 wraps the FileStream object fp inside the StreamWriter. The text the user enters is stored in the file using the WriteLine method of the StreamWriter class. When the user enters quit, the loop terminates, and the resources allocated to the streams are disposed of.

Note

The Dispose method called in the preceding program is essential to dispose of the resources allocated to the Stream.

If you are not concerned with opening the file in a specific mode (append, truncate, and so on), you can skip creation of a FileStream object. In other words, instead of creating a FileStream object and wrapping it inside StreamWriter, you can simply create a file directly by using the StreamWriter object.

You can modify the CreateCharacterFile.cs file shown in Listing 15.6 so that the file is created by using the StreamWriter object alone (without using the FileStream object). To do so, delete statements #1 and #2 and replace statement #3 with the following statement:

```
fstrm_out = new StreamWriter(args[0]);
```

That's all. The program now runs and creates a character-based file using the StreamWriter object.

Streams implement the IDisposable interface. All the objects that implement this interface must be disposed of manually by calling the Dispose method in the finally block to dispose or free up the allocated resources. Another way of disposing of the resources automatically is to utilize the using statement. The using statement opens and prepares the files. It also closes and disposes of the resources by calling the Dispose method automatically. The using statement calls the Dispose method even when an exception occurs.

The CreateUsingFile.cs file shown in Listing 15.7 demonstrates utilizing the using statement in freeing up the resources allocated to streams. The program uses StreamWriter to create a file with character-based content. The program does not use Dispose to dispose of the allocated resources because the using statement automatically does so.

Listing 15.7 Program Code in CreateUsingFile.cs File

```
using System;
using System.IO;
class CreateUsingFile {
    static void Main(string[] args) {
        string s;
        Console.WriteLine("Enter text to write into the file. Write quit to stop");
        using (StreamWriter fstream_out = new StreamWriter(args[0]))
        {
            try {
                do {
                    s = Console.ReadLine();
                    if(s != "quit") {
                        fstream_out.WriteLine(s);
                    }
                } while(s != "quit");
            } catch(IOException ex) {
                Console.WriteLine(ex.Message);
            }
        }
    }
}
```

Output:

```
D:\>CreateUsingFile characterfile.txt
Enter text to write into the file. Write quit to stop
```

```
I am fine
How are you?
Today is Monday
quit
```

You can see that StreamWriter opens the stream (the file whose name is supplied through the command-line argument) for output. StreamWriter opens and prepares the file with the using statement; consequently, the resources allocated to the stream are automatically released without calling the Dispose method. A few lines of text that the user enters through the ReadLine method are written into the file through the WriteLine method. When finished, the user exits the program by typing quit. Observe that the Dispose method is not called on the stream to free up the allocated resources; that task is done by the using statement.

Besides StreamWriter, there is one more class called StringWriter that writes characters to a stream. Both StreamWriter and StringWriter are derived from TextWriter, so before you learn about StringWriter, here's a quick look at TextWriter.

Implementing TextWriter

TextWriter is an abstract class that you use to write text (a sequential series of characters). It provides methods for converting any object into a string.

The TextWriterApp.cs file shown in Listing 15.8 demonstrates how the TextWriter class is implemented to write a series of characters in a file.

Listing 15.8 Program Code in TextWriterApp.cs File

```
using System;
using System.IO;
class TextWriterApp
{
    static void Main(string[] args)
    {
        string s;
        TextWriter twFilePointer = new StreamWriter(args[0]);    //#1
        Console.WriteLine("Enter text to write into the file. Write quit to stop");
        do {
            s = Console.ReadLine();
            if(s != "quit") {
                try {
                    twFilePointer.WriteLine(s);
                } catch(IOException ex) {
                    Console.WriteLine(ex.Message);
```

```
                        break;
                }
            }
        } while(s != "quit");
        twFilePointer.Close();
    }
}
```

Output:

```
D:\>TextWriterApp characterfile.txt
Enter text to write into the file. Write quit to stop
I am fine
How are you?
Today is Monday
quit
```

Statement #1 initializes a new instance of the StreamWriter class using default encoding and buffer size. The StreamWriter instance twFilePointer refers to the file whose name is passed through command-line arguments. The text the user enters is written into the file.

Using StreamReader

You use the StreamReader class to read characters from a byte stream in a particular encoding. The StreamReader class is derived from the TextReader class, which is abstract. For functionality, StreamReader implements the TextReader class.

To create a character-based input stream, a byte stream is wrapped inside a StreamReader. StreamReader defines several constructors. One is shown here:

StreamReader(Stream stream)

Here, stream is the name of an open stream such as a file, an I/O device, an interprocess communication pipe, or a TCP/IP socket. This constructor throws an ArgumentNullException if stream is null and an ArgumentException if stream is not opened for input.

As with StreamWriter, you can open a file directly using StreamReader (without using a byte stream like FileStream) via the following constructor:

StreamReader(string filename)

Here, filename specifies the name of the file to open. The following exceptions may be thrown after using the preceding constructor:

- ■ FileNotFoundException is thrown if the file does not exist.

- ■ ArgumentNullException is thrown if filename is null.

- ■ ArgumentException is thrown if filename is an empty string.

The commonly used methods for the StreamReader class are given here:

- ■ **Flush( )**—Immediately saves the file content from buffer to memory.

- ■ **Close( )**—Closes the file. It is mandatory to close the file.

- ■ **Read( )**—Reads content from the file stream.

- ■ **ReadLine( )**—Reads content from the given file stream line by line.

- ■ **ReadToEnd( )**—Reads all characters from the current position to the end of the stream.

- ■ **Peek( )**—Returns the next value in the stream without moving the file pointer. Returns a value of –1 when the file pointer reaches the end of the stream.

- ■ **Seek( )**—Sets the file pointer at the desired position in a file.

The ReadCharacterFile.cs file shown in Listing 15.9 displays the content in the character-based file (text file). The program uses StreamReader to open the input stream (to the file you want to read). To free up the resources automatically that will be allocated to the stream, use the using statement in the program.

Listing 15.9 Program Code in ReadCharacterFile.cs File

```
using System;
using System.IO;
class ReadCharacterFile {
    static void Main(string[] args) {
        string s;
        Console.WriteLine("Data in the file is as given below:");
        using (StreamReader fstrm_in = new StreamReader(args[0]))
        {
            try {
                while((s = fstrm_in.ReadLine()) != null) {
                    Console.WriteLine(s);
                }
            } catch(IOException ex) {
                Console.WriteLine(ex.Message);
            }
        }
    }
}
```

Output:

```
D:\>ReadCharacterFile characterfile.txt
I am fine
How are you?
Today is Monday
```

You can see that StreamReader opens the file (whose name is supplied through command-line arguments) for input (to read). When you use the ReadLine method in a loop, all the lines in the file are read and displayed on the screen.

Besides StreamReader, there is one more class called StringReader that is used for reading characters from the input stream. Both StreamReader and StringReader are derived from TextReader. Before you learn about StringReader, you'll read about the TextReader class.

Implementing TextReader

The TextReader class is an abstract one that reads data from the specified source in the form of characters. The class provides methods that enable you to read one character at a time, an entire line at a time, or the whole file at a time. The class takes care of the encoding while reading.

The TextReaderApp.cs file shown in Listing 15.10 demonstrates reading of a file by implementing the TextReader class. The program accesses all the text in the supplied file and displays it on the screen.

Listing 15.10 Program Code in TextReaderApp.cs File

```
using System;
using System.IO;

class TextReaderApp
{
    static void Main(string[] args)
    {
        TextReader trFilePointer=null;
        string s;
        try {
            trFilePointer = new StreamReader(args[0]);    //#1
        }
        catch(IOException ex) {
            Console.WriteLine(ex.Message);
        }
        try {
            while((s = trFilePointer.ReadLine()) != null) {
```

```
            Console.WriteLine(s);
        }
    } catch(IOException ex) {
        Console.WriteLine(ex.Message);
    }
    trFilePointer.Close();
    }
}
```

Output:

```
D:\>TextReaderApp characterfile.txt
I am fine
How are you?
Today is Monday
```

Statement #1 in Listing 15.10 initializes a new instance of the StreamReader class. The StreamReader instance trFilePointer refers to the file whose name is passed through command-line arguments. The sequential series of characters (text in the file) is accessed and displayed on the screen.

Now that you understand the role of StreamWriter and StreamReader, it's time to learn how StringWriter and StringReader manage the streams.

Using StringReader and StringWriter

The StringWriter class is derived from TextWriter and is used to write to a StringBuilder class. The strings in C# are immutable, so the StringBuilder class is used to build a string efficiently. StringWriter provides several methods, including Write and WriteLine, to write to the StringBuilder object. You use a StringBuilder object to store the input from the user using the StringWriter class. The StringReader class, on the other hand, is derived from TextReader and is used to read from the string that is built using the StringWriter class. The StringReader class provides several methods including Read and ReadLine to read from the given string.

The StringRWApp.cs file shown in Listing 15.11 demonstrates how StringWriter and StringReader are used to write and read strings, respectively. The program asks the user to enter a few lines of text, which are then written into the underlying StringBuilder through the StringWriter. The strings written into the StringBuilder are then read using the StringReader and displayed on the screen.

Listing 15.11 Program Code in StringRWApp.cs File

```
using System;
using System.IO;
```

```
using System.Text;
public class StringRWApp
{
    public static void Main()
    {
        string s;
        StringBuilder strngBldr = new StringBuilder();
        StringWriter strngWrter = new StringWriter(strngBldr);
        Console.WriteLine("Enter text to write using StringWriter. Write quit to
stop");
        do {
            s = Console.ReadLine();
            if(s != "quit") {
                strngWrter.WriteLine(s);
            }
        } while(s != "quit");
        strngWrter.Flush();
        strngWrter.Close();
        StringReader strngRdr = new StringReader(strngBldr.ToString());
        Console.WriteLine("\nReading data using StringReader");
        while (strngRdr.Peek() > -1)
        {
            Console.WriteLine(strngRdr.ReadLine());
        }
        strngRdr.Close();
    }
}
```

Output:

```
D:\>StringRWApp
Enter text to write using StringWriter. Write quit to stop
It might rain today
I am going
take care
quit

Reading data using StringReader
It might rain today
I am going
take care
```

You can see that the StringWriter object called strngWrter is created by passing the StringBuilder instance strnbBldr to the StringWriter's constructor. The text the user enters is written into the StringBuilder instance via StringWriter. To read the text, you create the StringReader object by passing the StringBuilder instance to the

StringReader's constructor. From the StringReader object, each line is read and displayed on the screen. The Peek method on the StringReader object returns the next available character without moving the position in the stream. The method returns −1 if no more characters are available.

You might be thinking that the only way to read the entire file is to use the ReadLine method in a loop. But you can also read the entire file through a single method. Read on.

READING AN ENTIRE FILE

To read an entire file, you can use either of the following two methods:

- **File.ReadAllLines**—This method reads all lines of the specified file and returns them as an array. In other words, all the lines of the file are accessed and assigned to an array in the form of array elements. The array containing all the lines of the file is then returned.

    Syntax:

    `string[] ReadAllLines(string filename_alongwith_path)`

    where `filename_alongwith_path` represents the file whose lines are returned in the form of a string array.

- **File.ReadAllText**—This method reads all lines of the specified file and returns them as a string. In other words, all the lines of the file are accessed and combined in a string format. The method closes the file and returns the string that contains all the lines of the file.

    Syntax:

    `string ReadAllText(string filename_alongwith_path)`

    where `filename_alongwith_path` represents the file whose lines are returned in the form of a string.

Note

Besides ReadAllLines and ReadAllText methods, the File class provides several static methods that you can use for opening, creating, copying, deleting, and moving.

Here are some of the most commonly used static methods of the File class:

- **Copy**—Copies a file to the specified location
- **Create**—Creates a file in the specified path
- **Delete**—Deletes a file

- **Open**—Opens the specified file and return a filestream object

- **Move**—Moves the specified file to a new location

- **Exists**—Returns a Boolean value indicating whether the specified file already exists

- **OpenRead**—Opens an existing file for reading

- **OpenWrite**—Opens an existing file or creates a new file for writing

The `ReadAllLinesApp.cs` file shown in Listing 15.12 demonstrates how an entire file is read through a single method. The program opens the file whose name is passed through command-line arguments. By calling the `File.ReadAllLines` method, all lines in the file are accessed and assigned to an array. The lines in the array are then accessed and displayed on the screen.

Listing 15.12 Program Code in ReadAllLinesApp.cs File

```
using System;
using System.IO;
class ReadAllLinesApp {
    static void Main(string[] args) {
        string[] lines=null;
        try {
            lines = File.ReadAllLines(args[0]);
        }
        catch(IOException ex) {
            Console.WriteLine(ex.Message);
        }
        foreach (string line in lines)
        {
            Console.WriteLine(line);
        }
    }
}
```

Output:

```
D:\CSharpBook>ReadAllLinesApp characterfile.txt
I am fine
How are you?
Today is Monday
```

All the lines from the file are accessed and assigned to the string array `lines`. Using the `foreach` loop, each line in the string array `lines` is accessed and displayed on the screen.

The `ReadAllTextApp.cs` file shown in Listing 15.13 demonstrates how a file is read completely through a single method. The program opens the specified file and calls the `File.ReadAllText` method to access all lines in the file and return them as an array. The string containing all lines of the file is then displayed on the screen.

Listing 15.13 Program Code in ReadAllTextApp.cs File

```
using System;
using System.IO;
class ReadAllTextApp
{
    static void Main(string[] args)
    {
        string completeFile = File.ReadAllText(args[0]);
        Console.WriteLine(completeFile);
    }
}
```

Output:

```
D:\CSharpBook>ReadAllTextApp characterfile.txt
I am fine
How are you?
Today is Monday
```

The filename that is passed through the command-line argument is opened, and its content is read through the `File.ReadAllText` method and assigned to a string object called `completeFile`. The string `completeFile` is then displayed on the screen.

HOLDING DATA TEMPORARILY USING MEMORYSTREAM

As the name suggests, `MemoryStream` represents the stream of data that is in memory. The data that you want to hold temporarily to manipulate it is managed through `MemoryStream`. The data in `MemoryStream` is kept as an unsigned byte array. After performing all the required updating to the data held in memory, the data in `MemoryStream` can be stored in the disk file. Shortly, to minimize frequent updating in a file, its data is read in the `MemoryStream`, and all modifications are applied to the data in memory. When complete, the data in memory is saved to the file for persistence. There are several constructors for creating the `MemoryStream` object. Two of them are listed here:

- **MemoryStream( )**—Creates a `MemoryStream` instance with an expandable capacity initialized to zero

- **MemoryStream(Byte[])**—Creates a nonresizable instance of the `MemoryStream` based on the supplied byte array

Note

MemoryStream enables random access to the available data.

The MemoryStreamApp.cs file shown in Listing 15.14 demonstrates storing of data in MemoryStream, reading of data from MemoryStream, and updating of data in MemoryStream.

Listing 15.14 Program Code in MemoryStreamApp.cs File

```
using System;
using System.IO;
using System.Text;

class MemoryStreamApp
{
    static void Main( string[] args )
    {
        string message = "Hello World!";
        byte[] byteArray = Encoding.ASCII.GetBytes( message );
        MemoryStream memStream = new MemoryStream( byteArray );
        StreamReader strmReader = new StreamReader(memStream);
        string str = strmReader.ReadToEnd();
        Console.WriteLine(str );
        memStream.Position = 0;
        int bite = memStream.ReadByte();
        do
        {
            Console.Write((char)bite);
            bite = memStream.ReadByte();
        } while (bite != -1);
        memStream.Position = 0;
        memStream.WriteByte(Convert.ToByte('b'));
        memStream.WriteByte(Convert.ToByte('y'));
        memStream.WriteByte(Convert.ToByte('e'));
        memStream.Position = 0;
        str = strmReader.ReadToEnd();
        Console.WriteLine("\n"+str );
    }
}
```

Output:

```
Hello World!
Hello World!
byelo World!
```

You create a byte array from the string message Hello World! The byte array then creates and initializes a MemoryStream object named memStream. The StreamReader object strmReader reads all the bytes from the memory stream. All the characters in the StreamReader object are read (from the current position to the end of the stream) and assigned to string str and displayed on the screen. After that, you set the position of the pointer in the stream to the beginning using the Position property. You read one byte at a time from the memory stream, cast it to the char type, and display it on the screen. To overwrite the first three bytes in the memory stream, set the pointer in the stream to the beginning. Overwrite the first three bytes by characters b, y, and e and display the content in the memory stream on the screen.

Managing a Directory Using DirectoryInfo

The DirectoryInfo class copies, moves, renames, creates, and deletes directories. Also, it can traverse any directory. To create and initialize a new instance of the DirectoryInfo class, use the following syntax:

```
public DirectoryInfo(string path)
```

where path can be a file or just a directory. An exception is thrown if the path is not entered or is entered incorrectly. For example, a fully qualified path that begins with a space will lead to an exception.

A few of the most commonly used methods of the DirectoryInfo class are listed here:

- **Create( )**—Creates a directory with the specified name
- **EnumerateDirectories( )**—Returns an enumerable collection of directory information in the current directory
- **EnumerateFiles( )**—Returns an enumerable collection of file information in the current directory
- **EnumerateFiles(String search_pattern)**—Returns an enumerable collection of file information that matches the supplied search_pattern
- **GetDirectories( )**—Returns the subdirectories of the current directory
- **GetDirectories(String search_pattern)**—Returns an array of directories in the current DirectoryInfo matching the given search_criteria
- **GetFiles( )**—Returns a list of files from the current directory
- **GetFiles(String search_pattern)**—Returns a list of files from the current directory that matches the given search pattern

A few of the commonly used DirectoryInfo properties are given here:

- **Exists**—Returns a Boolean value indicating whether the directory exists
- **Extension**—Returns the extension of the specified file
- **Name**—Returns the name of the DirectoryInfo instance
- **Parent**—Returns the parent directory of a specified subdirectory
- **Root**—Returns the root portion of the given directory

The ShowDirectoryApp.cs file shown in Listing 15.15 uses the DirectoryInfo class to display information about the specific directory. The program displays a list of subdirectories in the current directory and the list of files in the specific directory.

Listing 15.15 Program Code in ShowDirectoryApp.cs File

```
using System;
using System.IO;

public class ShowDirectoryApp
{
    static void Main()
    {
        try
        {
            DirectoryInfo dir = new DirectoryInfo("tmp");
            string[] files = Directory.GetFiles("tmp");
            DirectoryInfo[] dirs = dir.GetDirectories();
            Console.WriteLine("The subdirectories are:");
            foreach (DirectoryInfo subDir in dirs)
            {
                Console.WriteLine(subDir.Name);
            }
            Console.WriteLine("\The filenames are:");
            foreach (string fileName in files)
            {
                Console.WriteLine(fileName);
            }
        } catch (IOException ex)
        {
            Console.WriteLine(ex.Message);
        }
    }
}
```

Output:

```
The subdirectories are:
project
setup
The filenames are:
tmp\a.txt
tmp\doc.binary
```

You can see that the DirectoryInfo object is created named dir and is initialized to the tmp directory. The GetFiles method fetches all the filenames in the tmp directory and assigns them to the string array files. The GetDirectories method fetches all the sub-directories in the tmp directory and assigns them to the DirectoryInfo array dirs. Using the foreach loop, all the filenames and subdirectories in the tmp directory are displayed on the screen.

SUMMARY

In this chapter, you learned about file handling and about all the streams that manage files. You learned how to open a file, close a file, read a file randomly, and set the position of the file pointer in the file. You used the BinaryWriter and BinaryReader classes to read and write primitive types in a file. Also, you used the StreamWriter class to create text files, automatically dispose of resources through the using statement, and implement the TextWriter and TextReader abstract classes. You learned to use StreamReader, StringReader, and StringWriter classes to manage text files. You also reviewed the methods to read an entire file, hold data in MemoryStream, and manage a directory using the DirectoryInfo class.

The next chapter focuses on databases. You will learn to use SQL statements to retrieve and manipulate a database with SQL statements. In addition, you will learn about ADO.NET architecture, ADO.NET managed providers, and how data is accessed with ADO.NET. You will read about data readers, data adapters, and data sets. Finally, you will discover how to use stored procedures to edit database rows.

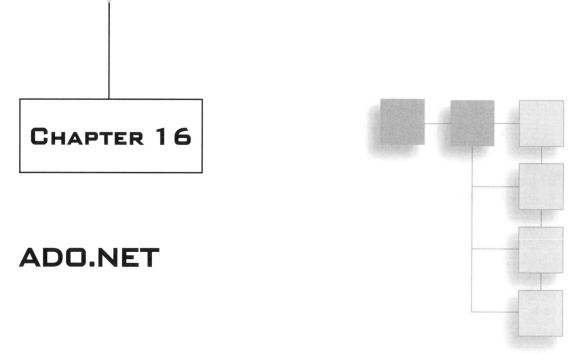

CHAPTER 16

ADO.NET

This chapter's topics include the following:

- Examining the major components of ADO.NET
- Connecting or creating a database
- Accessing data from the database
- Inserting rows in a table
- Updating a table

It is quite natural for a fully featured website to require data persistence. The information related to products, customers, users, pictures, and more needs to be stored for future reference. Databases store, retrieve, and manipulate data. Data in databases is maintained in terms of tables that in turn are divided into rows and columns. Each row in a table contains complete information related to products, clients, and users. The information stored in a row is composed of several attributes, such as product name, price, quantity, and manufacturing date. Data in databases can be stored and retrieved at runtime, encouraging the possibility for dynamic websites that fetch and display information according to the data the user enters. For storing, accessing, and manipulating information in databases, a query language called Structured Query Language (SQL) is used.

There are several types of databases, but the most popular and the one that is heavily used in websites is the relational database. A *relational database* is one in which rows in one table can be related to rows of other tables. Relations between the tables help to avoid repetitive or duplicated data in tables.

ADO stands for Active Data Objects, and the ADO.NET library is a rich framework that retrieves and updates information in various relational databases that include Microsoft SQL Server, Microsoft Access, Oracle, and XML. ADO.NET relies on the .NET Framework's various classes to process requests and transition between a database system and the user.

Note

ADO.NET Entity Framework provides easier access to database operations directly from code.

Examining the Major Components of ADO.NET

The two main components of ADO.NET that are used to access and manipulate data are `DataSet` and `Data Provider`. Table 16.1 shows a brief description of these ADO.NET components.

Table 16.1   ADO.NET Components

Component	Description
DataSet	The `DataSet` represents a local copy of related data tables. In other words, a `DataSet` is composed of one or more `DataTable` objects that are manipulated and updated as per the user requirement, and the modified data is then processed through the specific data adapters. `DataSet` can work with multiple and different data sources, including XML data.
	The `DataTable` manages information for any entity. Each `DataTable` contains zero or more rows of data. The individual data values shown in the table's row are identified by the `DataColumn` definitions. `DataColumn` definitions include a data type declaration based on the kind of data saved in each column. Besides rows and columns of data, `DataTable` includes primary key, foreign key, constraint, and relation information of different tables. The tables can be linked or related using `DataRelation` entries. `DataRelation` is a link between two `DataTable` classes within a `DataSet` class. The `Constraint` class defines a rule that a `DataColumn` class needs to follow. For example, a constraint that has only unique values can be applied to a `DataColumn`.
	`DataColumnMapping`—Maps the name of a column from the database to the name of a column within a `DataTable`.

	`DataTableMapping`—Maps a table name from the database to a `DataTable` within a `DataSet`. Depending on the requirement, information from the tables can be filtered before displaying it on the screen. `DataView` instances provide the desired view of the rows in a `DataTable`.
Data Provider	ADO.NET works with the help of data providers. Each database system that ADO.NET supports has a data provider that implements the mechanisms for connecting to a database, executing queries, and updating data. Database platforms that do not provide a specific provider can be accessed using generic Open Database Connectivity (ODBC) and Object Linking and Embedding (OLE) DB providers. Both ODBC and OLE DB providers are included with ADO.NET. The `Data Provider` class, therefore, performs all data management operations on specific databases. The .NET Framework currently ships with five data providers, each in its own namespace: ■ `Data Provider` for **SQL Server** (`System.Data.SqlClient`) ■ `Data Provider` for **OLE DB** (`System.Data.OleDb`) ■ `Data Provider` for **ODBC** (`System.Data.Odbc`) ■ `Data Provider` for **Oracle** (`System.Data.OracleClient`) ■ `EntityClient` **Provider** (`System.Data.EntityClient`)

To work with any data provider, you need to understand different objects defined in it.

Microsoft's .NET distribution has numerous data providers, including one for Oracle, SQL Server, and OLE DB/ODBC connectivity. A data provider defines the following set of objects that interact with a specific Database Management System (DBMS):

■ **Connection**—Lets you connect to and disconnect from the data source. All communication with the external data source occurs through a `Connection` object. ADO.NET also supports connection pooling to increase efficiency between queries.

■ **Command**—Offers the capability to run SQL commands and execute a stored procedure, which makes it possible to access and manipulate data. SQL queries and data management statements are wrapped in a `Command` object before being sent to the data source. Commands can include optional `Parameter` instances while calling stored procedures. `Parameter` instances represent named parameters that are used within a parameterized query.

- **DataReader**—Provides forward-only, read-only access to data using a server-side cursor. A `DataReader` object is obtained by invoking the `ExecuteReader` method of the `Command` object. The connection must be closed when operations with `DataReader` are performed.

- **DataAdapters**—Transfers `DataSets` between the caller and the data source. Acting as a bridge between `DataSet` and data source, the `DataAdapters` contain a connection and a set of `Command` objects that help in fetching and updating data between the `DataSets` and the data source. That is, both a `DataSet` and a `DataAdapter` enable two-way interaction with the database, enabling you to both read and write data. With the help of a `DataAdapter`, you can execute `SELECT`, `INSERT`, `UPDATE`, and `DELETE` statements to update the data source to match the `DataSet` content.

ADO.NET does not require a continuous connection to the database or data source and enables you to work in a disconnected manner. Periodically, the `DataSets` are connected to the parent databases to update them. The disconnected approach reduces the network traffic. When used in connected mode, ADO.NET interacts with the data source using `Connection`, `Command`, `DataReader`, and `DataAdapter` objects.

All the objects—`Connection`, `Command`, `DataReader`, and `DataAdapter`—in a specific data provider are prefixed with the name of the related DBMS. For SQL Server, the `Connection` object is prefixed with `Sql` to appear as `SqlConnection`. Similarly, for Oracle, the `Connection` object is prefixed as `OracleConnection`. `SqlDataReader` and `OracleDataReader` are the `DataReader` objects for the SQL Server and Oracle DBMS.

While accessing SQL Server database in your application, you need to include the `System.Data.SqlClient` namespace in your application. Table 16.2 shows the different database-specific classes contained in ADO.NET.

Table 16.2 Database-Specific Classes in ADO.NET

Database Classes	Description
`SqlCommand`, `OleDbCommand`, and `ODBCCommand`	Used as wrappers for SQL statements or stored procedure calls.
`SqlCommandBuilder`, `OleDbCommand Builder`, and `ODBCCommandBuilder`	Used to generate SQL commands for updating database tables. They automatically generate SQL commands from a `SELECT` statement.
`SqlConnection`, `OleDbConnection`, and `ODBCConnection`	Used to connect to the database.

`SqlDataAdapter, OleDbDataAdapter,` and `ODBCDataAdapter`	Used to handle interaction between `DataSet` and data source. Helps in executing different SQL commands to populate a `DataSet` and update the data source.
`SqlDataReader, OleDbDataReader,` and `ODBCDataReader`	Used as a forward-only, read-only access to data using a cursor.
`SqlParameter, OleDbParameter,` and `ODBCParameter`	Used to define a parameter to a stored procedure.
`SqlTransaction, OleDbTransaction,` and `ODBCTransaction`	Used to represent transactions to be made in data source.

© 2015 Cengage Learning®.

These classes implement a set of standard interfaces defined within the `System.Data` namespace. An outline of the namespaces included in ADO.NET is given here:

- **System.Data**—Includes all generic data access classes
- **System.Data.Common**—Includes classes that are shared or overridden by individual data providers
- **System.Data.EntityClient**—Includes Entity Framework classes
- **System.Data.Linq.SqlClient**—Includes LINQ to SQL provider classes
- **System.Data.Odbc**—Includes ODBC provider classes
- **System.Data.OleDb**—Includes OLE DB provider classes
- **System.Data.ProviderBase**—Includes new base classes and connection factory classes
- **System.Data.Sql**—Includes new generic interfaces and classes for SQL Server data access
- **System.Data.SqlClient**—Includes SQL Server provider classes
- **System.Data.SqlTypes**—Includes SQL Server data types

To understand the preceding concepts, you'll learn to create a database and see how data is stored and retrieved from it. You will be using SQL Server for this task.

CONNECTING OR CREATING A DATABASE

Launch Visual Studio and create a new website by selecting File, New Web Site. Select Visual C# as the programming language from the left tab. Because you want to create an empty website without default web pages in it, from the list of installed templates, select ASP.NET Empty Web Site. (ASP stands for Active Server Pages.) The Web location drop-down provides the following three options:

- **File System**—This creates the website folder on the physical file system, and the web application is executed with the help of the internal web server of Visual Studio and not on Internet Information Services (IIS). IIS is the web server usually used for running ASP.NET web applications.

- **HTTP**—This means the web pages you are going to create will be run using IIS, and the web application must be located in the IIS virtual directory. The virtual directory will be created automatically. Suppose that the name of your web application is Website1. Its web pages can be accessed from http://localhost/WebSite1/Default.aspx.

- **FTP**—FTP stands for File Transfer Protocol. When you want to develop your website on a remote location, use the FTP option. You are prompted to enter the remote server name, FTP user ID, and FTP password. Then the website is created on the remote server.

From the Web Location drop-down, select the File System option. Enter the name of the application as WebApp1 (see Figure 16.1). Click OK.

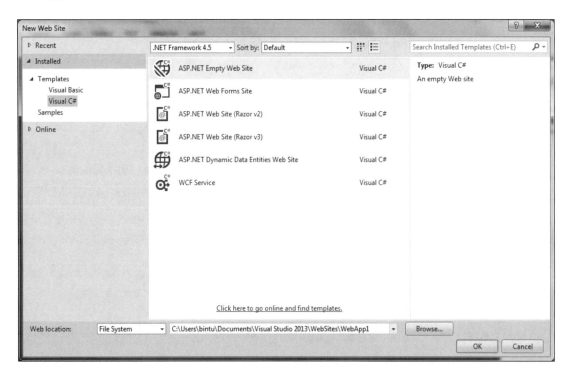

Figure 16.1
Creating a new empty website.
Used with permission from Microsoft.

Visual Studio creates a website named WebApp1 along with a configuration file called Web.config. To the empty website, you will add a web form by right-clicking your application in the Solution Explorer and selecting the Add, Add New Item option. From the Add New Item dialog that opens (see Figure 16.2), select the item Web Form. Let the default name of the web form be Default.aspx, and click the Add button.

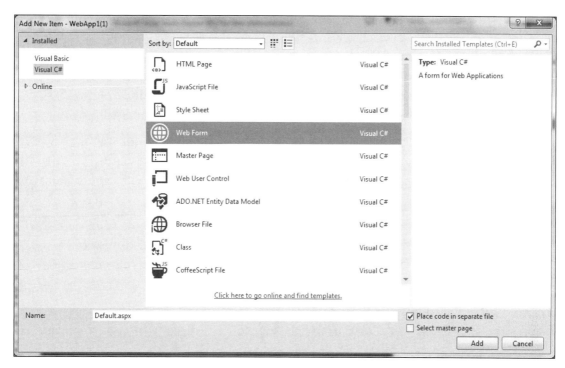

Figure 16.2
Adding a web form to the application.
Used with permission from Microsoft.

You get a design screen that is used to place controls from the toolbox to develop the user interface, as shown in Figure 16.3.

Figure 16.3
Default.aspx form in Design window.
Used with permission from Microsoft.

Two windows that help to connect to the SQL Server database in Visual Studio are SQL Server Object Explorer and Server Explorer. Here's a brief introduction:

- **SQL Server Object Explorer**—Used to connect to an available database or design or to browse its schema and query against its objects. It contains a SQL Server node, under which all connected SQL Server instances and their databases are displayed hierarchically. To open the SQL Server Object Explorer window, choose View, SQL Server Object Explorer. Right-click the SQL Server node in the SQL Server Object Explorer window and select Add SQL Server. In the Connect to Server dialog box, enter the server name of the server instance you want to connect to and the authentication details, and then click Connect. Once SQL Server is connected, expand its Databases node to see all the existing databases.

- **Server Explorer**—Server Explorer is the server management console that is used to open data connections, log onto servers, and access the databases. To open the Server Explorer window, choose View, Server Explorer. You will see the following three primary nodes in the Server Explorer window:

- **Data Connections**—Lists all the data connections to the server. Each data connection node displays the list of tables, views, stored procedures, and functions. You can also use the node to connect to a SQL Server database.

- **Servers**—Displays links to different available servers. The node can be expanded to display different resources, such as event logs, message queues, performance counters, and services. You can use these resources directly in your applications.

- **Windows Azure**—Lists available Windows Azure services to view and manage. Besides monitoring and learning the cloud services status, you can perform several tasks that include uploading blobs, editing table data, and using Windows Azure queues.

You can connect to a database through the Server Explorer window. In Server Explorer, right-click the Data Connections node and choose Add Connection. You get the dialog shown in Figure 16.4 (left).

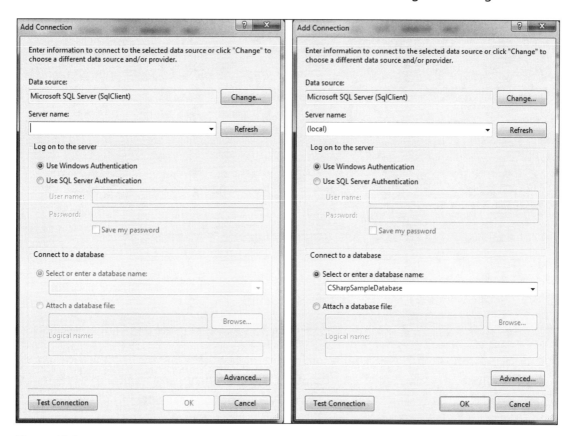

Figure 16.4
(left) Dialog for adding connection to the server and database. (right) Dialog after filling in server and database information.

Used with permission from Microsoft.

From the Data Source box, choose the kind of data source to which you need to connect. By default, the Data Source box shows the data source to which your application is connecting. Click the Change button to open the Change Data Source dialog that in turn provides different data sources and data providers to choose from (see Figure 16.5). Select Microsoft SQL Server from the Data Source drop-down and .NET Framework Data Provider for SQL Server from the Data Provider drop-down list. Click OK to go back to the Add Connection dialog.

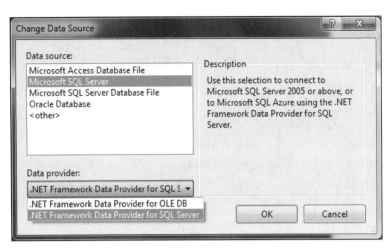

Figure 16.5
Dialog for changing data source information.
Used with permission from Microsoft.

Usage of other boxes and options shown in Add Connection dialog is detailed here:

- **Server Name**—Shows the name of the server for this connection. To choose a different server, select the desired option from the drop-down list. For SQL Server Express Edition instances, you need to type the local computer name with \SQLEXPRESS appended to the name. The \SQLEXPRESS suffix is not required while using the full SQL Server. For SQL Server instances hosted on the same system, you can use (local) as the server name. To specify the local instance of SQL Server Express, type .\sqlexpress in the text box. Enter (local) in the Server Name box to access the SQL Server hosted on the same system (see Figure 16.4 [right]).

- **Refresh**—Updates the list of available servers.

- **Use Windows Authentication**—Enables access to the database without supplying a user ID or password because the ones in Windows Authentication are used. You will employ this option in your example.

- **Use SQL Server Authentication**—Requires a valid username and password to open the database connection.
  - **User Name**—Text box to enter a user ID to access the database. The provided username must have enough permission to access the specified database.

  - **Password**—A text box to enter a password.

  - **Save My Password**—Saves and encrypts the password so that you don't have to enter a password every time you open the connection.

- **Select or Enter a Database Name**—Displays the available databases that you can connect to. To create a new database, you need to enter its name into the text box and then click the OK button. You'll create a new database called `CSharpSampleDatabase` (see Figure 16.4 [right]).

- **Attach a Database File**—Attaches the existing database name to the application. Click Browse to locate the database file.

- **Logical Name**—Displays the name for this database connection.

- **Advanced**—Displays the Advanced Properties dialog box that you use to specify or view settings for the connection.

- **Test Connection**—Tests the connection with the attached database without closing the dialog box. Displays the message `Test connection succeeded` if the settings for the selected database are correctly entered. Click OK to save the connection settings. Remember: the Test connection fails if you attempt to test with a database that does not exist.

After you enter the database name `CSharpSampleDatabase` in the Select or Enter a Database Name box and click OK, a message appears informing you that the database does not exist and prompts whether to create it. Click Yes to create the database. `CSharpSampleDatabase` is created and appears in the Server Explorer window under the Data Connections node, as shown in Figure 16.6.

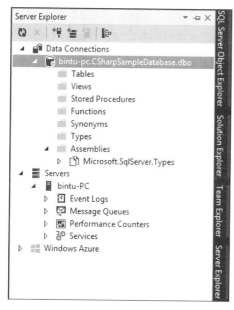

Figure 16.6
Server Explorer window showing newly created database along with its folders.

The newly created database, CSharpSampleDatabase, is empty now. To add a new database table, right-click the Tables node in Server Explorer and select Add New Table. Using the table editor, you can add the following five columns to the new table:

- **Code**—To be used for storing product code, so it is defined of int data type and is set as the primary key. After defining a primary key, you cannot assign a null value or a duplicate value to the Code column.

- **ProdName**—Defined of varchar(50) type, the ProdName column is used to store the product name.

- **Quantity**—Defined of int type, the Quantity column is used to store the available quantity of the product.

- **Category**—Defined of varchar(30) type, the Category column is used to store the category to which the current product belongs.

- **Price**—Defined of money type, the Price column is used to store the price of the product.

Don't forget to uncheck the Allow Nulls check box to compel users to fill all the columns while adding a new row. After you define the five columns, the table structure looks like Figure 16.7.

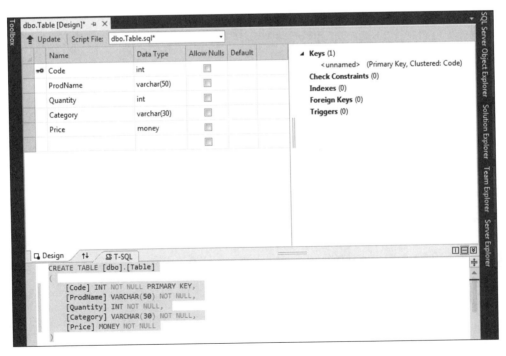

Figure 16.7
Defining structure for Products table.

After creating the table schema, you are prompted for the table's name when you save it. Name the table Products. The Products table will appear under the Tables node of the Server Explorer, as shown in Figure 16.8. Observe the key to the left of the Code column, which indicates that the Code column is a primary key field.

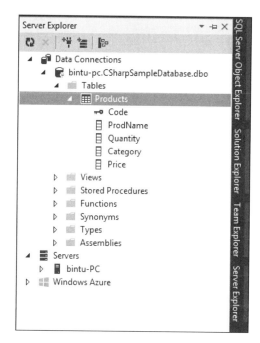

Figure 16.8
Products table and its columns in the Server Explorer window.
Used with permission from Microsoft.

To add records to your Products table, right-click the Products table icon and select Show Table Data. After you enter information for a few products, the Products table looks like Figure 16.9.

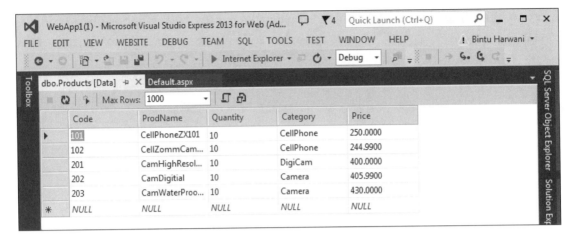

Figure 16.9
Products table after entering certain rows.

Used with permission from Microsoft.

You have created a database called `CSharpSampleDatabase` that contains a table called `Products`. You have even added a few rows to it. Now you'll learn how to access data in a database table through code.

Accessing Data from the Database

To interact with a database, you need to connect to the database server. The connection to the data source is represented through a `Connection` object. After a `Connection` object is created, it is shared with many different `Command` instances. A `Command` instance represents a database command (SQL statement, and so on) to apply on the connected database. To execute the SQL command, you can use different types of `Execute` methods.

Here are the steps to access data from a database:

1. Create a connection to the server.

2. Open the connection.

3. Create a `Command` object.

4. Create the `DataReader` or `DataAdapter` object.

5. Close the connection and release the resources.

You'll begin with the first step: creating a connection to the server.

Creating a Connection to the Server

To access the database, you need to connect to the server by providing connection parameters, such as the machine on which the database is running and login credentials (if any). Therefore, the first thing to do while working with the database is to create a `Connection` object and give it the necessary information through the connection string. The connection string contains the data source location, user ID, and password.

Specifically, to connect to a database, you first declare a `SqlConnection` variable using one of its two constructors. The constructor takes a connection string, as shown in the following syntax:

```
public SqlConnection(string connectionString);
```

The parameter `connectionString` is a string value that represents a connection with the database.

Example:

```
SqlConnection conSQL = new SqlConnection("");
```

To use the default constructor of `SqlConnection`, define a connection string, and then associate the connection string to the `SqlConnection` object using its `ConnectionString` property, as shown in the next code:

```
string strConnection = "";
SqlConnection conServer = new SqlConnection();
conServer.ConnectionString = strConnection;
```

To use a `SqlConnection` object, you need to provide a lot of information in the form of key/value pairs. These key/value pairs are separated from each other with a semicolon (;), as shown here:

```
key1=value1;key2=value2;key_n=value_n
```

This information is either passed to the `SqlConnection`'s constructor as shown here:

```
SqlConnection conn = new SqlConnection("key1=value1;key2=value2;key_n=value_n");
```

or it's assigned as a string to the `SqlConnection.ConnectionString` property like this:

```
SqlConnection conn = new SqlConnection();
string strConnection = "Key1=Value1;Key2=Value2;Key_n=Value_n";
conn.ConnectionString = strConnection;
```

Besides `ConnectionString`, there are some properties of the `Connection` object that are used while connecting with a database. Following are a few of the `Connection` properties:

- **ConnectionString**—Used to read or assign the connection string to be used by the `SqlConnection` object.

- **Datasource**—Read-only property that returns the name of the SQL Server instance that is used by the `SqlConnection` object.

- **Database**—Read-only property that returns the name of the database being used by the `Connection` object.

- **State**—Read-only property that returns the current state of the connection. The possible values are `Broken`, `Closed`, `Connecting`, `Executing`, `Fetching`, and `Open`.

A connection string includes information in the form of several key/value pairs or attributes. These attributes define the computer you are connecting to, the database name, and the level of security, among other things. Some of these attributes are essential, and some are optional. Table 16.3 shows a brief description of frequently used attributes in a connection string.

Table 16.3   Frequently Used Attributes in a Connection String

Attribute	Description
Server	To establish a connection, you need to specify the computer name to which you want to connect. Basically, the computer name where the desired database is installed is specified in the following format:
	`SqlConnection conn = new SqlConnection("Server=computer_name; ");`
	Example:
	`SqlConnection conn = new SqlConnection("Server=bintu-pc; ");`
	If the application is created on the same machine where the database is installed, the computer name can be specified as local:
	`SqlConnection conn = new SqlConnection("Server=(local); ");`
	The attribute for specifying the computer name is Server, Data Source, Address, or Addr. For example, the preceding statement can also be written as shown here:
	`SqlConnection conn = new SqlConnection("Data Source=(local); ");`
Database/ Initial Catalog	The attribute is used to specify the database to access on the specified server. The Database keyword can also be substituted for the Initial Catalog. For example, the following statement

establishes a connection with the `CSharpSampleDatabase` on the local computer:

```
SqlConnection conn = new SqlConnection("Server=(local); Initial
Catalog=CSharpSampleDatabase;");
```

This attribute is optional. In other words, it can be ignored when you to want to connect to a specific computer but not to any database.

Trusted_ Connection/ Integrated Security	This attribute implements the secure connection with the database. You can specify values `true`, `false`, `yes`, `no`, or `SSPI` for this attribute. While establishing a trusted connection or the connection that doesn't need to be verified, you can assign a value of `true` or `SSPI` (Security Support Provider Interface) for this attribute, as shown here:

```
SqlConnection conn = new SqlConnection("Server=(local);Initial
Catalog=CSharpSampleDatabase;Trusted_Connection=sspi");
```

When you use the `true` or `SSPI` value for this attribute, the username and the password (if any) of the person opening the application are used automatically. For example, if the application is being opened on a Windows operating system that has a default username and password, the connection to the database is established without checking security. To apply authentication, you can assign `false` or `no` to this attribute. In that case, you need to specify the username and the password, as shown in the following example:

```
SqlConnection conn = new SqlConnection("Server=(local);Initial
Catalog=CSharpSampleDatabase;Integrated Security=no");
```

After setting the security attribute to `false` or `no`, you must provide login credentials.

Username	To specify the username used in a connection, after assigning `false` or `no` to the `Integrated Security` attribute, you must use the `User ID` attribute and assign it a valid username. Here is an example:

```
SqlConnection conn = new SqlConnection("Server=(local);Initial
Catalog=CSharpSampleDatabase;Integrated Security=no;User
ID=David");
```

Password/Pwd	When establishing a secure connection to a database, in addition to a valid username, you need to provide a password. You can use the `Password` or `PWD` (not case sensitive) attribute to specify the password for the associated user ID, as shown in the following example:

```
SqlConnection conn = new SqlConnection("Server=(local);Initial
Catalog=CSharpSampleDatabase;Integrated Security=no; User
ID=David;PWD=gold2014");
```

Remember, the attributes shown in Table 16.3 are not case-sensitive.

Once you've created the connection string, when the application executes, each attribute in the connection string is validated. An unknown key, value, or invalid combination of key=value pair will result in throwing an ArgumentException exception; consequently, the connection will not be established.

It is better to store connection strings in the configuration file of the application so that you can write an application and then plug in various database providers without altering the main application. To define a database connection string, use the <connectionStrings> element of the configuration file. Here, you can specify a name for the connection and the actual database connection string parameters; in addition, you can specify the provider for the connection type. Here is an example:

```
<configuration>
   ...
   <connectionStrings>
      <add name="connectStringSample"
         providerName="System.Data.SqlClient"
         connectionString="server=(local);integrated security=SSPI;
            database=CSharpSampleDatabase" />
   </connectionStrings>
</configuration>
```

Once the database connection information has been defined within the configuration file, you can use it in the application immediately. You will soon learn to work with the configuration file Web.config.

Opening the Connection

To establish the connection with the database, you must call the SqlConnection.Open() method. Its syntax follows:

```
public virtual void Open();
```

The following code opens a connection to CSharpSampleDatabase on the local computer:

```
string source="Server=(local);Initial Catalog=CSharpSampleDatabase;Integrated
Security=True";
SqlConnection conn = new SqlConnection(source);
conn.Open();
```

If the connection fails, the compiler throws a SqlException exception. If the connection string doesn't contain the computer attribute or the connection is already opened, the compiler throws an InvalidOperationException exception.

Creating a Command Object

After creating a connection to the server, you create a `Command` object and provide SQL commands to perform the desired processing on the database. Using the `Command` object, you can execute any direct T-SQL or stored procedure on the server. To pass parameters to the server, you can even add a few input parameter objects to the `Command` and retrieve scalar values back via output parameters. Using the `ExecuteNonQuery` method on the `Command` object, you can execute T-SQL or a stored procedure on the server.

Note

> Transact-SQL (T-SQL) is Microsoft's and Sybase's proprietary extension to SQL, where SQL (Structured Query Language) is a standardized computer language that is used to query and update relational databases using declarative statements. T-SQL expands on the SQL standard and is focused on using Microsoft SQL Server. T-SQL includes procedural programming and several functions to make different processing tasks easier.

If the SQL command or the stored procedure returns a result, it is stored in the result set for further processing. To retain the result set, you must create a `DataAdapter` object and use it to fill a `DataSet` or `DataTable` object, which maintains the information in disconnected mode. The alternative method is to create a `DataReader` object, which keeps a live connection to the database and works as a forward-moving cursor.

A `Command` object is usually created by passing two parameters to the `Command` class constructor. The first is the SQL statement, and the second is the `Connection` instance, as shown in the next example:

```
string connstr="Server=(local);Initial Catalog=CSharpSampleDatabase;Integrated
Security=True";
string sqlstr = "SELECT Code, ProdName FROM Products";
SqlConnection conn = new SqlConnection(connstr);
conn.Open();
SqlCommand cmd = new SqlCommand(sqlstr, conn);
```

After defining the `Command` object, you can execute it through any of the following `Execute` methods:

- **ExecuteNonQuery**—Executes the command but does not return output. It is commonly used for `UPDATE`, `INSERT`, and `DELETE` statements. It returns the number of rows affected by the command.

- **ExecuteReader**—Executes the command and returns a `DataReader` object based on the SQL statement. In other words, when the `ExecuteReader` method executes on the `SqlCommand` object, it returns a `SqlDataReader` object. The `SqlDataReader` object is a read-only and forward-only cursor that can be iterated through to fetch the rows in it.

The following example creates a `SqlDataReader` object called `reader` by executing the `ExecuteReader` method on the `Command` object `cmd`:

```
string connstr="Server=(local);Initial Catalog=CSharpSampleDatabase;Integrated Security=True";
string sqlstr = "SELECT Code, ProdName FROM Products";
SqlConnection conn = new SqlConnection(connstr);
conn.Open();
SqlCommand cmd = new SqlCommand(sqlstr, conn);
SqlDataReader reader = cmd.ExecuteReader();
```

You can execute the `Read` method on the `SqlDataReader` object `reader` to obtain rows (the result of the query). In other words, you can access the data from SQL Server and use it directly in your application via a `SqlDataReader` object. `SqlDataReader` advances through the result set one row at a time, enabling you to extract the column values of each row. By default, the `SqlDataReader` object is positioned at the beginning of the result set.

- **ExecuteRow**—Executes the command and returns a `SqlRecord` object that contains a single returned row.

- **ExecuteScalar**—Executes the command and returns the first column of the first row in the result set. The remaining rows and columns in the result set are ignored.

- **ExecuteXmlReader**—Executes the command and returns an `XmlReader` object. (The result set is in the form of an XML document.)

Here are a few of the `Command` properties that are used while accessing the data from the database:

- **Connection**—Gets or sets the `SqlConnection` object to be used by the `Command` object.

- **CommandText**—Sets or gets either the T-SQL statement or the stored procedure name.

- **CommandType**—Indicates the way the `CommandText` property should be interpreted. The possible values are `StoredProcedure`, `TableDirect`, and `Text`.

- **CommandTimeout**—Gets or sets the number of seconds to wait while attempting to execute a command. The command is aborted after it times out and an exception is thrown. The default is 30 seconds.

Closing the Connection and Releasing the Resources

After accessing or updating the database, you close a connection by calling the `SqlConnection.Close()` method. The syntax follows:

```
public virtual void Close();
```

Example: The next example closes the current connection:

```
conn.Close();
```

To summarize, the following code snippet demonstrates the steps for accessing data from a database:

```
string connstr="connection_string";
string sqlstr = "SQL command";
// Creating a new SQL Connection object
SqlConnection conn = new SqlConnection(connstr);

// Opening the connection to the database
conn.Open();

// Creating the Command object
SqlCommand cmd = new SqlCommand(sqlstr, conn);

// Executing the SQL command
cmd.ExecuteNonQuery();

// Disposing the Command object
cmd.Dispose();

// Closing the database connection
conn.Close();

// Disposing the Connection object
conn.Dispose();
```

In addition to closing the connection, you need to release the resources that the disposable objects acquire. Disposable objects are those that allocate resources and implement the `IDisposable` interface.

The Garbage Collector (GC) cleans up the memory allocated to different objects when they are no longer required, but it can clean up the memory only when the resources allocated to the objects are released. You normally release resources by invoking the `Dispose` method.

The `IDisposable` interface specifies a `Dispose` method that you can call explicitly when the objects are no longer required. More specifically, the objects must implement the `IDisposable` interface to invoke the `Dispose` method to indicate that the requirement of the specific resource is over and is ready to be released. The using keyword makes this process simpler. You will learn to employ using in the following section.

Therefore, the Dispose method is called on Connection and Command objects in the preceding code snippet to release the resources acquired by the two objects. Dispose automatically closes the connection.

Using try . . . catch . . . finally

To ensure that resources are freed after use, use the try...catch...finally blocks. You call Dispose methods within the finally block to free up the resources even if the code fails, as shown in the next code snippet:

```
string connstr="connection_string";
string sqlstr = "SQL command";
try
{
    SqlConnection conn = new SqlConnection(connstr);
    conn.Open();
    SqlCommand cmd = new SqlCommand(sqlstr, conn);
    cmd.ExecuteNonQuery();
}
catch ( SqlException ex )
{
}
finally
{
    cmd.Dispose();
    conn.Dispose();
}
```

Within the finally block, you release the resources allocated to the Connection and Command objects by invoking the Dispose methods. This ensures that even if an exception is thrown, the memory allocated to the two object's resources is freed.

Utilizing the using Keyword

The using keyword is used to automatically free up the resources that the disposable objects acquired. You don't need to call the Dispose method explicitly to employ the using statement. Instead, the Dispose method is called automatically when the object falls out of scope. The following code snippet demonstrates utilizing the `using` keyword:

```
using (SqlConnection conn = new SqlConnection())
{
    conn.ConnectionString = "connection_string";
    try
    {
        using (SqlCommand cmd = new SqlCommand())
        {
            cmd.Connection = conn;
            cmd.CommandText = "SQL command";
            conn.Open();
            ......
        }
    }
    catch (SqlException ex)
    {
    }
}
```

Now you have sufficient knowledge to fetch and display information about the products in the `Products` table of `CSharpSampleDatabase`. In the code-behind file `Default.aspx.cs`, write the code as shown in Listing 16.1.

Listing 16.1 Program Code in Default.aspx.cs File

```
using System;
using System.Collections.Generic;
using System.Linq;
using System.Web;
using System.Web.UI;
using System.Web.UI.WebControls;
using System.Data.SqlClient;
public partial class _Default : System.Web.UI.Page
{
    protected void Page_Load(object sender, EventArgs e)
    {
        using (SqlConnection conn = new SqlConnection())
        {
            conn.ConnectionString = "server=(local);database=CSharpSampleDatabase;
Integrated Security=SSPI";
            try
            {
```

```
using (SqlCommand cmd = new SqlCommand())
{
    conn.Open();
    cmd.Connection = conn;
    cmd.CommandText = "SELECT Code, ProdName, Quantity, Category,
Price FROM Products";
    SqlDataReader reader = cmd.ExecuteReader();
    while (reader.Read())
    {
        Response.Write(reader[0].ToString() + " " +
reader[1].ToString() + " " + reader[2].ToString() + " " + reader[3].ToString() + " " +
reader[4].ToString() + " ");
    }
}
}
catch (SqlException ex)
{
    Console.WriteLine("An error occurred: {0}", ex.Message);
}
}
}
}
```

Note

The `SqlConnection` and `SqlCommand` classes are available in the `System.Data.SqlClient` namespace, so you need to include that namespace in the program through the `using` directive.

You can see that a new `SqlConnection` object is created and assigned to the variable conn. Similarly, a new `SqlCommand` object is created and assigned to the variable cmd. The `using` statement ensures that the `SqlConnection` and `SqlCommand` objects dispose of their resources when these objects are no longer needed. In other words, the `Dispose` method is called on both the `SqlConnection` and the `SqlCommand` objects even if an exception occurs. The `ConnectionString` property of the `SqlConnection` object conn is set to point at the CSharpSampleDatabase database running on the local SQL Server instance. The `Open` method is invoked on the `SqlConnection` object to establish the database connection. The `SqlCommand` object's (cmd) `Connection` property is associated with the open connection in conn, and its `CommandText` property is set to the TSql statement `SELECT` that you want to execute. Then the `ExecuteReader` method is invoked on the `SqlCommand` object, which passes the command to SQL Server. The `ExecuteReader` method creates the `SqlDataReader` object reader that contains the Product table's rows that are fetched upon execution of the SQL `SELECT` statement.

Once the reader object is created, it is positioned before the first row in the result set. Invoking the Read method advances the reader object to the first row. Basically, the reader object acts as an array in which each array element contains the data of the respective column. For example, reader[0] contains the value of the first column mentioned in the SQL SELECT statement (Code). Similarly, reader[1] contains the value of the second column (ProdName), and so on. Using the Response.Write method, the information in the table columns is displayed on the current HTTP output (on the browser screen). The while loop reads information in each table row and displays it on the screen.

After the command executes on the server, the inner using block closes, which implicitly disposes of the SqlCommand object and dereferences the cmd variable. Thereafter, the outer using block closes, which implicitly disposes of the SqlConnection object and dereferences the conn variable.

After you run the application, the information about all the products that are in the Products table is displayed on the screen (see Figure 16.10).

Note

Most of the data providers support connection pooling. A connection pool is a set of available database connections. When an application requires a connection, the provider extracts the next available connection from the pool. When the application closes the connection, it is returned to the pool to be used by the next application.

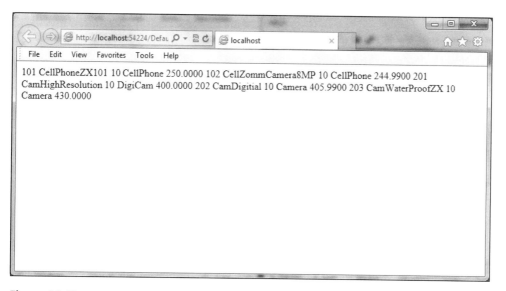

Figure 16.10
Products table information displayed on the screen.

Used with permission from Microsoft.

Displaying the Table Data Through GridView

The GridView control displays the data in tabular format. You can edit, update, or delete any row. Each row of the GridView control represents one table row, and each column represents the table column of that row. The GridView control also allows sorting and paging. As the name suggests, *sorting* arranges the rows in order of a particular column of the row. *Paging* divides the rows into groups (*chunks*). You can determine the number of rows you want in a group (*page*) and, accordingly, the whole list of rows is divided into pages. After dividing the rows into pages, the navigation tools automatically appear to navigate to the next or the previous page.

Now you'll learn to display the products information that is in the Products table of CSharpSampleDatabase through the GridView control. To display data through the GridView control, you must bind it to a data source. To associate a GridView to a data source, click its smart tag and select the Choose Data Source drop-down. Because you don't have any existing data source, select New Data Source (see Figure 16.11).

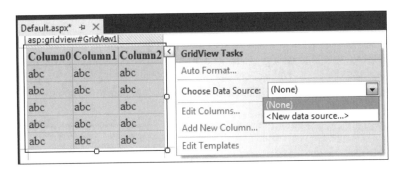

Figure 16.11
GridView control.
Used with permission from Microsoft.

A dialog box appears prompting you to select Data Source Type. Because you want to display the information in the Products table through the GridView, you'll bind the GridView control to SqlDataSource1, as shown in Figure 16.12.

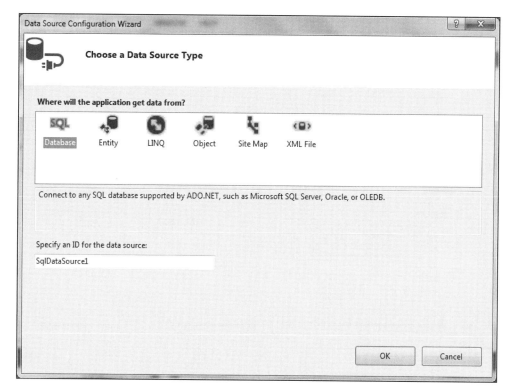

Figure 16.12
Dialog for choosing data source type.
Used with permission from Microsoft.

The next dialog asks you to select the connection string that you want to use to connect to the Products table. But because there is no existing connection string in the configuration file of the application, click New Connection in the dialog. The next dialog prompts you to choose the server name and the database that you want to connect to. Select (local) as the server name because you want to access the database from the local machine. Also, select CSharpSampleDatabase from the Select or Enter Database Name drop-down. Click OK (see Figure 16.13).

Figure 16.13
Dialog for adding connection to the CSharpSampleDatabase database.
Used with permission from Microsoft.

The next dialog confirms whether the server name and database name selected are correct. Click Next to move further. The next dialog prompts whether to save the connection in the application configuration file. The dialog also shows the default name by which the connection string will be saved (see Figure 16.14). Click Next to save the connection string by the specified name in the configuration file of the application: `Web.config`.

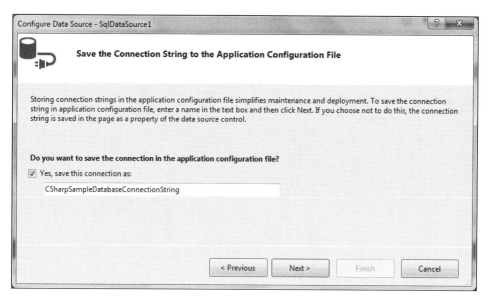

Figure 16.14
Saving connection string in the application configuration file.
Used with permission from Microsoft.

The next dialog asks you to select the columns that you want to display through the GridView control. Because you want to display all the columns of the Products table, check the check box associated to *. The SELECT statement box shows the SQL statement reflecting the table columns that are selected (see Figure 16.15). Click Next to move further.

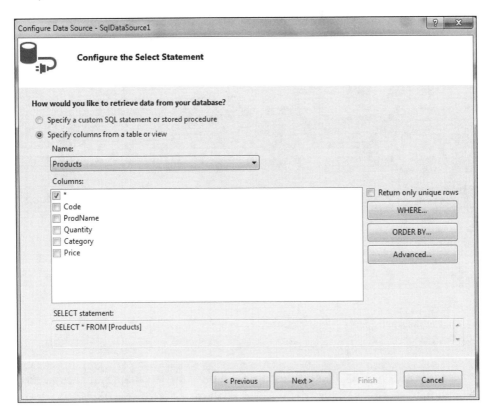

Figure 16.15
Choosing the Products table's columns to associate with the GridView control.
Used with permission from Microsoft.

The next dialog enables you to preview the data that will be returned by the data source and will be displayed through the GridView control. Click the Test Query button in the dialog to see the rows returned by the Products table on application of the specified SELECT statement (see Figure 16.16).

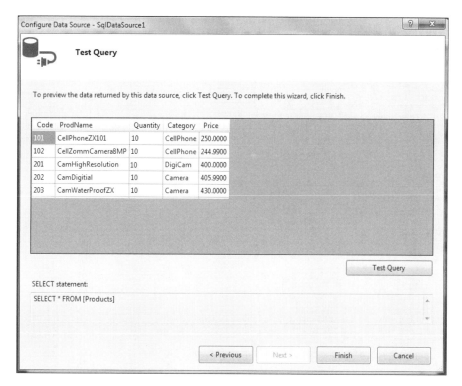

Figure 16.16
Test Query dialog showing the Products row that satisfies the SELECT statement.

Click Finish to close the Configure Data Source wizard. A data source called SqlDataSource1 appears in the Design window. The GridView control is associated with the data source SqlDataSource1 (see Figure 16.17). The Product table's columns appear in the GridView columns to confirm that the two are now connected.

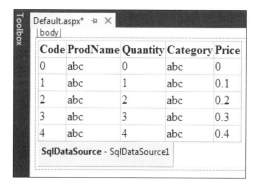

Figure 16.17
GridView control associated with the Products table.

Upon running the application, the contents of the `Products` table appear in the `GridView` control, as shown in Figure 16.18.

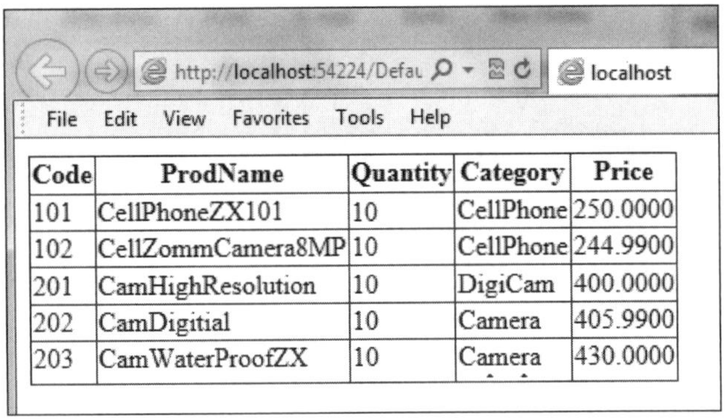

Figure 16.18
Screen showing all the rows of the Products table via the GridView control.
Used with permission from Microsoft.

The connection string that was created while associating a data source with the `GridView` is stored in the application's configuration file `Web.config`, as shown in Listing 16.2.

Listing 16.2 Program Code in Web.config File

```xml
<?xml version="1.0"?>
<configuration>
    <connectionStrings>
        <add name="CSharpSampleDatabaseConnectionString" connectionString="Data
Source=(local);Initial Catalog=CSharpSampleDatabase;Integrated Security=True"
providerName="System.Data.SqlClient" />
    </connectionStrings>
    <system.web>
      <compilation debug="true" targetFramework="4.5" />
      <httpRuntime targetFramework="4.5" />
    </system.web>
</configuration>
```

You saw how to add rows to the database table through the Solution Explorer window. Now you'll learn to insert rows into your `Products` table through coding.

INSERTING ROWS IN A TABLE

To your existing application `WebApp1`, you will add a new web form to create a user interface for inserting rows into the `Products` table. Right-click the application in the Solution Explorer window and select Add, Add New Item. From the dialog that pops up, select the Visual C# language from the left followed by the Web Form item. Name the new web form `AddProduct.aspx` and then click Add (see Figure 16.19).

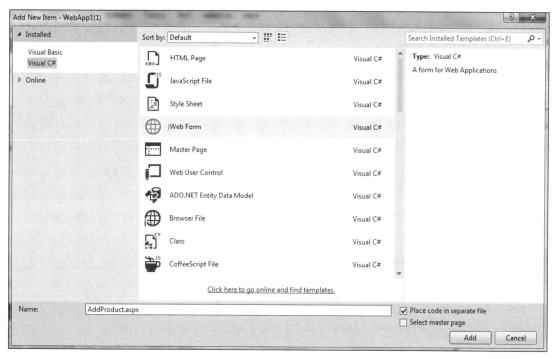

Figure 16.19
Adding the web form AddProduct.aspx to the application.
Used with permission from Microsoft.

The `AddProduct.aspx` form is opened in Design mode. Drag and drop seven `Label` controls, five `TextBox` controls, and a `Button` control on the web form (see Figure 16.20 [left]). Set the `Text` property of the first six `Label` controls to `Add Product`, `Product Code`, `Product Name`, `Quantity`, `Category`, and `Price`, respectively. Also, set the `Text` property of the `Button` control to `Add Product`. To access and identify the `TextBox` controls, set the `ID` property of the five `TextBox` controls to `txtCode`, `txtName`, `txtQuantity`, `txtCategory`, and `txtPrice`, respectively. Also, set the ID of the `Button` and the last `Label` control to `btnAdd` and `lblResponse`, respectively. After you apply all these changes, the `AddProduct.aspx` web form appears as shown in Figure 16.20 (right).

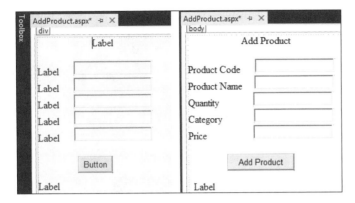

Figure 16.20
(left) Controls placed on the AddProduct.aspx form (right) Controls in AddProduct.aspx form after setting text
and ID properties.

Used with permission from Microsoft.

After you perform all the preceding tasks, the code in the AddProduct.aspx web form
appears, as shown in Listing 16.3.

Listing 16.3 Program Code in AddProduct.aspx File

```
<%@ Page Language="C#" AutoEventWireup="true" CodeFile="AddProduct.aspx.cs"
Inherits="AddProduct" %>
<!DOCTYPE html>
<html xmlns="http://www.w3.org/1999/xhtml">
<head runat="server">
    <title></title>
</head>
<body>
    <form id="form1" runat="server">
    <div>
        <asp:Label ID="Label1" runat="server" Font-Bold="True" Font-Size="X-Large"
Text="Add Product"></asp:Label>
        <br />
        <br />
        <asp:Label ID="Label2" runat="server" Text="Product Code"></asp:Label>
        <asp:TextBox ID="txtCode" runat="server"></asp:TextBox>
        <br />
        <br />
        <asp:Label ID="Label3" runat="server" Text="Product Name"></asp:Label>
        <asp:TextBox ID="txtName" runat="server"></asp:TextBox>
        <br />
        <br />
```

```
        <asp:Label ID="Label4" runat="server" Text="Quantity"></asp:Label>
        <asp:TextBox ID="txtQuantity" runat="server"></asp:TextBox>
        <br />
        <br />
        <asp:Label ID="Label5" runat="server" Text="Category"></asp:Label>
        <asp:TextBox ID="txtCategory" runat="server"></asp:TextBox>
        <br />
        <br />
        <asp:Label ID="Label6" runat="server" Text="Price"></asp:Label>
        <asp:TextBox ID="txtPrice" runat="server"></asp:TextBox>
        <br />
        <br />
        <br />
        <asp:Button ID="btnAdd" runat="server" OnClick="btnAdd_Click"
Text="Add Product" />
        <br />
        <br />
        <asp:Label ID="lblResponse" runat="server"></asp:Label>
        <br />
    </div>
    </form>
</body>
</html>
```

After you enter information about a new product in the respective TextBox controls, when the user clicks the Add Product button, the entered information should be inserted into the Products table. To accomplish that, double-click the Add Product button in the Design window to open the code-behind file. The code-behind file AddProduct.aspx.cs will open and the method btnAdd_Click will be added to it. The code written in the btnAdd_Click method executes when the user clicks the Add Product button. To insert a row in the Products table, write the code as shown in Listing 16.4 into the code-behind file AddProduct.aspx.cs.

Listing 16.4 Program Code in AddProduct.aspx.cs File

```
using System;
using System.Collections.Generic;
using System.Linq;
using System.Web;
using System.Web.UI;
using System.Data.SqlClient;
using System.Web.UI.WebControls;
```

```csharp
public partial class AddProduct : System.Web.UI.Page
{
    protected void Page_Load(object sender, EventArgs e)
    {
    }
    protected void btnAdd_Click(object sender, EventArgs e)
    {
        using (SqlConnection conn = new SqlConnection())
        {
            conn.ConnectionString = "server=(local);database=CSharpSampleDatabase;
Integrated Security=SSPI";
            try
            {
                using (SqlCommand cmd = new SqlCommand())
                {
                    cmd.Connection = conn;
                    conn.Open();
                    cmd.CommandText = "Insert into Products (Code, ProdName,
Quantity, Category, Price) Values (" + Convert.ToInt32(txtCode.Text) + ",'" +
txtName.Text + "'," + Convert.ToInt32(txtQuantity.Text) + ",'" + txtCategory.Text +
"'," + Convert.ToSingle(txtPrice.Text) + ")";                // #1
                    cmd.ExecuteNonQuery();
                    lblResponse.Text = "New product successfully added";
                    conn.Close();
                }
            }
            catch (SqlException ex)
            {
                lblResponse.Text="An error occurred: " + ex.Message;
            }
        }
    }
}
```

In the btnAdd_Click method, you can see that the SqlConnection and SqlCommand objects are created by employing the using keyword so that the resources allocated to them are automatically freed when their task is complete. The SQL INSERT statement is associated with the SqlCommand object that accesses the data entered into the TextBox controls and inserts it into the Products table. The SQL INSERT command is executed through the ExecuteNonQuery method. Recall that the ExecuteNonQuery method is commonly used for UPDATE, INSERT, and DELETE operations. The method returns the number of records affected. After successful insertion of a row in the Products table, the message New product successfully added is displayed through the last Label control.

When you run the application, the Add Product form appears on the screen. Enter information about the new product in the respective TextBox controls, and then click the Add Product button. The product's information is added to the Products table, and the message New product successfully added is displayed, as shown in Figure 16.21.

Figure 16.21
New product successfully added to the Products table.
Used with permission from Microsoft.

Using Parameters with the Command Object

You can pass parameters to the Command objects to pass values to SQL statements or stored procedures. To pass parameters to the Command objects, enlist the help of SqlParameterCollection. To add Parameter objects to a SqlParameterCollection, you can use the following two methods:

- **Add**—Adds the specified SqlParameter object to the SqlParameterCollection. Syntax:

```
public SqlParameter Add(SqlParameter value);
```

Before adding the SqlParameter in the Add method, specify its name and value using the two properties ParameterName and Value. For example, the following code defines a SQLParameter instance pcode whose ParameterName and Value properties are defined here:

```
SqlParameter pcode = new SqlParameter();
pcode.ParameterName = "@Code";
pcode.Value = txtCode.Text;
```

- **AddWithValue**—Adds a value to the end of the `SqlParameterCollection`. The method contains two arguments. The first one is a string that contains the `ParameterName`, and the second is an object that includes the value of that parameter, as shown in the following syntax:

```
public SqlParameter AddWithValue(string ParameterName, Object value);
```

The `ParameterName` is prefixed by an @ symbol and is filled in with the value when the `SqlCommand` executes.

Replace statement #1 in Listing 16.4 with the following code:

```
cmd.CommandText = "Insert into Products (Code, ProdName, Quantity, Category,
Price) Values (@Code, @ProdName, @Quantity, @Category, @Price )";
cmd.Parameters.AddWithValue("@Code", txtCode.Text);
cmd.Parameters.AddWithValue("@ProdName", txtName.Text);
cmd.Parameters.AddWithValue("@Quantity", txtQuantity.Text);
cmd.Parameters.AddWithValue("@Category", txtCategory.Text);
cmd.Parameters.AddWithValue("@Price",txtPrice.Text);
```

You can see that the INSERT statement that is assigned to the `CommandText` property of the `Command` object includes five parameters: @Code, @ProdName, @Quantity, @Category, and @Price. Values are assigned to the five parameters through the `AddWithValue` method. In other words, the data the user enters in the five `TextBox` controls is assigned to the five parameters, respectively.

Specifically, the parameter names, along with their values that the user enters in the respective `TextBox` controls, are added to the `Parameters` collection of the `SqlCommand` object. The `ExecuteNonQuery()` method, when executed on the `SqlCommand` object, inserts a new row in the `Products` table based on the data the user enters into the `TextBox` controls.

Calling Stored Procedures

Stored procedures are T-SQL commands that are compiled and stored inside the database. You can separate the .NET code from the T-SQL code by using stored procedures. Primary benefits to this approach include maintainability, reusability, and security. The commands in a stored procedure are parsed and optimized and result in efficient execution of SQL code. To understand the concept practically, you need to learn to add a new product to the `Products` table through a stored procedure.

To add a new stored procedure to `CSharpSampleDatabase`, expand the database in the Server Explorer window. Right-click the Stored Procedure node and select the Add New Stored Procedure option. You get a screen with some default code for the new procedure, as shown in Figure 16.22.

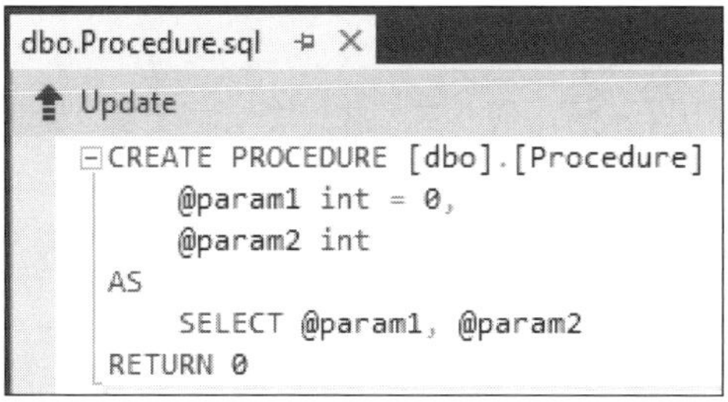

Figure 16.22
Default code of the newly created stored procedure.

Used with permission from Microsoft.

Replace the default procedure code with the one shown in Listing 16.5.

Listing 16.5 Program Code in InsertProductProc File

```
CREATE PROCEDURE [dbo].[InsertProductProc]
    @Code int,
    @ProdName varchar(50),
    @Quantity int,
    @Category varchar(30),
    @Price money
AS
Insert into Products (Code, ProdName, Quantity, Category, Price) Values (@Code,
@ProdName, @Quantity, @Category, @Price )
RETURN 0
```

You can see that the stored procedure is named InsertProductProc, and it takes five parameters: @Code, @ProdName, @Quantity, @Category, and @Price of type int, varchar(50), int, varchar(30), and money, respectively. The values passed for these parameters are inserted into the Products table.

After you write the code of the stored procedure, click the Update button shown along with the Up arrow key. Upon clicking the Update button, you get a dialog titled Preview Database Updates, as shown in Figure 16.23. The dialog shows three buttons: Generate Script, Update Database, and Cancel.

Figure 16.23
Dialog prompting to update the database and to generate a script.

When you click the Update Database button, the InsertProductProc stored procedure is created in the CSharpSampleDatabase and appears under the Stored Procedures node. If you click the Generate Script button, an SQL script is generated. When the script is executed, it creates a stored procedure, InsertProductProc, for you, as shown in Figure 16.24.

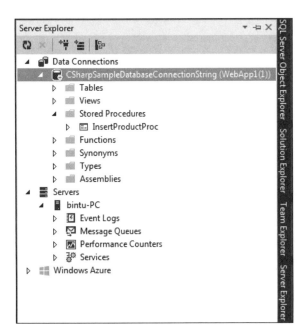

Figure 16.24
Stored procedure InsertProductProc appears under the Stored Procedures node.

To use the stored procedure, you need to set the command object's `CommandType` property to the stored procedure name:

```
cmd.CommandType = CommandType.StoredProcedure;
```

Also, you need to add the parameters to the `SqlCommand` object using the `Parameters` collection. For example, the following statement assigns the data the user enters into the `txtCode` text box to the `@Code` parameter:

```
cmd.Parameters.Add("@Code", SqlDbType.Int).Value=txtCode.Text.Trim();
```

The `@Code` parameter takes an integer value. Similarly, you need to assign the values to be passed for other parameters used in the stored procedure. Finally, you use `ExecuteNonQuery` to execute the stored procedure. To add new product to the `Products` table through the stored procedure, modify the code-behind file `AddProduct.aspx.cs` to appear as shown in Listing 16.6.

Listing 16.6 Program Code in AddProduct.aspx.cs File

```
using System;
using System.Data;
using System.Collections.Generic;
using System.Linq;
using System.Web;
using System.Web.UI;
using System.Data.SqlClient;
using System.Web.UI.WebControls;
public partial class AddProduct : System.Web.UI.Page
{
    protected void Page_Load(object sender, EventArgs e)
    {
    }
    protected void btnAdd_Click(object sender, EventArgs e)
    {
        using (SqlConnection conn = new SqlConnection())
        {
            conn.ConnectionString = "server=(local);database= CSharpSampleDatabase;
Integrated Security=SSPI";
            try
            {
                using (SqlCommand cmd = new SqlCommand())
                {
                    cmd.Connection = conn;
                    conn.Open();
                    cmd.CommandText = "InsertProductProc";
```

```
                    cmd.CommandType = CommandType.StoredProcedure;
                    cmd.Parameters.Add("@Code", SqlDbType.Int).Value=
txtCode.Text.Trim();
                    cmd.Parameters.Add("@ProdName", SqlDbType.VarChar).
Value=txtName.Text.Trim();
                    cmd.Parameters.Add("@Quantity", SqlDbType.Int).Value =
txtQuantity.Text.Trim();
                    cmd.Parameters.Add("@Category", SqlDbType.VarChar).Value =
txtCategory.Text.Trim();
                    cmd.Parameters.Add("@Price", SqlDbType.Money).Value =
txtPrice.Text.Trim();
                     cmd.ExecuteNonQuery();
                    lblResponse.Text = "New product successfully added";
                    conn.Close();
                }
            }
            catch (SqlException ex)
            {
                lblResponse.Text="An error occurred: " + ex.Message;
            }
        }
    }
}
```

The code for adding the new product row, including the actual INSERT statement, is contained in the stored procedure. The CommandText property of the SqlCommand object is set to the name of a stored procedure. Also, its CommandType property is set to CommandType.StoredProcedure. The InsertProductProc stored procedure executes the INSERT statement to add the new product row. When the new product is successfully inserted into the Products table, the message New product successfully added is displayed on the screen.

Now that you understand listing and inserting of rows in the Products table, you'll learn to update content for a database table.

UPDATING A TABLE

To update data in a database table, you will use the SQL UPDATE command. Because Code is the primary key in your Products table, the user will be prompted to enter code for the product whose information is required to be updated. To make the user's task easier, you will use a drop-down list that displays codes of all the existing products. When a user selects any product code from the drop-down list, the information for that product can be displayed in the TextBox controls. The user can see and modify the product information that is displayed in the TextBox controls. After performing the desired modification, when the user selects Update, the information about that product is updated in the Products table.

You'll add a new web form for updating the Products table. Right-click the application in the Solution Explorer window and select Add, Add New Item. Name the new web form UpdateProduct.aspx. Drag and drop a drop-down, eight Label controls, five TextBox controls, and a Button control on the web form. To access and identify the TextBox controls, set the ID property of the five TextBox controls to txtCode, txtName, txtQuantity, txtCategory, and txtPrice, respectively. Also, set the ID property of the Button and the last Label control to btnUpdate and lblResponse, respectively. Set the Text property of the Label and Button control to appear as shown in Figure 16.25.

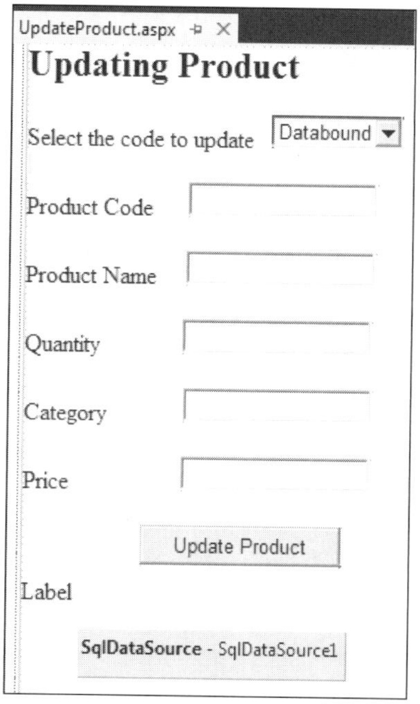

Figure 16.25
Controls after setting the Text and ID properties of the controls placed on UpdateProduct.aspx form.
Used with permission from Microsoft.

Associate the drop-down control to the Code column of the Products table by performing the following steps:

1. Click the smart tag of the drop-down list.

2. Select the Choose Data Source drop-down followed by the New Data Source option.

3. Select Database as the Data Source Type. The data source is assigned a default named `SqlDataSource1`.

4. The next dialog prompts you to choose the data connection. Click New Connection.

5. The next dialog prompts you to choose the server name and the database that you want to connect to. Select `(local)` as the server name and `CSharpSampleDatabase` as the database name. Click OK.

6. Save the connection in the application configuration file. Click Next.

7. Select the Code column of the `Products` table. You want to display only the product codes through the drop-down list. Click Next.

8. Click the Text Query button to preview and confirm that data in the Code column is accessed from the `Products` table.

9. Clicking the Finish button to close the Configure Data Source wizard.

A data source called `SqlDataSource1` appears in the Design window. Because you don't want the user to update code of the product—except for the product name, quantity category, and price—right-click the txtCode TextBox from the Design window and select Properties. Change the `Enabled` property of the txtCode from `true` to `false`.

The code in `UpdateProduct.aspx` appears as shown in Listing 16.7.

Listing 16.7 Program Code in UpdateProduct.aspx File

```
<%@ Page Language="C#" AutoEventWireup="true" CodeFile="UpdateProduct.aspx.cs"
Inherits="UpdateProduct" %>

<!DOCTYPE html>
<html xmlns="http://www.w3.org/1999/xhtml">
<head runat="server">
    <title></title>
</head>
<body>
    <form id="form1" runat="server">
        <div>
            <asp:Label ID="Label1" runat="server" Font-Bold="True" Font-Size="X-Large"
Text="Updating Product"></asp:Label>
            <br />
            <br />
            <asp:Label ID="Label8" runat="server" Text="Select the code to
update"></asp:Label>
            <asp:DropDownList ID="DropDownList1" runat="server" DataSourceID=
"SqlDataSource1" OnSelectedIndexChanged="DropDownList1_SelectedIndexChanged"
AutoPostBack="True" DataTextField="Code">
```

```
        </asp:DropDownList>
        <asp:SqlDataSource ID="SqlDataSource1" runat="server" ConnectionString="<%$
ConnectionStrings:CSharpSampleDatabaseConnectionString2 %>" SelectCommand="SELECT
[Code] FROM [Products]"></asp:SqlDataSource>
        <br />
        <br />
        <asp:Label ID="Label2" runat="server" Text="Product Code"></asp:Label>
        <asp:TextBox ID="txtCode" runat="server" Enabled="False"></asp:TextBox>
        <br />
        <br />
        <asp:Label ID="Label3" runat="server" Text="Product Name"></asp:Label>
        <asp:TextBox ID="txtName" runat="server"></asp:TextBox>
        <br />
        <br />
        <asp:Label ID="Label4" runat="server" Text="Quantity"></asp:Label>
        <asp:TextBox ID="txtQuantity" runat="server"></asp:TextBox>
        <br />
        <br />
        <asp:Label ID="Label5" runat="server" Text="Category"></asp:Label>
        <asp:TextBox ID="txtCategory" runat="server"></asp:TextBox>
        <br />
        <br />
        <asp:Label ID="Label6" runat="server" Text="Price"></asp:Label>
        <asp:TextBox ID="txtPrice" runat="server"></asp:TextBox>
        <br />
        <br />
        <asp:Button ID="btnUpdate" runat="server" OnClick="btnUpdate_Click"
Text="Update Product" />
        <br />
        <br />
        <asp:Label ID="lblResponse" runat="server" Text="Label"></asp:Label>
        <br />
         <br />
    </div>
    </form>
</body>
</html>
```

Next, you need to write the code in the code-behind file UpdateProduct.aspx.cs to perform the following tasks:

- Access the code the user selects from the drop-down list.

- Fetch the product's information from the Products table, whose code is selected from the drop-down list.

- Display the information fetched from the Products table through the respective TextBox controls.

- Access the updated information from the TextBox controls and apply the changes to the Products table when the user clicks the Update button.

To perform all the preceding tasks, write the code as shown in Listing 16.8 in the code-behind file UpdateProduct.aspx.cs.

Listing 16.8 Program Code in UpdateProduct.aspx.cs File

```
using System;
using System.Collections.Generic;
using System.Linq;
using System.Web;
using System.Web.UI;
using System.Web.UI.WebControls;
using System.Data.SqlClient;
public partial class UpdateProduct : System.Web.UI.Page
{
    protected void Page_Load(object sender, EventArgs e)
    {
    }
    protected void btnUpdate_Click(object sender, EventArgs e)
    {
        using (SqlConnection conn = new SqlConnection())
        {
            conn.ConnectionString = "server=(local);database=CSharpSampleDatabase;
Integrated Security=SSPI";
            try
            {
                using (SqlCommand cmd = new SqlCommand())
                {
                    cmd.Connection = conn;
                    conn.Open();
                    cmd.CommandText = "Update Products Set ProdName=@ProdName,
Quantity=@Quantity, Category=@Category, Price=@Price where Code=@Code";
                    cmd.Parameters.AddWithValue("@Code", txtCode.Text);
                    cmd.Parameters.AddWithValue("@ProdName", txtName.Text);
                    cmd.Parameters.AddWithValue("@Quantity", txtQuantity.Text);
                    cmd.Parameters.AddWithValue("@Category", txtCategory.Text);
                    cmd.Parameters.AddWithValue("@Price",txtPrice.Text);
                    cmd.ExecuteNonQuery();
                    lblResponse.Text = "Product successfully updated";
                    conn.Close();
```

```
                    }
                }
                catch (SqlException ex)
                {
                    lblResponse.Text="An error occurred: " + ex.Message;
                }
            }
        }
    protected void DropDownList1_SelectedIndexChanged(object sender, EventArgs e)
    {
        String code = DropDownList1.SelectedItem.Text;
        using (SqlConnection conn = new SqlConnection())
        {
            conn.ConnectionString = "server=(local);database=CSharpSampleDatabase;
Integrated Security=SSPI";
            try
            {
                using (SqlCommand cmd = new SqlCommand())
                {
                    cmd.Connection = conn;
                    cmd.CommandText = "SELECT Code, ProdName, Quantity, Category,
Price    FROM Products where Code=" + Convert.ToInt32(code);
                    conn.Open();
                    SqlDataReader reader = cmd.ExecuteReader();
                    while (reader.Read())
                    {
                        txtCode.Text = reader[0].ToString();
                        txtName.Text = reader[1].ToString();
                        txtQuantity.Text = reader[2].ToString();
                        txtCategory.Text = reader[3].ToString();
                        txtPrice.Text = reader[4].ToString();
                    }
                }
            }
            catch (SqlException ex)
            {
                Console.WriteLine("An error occurred: {0}", ex.Message);
            }
        }
    }
}
```

After you run the web form, the drop-down list shows all the existing product codes. Upon selecting a product code, you can access its information from the Products table displayed in the TextBox control below. A user can modify content in any of the

TextBox controls except the code text box. After modifying the desired data, when the user clicks the Update Product button, the Products table is updated with the supplied modified data and the message Product successfully updated (see Figure 16.26).

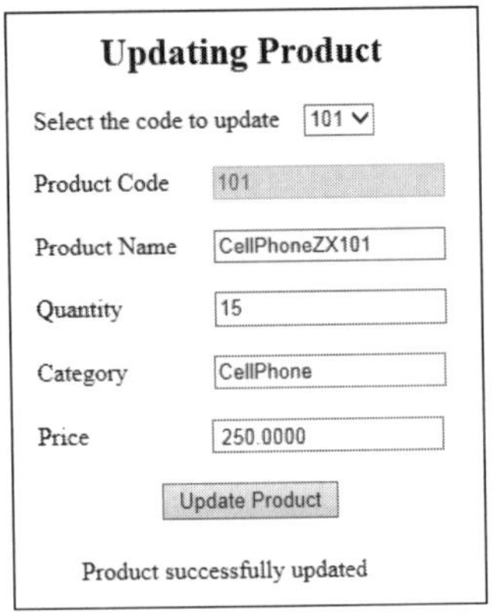

Figure 16.26
Message confirming that the product's information has been successfully updated.
Used with permission from Microsoft.

The preceding program can be modified easily to delete any product from the Products table. To do so, in the btnUpdate_Click function, you just need to replace the SQL UPDATE statement with the SQL DELETE statement in the cmd.CommandText property.

SUMMARY

In this chapter, you learned the major components of ADO.NET and different data providers. You reviewed the steps to connect or create a database, create a database table, access data from a database, create a connection to the server, open the connection, create a Command object, execute commands, close the connection, and release the resources. You learned to apply try . . . catch . . . finally, utilize the using keyword, display the table data through GridView, and insert rows in a database table. Finally, you learned the technique to use parameters with the Command object, call stored procedures, and update a database table.

The next chapter is focused on LINQ queries. You learn about query expressions, LINQ operators, deferred execution, and subqueries. In addition, you read about composition and projection strategies. You also discover how to build query expressions, apply filtering, project, join, order, and group. Finally, you learn to use conversion methods, aggregation methods, and generation methods.

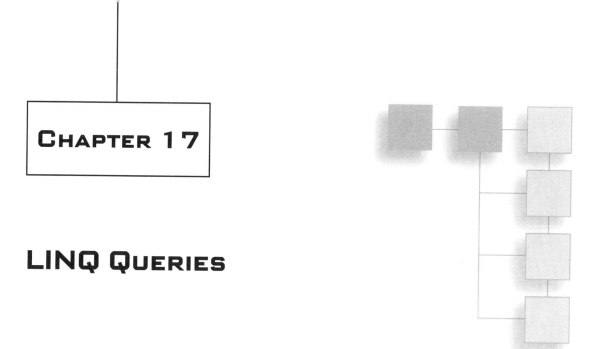

CHAPTER 17

LINQ QUERIES

This chapter's topics include the following:

- Implicitly typed local variables
- Object and collection initializers
- Lambda expressions
- Extension methods
- Anonymous types
- LINQ categories

LINQ is an acronym for the Language Integrated Query, and it's defined as a set of language and framework features used for writing structured type-safe queries as part of a programming language. It defines a set of standard query operators that make it possible to write queries in any of the .NET supported languages. LINQ was introduced in C# 3.0 and Framework 3.5.

The following are the benefits of using LINQ:

- It is available in all .NET platform languages such as C#.NET, VB.NET, and F#. NET.
- It makes it easier to extract data from several data sources (XML, SQL, objects, and so on).
- It provides support for querying in-memory collections like arrays, lists, XML, and datasets.

- It easily transforms data into objects and vice versa.

- It reduces SQL injection attacks, so it is more secure.

- It reduces the code size because it provides relatively short code for queries.

Precisely, LINQ is a strongly typed query language that you can embed directly into the C# programming language. Several programming constructs are added to .NET languages to support the LINQ technology set. Specifically, the C# language uses the following core LINQ-centric features:

- Implicitly typed local variables

- Object and collection initializers

- Lambda expressions

- Extension methods

- Anonymous types

You'll learn LINQ features one by one. You begin with implicitly typed local variables.

IMPLICITLY TYPED LOCAL VARIABLES

You can declare a local variable without specifying its type by using the keyword var. When the var keyword is used to declare a local variable, the compiler determines the type of the variable from its initialization. Following are a few implicitly typed variables:

```
var n = 10;
var msg = "Hello World!";
var price = 14.99;
var arrayInt = new[] {1, 2, 3};
```

To display the types of these variables, you can use the following statements:

```
Console.WriteLine("n is a: {0}", n.GetType().Name);
Console.WriteLine("msg is a: {0}", msg.GetType().Name);
Console.WriteLine("price is a: {0}", price.GetType().Name);
Console.WriteLine("arrayInt is a: {0}", arrayInt.GetType().Name);
```

This language feature is useful because many LINQ queries return a sequence of data types, which are not known until compile time. Therefore, you can't declare a variable explicitly. Using a var keyword simplifies the code and provides the benefits of strong types, such as compile-time validation and IntelliSense.

Next, you'll learn about the object and collection initializers.

OBJECT AND COLLECTION INITIALIZERS

Object initializers allow you to create a structure or a class and set one or more properties in one step. In other words, you can make an object ready to use through minimum and compact code. The following code initializes an object of the `Product` class using an initialization approach:

```
var prod = new Product {Code = 123, Name = "Laptop", Price = 310.99};
```

The preceding statement initializes the object `prod` and sets its three properties: `Code`, `Name`, and `Price`. This code is quite compact compared to the earlier traditional approach. The following statements initialize the `prod` object and its three properties through the traditional approach:

```
Product prod = new Product();
prod.Code = 123;
prod.Name = "Laptop";
prod.Price = 310.99;
```

The collection initializer, as the name suggests, initializes different types of collections. For example, the following statement initializes a `List` collection with certain `int` values:

```
var evennums = new List<int> {0, 2, 4, 6, 8};
```

Without the collection initializer, the code for initializing a collection would be too long, as shown in the following code:

```
List<int> evennums = new List<int>();
evennums.Add(0);
evennums.Add(2);
evennums.Add(4);
evennums.Add(6);
evennums.Add(8);
```

The next code demonstrates object and collection initializers. The code initializes a `List` collection that contains several objects of the `Product` class:

```
var prods = new List<Product> {
  new Product {Code=123, Name="Laptop", Price=310.99},
  new Product {Code=124, Name="Camera", Price=400.50}
}
```

The preceding code is compact. This syntax, when combined with implicit typing of local variables, allows you to declare an anonymous type, which is useful when creating a LINQ projection. You will learn about anonymous types later in this chapter.

Again, without collection and object initializers, the code would become quite long. For example, the following statements initialize a `List` collection that contains objects of the `Product` class without using object and collection initializers. You can see that the code is quite long compared to the compact code given earlier:

```
ProcessData tmp;
var prods = new List<Product>();
tmp = new Product();
tmp.Code = 123;
tmp.Name = "Laptop";
tmp.Price = 310.99;
prods.Add(tmp);
tmp = new Product();
tmp.Code = 124;
tmp.Name = "Camera";
tmp.Price = 400.50;
prods.Add(tmp);
```

Now that you understand the role of object and collection initializers, it's time to explore the benefit of using lambda expressions.

LAMBDA EXPRESSIONS

A *lambda expression* refers to an anonymous function that can contain expressions and statements. More precisely, a lambda expression is an inline delegate that represents an anonymous method.

Note

Delegates enable a method to be passed as an argument to other methods. Anonymous methods are unnamed inline statement blocks that you can execute in a delegate invocation.

A lambda expression consists of parameters followed by execution code in the following format:

```
Parameter => executioncode
```

The => symbol in the preceding format is known as a lambda operator and is read as "goes to." The left side of the lambda operator represents zero or more parameters, and the right side represents the execution code (the method body).

Example:

```
product =>product.Category == "Laptop", is read as "product goes to product.Category
equals Laptop".
```

Lambdas greatly simplify working with delegates. You can use a lambda expression to invoke a method that requires a delegate as an argument. The following example shows using a lambda expression to filter desired digits. There is an array with 10 digits in it, and even digits in the array are filtered out:

```
static void LambdaExpression()
{
    List<int> list = new List<int>{8, 5, 1, 0, 2,10, 6, 23, 18, 4};
    List<int> evenNums = list.FindAll(i => i % 2 == 0);
    Console.WriteLine("List of even numbers are:");
    foreach (int evenNumber in evenNums)
    {
        Console.WriteLine("{0}", evenNumber);
    }
}
```

The FindAll method in the preceding code uses the lambda expression to filter out the even values in the list. Parentheses are not required if the number of parameters is one. You can also define the return type in the lambda expression if required.

The following example explains delegates, the anonymous method, and their relation to the lambda expression:

```
// Defining a delegate that takes two int types and returns an int
public delegate int Calculate(int x, int y);

// Defining a method to which the delegate can point
static public int Rect(int x, int y)
{
    return x * y;
}
//Creating and initializing an instance of the delegate, and then calling it:
Calculate r = new Calculate(Rect);
Console.WriteLine ("Area of rectangle is "+ r(5,8));
```

You can see that the Rect method matches the delegate's method signature and takes two parameters of int type. Also, an instance named r is created of the delegate Calculate class and is set to refer to the Rect method.

An anonymous method is an inline, unnamed method in the code. It is created using the delegate keyword and doesn't require a name and return type. In other words, an anonymous method has only body without name, optional parameters, and return type. An anonymous method behaves like a regular method and allows you to write inline code in place of explicitly named methods.

Following is an anonymous method that takes two parameters and returns their multiplication:

```
Calculate r = new Calculate(
    delegate(int x, int y)
    {
        return x * y;
    }
);
Console.WriteLine ("Area of rectangle is "+ r(5,8));
```

With lambda expressions, the syntax becomes compact. The following lambda expression is an anonymous method that takes two arguments, x and y, and returns x * y.

```
Calculate r = (x, y) => x * y;
Console.WriteLine ("Area of rectangle is "+ r(5,8));
```

The data types of x and y and the return type of the lambda are inferred from the type of the delegate to which the lambda is assigned. You can even specify the type of the arguments, as shown in the following code:

```
Calculate r = (int x, int y) => x * y;
Console.WriteLine ("Area of rectangle is "+ r(5,8));
```

The types of x and y parameters are specified in the lambda expression.

Extension Methods

C# extension methods enable you to add new functionality to existing classes or types without deriving or recompiling them. The first parameter in an extension method is qualified with the this keyword and marks the type being extended. The extension methods must always be defined within a static class and must, therefore, also be declared using the static keyword. For example, suppose you want to check whether a string variable is a valid email address. You would do this by writing a function that takes a string as an argument and returns true or false. With extension methods, you can do the following:

```
namespace MyExtensions
{
    public static class Extensions {
        public static bool IsValidEmailAddress(this string s) {
            Regex regex = new Regex(@"^[\w-\.]+@([\w-]+\.)+[\w-]{2,4}$");
            return regex.IsMatch(s);
        }
    }
}
```

You defined a static class with a static method containing the extension method. Observe that the static method shown here has a `this` keyword before the first parameter argument of type `string`. The `this` keyword informs the compiler that this extension method (`IsValidEmailAddress`) should be added to objects of type `string`. The extension method can then be called from the `string` as a member function. To use the extension, an application must import the namespace defining the extension method:

```
using MyExtensions;

Console.Write("Enter your email address ");
string emailaddr = Console.ReadLine();
if ( emailaddr.IsValidEmailAddress() ) {
    .....
}
```

You can use several built-in extension methods to create LINQ query expressions.

LINQ query operators call and use the built-in extension methods. The LINQ standard query operators allow queries to be applied to the existing `System.Collections.IEnumerable` and `System.Collections.Generic.IEnumerable<T>` types.

You can use query expressions to filter out undesired information from any collection or database table. To use the standard query operators in building query expressions, you need to import the `System.Linq` namespace. Once you've imported `System.Linq`, any type that implements `IEnumerable<T>` can use extension methods, such as `GroupBy`, `OrderBy`, and `Average`.

The following example uses the standard query operators to process the contents of an array. The example defines a string array containing certain fruit names. The LINQ operators `where` and `orderby` are used to display the fruit names whose length is >=6 characters.

```
using System;
using System.Linq;
using System.Collections.Generic;

class queryop {
    static void Main() {
        string[] fruits = { "Apple", "Grapes", "Mango", "Banana", "Pineapple" };
        IEnumerable<string> selectedFruits = from f in fruits
            where f.Length >= 6
            orderby f
            select f;
        foreach (string fruit in selectedFruits)
            Console.WriteLine(fruit);
    }
}
```

The preceding code alphabetically displays the fruit names whose length is more than or equal to six characters.

Anonymous Types

Anonymous types represent the variables for which you don't need to define a data type in advance. The keyword var is used to define anonymous types. The compiler infers the type of the variable automatically by the expression that is written after the equal sign. Precisely, the var keyword informs the compiler to emit a strong type based on the value assigned to the variable.

For instance:

```
var str = "Hello World!";
```

The preceding statement defines an anonymous type and assigns the string value Hello World!.

You can also create a composite anonymous type by specifying the name of the object, followed by the = operator and the keyword new. You enumerate the names and the values of the properties of the anonymous type in curly braces.

```
var product = new { Code = 101, Name = "Laptop", Price = 310.99 };
```

The basic units of data in LINQ are sequences and elements. A *sequence* is any object that implements IEnumerable<T>, and an *element* is each item in the sequence. In the following example, products is a sequence, and Laptop, CellPhone, and Tablet are elements:

```
string[] products = { "Laptop", "CellPhone", "Tablet" };
```

You call this a local sequence because it represents a local collection of objects in memory. A *query operator* is a method that transforms an input sequence into an output sequence. Queries that operate over local sequences are called *local queries,* or LINQ-to-objects queries. A *query* is an expression that transforms sequences with query operators. The simplest query comprises one input sequence and one operator. For example, the following code creates a query named RequiredProducts that uses the where operator to fetch all the rows from the Products table whose price is >=$250.

Example:

```
var RequiredProducts =
    from s in Products
    where s.Price >=250
    select s;
```

```
Console.WriteLine("Products whose price is more than 250 dollars are:");
foreach (var f in RequiredProducts) {
    Console.WriteLine("{0} {1} {2} ", f.Code, f.Name, f.Price);
}
```

Similarly, the following example extracts the array elements whose length (number of characters) is greater than or equal to four digits:

```
string[] products = { "Laptop", "CellPhone", "Tablet" };
IEnumerable<string> selectedprods = System.Linq.Enumerable.Where
(products, n => n.Length >= 4);
foreach (string n in selectedprods)
    Console.WriteLine (n);
```

What follows is a quick look at the LINQ categories.

LINQ CATEGORIES

As mentioned earlier, LINQ simplifies the interaction between different data sources and .NET-supported programming languages. Specifically, LINQ is a toolset that you can use to access data coming from different resources. Based on its application, LINQ is categorized as follows:

- **LINQ to Objects**—Used to apply LINQ queries to in-memory objects like arrays and collections
- **LINQ to XML**—Used to apply LINQ to manipulate and query XML documents
- **LINQ to SQL**—Used to apply LINQ queries to databases
- **LINQ to DataSet**—Used to apply LINQ queries to ADO.NET `DataSet` objects
- **LINQ to Entities**—Used to apply LINQ queries within the ADO.NET Entity Framework (EF) application programming interface (API)

Remember, LINQ can be applied to any type of data.

LINQ to Objects

You'll learn to apply LINQ queries to the arrays. To do so, launch Visual Studio for Web and create a new class library project called `LINQToObjectApp`.

Assume that a string array exists containing some fruit names, and you want to filter the fruit names whose length is more than six characters. Prior to LINQ, this task was done by writing the code as shown in Listing 17.1 in the `Class1.cs` file.

Listing 17.1 Program Code in Class1.cs File

```csharp
using System;
using System.Collections.Generic;
using System.Linq;
using System.Text;
using System.Threading.Tasks;

namespace LINQToObjectApp
{
    public class Class1
    {
        static void Main(string[] args)
        {
            string[] fruits = { "Apple", "Grapes", "Mango", "Banana", "Pineapple" };
            string[] selectedFruits = new string[5];
            for (int i = 0; i < fruits.Length; i++)
            {
                if (fruits[i].Length >=6)
                    selectedFruits[i] = fruits[i];
            }
            Array.Sort(selectedFruits);
            foreach (string fruit in selectedFruits)
            {
                if (fruit != null)
                    Console.WriteLine(fruit);
            }
            Console.ReadKey();
        }
    }
}
```

To filter the fruit names whose length is greater than or equal to six characters, you use a for loop, where the length of each fruit name is computed, and the ones whose length is greater than or equal to six characters are stored in a temporary array called selectedFruits. The selectedFruits array is then sorted alphabetically. Thereafter, using the foreach loop, the fruit names in the selectedFruits array are accessed and displayed on the screen.

This task of filtering out the desired elements from the array can be greatly simplified by applying LINQ operators. To apply LINQ operators, modify the Class1.cs file to appear as shown in Listing 17.2.

Listing 17.2 Program Code in Class1.cs File

```
using System;
using System.Collections.Generic;
using System.Linq;
using System.Text;
using System.Threading.Tasks;

namespace LINQToObjectApp
{
    public class Class1
    {
        static void Main(string[] args)
        {
            string[] fruits = { "Apple", "Grapes", "Mango", "Banana", "Pineapple" };
            IEnumerable<string> selectedFruits = from f in fruits     // #1
                where f.Length >= 6
                orderby f
                select f;
            foreach (string fruit in selectedFruits)
                Console.WriteLine(fruit);
            Console.ReadKey();
        }
    }
}
```

The query expression created in Listing 17.2 uses the `from`, `in`, `where`, `orderby`, and `select` LINQ query operators. The returned sequence is held in a variable named `selectedFruits`, of a type that implements the generic version of `IEnumerable<T>`, where `T` is of type `System.String`. From the obtained result set, you simply print each item using a standard `foreach` construct.

The LINQ expression through statement #1 in Listing 17.2 can be replaced by the lambda expression shown here:

```
IEnumerable<string> selectedFruits = fruits
    .Where(n => n.Length >=6)
    .OrderBy(n => n);
```

After running the application, the fruit names that satisfy the specified criteria are displayed as shown in Figure 17.1.

Note

To execute the class library project, you need to set its output type to Console Application. To do so, right-click the project in Solution Explorer and select the Properties option. From the Properties dialog, click the Application tab and in the Output Type drop-down, select Console Application.

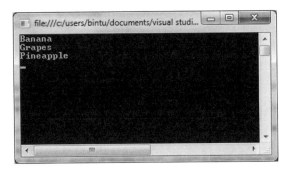

Figure 17.1
Displaying fruit names whose length is greater than or equal to six characters.
Used with permission from Microsoft.

Therefore, you see that the LINQ query expressions greatly simplify the task of accessing required data from the arrays.

LINQ to XML

Traditionally, XML APIs are used to deal with XML data. These APIs include `XmlDocument`, `XmlReader`, `XPathNavigator`, `XslTransform` for `XSLT`, and `SAX` and `XQuery` implementations. Several lines of code are required to use these APIs in applications. LINQ to XML, on the other hand, enables application of XML query in any of the .NET programming languages with minimum code. LINQ to XML also facilitates editing of XML documents and element trees. In other words, you can perform XML processing tasks, exchange data between applications, store configuration information, persist temporary data, and generate web pages or reports with ease.

You can work with entire XML documents as well as fragments like elements and attributes. To work with XML, LINQ to XML uses two classes called `XmlReader` and `XmlWriter`.

To understand how an XML document composed of certain elements and attributes can be created, launch Visual Studio for Web and create a new class library project called `LINQToXMLApp`.

In this application, you create an XML document that displays information about three products. The product's code, name, and price are displayed in the form of XML elements and attributes. To manage the code, name, and price of the product, you create a class called `Product`, along with a constructor, to initialize class members. To display product information in the XML format, write the code as shown in Listing 17.3 into the `Class1.cs` file.

Listing 17.3 Program Code in Class1.cs File

```csharp
using System;
using System.Collections.Generic;
using System.Linq;
using System.Text;
using System.Threading.Tasks;
using System.Xml;
using System.Xml.Linq;

class Product
{
    public string Code;
    public string Name;
    public float Price;
    public Product(string code, string name, float price)
    {
        Code = code;
        Name = name;
        Price = price;
    }
}

namespace LINQToXMLApp
{
    public class Class1
    {
        static void Main()
        {
            Product[] Products = new Product[] {
                new Product("C101", "Laptop", 299.99f),
                new Product("C102", "CellPhone", 249.99f),
                new Product("C103", "Tablet", 275.99f)
            };
            XElement xml = new XElement("Products",
                from Product in Products
                where Product.Price >=250
                select new XElement("Product",
                    new XAttribute("Code", Product.Code),
                        new XElement("Name", Product.Name),
                        new XElement("Price", Product.Price)
                    )
                );
            Console.WriteLine(xml);
            Console.ReadLine();
        }
    }
}
```

You can see that an array of objects of the Product class is created named Products. Three Product objects are initialized and assigned to the Products array. An XML element is defined called xml, in which the products whose price is greater than or equal to $250 are assigned. The product's code, name, and price are finally displayed on the screen in XML format. When you run the application, the product information is displayed in XML format, as shown in Figure 17.2.

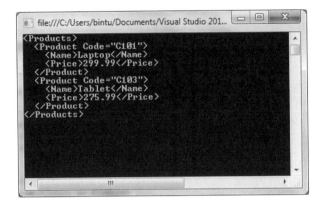

Figure 17.2
Displaying products information in XML format.
Used with permission from Microsoft.

Now you'll learn to use LINQ to SQL.

LINQ to SQL

LINQ to SQL is an Object Relational Mapping (ORM) implementation that enables you to model a relational database using .NET classes. It enables mapping of a table to a class, table's columns to properties of the class, and relationships between tables through additional properties. Once a table is mapped, you can query the database using LINQ and update, insert, and delete data from it. Using LINQ to SQL, you can easily apply database transactions, validations, and business logics to the data model. LINQ to SQL automatically tracks changes made to the objects and updates the database accordingly through dynamic SQL queries or stored procedures.

To understand the concept through a running example, launch Visual Studio for Web and create a new class library project called LINQToSQLApp. In this application, you will use the Products table that you created in the CSharpSampleDatabase database in Chapter 16, "ADO.NET." The application displays all the product names whose price is greater than or equal to $250.

To work with LINQ to SQL, you need classes that represent the database tables and the relationships between them, if any. Such classes are known as `DataContext`, and all the queries and other database management tasks are implemented through these modeled classes. To create a `DataContext`, you use the LINQ to SQL Classes template. So right-click the application in the Solution Explorer window and select Add, New Item. Select LINQ to SQL Classes. The default name of the file, `DataClasses1.dbml`, appears. Assign the filename as `ProductsClasses.dbml` (see Figure 17.3), and then click Add.

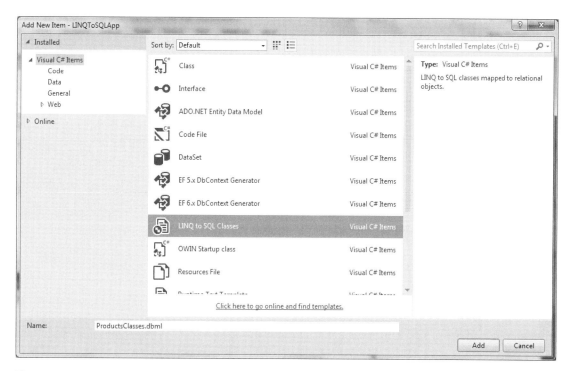

Figure 17.3
Adding the LINQ to SQL class called ProductsClasses.dbml to the application.
Used with permission from Microsoft.

The Object Relational Designer will open. From Server Explorer, drag and drop the `Products` table from `CSharpSampleDatabase` into the left pane of the designer surface. It should appear as shown in Figure 17.4.

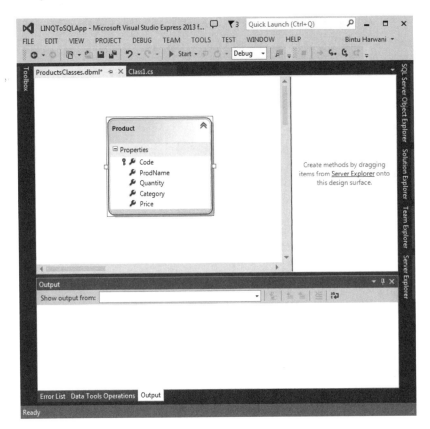

Figure 17.4
Dropping the Products table to the left pane of the Object Relational Designer.
Used with permission from Microsoft.

When you click the Save button, Visual Studio generates a DataContext class that represents the entities and database relationships you modeled. The DataContext class will have properties that represent each table modeled within the database, as well as methods for each stored procedure (if any) that has been added. It is through this DataContext class that you will query entities from the database and apply database management tasks.

Note

The purpose of DataContext is to translate requests for objects into SQL queries made against the database and then assemble objects out of the results.

The preceding step automatically creates a connection string for you in the app.config file, as shown here:

```
<connectionStrings>
    <add name="LINQToSQLApp.Properties.Settings.CSharpSampleDatabaseConnectionString"
        connectionString="Data Source=(local);Initial Catalog=CSharpSampleDatabase;
        Integrated Security=True"
        providerName="System.Data.SqlClient" />
</connectionStrings>
```

The connection string helps to connect with the desired tables in the database. To display the products whose price is more than or equal to $250, open the Class1.cs file and write the code as shown in Listing 17.4.

Listing 17.4 Program Code in Class1.cs File

```
using System;
using System.Collections.Generic;
using System.Linq;
using System.Text;
using System.Threading.Tasks;
using System.Data.Linq;

namespace LINQToSQLApp
{
    public class Class1
    {
        static void Main(string[] args)
        {
            ProductsClassesDataContext db = new ProductsClassesDataContext();
            Table<Product> Productstab = db.GetTable<Product>();
            IQueryable<string> query = from c in Productstab
                where c.Price >= 250
                select c.ProdName;
            Console.WriteLine("Products whose price is more than 250 dollars are:");
            foreach (string ProdName in query) Console.WriteLine(ProdName);
            Console.ReadLine();
        }
    }
}
```

You can see that a context object is created called db. The GetTable() method is called on the db context to access the Products table, and it's assigned to Productstab. From Productstab, all the rows of the products that have price >=250 are accessed, and only the ProdName column is assigned to the IQueryable object query. Finally, using the foreach loop, all the names of the products in the query object are accessed and displayed on the screen, as shown in Figure 17.5.

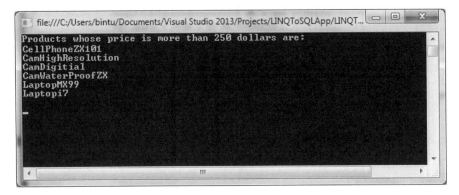

Figure 17.5
Showing product names that have a price greater than $250.
Used with permission from Microsoft.

To display all the columns or fields of the products whose price >=250, modify the code in Class1.cs file to appear as shown in Listing 17.5.

Listing 17.5 Program Code in Class1.cs File

```
using System;
using System.Collections.Generic;
using System.Linq;
using System.Text;
using System.Threading.Tasks;
using System.Data.Linq;

namespace LINQToSQLApp
{
    public class Class1
    {
        static void Main(string[] args)
        {
            ProductsClassesDataContext db = new ProductsClassesDataContext();
            var query = from c in db.Products
                where c.Price >= 250
                select new { c.Code, c.ProdName, c.Quantity, c.Category, c.Price };
            Console.WriteLine("Products whose price is more than 250 dollars are:");
            Console.WriteLine("Code\tName\tQuantity\tCategory\tPrice");
```

```
    foreach (var product in query)
        Console.WriteLine("{0}\t{1}\t{2}\t{3}\t{4}", product.Code,
            product.ProdName, product.Quantity, product.Category, product.Price);
    Console.ReadLine();
    }
  }
}
```

You can see that the select clause in Listing 17.5 includes Code, ProdName, and Price. Hence, all three fields—Code, ProdName, and Price—of the rows of the products that have a price >=250 are accessed from the query object and displayed on the screen, as shown in Figure 17.6.

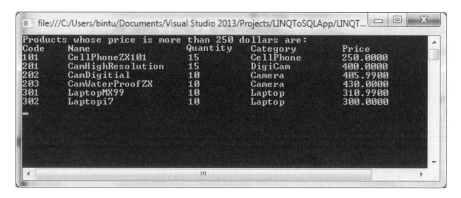

Figure 17.6
Showing complete Products rows that have a price greater than $250.
Used with permission from Microsoft.

You might be wondering if, instead of console applications, you can create websites that use LINQ. Yes, of course! The following example creates a website that accesses all rows of the Products table using LINQ and displays them through the GridView control.

Create an empty website called LINQToSQLSite. Add a web form called Default.aspx to the site, and drag and drop a GridView control on the form. To add DataContext to the application, right-click the application in the Solution Explorer window and select Add, Add New Item. Select the LINQ to SQL Classes template. Assign the filename as ProductsClasses.dbml, and click the Add button (see Figure 17.7). The Object Relational Designer opens. From the Server Explorer, drag and drop the Products table from the CSharpSampleDatabase into the left pane of the designer surface. This creates all the mappings and settings for your `Products` table and its entities. It also creates a connection string for you in the `Web.config` file, as shown here:

```
<connectionStrings>
    <add name="CSharpSampleDatabaseConnectionString" connectionString="Data Source
        =(local);Initial Catalog=CSharpSampleDatabase;Integrated Security=True"
        providerName="System.Data.SqlClient" />
</connectionStrings>
```

The connection string helps connect with your `Products` table in `CSharpSampleDatabase`. Now open the `Default.aspx` web form and drag and drop a `GridView` control on it. To display the products that have a price greater than or equal to $250 through the `GridView` control, open the code file `Default.aspx.cs` and write the code as shown in Listing 17.6.

Listing 17.6 Program Code in Default.aspx.cs File

```
using System;
using System.Collections.Generic;
using System.Linq;
using System.Web;
using System.Web.UI;
using System.Web.UI.WebControls;
public partial class _Default : System.Web.UI.Page
{
    protected void Page_Load(object sender, EventArgs e)
    {
        ProductsClassesDataContext db = new ProductsClassesDataContext();
        var products = from c in db.Products
            where c.Price >= 250
            select c;
        GridView1.DataSource = products;
        GridView1.DataBind();
    }
}
```

A context called `db` is created. Using the `db` context, the `Products` table is accessed, and all the rows that have a price >=250 are assigned to `products`. The data source `products` is bound to the `GridView` control to display rows on the screen, as shown in Figure 17.7.

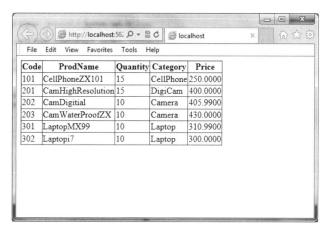

Figure 17.7
Displaying products rows displayed through GridView control.
Used with permission from Microsoft.

SUMMARY

In this chapter, you learned to use LINQ in the C# programming language. You saw how LINQ shrinks code and performs different tasks with ease. You explored LINQ-centric features such as implicitly typed local variables, object and collection initializers, and lambda expressions. You saw how anonymous methods, extension methods, and anonymous types are used in .NET applications. Finally, you explored LINQ categories like LINQ to Objects, LINQ to XML, and LINQ to SQL through step-by-step running applications.

In the next chapter, you learn how to develop web applications and how to handle sessions. You also learn about some frequently used tools and their implementations and how to program web services. Finally, you learn to create server-side and client-side ASP.NET web services and learn the procedure to test them.

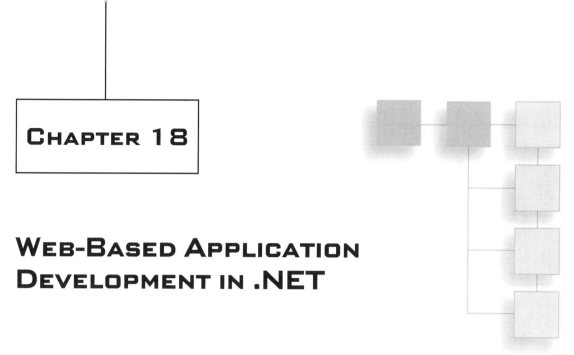

CHAPTER 18

WEB-BASED APPLICATION DEVELOPMENT IN .NET

This chapter's topics include the following:

- Examining the Visual Studio toolbox
- Building your first web application
- Using the CheckBox control
- Using the RadioButton control
- Using the ListBox control
- Using the LinkButton control
- Using the HyperLink control
- Using the ImageButton control
- Working with WCF
- Creating a client application

Visual Studio has several tools that make the task of creating websites much easier. To design a great user interface, you don't have to write code; all you need to do is drag the desired tools from the respective toolbox and drop them on the web form. From there, you can configure the tools as per your requirement. Visual Studio automatically generates code for the user tools and their configurations. Before you develop websites in Visual Studio, you'll look at different tools provided in the Visual Studio toolbox.

EXAMINING THE VISUAL STUDIO TOOLBOX

The toolbox in Visual Studio 2013 is divided into several tabs, as shown in Figure 18.1.

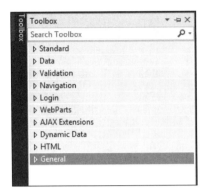

Figure 18.1
Different tools in the toolbox.
Used with permission from Microsoft.

Table 18.1 contains the overview of different tabs in the toolbox.

Table 18.1   Different Tabs in the Toolbox

Tab	Controls Included in the Section
Standard	Contains the standard `<asp:>` controls, such as `TextBox`, `Button`, `RadioButton`, `CheckBox`, and so on, which are usually required in standard web applications.
Data	Includes all the controls that deal with the retrieval and display of data from any database. This section includes the data source controls `SqlDataSource`, `AccessDataSource`, and so on, as well as `GridView`, `DetailsView`, and `DataList`, to display the retrieved data in tabular format.
Validation	Includes all the validation controls, such as `RequiredFieldValidator` and `RegularExpressionValidator`, which validate the data the user enters before it's processed.
Navigation	Includes controls that allow users to navigate to various pages of a website. It includes controls like `SiteMapPath`, `Menu`, and `TreeView`. These controls offer menus on your website or supply pages of your website in the form of nodes. Users can easily go to any web form by selecting either the respective menu item from the menu or the desired node from the `TreeView`.
Login	Contains all controls that deal with adding user login and password capabilities to your ASP.NET applications, such as `Login`, `CreateUserWizard`, and `PasswordRecovery`.

WebParts	Includes controls like `WebPartManager`, `WebPartZone`, and `CatalogZone`, which are used to make *portals* (web pages having modular contents that the user can customize).
AJAX Extensions	AJAX stands for Asynchronous JavaScript and XML. These controls are meant for building highly responsive web apps with the least effort.
Dynamic Data	Used to obtain schema information at runtime. These controls also provide default display formats and enable you to easily customize these formats at runtime.
HTML	Includes the Hypertext Markup Language (HTML) server controls. While doing ASP.NET programming, in addition to web server controls, you can use HTML server controls.
General	Remains empty so you can place your own custom controls in it.

© 2015 Cengage Learning®.

The Standard toolbox tab contains several controls. A few of the commonly used standard controls are mentioned next:

- **Label control**—Displays simple text on the web form that can be made invisible or visible to display desired information to the user. To display text through the `Label` control, you use its `Text` property. You can configure the `Text`, `Font`, `BackColor`, and `ForeColor` properties to display the text in a desired font and color.

- **TextBox control**—Accepts data from the user. The data entered in this control is in `Text` form which, if desired, can be converted to integer or float by the respective conversion functions `Convert.ToInt32()`, `Convert.ToSingle()`, `Convert.ToDecimal()`, and so on. By using the `TextMode` property of this control, you can make a `TextBox` accept a single line or multiple lines of text. You can avoid alteration of contents of any `TextBox` by setting its `ReadOnly` property to `true`. The facility of setting the `Font`, `Size`, `Backcolor`, and `Forecolor` is always available.

- **Button control**—Fires an event. Through this control, you can execute a block of statements when a click or some other event takes place on the `Button` control. Most commonly, you use the `Button` controls to submit the web forms (for posting the form back to the server). In ASP.NET, there are three types of buttons:
  - **Button**—Standard button that you usually find as a pressable control on a web form.
  - **LinkButton**—Button that behaves as a hyperlink and helps you navigate to the desired web form.

- **ImageButton**—Button that displays a graphics image instead of text on a button. In other words, it is a graphical button.

- **DropDown List control**—Displays a list of options to the user. This control takes less space because it is in collapsed mode when it is not in use.

- **ListBox control**—Offers a fixed-size list of items to choose from.

- **CheckBox and RadioButton controls**—`CheckBox` allows you to choose more than one option. `RadioButton` controls, in contrast, are exclusive, which means you can select only one option from a set of those available.

- **HyperLink control**—Helps you navigate to another web form of the same website or to any other resources on the Internet.

- **Image control**—Displays images on a page.

- **Calendar control**—Displays a fully featured calendar on your web form. You can easily move to any month and select any specific day. You can double-click on any date to retrieve it. To get the date in the format you want, you can use several methods, including `ToLocalTime` and `ToShortDateString`.

You can configure each control through the properties attached to it. Also, each control has a certain event associated to it. These events are linked with respective event handlers to take action when events occur. For example, a click event is associated to a `Button` control that is fired when a user clicks on it. Each event is represented by a unique method, and the code that you want to execute on occurrence of that event must be written in that method. The `Button1_Click()` method, for example, is associated to the `Button1` control, which is invoked when a click event occurs on the `Button1` control. So you must write the code that you want to execute when the `Button1` control is clicked in the `Button1_Click()` method.

Almost all controls have certain properties in common. Table 18.2 briefly describes those common properties of controls.

Table 18.2   Common Properties of Controls

Property	Description
AccessKey	Assigns shortcut keys to a control. If you assign AccessKey say, as b, to any control, you can access that control by using the shortcut key Alt+b.
BackColor	Controls the background color of the selected control.
BorderColor	Assigns a specified color to the physical edge of the server control.

BorderWidth	Specifies the width in pixels to the border of the control.
BorderStyle	Assigns a design to the border of the selected server control. By default, the border is created as a straight line, but a number of different styles, such as Dotted, Dashed, Solid, Double, Groove, Ridge, Inset, and Outset, are available.
Enabled	Enables or disables any control. If Enabled is set to false, that control is disabled (meaning no event takes place on that control). By default, the Enabled property is set to true.
EnableTheming	Enables you to turn on theming capabilities for the selected server control. The default value is true.
Font	Sets the font of the text that appears in the control.
ForeColor	Sets the foreground color of the text that appears on the control.
Height	Sets the height of the control.
SkinID	Sets the skin to use when applying themes to the control.
CssClass	Enables you to apply CSS (Cascading Style Sheet) classes to the control.
TabIndex	Sets the control's tab position in the ASP.NET page. This property works in conjunction with other controls on the page.
ToolTip	Assigns ToolTip text to the selected control, which provides information to the user about the control.
Width	Sets the width of the control.

© 2015 Cengage Learning®.

After using any control in the web form, Visual Studio auto-generates its code representing the control and the properties that are set for it. For example, the following code is auto-generated when you drag and drop a Button control onto the web form:

```
<asp:Button ID="btnCalculate" runat="server" Text="Calculate Bill"/>
```

The preceding statement informs you that btnCalculate is the ID of the Button control. A unique ID is essential to identify and access a control. The runat attribute indicates that this control is a server control. (It executes on the server, not on the client machine.) When a web form containing certain server controls is accessed from a web server (either from IIS or a built-in server of Visual Studio 2013), the server controls are converted to HTML elements dynamically so that the client's browser can understand them. The Text property indicates that the Button control has the caption Calculate Bill.

Server controls have certain events attached to them that specify the code you want to execute when the particular event occurs on that control. The following code states that the method `btnCalculate_Click` will be invoked when the click event occurs on the `Button` control:

```
<asp:Button ID="btnCalculate" runat="server" Text="Calculate Bill"
OnClick="btnCalculate_Click" />
```

Now that you know about basic controls, you'll begin developing small websites.

BUILDING YOUR FIRST WEB APPLICATION

You are going to make a website in which a user enters the product name, the quantity of products purchased, and the cost of the product. After you click the Calculate Bill button, the bill of the products purchased (cost*quantity) is displayed.

To create a new empty website, launch Visual Studio and select File, New Web Site. Select the Visual C# language from the left tab and the ASP.NET Empty Web Site template from the right tab. Assign the name `CalculateBillApp` to the website, and click OK, as shown in Figure 18.2.

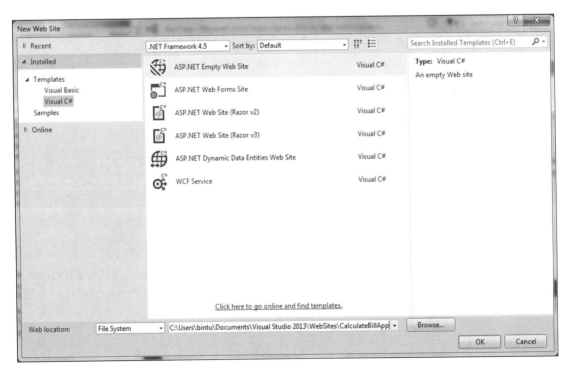

Figure 18.2
Creating a new website named CalculateBillApp.
Used with permission from Microsoft.

Initially, your website is empty, so you need at least one web form to create a user interface. You'll add a web form named `Default.aspx` to the website by right-clicking it in the Solution Explorer window and selecting Add, Add New Item from the pop-up menu. After you add a web form, its code-behind file `Default.aspx.cs` is automatically added to your `CalculateBillApp` website.

ASP.NET provides the following two types of coding styles:

- **Inline coding**—In this coding style, the same file contains standard HTML code, Active Server Pages (ASP) tags that define the server controls used on the web form, and the coding that controls the operation of the controls used on the web form.

- **Code-behind file**—In this coding style, a web form is divided into two files. The first file contains standard HTML code and ASP tags that define the server controls used on the web form. This file is saved with the extension `.aspx`. The second file contains the coding in the selected programming language that controls the operation of the controls used on the web form. This file is saved with the extension `.aspx.cs` (because you are using C# programming language in this book) and is called the code-behind file because it provides the code behind the web form.

You can open a web form in the following three modes:

- **Design**—Creates a user interface. In Design mode, you can drag and drop controls onto the web form.

- **Code**—Displays the code that is auto-generated for the controls dropped on the web form. The code also represents properties and events that are associated with the controls.

- **Split**—Enables dragging and dropping of controls and simultaneously displays the generated code.

You open your `Default.aspx` web form in Design mode and drag and drop five `Label`, four `TextBox`, and a `Button` control on it, as shown in Figure 18.3.

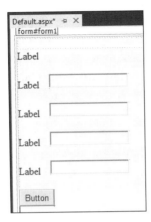

Figure 18.3
Controls placed in Default.aspx web form of CalculateBillApp website.
Used with permission from Microsoft.

Set the Text property of the Label1 control to Online Store, as shown in Figure 18.4.
Also, set its Font to X-Large and its Bold property to True.

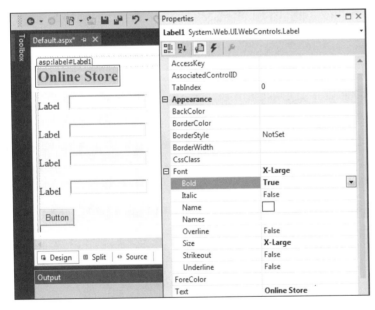

Figure 18.4
Setting the Text property of the Label1 control.
Used with permission from Microsoft.

Similarly, set the `Text` properties of the `Label` and `Button` controls as shown in Table 18.3.

Table 18.3   Setting the Text Property of Controls

Control	Text Property
Label2	Product Name
Label3	Quantity
Label4	Cost
Label5	Amount
Button1	Calculate Bill

© 2015 Cengage Learning®.

Also, set the `ID` properties of the `TextBox` and `Button` controls as shown in Table 18.4.

Table 18.4   Setting the ID Property of Controls

Control	ID
TextBox1	txtProductName
TextBox2	txtQuantity
TextBox3	txtCost
TextBox4	txtAmount
Button1	btnCalculate

© 2015 Cengage Learning®.

After you set the `Text` and `ID` properties of the controls, the `Default.aspx` web form appears like what's shown in Figure 18.5.

Figure 18.5
Controls in Default.aspx web form.
Used with permission from Microsoft.

After you place the said controls in the Default.aspx web form and set their Text and ID properties, the auto-generated code appears, as shown in Listing 18.1. The code represents the controls, their locations on the web form, and their Size, Font, Text, ID, and other properties.

Listing 18.1 Program Code in Default.aspx File

```
<%@ Page Language="C#" AutoEventWireup="true" CodeFile="Default.aspx.cs"
Inherits="_Default" %>
<!DOCTYPE html>
<html xmlns="http://www.w3.org/1999/xhtml">
<head runat="server">
    <title></title>
</head>
<body>
    <form id="form1" runat="server">
    <div>
    </div>
        <asp:Label ID="Label1" runat="server" Font-Bold="True" Font-Size="X-Large"
Text="Online Store"></asp:Label>
        <br />
        <br />
        <asp:Label ID="Label2" runat="server" Text="Product Name"></asp:Label>
        <asp:TextBox ID="txtProductName" runat="server"></asp:TextBox>
        <br />
        <br />
        <asp:Label ID="Label3" runat="server" Text="Quantity"></asp:Label>
        <asp:TextBox ID="txtQuantity" runat="server"></asp:TextBox>
        <br />
        <br />
```

```
            <asp:Label ID="Label4" runat="server" Text="Cost"></asp:Label>
            <asp:TextBox ID="txtCost" runat="server"></asp:TextBox>
            <br />
            <br />
            <asp:Label ID="Label5" runat="server" Text="Amount"></asp:Label>
            <asp:TextBox ID="txtAmount" runat="server"></asp:TextBox>
            <br />
            <br />
            <asp:Button ID="btnCalculate" runat="server" Text="Calculate Bill" />
            <br />
            <br />
    </form>
</body>
</html>
```

Most of the code is easy to understand. It simply represents the controls placed on the web form and their respective properties. The first statement, the Page directive, does need an explanation.

The Page directive begins with <%@ and ends with %>. This special sequence of characters is called a *directive block*. It is not sent to the browser in HTML format when the page is displayed. ASP.NET processes directive blocks when the page is compiled. This block contains the following attributes:

- **Language**—This is used to specify the language in which the web form is coded.

- **AutoEventWireup**—This causes the page event handlers, such as Init and Load, to be executed automatically whenever these events occur. This attribute is usually set to Boolean value true.

- **CodeFile**—This is for specifying the code-behind file. The concept of a code-behind file leads to creation of two files. One of the files contains the standard HTML code and ASP tags that represent the controls used on the web form. This file is saved with the extension .aspx. The second file contains the coding in the selected programming language that defines the operation of the controls placed on the web form. This file is saved with the extension .aspx.cs and is called the code-behind file.

- **Inherits**—This provides the name of the compiled class that the page inherits at runtime.

The set of tags that defines the DOCTYPE declaration tells the browser about the HTML version that is being used. An HTML document body consists of a single div element within a form element. The `div` element contains all the ASP and HTML elements for the form. It can also be used to apply formatting to all its elements. Recall that the attribute `runat=server` means the control will be processed on the server by ASP.NET.

The user interface is ready. Next, you want to write the code that accesses the values entered into the Quantity and Cost boxes, multiplies the values, and displays the result in the Amount text box. But you want this computation and result to appear when a user clicks the `Button` control. In short, you want to make an event-driven program that displays the result when an event occurs. Because you want the result to appear when the user clicks the `Button` control, you have to write code in the `Click` method of the `Button` control. So double-click the `Button` control to write the code for its `btnCalculate_Click()` method in the code-behind file `Default.aspx.cs`. Make the `Default.aspx.cs` file look like Listing 18.2.

Listing 18.2 Program Code in Default.aspx.cs File

```
using System;
using System.Collections.Generic;
using System.Linq;
using System.Web;
using System.Web.UI;
using System.Web.UI.WebControls;
public partial class _Default : System.Web.UI.Page
{
    protected void Page_Load(object sender, EventArgs e)
    {
    }
    protected void btnCalculate_Click(object sender, EventArgs e)
    {
        int q;
        float r,a;
        q = Convert.ToInt32(txtQuantity.Text);
        r = Convert.ToSingle(txtCost.Text);
        a = q * r;
        txtAmount.Text = a.ToString();
    }
}
```

In Listing 18.2, an integer variable, `q`, and two float variables, `r` and `a`, are defined. The quantity of products the user enters in the `txtQuantity` control is retrieved and assigned to variable q after converting the text to integer format. The `Convert.ToInt32()` function converts text to an integer. Similarly, the cost of products entered into `txtCost` is retrieved and stored in variable r after converting the `Text` data type into a `Single` type (into a single-precision floating-point number). Then the values in the q and r variables are multiplied, and the resultant amount is assigned to variable a. The amount in variable a is assigned to the `Text` property of the control `txtAmount`. The float value in variable a is converted into a string before assigning it to the `Text` property of the `txtAmount` control.

The `btnCalculate_Click()` method in Listing 18.2 is an event handler method that contains the code that you want to execute on occurrence of the click event on the `Button` control. Table 18.5 shows the list of events and the controls to which they are associated.

Table 18.5   List of Controls and Their Common Events

Event	Attribute	Controls
Click	OnClick	Button, ImageButton, LinkButton, ImageMap
Command	OnCommand	Button, ImageButton, LinkButton
TextChanged	OnTextChanged	TextBox
SelectedIndexChanged	OnSelectedIndexChanged	DropDownList, ListBox, RadioButtonList, CheckBoxList
CheckedChanged	OnCheckedChanged	CheckBox, RadioButton

© 2015 Cengage Learning®.

One more thing that requires explanation in Listing 18.2 is the `Page_Load` method. When a page is requested from the server, two events take place: `Init` and `Load`. Of these two events, an `Init` event occurs first and is raised so that the view state of the page and its controls can be restored. After all controls have been initialized, a `Page_Load` event is invoked to perform initialization of form controls, defining `SqlConnection` (if any), retrieving some data, and so on. Therefore, the `Page_Load` method is invoked whenever the page is loaded for processing. Here's the syntax of `Page_Load`:

```
protected void Page_Load(object sender, System.EventArgs e)
```

- The protected access specifier designates that only those programs that are within the same class can use this method.

- The void keyword means that this event-handling method is not going to return a value.

- The parameters in parentheses (object sender, System.EventArgs e) are variables that ASP.NET passes to the event method. The sender is the object that raises the event. And the second parameter, e, contains the additional information that the event-handling method may require.

After running the website, you get the output shown in Figure 18.6.

Figure 18.6
Output of CalculateBillApp website.
Used with permission from Microsoft.

After you enter the product name, quantity, cost, and amount, when you click Calculate Bill, the btnCalculate_Click method is invoked and displays the amount.

Now you'll add one feature to your website: CalculateBillApp. You want to compute the discount on the total amount of the products sold. To calculate the discount, you'll add two more Label and TextBox controls to the Default.aspx web form. Change the Text properties of the Label6 and Label7 controls to Discount and Net Amount, respectively. Set the ID of the TextBox5 and TextBox6 controls to txtDiscount and txtNetAmount. After you add these controls and set the properties, your Default.aspx web form appears as shown in Figure 18.7.

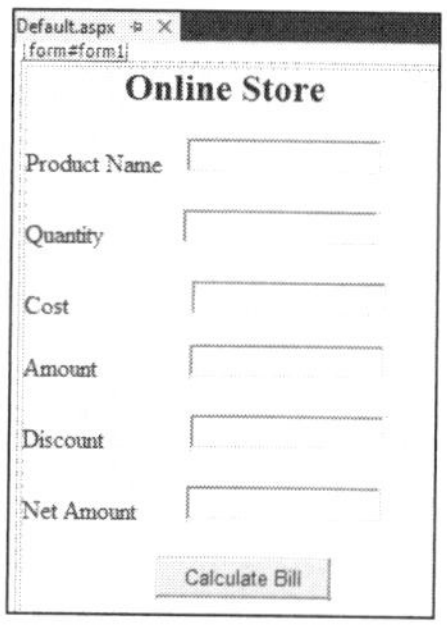

Figure 18.7
Default.aspx web form after setting the Text property of two Label and TextBox controls.
Used with permission from Microsoft.

After you click the Calculate Bill button, you want to compute the Amount, Discount, and Net Amount based on the formula given here:

```
Amount=Quantity * Cost
Discount=10% of Amount
Net Amount=Amount-Discount
```

Because you want these things to be computed and displayed after you click the Calculate Bill button, you need to write the code in the click event handler method of the Button control. So double-click the Calculate Bill button and write the code as shown here:

```
protected void btnCalculate_Click(object sender, EventArgs e)
{
    int q;
    float d,n, r,a;
    q = Convert.ToInt32(txtQuantity.Text);
    r = Convert.ToSingle(txtCost.Text);
    a = q * r;
    d = (float)a * 10 / 100;
    n = a - d;
    txtAmount.Text = a.ToString();
    txtDiscount.Text = d.ToString();
    txtNetAmount.Text = n.ToString();
}
```

You have included two more float variables: d and n (for storing values of Discount and Net Amount, respectively). The Quantity the user enters in the txtQuantity control is retrieved and stored in variable q after converting text to an integer. Similarly, the cost entered in txtCost is retrieved and stored in variable r after converting the Text data type to Single (single-precision floating-point number). Then q and r are multiplied to calculate the gross amount, which is stored in variable a. After that, a discount is computed that is 10 percent of the gross amount, and that is assigned to float variable d. The Net Amount is then easily computed by subtracting discount d from gross amount a. The Net Amount is assigned to float variable n. The gross amount in variable a is then assigned to the txtAmount text box. The integer value in variable a is converted to a string before assigning it to txtAmount. Similarly, the Discount and Net Amount in variables d and n are assigned to TextBox controls txtDiscount and txtNetAmount. After running the website, you get the output shown in Figure 18.8.

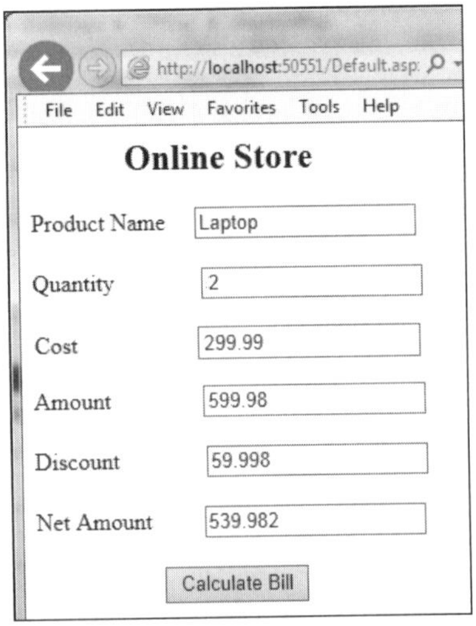

Figure 18.8
Output after running the CalculateBillApp website.
Used with permission from Microsoft.

By now, you know how to use Label, TextBox, and Button controls. Now you'll learn to display different options or choices through the DropDownList control.

Using the DropDownList Control

A DropDownList control offers options in which a user can select any one option. The options displayed in a DropDownList control can be retrieved from a table, from an array list, or from any other data source. When any item from the DropDownList control is selected, you get the index of the selected item through its `SelectedIndex` property. You can access the name of the selected item from the `DropDownList` control by using the `SelectedItem` property. Initially, the `SelectedIndex` property of the `DropDownList` control is zero, which depicts that, by default, the first item of the `DropDownList` control is selected.

To understand how `DropDownList` is used practically, you'll apply it to the `CalculateBillApp` you created earlier. You will display three types of customer categories through the `DropDownList` control. Instead of a flat 10 percent discount, you will compute a discount based on the category to which the customer belongs. The three categories that you will display through the `DropDownList` control are Individual, Non Profit Organization, and Corporate. The discount will be 10 percent, 20 percent, and 15 percent for Individual, Non Profit Organization, and Corporate customers, respectively.

Launch Visual Studio and open `CalculateBillApp`. Drag and drop a `Label` and a `DropDownList1` control to the `Default.aspx` web form. Set the `Text` property of the `Label` control to `Category`, as shown in Figure 18.9.

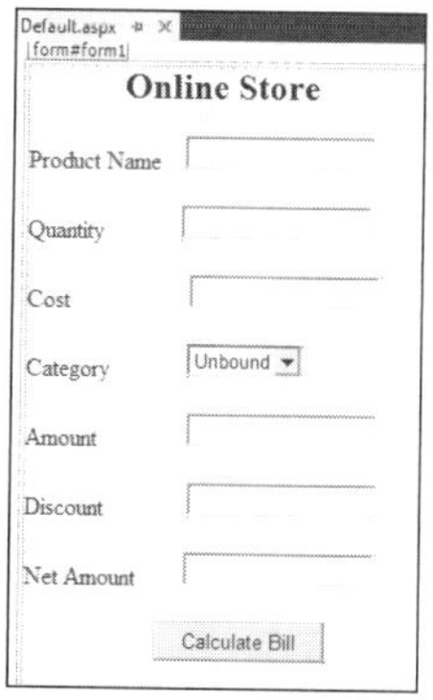

Figure 18.9
Label and DropDownList control added to Default.aspx web form of CalculateBillApp website.
Used with permission from Microsoft.

Set the `ID` property of the `DropDownList` control to `drpdnCategory`. To display three choices through the `DropDownList` control, add the following code to the code-behind file `Default.aspx.cs`:

```
protected String[] category = { "Individual", "Non Profit Organization", "Corporate" };
protected void Page_Load(object sender, EventArgs e)
```

```
{
    if (!IsPostBack)
    {
        drpdnCategory.DataSource = category;
        drpdnCategory.DataBind();
    }
}
```

As mentioned earlier, you want to display three string options—Individual, Non Profit Organization, and Corporate, through the DropDownList control. To do so, you use the string array category (to designate category of customers) and store the three options as array elements in the category array. After that, the DropDownList control is bound to the string array category. By using the DataBind method, the contents of DataSource (category array) are assigned to the DropDownList control. The IsPostback method used in the preceding code needs explanation. Read on.

The Page_Load event executes even if a button is clicked. That means the Page_Load event executes when the web form is loaded for the first time and every time an event occurs on any control of the web form. But sometimes you want a specific code to execute only once. For example, a variable is initialized in the Page_Load method, and you don't want it to reinitialize when an event occurs. In that case, you write that code in the following if block:

```
if (!IsPostBack)
{
    ..........................
    ..........................
}
```

IsPostBack identifies whether the page has been posted back. If the page is loaded for the first time, IsPostBack returns false, and if the page is already loaded, IsPostBack returns true. When you write the set of statements in the preceding if block, that set of statements executes only once (for the time IsPostBack returns false—when the page is loaded). This set of statements does not execute when an event occurs on any control.

Note

IsPostBack is reset when you move to another page.

Besides the `IsPostBack` method, there is one more way to handle page postback: by using the `AutoPostBack` property.

Understanding the AutoPostBack Property

The `AutoPostBack` property is set to `true` for non-postback controls. The postback controls cause the form to be posted back or submitted to the server immediately. For example, a `Button` is a postback control; it has a postback event, `Button.Click`, that causes the form to be posted back or submitted to the server immediately when the click event occurs. Non-postback controls like `CheckBox` and `DropDownList` have non-postback events, which means, when an event occurs, the form is not posted back to the server immediately but is cached until the next time posting occurs. By making the `AutoPostBack` property `true` for these non-postback controls, you can ensure the form is submitted immediately, even when non-postback events occur.

Following are postback controls:

- `Button`
- `Calendar`
- `DataGrid`
- `DataList`
- `FileUpload`
- `GridView`
- `ImageButton`
- `ImageMap`
- `LinkButton`
- `Menu`
- `Repeater`

And here are non-postback controls:

- `BulletedList`
- `CheckBoxList`
- `DropDownList`
- `ListBox`

- RadioButtonList

- RadioButton

- TextBox

You assume that the customer belongs to an Individual, Corporate, or Non Profit Organization and that her discount is computed as per the following rules:

- 10 percent discount is given to the Individual category

- 15 percent discount is given to the Corporate category

- 20 percent discount is given to the Non Profit Organization category

To display the options through the DropDownList control and to compute the discount based on the category chosen from the DropDownList control, modify the code-behind file Default.aspx.cs to appear as shown in Listing 18.3.

Listing 18.3 Program Code in Default.aspx.cs File

```
using System;
using System.Collections.Generic;
using System.Linq;
using System.Web;
using System.Web.UI;
using System.Web.UI.WebControls;
public partial class _Default : System.Web.UI.Page
{
    protected String[] category = { "Individual", "Non Profit Organization",
"Corporate" };
    protected void Page_Load(object sender, EventArgs e)
    {
        if (!IsPostBack)
        {
            drpdnCategory.DataSource = category;
            drpdnCategory.DataBind();
        }
    }
    protected void btnCalculate_Click(object sender, EventArgs e)
    {
        String c;
        int q;
        float d,n, r,a;
        d = 0;
```

```
q = Convert.ToInt32(txtQuantity.Text);
r = Convert.ToSingle(txtCost.Text);
a = q * r;
c = drpdnCategory.SelectedItem.Text;
if (String.Compare(c, "Individual") == 0)
{
    d = (float)a * 10 / 100;
}
if (String.Compare(c, "Non Profit Organization") == 0)
{
    d = (float)a * 20 / 100;
}
if (String.Compare(c, "Corporate") == 0)
{
    d = (float)a * 15 / 100;
}
n = a - d;
txtAmount.Text = a.ToString();
txtDiscount.Text = d.ToString();
txtNetAmount.Text = n.ToString();
    }
}
```

The string array category is defined and assigned three strings—Individual, Non Profit Organization, and Corporate—as array elements. In a Page_Load event, that string array category is bound to a DropDownList control, so the three string options can be assigned to it.

Three variables—q, r, and a—are declared, and you have included two float variables: d and n (for storing values of discount and net amount). To decide which option to choose from the DropDownList control, declare one local string variable: c. The quantity of products the user enters in the txtQuantity control is retrieved and stored in variable q after converting the Text type into the Integer type. Similarly, the cost of products entered into txtCost is retrieved and stored in variable r after converting the Text data type to Single. Then q and r are multiplied to calculate the gross amount, which is then stored in variable a. Thereafter, with the help of the SelectedItem.Text property of the DropDownList control, you determine which option (Individual, Non Profit Organization, or Corporate) the user has chosen. The chosen item is stored in string variable c.

Then the string in variable c is checked. If Category is Individual, the discount is computed as 10 percent of the gross amount. If the string in variable c is Non Profit Organization, the discount is calculated as 20 percent of the gross amount. If the Category is Corporate, the discount computed is 15 percent of the gross amount. The computed discount is stored in float variable d. The Net Amount is then easily computed by subtracting discount d from gross amount a and storing it in float variable n. The gross amount in variable a is then assigned to the txtAmount control. The value in float variable a is converted to a string before assigning it to txtAmount. Similarly, the Discount and Net Amounts in variables d and n are assigned to TextBox controls txtDiscount and txtNetAmount.

After running the website, you find the DropDownList control along with other controls. The DropDownList control displays three options, as shown in Figure 18.10 (left). The Discount and Net Amount are computed based on the option selected from the DropDownList control (see Figure 18.10 [right]). You can see in the figure that a Non Profit Organization gets a discount of 20 percent off the gross amount.

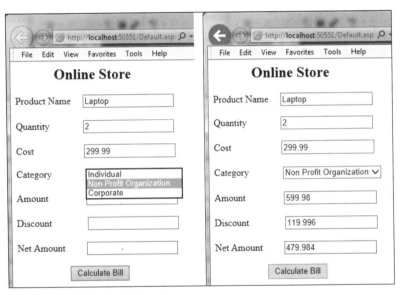

Figure 18.10
(left) DropDownList control displaying different options (right) Discount and Net Amount computed based on the customer category selected from the DropDownList control.
Used with permission from Microsoft.

The DropDownList can also be assigned values or items from a database table, from an ArrayList, or from any other data source. Now you'll learn how the content of ArrayList is assigned to the DropDownList control.

Using the ArrayList Class to Display Data in DropDownList

Recall that the ArrayList class is an enhanced form of an array that is automatically sized according to data supplied to it. It has several methods, including Add, Insert, Remove, Sort, and BinarySearch, that can be used directly to make your task easier. You need to import the System.Collections namespace to use the ArrayList class in an application.

To assign or bind the content of an ArrayList object to the DropDownList control, open the code-behind file Default.aspx.cs and modify it to appear as shown in Listing 18.4. Only the code in bold is modified; the rest is the same as what you saw in Listing 18.3.

Listing 18.4 Program Code in Default.aspx.cs File

```
using System;
using System.Collections.Generic;
using System.Linq;
using System.Web;
using System.Web.UI;
using System.Web.UI.WebControls;
using System.Collections;

public partial class _Default : System.Web.UI.Page
{
        ArrayList category = new ArrayList();
    protected void Page_Load(object sender, EventArgs e)
    {
        category.Add("Individual");
        category.Add("Non Profit Organization");
        category.Add("Corporate");
        if (!IsPostBack)
        {
            drpdnCategory.DataSource = category;
            drpdnCategory.DataBind();
        }
    }
    protected void btnCalculate_Click(object sender, EventArgs e)
    {
        String c;
        int q;
        float d,n, r,a;
        d = 0;
        q = Convert.ToInt32(txtQuantity.Text);
        r = Convert.ToSingle(txtCost.Text);
        a = q * r;
        c = drpdnCategory.SelectedItem.Text;
```

```
        if (String.Compare(c, "Individual") == 0)
        {
            d = (float)a * 10 / 100;
        }
        if (String.Compare(c, "Non Profit Organization") == 0)
        {
            d = (float)a * 20 / 100;
        }
        if (String.Compare(c, "Corporate") == 0)
        {
            d = (float)a * 15 / 100;
        }
        n = a - d;
        txtAmount.Text = a.ToString();
        txtDiscount.Text = d.ToString();
        txtNetAmount.Text = n.ToString();
    }
}
```

You can see that an ArrayList object called category is created and, using the Add method, three strings—Individual, Non Profit Organization, and Corporate—are added to it. Thereafter, the content in the ArrayList object is assigned to the DropDownList control by using its DataSource property and then invoking the DataBind method. The output of this program is the same as in Figure 18.10.

Now you'll learn about a control that enables you to select more than one option or choice: the CheckBox control.

USING THE CHECKBOX CONTROL

You use the CheckBox control to select more than one item from the range of available choices. The next statement displays a CheckBox control with the ID chkAirPostPickup. The CheckBox control displays the text Airport Pickup $20.

```
<asp:CheckBox ID="chkAirportPickup" runat="server" Text="Airport Pickup $20" />
```

The most commonly used properties of the CheckBox control are described in Table 18.6.

Table 18.6 Commonly Used Properties of the CheckBox Control

Property	Description
Checked	It returns true if the CheckBox is checked; otherwise, it returns false.
Text	You write the text to be displayed, along with the CheckBox.
AutoPostBack	If it is true, automatic postback to the server occurs if the user changes the contents of the control. If false, the postback to the server occurs only with the help of a button or by using a control with its AutoPostBack property set to true.
CheckChanged	This event is raised when the Checked property is changed.

© 2015 Cengage Learning®.

To understand the working of CheckBox controls, you'll create a small website. Launch Visual Studio and create a new empty website called HotelReservApp. Add a web form named Default.aspx to the website. Drag and drop a CheckBox control on the Default.aspx web form and, using the Properties window, set its Text property to Airport Pickup $20. The CheckBox control appears as in Figure 18.11.

Figure 18.11
Setting the Text property of the CheckBox control.
Used with permission from Microsoft.

Similarly, drag two more CheckBox controls and drop them on the Default.aspx web form. Also, set their Text property to WiFi $10 and BuffetFood $15, respectively. Drag and drop two Label controls, a TextBox control, and a Button control on the web form. Set the Text property of the two Label controls to Hotel Room Reservation and Bill, respectively. Also, set the Text property of the Button control to Show Bill. Increase the font size of the first Label control and make it bold, as shown in Figure 18.12.

Figure 18.12
The controls after setting the respective properties.
Used with permission from Microsoft.

To identify and access the three CheckBox controls in the code, set their ID property to chkAirportPickup, chkWiFi, and chkBuffetFood, respectively. Also, set the ID property of the TextBox and Button control to txtBill and btnShowBill, respectively. After placing all the controls and setting their properties, the source code of the web form Default.aspx appears, as shown in Listing 18.5.

Listing 18.5 Program Code in Default.aspx File

```
<%@ Page Language="C#" AutoEventWireup="true" CodeFile="Default.aspx.cs"
Inherits="_Default" %>

<!DOCTYPE html>
<html xmlns="http://www.w3.org/1999/xhtml">
<head runat="server">
    <title></title>
</head>
<body>
    <form id="form1" runat="server">
    <div>
        <asp:Label ID="Label1" runat="server" Text="Hotel Room Reservation" Font-
Bold="True" Font-Size="X-Large"></asp:Label>
        <br />
        <asp:CheckBox ID="chkAirportPickup" runat="server" Text="Airport Pickup $20" />
        <br />
        <asp:CheckBox ID="chkWiFi" runat="server" Text="WiFi $10" />
        <br />
        <asp:CheckBox ID="chkBuffetFood" runat="server" Text="Buffet Food $15" />
        <br />
        <asp:Label ID="Label2" runat="server" Text="Bill"></asp:Label>
```

```
        <asp:TextBox ID="txtBill" runat="server"></asp:TextBox>
        <br />
        <asp:Button ID="btnShowBill" runat="server" Text="Show Bill"
OnClick="btnShowBill_Click" />
        <br />
    </div>
    </form>
</body>
</html>
```

When a user checks any of the desired CheckBox controls and clicks the Show Bill button, you want the total amount of the checked items to be displayed in the Bill text box. Because you want the bill to be displayed when the click event occurs on the Button control, you need to associate the click event handler with the Button control. So double-click the Button control btnShowBill, and in the code-behind file Default.aspx.cs, write the code shown in Listing 18.6.

Listing 18.6 Program Code in Default.aspx.cs File

```
using System;
using System.Collections.Generic;
using System.Linq;
using System.Web;
using System.Web.UI;
using System.Web.UI.WebControls;

public partial class _Default : System.Web.UI.Page
{
    protected void Page_Load(object sender, EventArgs e)
    {
    }
    protected void btnShowBill_Click(object sender, EventArgs e)
    {
        int amount = 0;
        if (chkAirportPickup.Checked == true)
        {
            amount = amount + 20;
        }
        if (chkWiFi.Checked == true)
        {
            amount = amount + 10;
        }
        if (chkBuffetFood.Checked == true)
```

```
        {
            amount = amount + 15;
        }
        txtBill.Text = amount.ToString();
    }
}
```

You can see in Listing 18.6 that if a CheckBox control is checked, the amount of that item is added to the integer variable amount, which is finally displayed in the TextBox control. After running the application, you'll find that only the sum of the items whose CheckBox controls are checked is displayed through the Bill text box (see Figure 18.13 [left] and [right]).

Figure 18.13
(left) and (right) The bill of the selected items is displayed through the Bill text box.
Used with permission from Microsoft.

You get the result (bill) only when you click the Button control. If you want the bill to appear without clicking the Button control (immediately after checking or unchecking any CheckBox control), you need to use the AutoPostBack property of the three CheckBox controls. Recall that when the AutoPostBack property is set to true for non-postback controls, the web form is posted back or submitted to the server immediately after any event occurs on the non-postback control. The CheckBox controls are non-postback. Click each of the three CheckBox controls, and set their AutoPostback property to true, as shown in Figure 18.14.

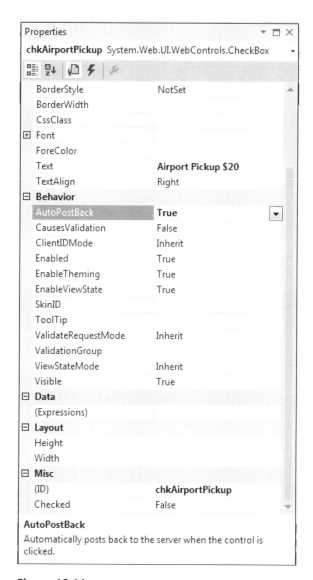

Figure 18.14
Setting the AutoPostBack property of the CheckBox controls for a quick response.
Used with permission from Microsoft.

Now, because the bill will be computed and displayed immediately after checking or unchecking the CheckBox controls, you no longer need the Button control. So delete the Button control from the web form and shift the code that is meant for computing the bill from the btnShowBill_Click method to the Page_Load method, as shown in Listing 18.7.

Listing 18.7 Program Code in Default.aspx.cs File

```
using System;
using System.Collections.Generic;
using System.Linq;
using System.Web;
using System.Web.UI;
using System.Web.UI.WebControls;

public partial class _Default : System.Web.UI.Page
{
    protected void Page_Load(object sender, EventArgs e)
    {
        int amount = 0;
        if (chkAirportPickup.Checked == true)
        {
            amount = amount + 20;
        }
        if (chkWiFi.Checked == true)
        {
            amount = amount + 10;
        }
        if (chkBuffetFood.Checked == true)
        {
            amount = amount + 15;
        }
        txtBill.Text = amount.ToString();
    }
}
```

Now, when you run the application, you'll find that the bill will be computed and displayed through the TextBox control immediately when the CheckBox control is checked or unchecked, as shown in Figure 18.15.

Figure 18.15
Bill displayed after checking or unchecking the CheckBox controls.
Used with permission from Microsoft.

Now that you understand the working of the `CheckBox` control, you'll learn to use `RadioButton` control in a website.

Using the RadioButton Control

The `RadioButton` control is a server control that displays several options or choices to the user but allows selection of only a single option. In other words, after selecting an option, any previously selected option is automatically deselected. The following statements create two `RadioButton` controls showing the options Queen Bed $125 and King Bed $150:

```
<asp:RadioButton ID="radioQueenBed" runat="server" GroupName="BedType" Text="Queen
Bed $125" />
<asp:RadioButton ID="radioKingBed" runat="server" GroupName="BedType" Text="King Bed
$150" />
```

The preceding example creates two `RadioButton` controls under the `GroupName=BedType`. To ensure that only one `RadioButton` control can be selected, you must assign two or more `RadioButton` controls to the same group name. Remember, you can have any number of `RadioButton` controls assigned to a single group, but only one `RadioButton` can be selected at a time from each group. In other words, after selecting a `RadioButton`, any of the previously selected `RadioButton` controls in that group will be automatically deselected.

Note

When you want to select only one item from a set of options, you use the `RadioButton` control. When you want to select more than one option, your preference should be the `CheckBox` control.

To better understand the concept of `RadioButton` controls, you'll apply them to the `HotelReservApp` website that you created earlier. Assuming that the website is for a hotel that provides different types of rooms, such as Standard, Deluxe, and Honeymoon Suite, and that also of Queen Bed and King Bed, you will add two groups of `RadioButton` controls to the application. One group will contain two `RadioButton` controls showing the text `Queen Bed` and `King Bed`. The second group will contain three `RadioButton` controls showing the text `Standard Room`, `Deluxe Room`, and `Honeymoon Suite`. You will be using five `RadioButtons` divided into two groups:

- `BedType`
- `RoomType`

Drag and drop five `RadioButton` controls on the web form. Set the `Text` property of the five `RadioButton` controls to `Queen Bed 125$`, `King Bed 150$`, `Standard Room 125$`, `Deluxe Room 150$`, and `Honeymoon Suite 225$`, respectively. To identify and access the RadioButton controls, set the IDs of the five `RadioButton` controls to `radioQueenBed`, `radioKingBed`, `radioStandardRoom`, `radioDeluxeRoom`, and `radioHoneymoonSuite`, respectively. Assign `radioQueenBed` and `radioKingBed` controls to the `BedType` group (see Figure 18.16).

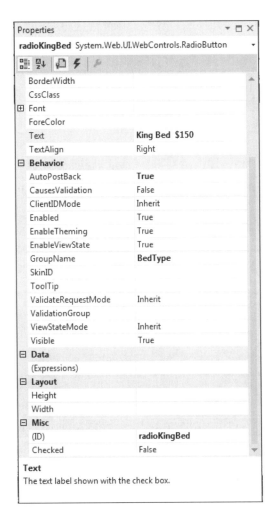

Figure 18.16
Setting the GroupName property of the RadioButton control radioKingBed to BedType.
Used with permission from Microsoft.

Assign the `radioStandardRoom`, `radioDeluxeRoom`, and `radioHoneymoonSuite` to the `RoomType` group. Select any one `RadioButton` control from each group and set their `Checked` property to `true` to make them appear checked by default (see Figure 18.17).

Figure 18.17
Screen showing two groups of RadioButtons.
Used with permission from Microsoft.

Because you want the bill to be computed immediately, the moment any RadioButton control is selected, set the AutoPostBack property of all the RadioButton controls to true. To calculate and display the bill when any of the RadioButton controls is selected from either or both groups, modify the code in the Default.aspx.cs file to appear as shown in Listing 18.8. Only the code in bold is new; the rest is the same as what you saw in Listing 18.7.

Listing 18.8 Program Code in Default.aspx.cs File

```
using System;
using System.Collections.Generic;
using System.Linq;
using System.Web;
```

```csharp
using System.Web.UI;
using System.Web.UI.WebControls;

public partial class _Default : System.Web.UI.Page
{
    protected void Page_Load(object sender, EventArgs e)
    {
        int amount = 0;
        if (chkAirportPickup.Checked == true)
        {
            amount = amount + 20;
        }
        if (chkWiFi.Checked == true)
        {
            amount = amount + 10;
        }
        if (chkBuffetFood.Checked == true)
        {
            amount = amount + 15;
        }
        if (radioKingBed.Checked == true)
        {
            amount = amount + 150;
        }
        else
        {
            amount = amount + 125;
        }
        if (radioStandardRoom.Checked == true)
        {
            amount = amount + 125;
        }
        else
        {
            if (radioDeluxeRoom.Checked == true)
            {
                amount = amount + 150;
            }
            else
            {
                amount = amount + 225;
            }
        }
        txtBill.Text = amount.ToString();
    }
}
```

As you can see in Listing 18.8, if any of the RadioButton controls is found selected, the amount of that item is added to the integer variable amount. Because only one RadioButton control can be selected in a group, you have used if else statements while dealing with RadioButton controls in Listing 18.8, unlike the if statements that you used with the CheckBox controls. Finally, the value in the amount variable is displayed in a TextBox control. After running the application, the output that you may get is shown in Figure 18.18 (left) and (right).

Figure 18.18
(left) and (right) When you select any RadioButton from each group, the bill amount appears accordingly.
Used with permission from Microsoft.

When you want to enable a user to select one or more options beyond the CheckBox control, you have one more handy control called ListBox.

USING THE LISTBOX CONTROL

You can use the ListBox control to display a collection of items in a limited space. Not only does it display more items within the confined space, but it allows the user to make multiple selections. Common properties of the ListBox control are briefly described in Table 18.7.

Table 18.7 Common Properties of the ListBox Control

Property	Description
Items	Returns the collection of ListItem objects that correspond to the items in the control. This property returns an object of type ListItemCollection.
Rows	Returns the number of items that are displayed in a ListBox at one time. If the list contains more rows than can be displayed, a scrollbar is added automatically.
SelectedItem	Returns the ListItem object for the currently selected item, or the ListItem object for the item with the lowest index if more than one item is selected.
SelectedIndex	Returns the index of the currently selected item, or the index of the first selected item if more than one item is selected in a ListBox. If no item is selected in the ListBox, the value of this property is -1.
SelectedValue	Returns the value of the currently selected item, or the value of the first selected item if more than one item is selected in a ListBox. If no item is selected, the value of this property is an empty string ("").
SelectionMode	Determines if the ListBox allows single selections (Single) or multiple selections (Multiple).

© 2015 Cengage Learning®.

To understand the practical usage of the ListBox control, you'll apply it in the HotelReservApp website that you created earlier. Launch Visual Studio and open the HotelReservApp website. On the Default.aspx web form, drag and drop a Label and a ListBox control. Initially, the ListBox control appears as shown in Figure 18.19.

Figure 18.19
Appearance of ListBox control.
Used with permission from Microsoft.

You will display the options that represent the purpose of the guest's visit to the hotel. In other words, you will display options such as Tourism and Business through the

ListBox control. The user can select an option from the list of those available to indicate the purpose of his visit.

Set the Text property of the Label control to Purpose of visit. To display different choices through the ListBox control, select the control in the Design window and then select the Items property from the Properties window. Add the items Tourism, Business, Education, Research, and Other by choosing the Add button in the ListItem Collection Editor dialog box shown in Figure 18.20.

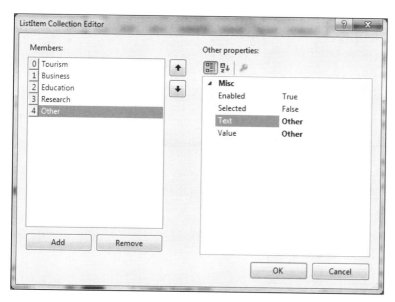

Figure 18.20
Adding items and specifying their values using the ListItem Collection Editor in the ListBox control.
Used with permission from Microsoft.

Set the ID of the ListBox control to listboxPurpose. Also, set the value of the AutoPostBack property to true. You can set the SelectionMode to Single or Multiple mode. Initially, keep the SelectionMode property to its default value (Single), as shown in Figure 18.21.

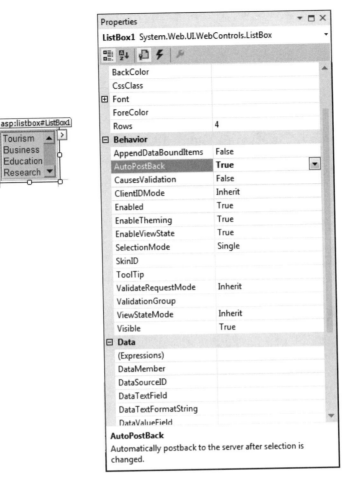

Figure 18.21
Setting ID, AutoPostBack, and SelectionMode properties of the ListBox control.

Drag and drop a Label control on the web form and set its ID property to lblPurpose. The web form now appears as shown in Figure 18.22.

Figure 18.22
Web form with ListBox control.
Used with permission from Microsoft.

The moment the user selects any option from the ListBox control, you want the chosen item to be displayed through the Label lblPurpose, so double-click the ListBox control in the Design window and type the following statements in the open code-behind file:

```
protected void listboxPurpose_SelectedIndexChanged(object sender, EventArgs e)
{
    lblPurpose.Text = "Your purpose of visit is "+listboxPurpose.Text;
}
```

The preceding code displays the text that is selected from the ListBox control through the Label control, as shown in Figure 18.23.

Figure 18.23
The option selected from the ListBox control is displayed through the Label control.
Used with permission from Microsoft.

To select more than one item from the ListBox control, set its SelectionMode property to Multiple. To display all the options that are selected from the ListBox control, double-click in the Design window and modify the code to appear as shown here:

```
protected void listboxPurpose_SelectedIndexChanged(object sender, EventArgs e)
{
    String str = "";
    foreach (ListItem purpose in listboxPurpose.Items)
    {
        if (purpose.Selected == true)
        {
            str = str + purpose.Text + " ";
        }
    }
    lblPurpose.Text = "Your purpose of visit is "+str;
}
```

As you can see in the preceding code, each of the Items property of the ListBox control is tested with the help of the ListItem object purpose. You make the string variable str blank. If the purpose object (the ListItem) is selected, its Text property is concatenated to string variable str, with a space in between. When all the ListItem objects are tested, the content of string variable str (containing the list items that are selected) is displayed through the Label control lblPurpose. After running the application, you see that all the items selected from the ListBox control are displayed through the Label control shown in Figure 18.24.

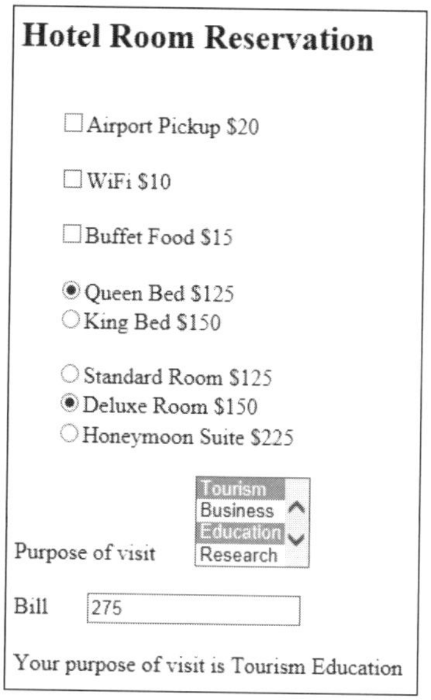

Hotel Room Reservation

☐ Airport Pickup $20

☐ WiFi $10

☐ Buffet Food $15

◉ Queen Bed $125
○ King Bed $150

○ Standard Room $125
◉ Deluxe Room $150
○ Honeymoon Suite $225

Purpose of visit | Tourism
Business
Education
Research

Bill   275

Your purpose of visit is Tourism Education

Figure 18.24
Output when multiple selections are made in the ListBox control.
Used with permission from Microsoft.

What if you want to navigate from one web form to another? Several controls enable you to do just that. You'll begin with LinkButton control.

USING THE LINKBUTTON CONTROL

The LinkButton control displays text that looks like a hyperlink which, when clicked, submits the web form to the server for processing. This control initially appears as shown in Figure 18.25.

Figure 18.25
LinkButton control.
Used with permission from Microsoft.

When you click the LinkButton control, the web form specified in its PostBackUrl property is loaded. (You are navigated from the current web form to the web form that is specified in the PostBackUrl property.) You then apply the LinkButton control to the HotelReservApp website that you created earlier.

Launch Visual Studio and open the HotelReservApp website. On the Default.aspx web form, drag and drop a LinkButton control. When a user clicks the LinkButton control, you want the web form mentioned in its PostBackUrl property to be loaded. Before using the PostBackUrl property, you need to create a web form that you want to navigate to. Add a new web form to your website named Checkout.aspx. Also, drag and drop a Label control on the Checkout.aspx web form. Set the Text property of the Label control to Please enter your credit card details, as shown in Figure 18.26. This Label control informs the user that the navigation is performed and the destination web form is loaded.

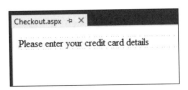

Figure 18.26
Label control after setting its Text property in the Checkout.aspx file.
Used with permission from Microsoft.

After creating the destination web form, you can go back to your Default.aspx web form and set the PostBackUrl property of the LinkButton control. Click the LinkButton control and select its PostBackUrl property from the Properties window. A dialog box opens that displays all the available web forms in the website. Select the Checkout.aspx web form that you want to navigate to, and then click OK. The name of the Checkout.aspx web form appears in the PostBackUrl property of the LinkButton control along with the path, as shown in Figure 18.27.

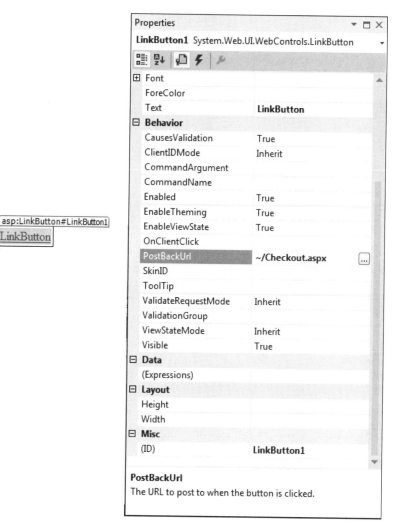

Figure 18.27
LinkButton control and its properties.
Used with permission from Microsoft.

Also, set the Text property of the LinkButton control to Payment Info so the user knows he can click it to navigate to a web form that enables entering of payment information. After you run the website, a Payment Info link appears at the bottom (see Figure 18.28 [left]). When you click that link, you are navigated to the Checkout.aspx web form, where its Label control displays the message Please enter your credit card details (see Figure 18.28 [right]).

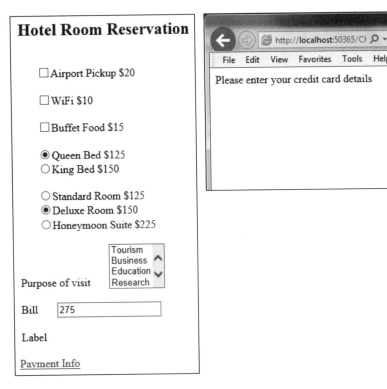

Figure 18.28
(left) LinkButton control displayed with text Payment Info (right) Checkout.aspx web form loaded after clicking the LinkButton control.

Used with permission from Microsoft.

There is one more control that is similar to LinkButton control: the HyperLink control.

USING THE HYPERLINK CONTROL

You use the HyperLink control to navigate to the target URL without a postback. In other words, after you click the HyperLink control, the destination web form is loaded without submitting the current web form to the server. The HyperLink control looks like Figure 18.29.

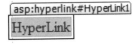

Figure 18.29
HyperLink control.

Used with permission from Microsoft.

Here are the most common properties of the HyperLink control:

- **ImageUrl**—Specifies the path of the image that you want to appear as a link for the target URL. When the image is clicked, you are navigated from the current to the target web form.

- **NavigateUrl**—Specifies the path and the name of the target web form.

- **Text**—Specifies the text to appear as a link on the screen.

- **Target**—Specifies the target window or frame where you want to load the linked page. The target value can be any of the ones that are mentioned in Table 18.8.

Table 18.8   Valid Values for the Target Property of the HyperLink Control

Target Value	Description
_blank	Displays the content in a new unnamed window without frames.
_new	Same as _blank.
_parent	Displays the content in the parent window or frameset of the window or frame with the hyperlink.
_self	Displays the content in the current frame or window with focus. This is the default value.
_top	Displays the content in the current full window without frames.

© 2015 Cengage Learning®.

When you click the HyperLink control, navigation takes place from the current web form to the web form that is specified in its NavigateUrl property. You can display an image or text in the HyperLink control. The text assigned to the HyperLink control appears as underlined, and the image is set by using the ImageUrl attribute.

To understand how the HyperLink control works, apply it to your HotelReservApp website that you created earlier. Launch Visual Studio and open the HotelReservApp website. From the Default.aspx web form, delete the LinkButton control because, this time, you want to navigate to the Checkout.aspx web form by using the HyperLink control. Drag and drop the HyperLink control on the web form. Set the Text property of the HyperLink control to Payment Info. Also, set its NavigateUrl property to point to the Checkout.aspx web form, the form that you want to navigate to, as shown in Figure 18.30.

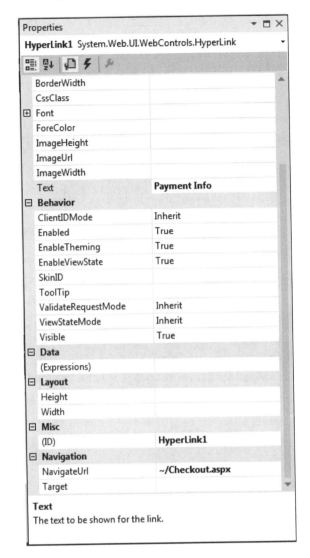

Figure 18.30
Setting the Text and NavigateUrl property of the HyperLink control.
Used with permission from Microsoft.

After running the application, you get a link with the text Payment Info (the same as in Figure 18.28 [left]). When you click the Payment Info link, you are navigated from the current web form at Default.aspx to the Checkout.aspx web form.

In addition to text, you can make an image act as a hyperlink. To accomplish this, you need to add some images to your website. Right-click HotelReservApp in the Solution Explorer window and select Add, New Folder. You are prompted for the name of the newly added folder. Assign the name images to the newly added folder. Copy and paste any image that you want to appear as a hyperlink into the images folder of the website. Assuming that the image filename is mastercard.jpg that is copied into the images folder, set the ImageUrl, ImageHeight, and ImageWidth properties to appear as shown in Figure 18.31. The NavigateUrl property should point to the same web form, Checkout.aspx.

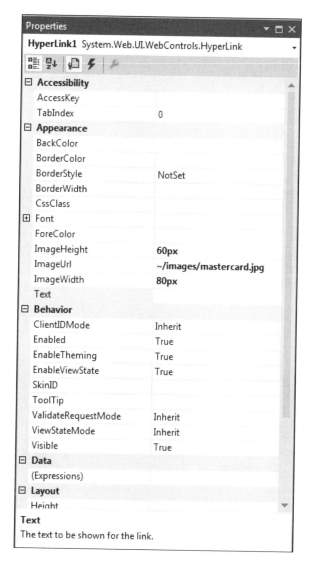

Figure 18.31
Setting the ImageUrl, ImageHeight, and ImageWidth properties of the HyperLink control.
Used with permission from Microsoft.

After you set the ImageUrl property, the text Payment Info is replaced by the specified image (see Figure 18.32 [left]). In other words, the image does not act as a hyperlink.

When you click the image, you are navigated from the current web form to the Checkout.aspx web form, as shown in Figure 18.32 (right).

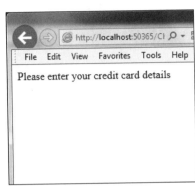

Figure 18.32
(left) Hyperlink appears in image format (right) Navigating to the destination web form after clicking the image.
Used with permission from Microsoft.

You can also dynamically change the link text or target page based on conditions. In addition, you can use data binding to specify the target URL for the link (and parameters to be passed with the link, if necessary).

Note

The HyperLink control does not raise an event in server code when users click it. Instead, navigation takes place from the current web form to the one that is specified in the NavigateUrl property.

There is one more control called ImageButton that displays an image resulting in navigation when it's clicked. It's covered next.

Using the ImageButton Control

The ImageButton control displays a clickable image. You can use the control to display an image that performs the desired action when it's clicked. The image can also perform navigation from the current web form to the desired web form. The ImageButton control is shown in Figure 18.33.

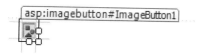

Figure 18.33
ImageButton control.
Used with permission from Microsoft.

Following are the two properties that are commonly used for working with the ImageButton control:

- **PostBackUrl**—Used for specifying the path of the web form that you want to navigate to.

- **ImageUrl**—Used for specifying the image filename that you want to display through the ImageButton control. The image needs to exist in the images folder of the website.

Suppose that you want to navigate to the Checkout.aspx web form and set its name in the PostBackUrl property. To display an image, copy the image filename contactus.jpg into the images folder of the website. After that, set the ImageUrl property to point at it. You can use the Height and Width properties to display the image in the desired height and width (see Figure 18.34).

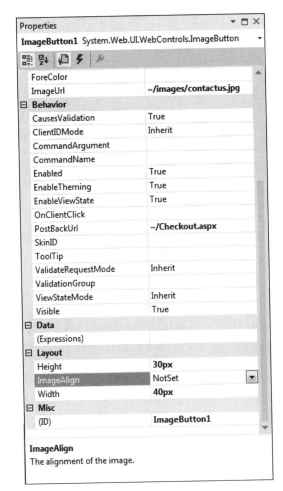

Figure 18.34
Setting ImageUrl and PostBackUrl properties of the ImageButton control to display an image and to navigate to the selected web form.
Used with permission from Microsoft.

After you run the application, an image appears in the top-right corner (Figure 18.35 [left]) that the user can click to navigate at the destination web form (Figure 18.35 [right]).

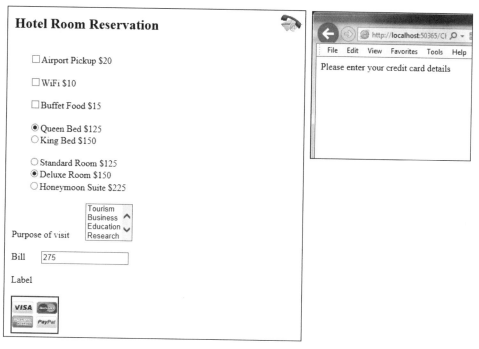

Figure 18.35
(left) Image displayed through ImageButton control (right) Checkout.aspx page opens after you click the image.
Used with permission from Microsoft.

Now that you understand the controls that are commonly used for developing web-sites, you'll learn how web services are created and consumed.

WORKING WITH WCF

Windows Communication Foundation (WCF) is a framework used for building, configuring, and deploying service-oriented applications. Some of the WCF features are listed here:

- WCF supports varieties of network communication technologies such as Hypertext Transfer Protocol (HTTP), .NET Remoting, and Microsoft Message Queuing. Therefore, it enables exchanging of data on different types of systems and networks, including the Internet.

- It enables you to send data as asynchronous messages from one service endpoint to another. The architecture used to send and receive data is Service-Oriented architecture (SOA). Services work by passing messages using specific interfaces.

- Messages are usually encoded in Simple Object Access Protocol (SOAP) format and passed over HTTP protocol. Although, messages can be sent on

Transmission Control Protocol (TCP) and Microsoft Message Queuing (MSMQ), too.

■ The reliability of message exchange is implemented by using WS-Reliable Messaging and MSMQ.

■ Secure message exchange happens by encrypting the messages using the Secure Sockets Layer (SSL) or WS-SecureConversation standard.

■ Service metadata is published in Web Service Definition Language (WSDL) and XML Schema formats. The metadata displays information that enables clients to understand different methods of services and their input and output parameters. It provides complete information to the client that it might need in accessing services.

You'll learn the concept of WCF through a running example. Launch Visual Studio and select File, New Project. Select WCF from the list of Templates followed by WCF Service Application. Assign the name as WCFAvgServiceApp, and click OK (see Figure 18.36).

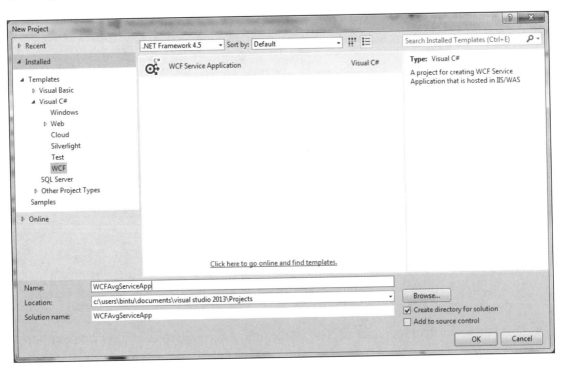

Figure 18.36
Creating a new WCF Service Application.
Used with permission from Microsoft.

Visual Studio automatically generates default class files for the service (see Figure 18.37). A standard web service requires interface declaration and service implementation code. In the figure, you see that the following two important class files are auto-generated:

- **IService1.cs**—Interface declaration
- **Service1.svc**—Service implementation code

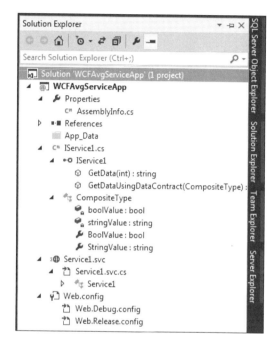

Figure 18.37
Solution Explorer window showing different application files and folders.
Used with permission from Microsoft.

Because web services deal with passing messages between two applications, you need to define a contract. A contract is an agreement between two applications that defines what the service is supposed to do. It can be a service contract or an operation contract.

- **Service contract**—Exposes one or more endpoints, with each endpoint exposing one or more service operations. IService1.cs, which you see in Figure 18.37, is an interface file. You call this interface a service contract.

- **Operation contract**—Defines the methods, parameters, and return type of an operation.

You'll create a service that calculates the average of the three numbers supplied to it. As expected, you need to define a service contract (interface) that declares this task. You will use the existing interface, IService1.cs, for this purpose. Modify IService1.cs to appear as shown in Listing 18.9.

Listing 18.9 Program Code in IService1.cs File

```
using System;
using System.Collections.Generic;
using System.Linq;
using System.Runtime.Serialization;
using System.ServiceModel;
using System.ServiceModel.Web;
using System.Text;

namespace WCFAvgServiceApp
{
    [ServiceContract]
    public interface IService1
    {
        [OperationContract]
        double GetAverage(int valueOne, int valueTwo, int valueThree);
    }
}
```

You can see that in a service file, you define a service contract and an operation contract. The service contract defines the overall service, and the operation contract defines the various methods that are available on the service. A service contract is defined by applying a ServiceContract attribute wrapped in square brackets to the class. Each method of the service that you want to expose is marked with the OperationContract attribute. GetAverage is the method that you want to be exposed and used by the client application.

Note

An interface is usually termed a service contract, and the corresponding methods are called operation contracts.

After interface declaration, it is time to write code for service implementation. Open the service implementation file Service1.svc.cs and define the code for the GetAverage method (that was declared in the interface IService1.cs file). Modify Service1.svc.cs to appear as shown in Listing 18.10.

Listing 18.10 Program Code in Service1.svc.cs File

```
using System;
using System.Collections.Generic;
using System.Linq;
using System.Runtime.Serialization;
using System.ServiceModel;
using System.ServiceModel.Web;
using System.Text;

namespace WCFAvgServiceApp
{
    public class Service1 : IService1
    {
        public double GetAverage(int valueOne, int valueTwo, int valueThree)
        {
            double result = 0;
            try
            {
                result = (valueOne + valueTwo + valueThree) / 3;
            }
            catch (Exception Ex)
            {
                throw new FaultException(new FaultReason(Ex.Message));
            }
            return result;
        }
    }
}
```

You can see that GetAverage is defined to take three integer parameters: valueOne, valueTwo, and valueThree. The average of the three passed parameters is computed and returned. If an error occurs while you're computing the average, an exception is thrown.

To test a WCF service, press F5. A WCF Test Client dialog is displayed to load the service. In the WCF Test Client dialog, double-click the GetAverage() method under the IService1 node. The GetAverage tab is displayed, as shown in Figure 18.38. In the Request box, select the Value field and enter three values. Then click the Invoke button. If a Security Warning dialog box is displayed, click OK. The result is displayed in the Response box.

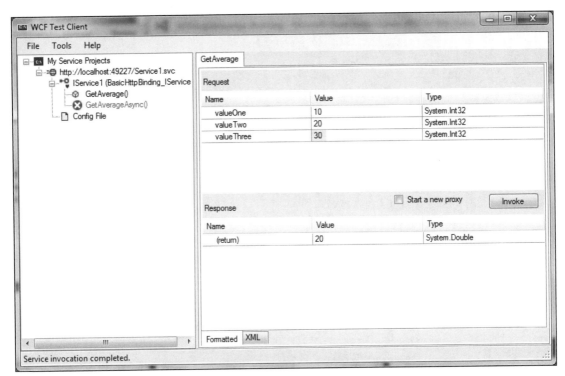

Figure 18.38
Values for the three parameters of the GetAverage() method supplied in the WCF Test Client form.

Observe the value in the Response box to see if the result is correct. To make the service accessible to clients, it needs to be publicly available, so you must publish it. Before initiating the publish procedure, close the WCF Test Client dialog by selecting File, Exit.

To begin publishing the service, right-click the application in Solution Explorer and select the Publish option. The Publish Web dialog opens. The first step is to create a publish profile, so select New Profile from the drop-down list to create a new profile (see Figure 18.39).

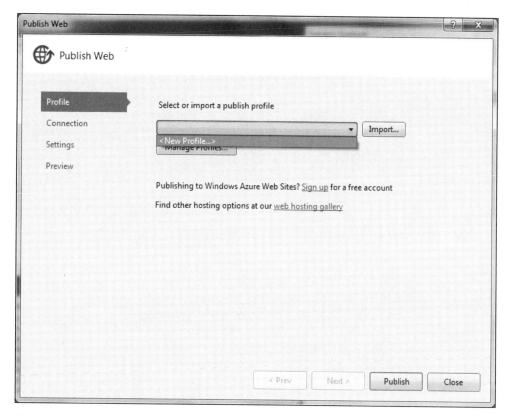

Figure 18.39
Dialog for publishing the web service.
Used with permission from Microsoft.

You are prompted to specify the name for the new publish profile. Specify the name as CalculateService, as shown in Figure 18.40. The publishing profile is meant to contain several details that include various web publishing methods, build configurations, publishing URLs or paths, and so on. This profile contains settings or configurations that are required before publishing.

Figure 18.40
Assigning a name to the new profile.
Used with permission from Microsoft.

The next dialog is Publish Web, which contains several tabs. Click the Connection tab to configure the web service. Fill the following information in the respective boxes (see Figure 18.41):

- **Publish Method**—Select Web Deploy from the drop-down list. Web Deploy is recommended because it automates the widest range of deployment tasks.

- **Server**—Enter the server URL where the web service will be hosted. If the web service is to be published locally on the Internet Information Services (IIS) server, enter `localhost` or the name of your computer in this box.

- **Site Name**—Enter the website URL followed by the service name with a forward slash in between. Here's the syntax:
  `http://ServerName/servicename`

- **User Name and Password**—Credentials are required to deploy the web service on the web server. These credentials are provided by the hosting company and are not required for publishing locally.

- **Save Password**—Check this check box to avoid being prompted for a password every time you publish.

- **Destination URL**—Visual Studio automatically opens the default browser and points at the supplied URL on successful deployment.

After you enter the preceding information, click the Validate Connection button to verify that the provided information is correct. Once the connection is validated, click Publish to publish the service to the server.

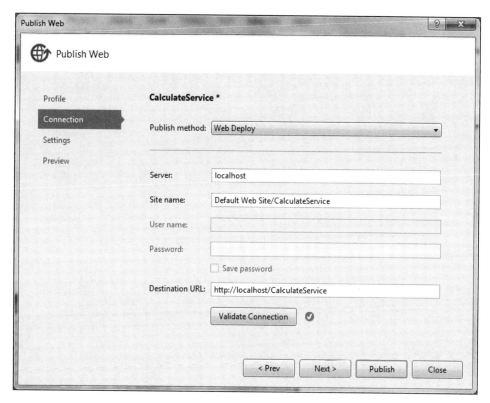

Figure 18.41
Page prompting for connection information before publishing the service.
Used with permission from Microsoft.

If you get any error while publishing the service, open your IIS server and ensure that the .NET version of the default pool is .NET 4.0.

If the service has published successfully, the default browser launches and points at the service URL (see Figure 18.42). The web page displays the links to create a client and call the service. The web page also displays the link to display a service description file.

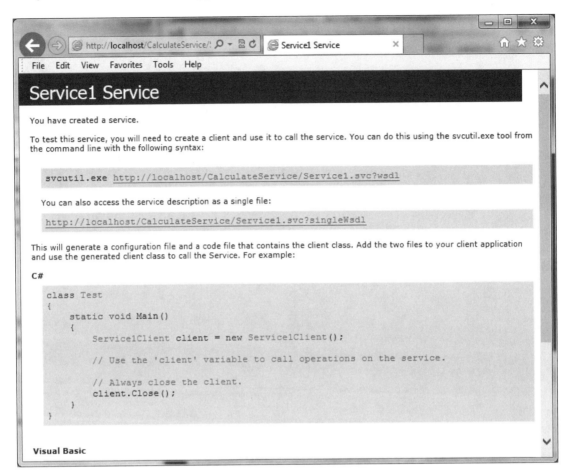

Figure 18.42
Web page pointing at the service URL showing links for creating the client, testing the service, and showing the service description file.

Used with permission from Microsoft.

On clicking the link to display the service description file, the service description file will be displayed as shown in Figure 18.43. Web Services Description Language (WSDL) is an XML document that describes the Web service. It specifies the location of the service and the operations i.e., the methods that the service exposes. It is the WSDL that the client uses to determine the methods that are available on the server.

Figure 18.43
Web Description File of the service.
Used with permission from Microsoft.

After successful creation and publishing of the web service, the next task is to create a client application and access the service.

CREATING A CLIENT APPLICATION

To consume the created web service, you'll create a client application. The client application that you will create is a website that accesses the web service and uses it to compute the average of three numerical values. Launch Visual Studio and select File, New Website. Select the ASP.NET Empty Web Site option, name the website AccessingCalcService, and click OK. Add a web form to the application by right-clicking the application in Solution Explorer and selecting Add, Add New Item. From the dialog that opens, select Web Form. The default name that is assigned to the new web form is `Default.aspx`. Keeping the default name of the web form, click the Add button to add it to the application.

To add a reference for the web service you want to access, right-click the application in Solution Explorer and select Add, Service Reference. An Add Service Reference dialog box opens. In the Address box, add the URL of the service (http://localhost/ CalculateService/Service1.svc), and then click Go. If any service is found that is published and available at the given URL, that service will be detected and displayed. In the Services pane, the service name appears as `Service1`, and in the Operations pane, the `GetAverage` method (which was exposed while creating the service) appears (see Figure 18.44). Click the service and then click OK to add the service to the client application. The selected service is added to your client application.

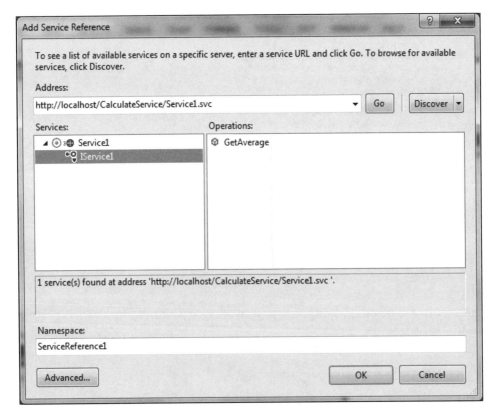

Figure 18.44
Dialog for adding Service Reference to the client application.
Used with permission from Microsoft.

In the Design window of the web form `Default.aspx`, drag and drop five `Label`, three `TextBox`, and a `Button` control on the web form. The three `TextBox` controls are used to enter three values, which in turn are supplied to the service for calculating the average.

The Label control at the bottom is used to display the result (average returned by the service). Set the Text properties of the first four Label controls to Finding Average, First Value, Second Value, and Third Value. Also, set the Text property of the Button control to Calculate Average. To be able to access and identify it in the code, set the ID of the three TextBox controls to txtFirstValue, txtSecondValue, and txtThirdValue, respectively. Also, set the ID of the Button and the Label control (at the bottom) to btnCalculateAvg and lblResponse. After performing all these tasks, the Default.aspx web form appears as shown in Figure 18.45.

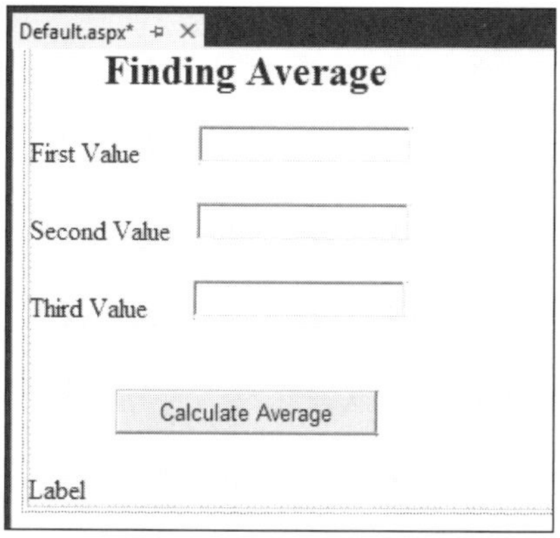

Figure 18.45
Controls placed in the Default.aspx web form.
Used with permission from Microsoft.

The code for the controls and their configured properties is auto-generated and can be seen from the Code window of the Default.aspx web form. The code in Default.aspx appears as shown in Listing 18.11.

Listing 18.11 Program Code in Default.aspx File

```
<%@ Page Language="C#" AutoEventWireup="true" CodeFile="Default.aspx.cs"
Inherits="_Default" %>

<!DOCTYPE html>
<html xmlns="http://www.w3.org/1999/xhtml">
<head runat="server">
    <title></title>
</head>
<body>
    <form id="form1" runat="server">
    <div>
        <asp:Label ID="Label1" runat="server" Font-Bold="True" Font-Size="X-Large"
Text="Finding Average"></asp:Label>
```

```
        <br />
        <br />
        <asp:Label ID="Label2" runat="server" Text="First Value"></asp:Label>
        <asp:TextBox ID="txtFirstValue" runat="server"></asp:TextBox>
        <br />
        <br />
        <asp:Label ID="Label3" runat="server" Text="Second Value"></asp:Label>
        <asp:TextBox ID="txtSecondValue" runat="server"></asp:TextBox>
        <br />
        <br />
        <asp:Label ID="Label4" runat="server" Text="Third Value"></asp:Label>
        <asp:TextBox ID="txtThirdValue" runat="server"></asp:TextBox>
        <br />
        <br />
        <br />
        <asp:Button ID="btnCalculateAvg" runat="server" Text="Calculate Average" />
        <br />
        <br />
        <asp:Label ID="lblResponse" runat="server" Text="Label"></asp:Label>
    </div>
    </form>
</body>
</html>
```

Because you want the service to be invoked after clicking the btnCalculateAvg button, you need to write code in its Click event. Double-click the button and write the code as shown in Listing 18.12.

Listing 18.12 Program Code in Click Event of Calculate Average Button

```
protected void btnCalculateAvg_Click(object sender, EventArgs e)
    {
        int a, b, c;
        ServiceReference1.Service1Client objService = new
ServiceReference1.Service1Client();
        a = Convert.ToInt32(txtFirstValue.Text);
        b = Convert.ToInt32(txtSecondValue.Text);
        c = Convert.ToInt32(txtThirdValue.Text);
        double result = objService.GetAverage(a, b, c);
        lblResponse.Text = "Average is " + result.ToString();
    }
```

You can access the web service by creating an instance called objService. The numerical values that the user enters in the three TextBox controls are accessed and assigned to integer variables a, b, and c, respectively. The three variables are then passed to the

GetAverage method of the service, and the result that is returned by the method is assigned to the variable, a result of the double type. The average in the result variable is displayed through the Label control. When you run the application, you find three TextBox controls prompting for values. After you click the Calculate Average button, the average of the three values is displayed (see Figure 18.46).

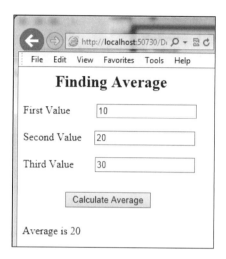

Figure 18.46
Client application displaying average that is computed by accessing the web service.
Used with permission from Microsoft.

SUMMARY

This chapter focused on using Visual Studio to develop websites. You learned about different tools that make up the Visual Studio toolbox and developed your first web application by using the Label, TextBox, and Button controls. Thereafter, you used the DropDownList control, AutoPostBack property, and ArrayList class to display data in the DropDownList control. Also, you learned to use the CheckBox, RadioButton, and ListBox controls in websites. From there, you discovered how to navigate from one web form to another by using the LinkButton, HyperLink, and ImageButton controls. Finally, you learned to develop web services with WCF and create a client application that can access and use web services.

In the next chapter, you will learn about the roles and benefits of assemblies. In addition, you will learn the difference between private and public assemblies. Finally, you will learn to create and use a public assembly.

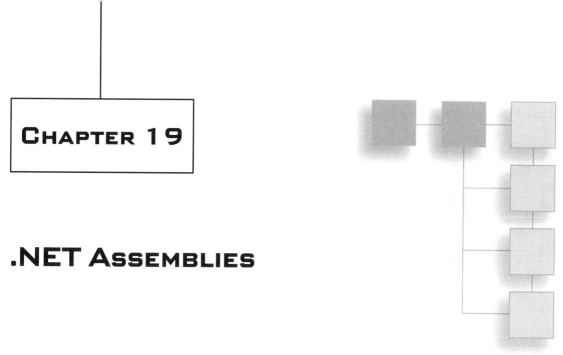

CHAPTER 19

.NET ASSEMBLIES

This chapter's topics include the following:

- Using assemblies
- Creating and using a shared assembly

USING ASSEMBLIES

Assemblies are the files that contain compiled code targeted at the .NET Framework. They are basically physical packages meant for distributing code. The .NET classes are actually contained in a number of assemblies. Here are some facts about assemblies:

- They contain all deployment and version information for a program. They provide mechanisms that support safe component interaction, cross-language interoperability, and versioning.

- They are logical units that can be stored across more than one file. If an assembly is stored in more than one file, there will be one main file that contains the entry point and describes the other files in the assembly.

- Assemblies contain metadata that describes the types and methods defined in the corresponding code. The assembly metadata is contained in an area called the *manifest*, which enables you to check the assembly version and maintain its integrity. Here are the two important sections of an assembly:

  - **Manifest**—Contains information about the assembly that includes the name of the assembly, its version number, and its type mapping information.

- **Metadata**—Includes the information about the data types the program uses.

- Assembly files have the extension `.exe` if they are standalone applications, or `.dll` if they're reusable components.

The core assemblies for the .NET Framework are found in the folder `C:\Windows\Assembly`. An assembly can contain multiple namespaces. Conversely, more than one assembly file can contain classes in the same namespace. Precisely, all .NET classes are contained in assemblies. Therefore, assemblies enable you to use the class library namespaces in a .NET program.

To develop applications, you can use .NET assemblies as well as third-party assemblies. While compiling an application, you need to specify the assemblies that the application is using. You can add the assemblies to the application by defining them in the configuration file. The assemblies can be automatically defined in the configuration file of the application by using the Website, Add Reference command.

Assemblies come in two types: private and shared.

Private Assemblies

Private assemblies are the simplest type. They are intended to be used only with the software with which they are shipped. Other software cannot use private assemblies because an application loads the private assemblies only if they are located in the same folder (or in a subfolder) where the main executable file is kept. Because private assemblies can be used only by the software package they are intended for, you don't have to worry much about their security. There are no chances of name collisions and no chances of some other software overwriting the private assemblies. Even two private assemblies having the same class names isn't a problem because an application can see only the classes that are mentioned in its private assemblies. Because a private assembly is entirely self-contained, the process to deploy it is simple. You simply place the appropriate file(s) in the appropriate folder in the file system. No registry entries are required.

Shared Assemblies

Shared assemblies, as the name suggests, are the libraries that other applications can commonly use. Because any other software can access a shared assembly, security precautions are necessary. There can be several security problems, such as name collisions. A name collision occurs when another shared assembly has classes or variables with the same names matching the shared assembly. A different version of the same assembly might overwrite a shared assembly, and the new version might be incompatible with the existing code. To prevent name collisions, shared assemblies are given a strong name, which is unique based on the private key cryptography. To avoid overwriting the shared assembly, their version information is specified in the assembly manifest.

To enable several applications to share a shared assembly, you need to add the assembly to the special directory known as the Global Assembly Cache (GAC). The GAC provides a centralized storage location for .NET assemblies. Using one of the .NET utilities, the shared assembly must be installed into the cache.

Note

Each assembly is uniquely identified by its strong name.

CREATING AND USING A SHARED ASSEMBLY

Here are the steps to create a shared assembly:

1. Create a project containing a class file. The class file may contain the methods and properties that you want other applications to access.

2. Generate a strong name for the project. The strong name is saved in a strong key filename.

3. Specify the key filename in the project by indicating its strong key filename in the AssemblyInfo.cs file.

4. Compile the project to generate an assembly. The assembly is generated with the extension .dll.

5. Register or add the compiled class file .dll into the GAC.

After these steps, any application can share the assembly. The application that is supposed to use an assembly just needs to specify it in its configuration file by invoking the Add Reference command.

Now you'll create an assembly called MySharedAssembly that contains a class called SharedAssembClass containing a method called WelcomeMsg. WelcomeMsg displays a welcome message and the supplied name. Launch Visual Studio, and create a new class library project called MySharedAssembly, as shown in Figure 19.1.

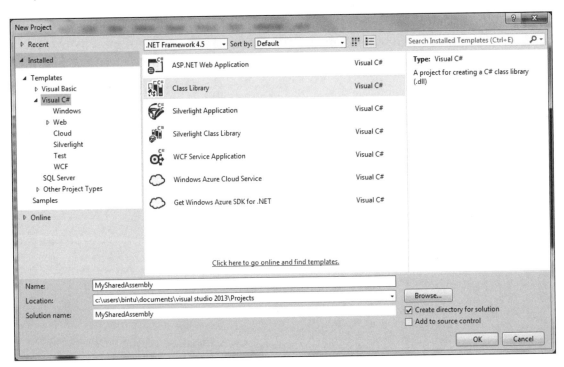

Figure 19.1
Creating a class library project called MySharedAssembly.
Used with permission from Microsoft.

To create a method that accepts a name as a parameter and returns it along with a welcome message, write the code as shown in Listing 19.1 in the class file Class1.cs.

Listing 19.1 Program Code in Class1.cs File

```csharp
using System;
using System.Collections.Generic;
using System.Linq;
using System.Text;
using System.Threading.Tasks;

namespace MySharedAssembly
{
    public class SharedAssembClass
    {
        public string WelcomeMsg(string name)
        {
            return ("Welcome " + name);
        }
    }
}
```

You can see that a class named SharedAssembClass is defined. The class contains the method WelcomeMsg that takes a string parameter and returns the string along with a welcome message. After creating a class that you want to act as assembly, you need to create a strong name for it. The command-line utility for doing so is sn.exe. Through Visual Studio, you can assign a strong name from the application's properties. Right-click the application in the Solution Explorer window and select the Properties option. Select the Signing tab from the Properties page (see Figure 19.2). From the drop-down list, select Browse to select a strong name key file (if it is already created), or select New to create a new strong name key file.

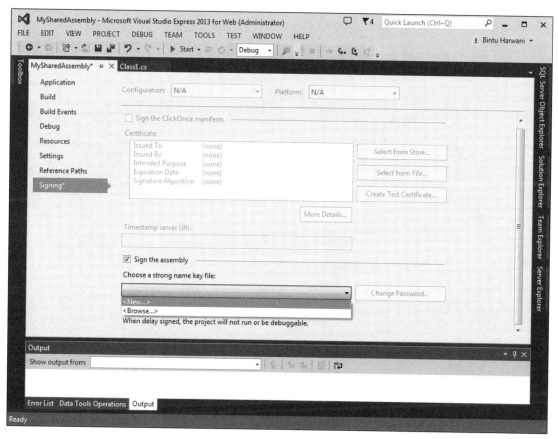

Figure 19.2
Properties page for creating strong name key file for the assembly.
Used with permission from Microsoft.

Enter the strong key filename into the dialog that pops up. Here, the name MySharedAssemblyKeyFile has been assigned to the key filename (see Figure 19.3). Don't protect the file with a password because, as a shared assembly, it will be shared by external developers. Click OK to continue.

Figure 19.3
Entering information for the strong name key file of the assembly.
Used with permission from Microsoft.

The strong key file is created named `MySharedAssemblyKeyFile.snk`. It appears in the Solution Explorer window, as shown in Figure 19.4.

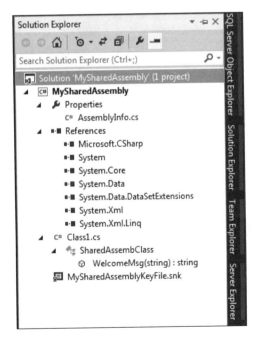

Figure 19.4
Strong name key file of the assembly appears in the Solution Explorer window.
Used with permission from Microsoft.

To inform the application about the presence of the assembly, specify its strong key filename in the `AssemblyInfo.cs` file. From the Solution Explorer window, open the `AssemblyInfo.cs` file and add the following line (see Figure 19.5):

```
[assembly: AssemblyKeyFile("MySharedAssemblyKeyFile.snk")]
```

```
AssemblyInfo.cs*  ⊕ ×  Class1.cs

    using System.Reflection;
    using System.Runtime.CompilerServices;
    using System.Runtime.InteropServices;

    // General Information about an assembly is controlled through the following
    // set of attributes. Change these attribute values to modify the information
    // associated with an assembly.
    [assembly: AssemblyKeyFile("MySharedAssemblyKeyFile")]
    [assembly: AssemblyTitle("MySharedAssembly")]
    [assembly: AssemblyDescription("")]
    [assembly: AssemblyConfiguration("")]
    [assembly: AssemblyCompany("")]
    [assembly: AssemblyProduct("MySharedAssembly")]
    [assembly: AssemblyCopyright("Copyright © 2014")]
    [assembly: AssemblyTrademark("")]
    [assembly: AssemblyCulture("")]

    // Setting ComVisible to false makes the types in this assembly not visible
    // to COM components.  If you need to access a type in this assembly from
    // COM, set the ComVisible attribute to true on that type.
    [assembly: ComVisible(false)]

    // The following GUID is for the ID of the typelib if this project is exposed to COM
    [assembly: Guid("eae207ff-b1fb-4aa6-9095-18d7e2cd32c5")]
```

Figure 19.5
Specifying the strong name key file in the AssemblyInfo.cs file.
Used with permission from Microsoft.

Save the `AssemblyInfo.cs` file. The next step is to compile your application into a `.dll` file. To get the assembly, set the output type of the application to the class library. Right-click the project in Solution Explorer and select Properties. From the Properties dialog, click the Application tab, and in the Output Type drop-down, select Class Library. You can now go ahead and build the project. After you do so, a `MySharedAssembly.dll` file is generated in the `bin\Debug` folder of the project.

To make your newly generated assembly visible to other applications, you need to add it to the GAC directory. The command-line utility to add an assembly to GAC is `gacutil.exe`. Run the Developer Command Prompt for VS2013, change the directory to the `bin\Debug` folder of the application (because the `.dll` file is created in that directory by default), and type the command with the following syntax:

```
gacutil /i <assembly name>
```

Figure 19.6 shows the output of using `gacutil.exe` to add the assembly to the GAC directory.

Figure 19.6
Executing the gacutil.exe command to add the assembly into the GAC.
Used with permission from Microsoft.

After you place the assembly in the GAC, you can use it in any application by referencing it. To see it practically, you'll create another class library project named `ClientforSharedAssembly`, as shown in Figure 19.7.

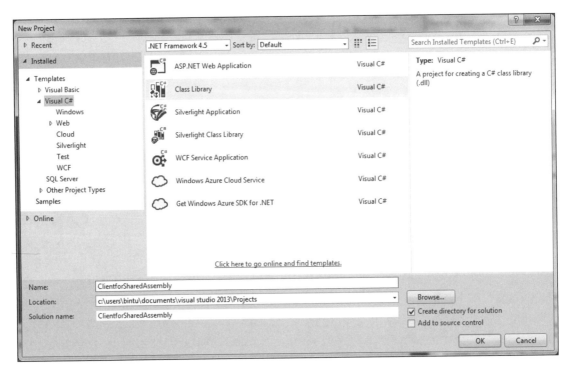

Figure 19.7
Creating a new application called ClientforSharedAssembly for using the assembly.
Used with permission from Microsoft.

To use MySharedAssembly in your client application, you need to import it with a command. Also, you need to create an instance of the SharedAssembClass (that you defined in the MySharedAssembly) and invoke its WelcomeMsg method. To do so, write the code as shown in Listing 19.2 in the Class1.cs file.

Listing 19.2 Program Code in Class1.cs File

```
using System;
using System.Collections.Generic;
using System.Linq;
using System.Text;
using System.Threading.Tasks;
using MySharedAssembly;

namespace ClientforSharedAssembly
{
    public class Class1
    {
        public static void Main(string[] args)
        {
            string uname;
            Console.Write("Enter your name ");
            uname = Console.ReadLine();
            SharedAssembClass sharedObj = new SharedAssembClass();
            Console.WriteLine(sharedObj.WelcomeMsg(uname));
            Console.Read();
        }
    }
}
```

The user is prompted for a name assigned to the string variable uname. An instance of the SharedAssembClass class is created named sharedObj. Using the sharedObj instance, the WelcomeMsg method is called to display the welcome message to the user. As mentioned earlier, the assemblies are added to an application by defining them in the configuration file. The assemblies can be automatically defined in the configuration file of the application by using the Add Reference command. Right-click the application in Solution Explorer and select Add, Reference. Select Browse, and then select the MySharedAssembly.dll file (see Figure 19.8).

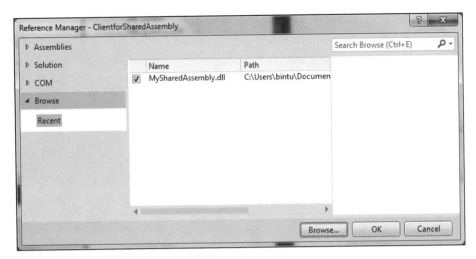

Figure 19.8
Adding a reference to the assembly in the new application.
Used with permission from Microsoft.

To execute the class library project ClientforSharedAssembly, you need to set its output type to Console Application. To do so, right-click the project in Solution Explorer and select Properties. From the Properties dialog, click the Application tab, and in the Output Type drop-down, select Console Application.

After you run the application, it prompts you for a name that is then passed to the WelcomeMsg method of your assembly. The WelcomeMsg method returns the name along with a welcome message that is displayed on the screen (see Figure 19.9).

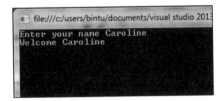

Figure 19.9
The application using the assembly and invoking its WelcomeMsg method to display a welcome message.
Used with permission from Microsoft.

SUMMARY

In this chapter, you learned about assemblies and their usage in .NET applications. You also discovered the difference between private and shared assemblies. Finally, you learned the steps to create a shared assembly and the procedure to use it in an application.

In this book, I've tried to keep things easy to understand. I hope I've succeeded. You now have all the necessary information related to object-oriented programming in C# 5.0. You also know how to develop web applications in .NET.

Have fun creating your own C# programs, and thanks for reading!

INDEX